IN SECRECY'S SHADOW

Traditions in American Cinema
Series Editors Linda Badley and R. Barton Palmer

Titles in the series include:

The 'War on Terror' and American Film: 9/11 Frames Per Second
by Terence McSweeney

American Postfeminist Cinema: Women, Romance and Contemporary Culture
by Michele Schreiber

Film Noir
by Homer B. Pettey and R. Barton Palmer (eds)

In Secrecy's Shadow: The OSS and CIA in Hollywood Cinema 1941–1979
by Simon Willmetts

www.edinburghuniversitypress.com

IN SECRECY'S SHADOW
*The OSS and CIA in Hollywood Cinema
1941–1979*

Simon Willmetts

EDINBURGH
University Press

For my Family, Sally and Richard Aldrich.
This book would not exist without you.

Edinburgh University Press is one of the leading university presses in the UK. We publish academic books and journals in our selected subject areas across the humanities and social sciences, combining cutting-edge scholarship with high editorial and production values to produce academic works of lasting importance. For more information visit our website: www.edinburghuniversitypress.com

© Simon Willmetts, 2016, 2017

Edinburgh University Press Ltd
The Tun – Holyrood Road
12 (2f) Jackson's Entry
Edinburgh EH8 8PJ

First published in hardback by Edinburgh University Press 2016

Typeset in 10/12.5pt Sabon by
Servis Filmsetting Ltd, Stockport, Cheshire,
and printed and bound in Great Britain by
CPI Group (UK) Ltd, Croydon CR0 4YY

A CIP record for this book is available from the British Library

ISBN 978 0 7486 9299 6 (hardback)
ISBN 978 1 4744 2594 0 (paperback)
ISBN 978 0 7486 9300 9 (webready PDF)
ISBN 978 0 7486 9301 6 (epub)

The right of Simon Willmetts to be identified as author of this work has been asserted in accordance with the Copyright, Designs and Patents Act 1988 and the Copyright and Related Rights Regulations 2003 (SI No. 2498).

CONTENTS

List of Illustrations	vii
Acknowledgements	x
Introduction	1

1. The Facts of War: Cinematic Intelligence and the Office of Strategic Services — 22
   - John Ford's Navy — 30
   - Weaponising Cinema — 34
   - Hollywood's Intelligence Archive — 36
   - Wild Bill Donovan and the Origins of the OSS Field Photographic Unit — 42
   - *December 7th*: Scripting an Intelligence Failure — 46
   - Zanuck, Ford and the Filming of the North African Invasion — 51
   - The Authority of Cinema at the Nuremberg Trials — 57

2. 'What is Past is Prologue': Hollywood's History of the OSS and the Establishment of the CIA — 77
   - Hollywood Enlists in General Donovan's Campaign for a Permanent Peacetime Intelligence Agency — 79
   - *O.S.S.* (1946) — 85
   - *Cloak and Dagger* (1946) — 89
   - *13 Rue Madeleine* (1947) — 102

3. Quiet Americans: The CIA and Hollywood in the Early Cold War — 121
    Cherishing Anonymity: Hollywood and the CIA in the Early Cold War — 127
    Dangerous Liaisons: The CIA in Hollywood — 138
    Joseph Mankiewicz's *The Quiet American* (1958) — 142
    Figaro Entertainment's Unmade CIA Semi-documentary TV Series — 159

4. The Death of the 'Big Lie' and the Emergence of Postmodern Incredulity in the Spy Cinema of the 1960s — 170
    Our Man in Havana and the Origins of Cold War Satire — 181
    North by Northwest (1959) — 185
    The Man from U.N.C.L.E. and TV Spy Satire in the 1960s — 193
    Parody Turns Political in *The President's Analyst* (1967) — 204

5. Secrecy, Conspiracy, Cinema and the CIA in the 1970s — 222
    Scorpio (1973) and CIA Public Relations — 232
    The Spook Who Sat by the Door (1973) — 236
    Watergate, *The Parallax View* (1974) and the Emergence of the Conspiracy Thriller — 241
    Three Days of the Condor (1975) — 248
    Emile de Antonio and Philip Agee: The Radical CIA Film that Never Was — 253
    Fighting Back: The Birth of CIA Public Relations — 261

Conclusion — 272

Select Filmography — 280
Bibliography — 282
Film and TV Index — 297
General Index — 299

ILLUSTRATIONS

Figure I.1	*13 Rue Madeleine* opens with a scene celebrating the centrality of the US National Archives	2
Figure I.2	Records of America's secret Second World War intelligence activities are safely filed	3
Figure I.3	Oliver Stone places American history on trial in *JFK*	5
Figure 1.1	The Cunningham Combat Camera, introduced late in the war in 1945	24
Figure 1.2	John Ford poses with film stock at Midway	27
Figure 1.3	John Ford with members of his photographic unit aboard his yacht, *Araner*	30
Figure 1.4	Use of the viewfinder in photography is illustrated by Lt Gregg Toland, USNR	32
Figure 1.5	Members of the special photographic unit of the Naval Reserve learn to handle sound equipment at the Twentieth Century-Fox studios in Los Angles	33
Figure 1.6	Richard de Rochemont, photographed on 15 June 1945	38
Figure 1.7	Head of OSS, William 'Wild Bill' Donovan	43
Figure 1.8	US Navy planes and a hangar burning at the Ford Island Naval Air Station's seaplane base, 7 December 1941	48
Figure 1.9	Twentieth Century-Fox studio boss Darryl F. Zanuck	52
Figure 1.10	OSS Field Photographic Officer Ray Kellogg shoots footage from the tail of a German plane, Tunisia, November 1942	54

Figure 1.11	22 November 1945: Hitler's photographer Heinrich Hoffmann (1885–1957) inspecting evidence during the Nuremberg War Crimes Trial	60
Figure 1.12	The OSS installed a screen in the Nuremberg courtroom	62
Figure 1.13	Nuremberg Trial defendants in their dock, circa 1945–6	63
Figure 2.1	Alan Ladd and Geraldine Fitzgerald star in *O.S.S.*	84
Figure 2.2	Fritz Lang's *Cloak and Dagger*, starring Gary Cooper as OSS agent Alvah Jesper	90
Figure 2.3	Film director Fritz Lang, photographed in 1969	91
Figure 2.4	James Cagney as OSS agent Bob Sharkey in *13 Rue Madeleine*	102
Figure 2.5	Louis de Rochemont made his name as the producer of the *March of Time* newsreel service	105
Figure 3.1	Allen Dulles, the longest-serving Director of Central Intelligence (from 1953 to 1961)	123
Figure 3.2	J. Edgar Hoover maintained close ties to Hollywood throughout his tenure as head of the FBI	129
Figure 3.3	*John Goldfarb, Please Come Home!* was a screwball comedy based loosely on the Gary Powers incident	133
Figure 3.4	Partially concealed plaque from *North by Northwest*	136
Figure 3.5	Allen Dulles with Eric Johnston, President of the Motion Picture Association of America, and James A. Mulvey, President of the Society of Independent Motion Picture Producers	137
Figure 3.6	The CIA sponsored the 1954 animated adaptation of George Orwell's *Animal Farm*	140
Figure 3.7	Michael Redgrave plays British journalist Thomas Fowler alongside war hero Audie Murphy as Alden Pyle in Mankiewicz's *The Quiet American*	143
Figure 3.8	Michael Redgrave as Thomas Fowler, inspecting a tub of 'dialacton', in Mankiewicz's *The Quiet American*	146
Figure 3.9	Fowler pleads with Phuong, played by Italian actress Giorgia Moll, in Mankiewicz's *The Quiet American*	148
Figure 3.10	French inspector Vigot interrogates Fowler in the final scene of Mankiewicz's *The Quiet American*	149
Figure 3.11	Hollywood censor Geoffrey Shurlock, head of the Production Code Administration from 1954 to 1968	152
Figure 4.1	Captured Cuban counter-revolutionaries after their failed invasion attempt at the Bay of Pigs	175
Figure 4.2	David McCallum (Illya Kuryaking), Leo Carroll (Alexander Waverley) and Robert Vaughn (Napoleon Solo) star in *The Man from U.N.C.L.E.* television series	178

ILLUSTRATIONS

Figure 4.3	Camp spy satire *In Like Flint*	180
Figure 4.4	*Our Man in Havana* co-stars Alec Guinness and Maureen O'Hara meeting Fidel Castro while filming in Havana	185
Figure 4.5	Cary Grant as mistaken CIA agent Roger Thornhill confronting spy chief 'The Professor', played by Leo G. Carroll in Hitchcock's *North by Northwest*	189
Figure 4.6	Robert Vaughn as Napoleon Solo starred alongside David McCallum in *The Man from U.N.C.L.E.*	195
Figure 4.7	David McCallum as Russian-born U.N.C.L.E. agent Ilya Kuryakin in *The Man from U.N.C.L.E.*	197
Figure 4.8	Don Adams playing Maxwell Smart in spy spoof television series *Get Smart*	203
Figure 4.9	James Coburn taking on the phone company in psychedelic 60s spy satire *The President's Analyst*	204
Figure 4.10	James Coburn, playing psychoanalyst Dr Sidney Schaefer, counselling CIA agent Don Masters (Godfrey Cambridge) in *The President's Analyst*	210
Figure 4.11	Dr Schaeffer (Coburn), sitting in between head of the 'CEA' Ethen Allen Crcoket (Eduard Franz) and 'FBR' chief Henry Lux (Walter Burke), in *The President's Analyst*	213
Figure 5.1	Senator Frank Church holds up a CIA poisoned-dart gun during the Senate Church Committee hearings	224
Figure 5.2	Promotional poster for *Scorpio*	233
Figure 5.3	Poster for Ivan Dixon's bold adaptation of Sam Greenlee's novel, *The Spook Who Sat by the Door*	237
Figure 5.4	Poster for *The Parallax View*, starring Warren Beatty as intrepid reporter Joseph Frady	245
Figure 5.5	Faye Dunaway and Robert Redford co-star in *Three Days of the Condor*	248
Figure 5.6	Former CIA Director Richard Helms chats with Robert Redford on the set of *Three Days of the Condor*	254
Figure 5.7	CIA apostate Philip Agee, whose memoir, *Inside the Company*, was published in 1975	256
Figure 5.8	Radical filmmaker Emile de Antonio, who tried to make a fictional feature based on Agee's memoir.	258

ACKNOWLEDGEMENTS

Writing this book has been an uphill struggle. It has taken shape over the course of seven long years during a formative period of my life. Writing can be a lonely experience, but no book is an island. The people who have helped me get to this stage – and there are too many for me to include all of them here – have not only offered encouragement and support, but true mentorship; their guidance has helped me grow both personally and professionally, and their patience has given me the space and time in which to hone my craft – space and time that is sadly increasingly limited for young scholars who are today expected to perform feats few would have expected from end-of-career professors only a few decades previously. I have been lucky to have had so much support at such a crucial phase of my career and life, and for that I am thankful.

A number of people and institutions deserve special mention. This book, and the research upon which it is based, would not have been possible without the generous financial support of the UK's Arts and Humanities Research Council (AHRC). As a PhD student I was attached to the AHRC-funded project entitled *The Landscapes of Secrecy: The CIA and the Contested Record of US Foreign Policy, 1947–2001*. This book is the culmination of years of research I conducted while on that project. My colleagues on the project were generous with their time and patient with their support of a younger and less-experienced collaborator. Paul McGarr and Matthew Jones worked tirelessly on their part of the project based at The University of Nottingham, and were largely responsible for the organisation of a successful end-of-project conference. Kaeten

ACKNOWLEDGEMENTS

Mistry, a later addition to the project thanks to a grant from the Leverhulme Trust (supporting scholarships for the purposes of education and research), also deserves a special mention for his scholarly advice, keen wit, friendship and encyclopaedic knowledge of Winston Churchill quotes.

The University of Warwick, where I completed my undergraduate studies, master's degree and PhD, is an institution of the highest order, which on countless occasions went above and beyond the call of duty in providing opportunities for young scholars such as myself. In particular I would like to thank Warwick's History Department, and especially Roger Fagge, for first inspiring me. I am not the only young scholar whose ambition to become an academic was first forged by a particularly inspiring seminar taught by Roger, or the many equally excellent seminars and lectures that Warwick history students are lucky enough to experience and should never take for granted. Thank you, Roger.

Warwick's Politics and International Studies (PAIS) Department, where I studied for my PhD, was likewise crucial to my personal and professional development. Special thanks goes to Matthew Watson for his dedicated stewardship of their postgraduate programme. PAIS always put its young scholars first, in the process helping to create a vibrant atmosphere within its PhD and post-doctorate community. It is difficult not to be overcome with nostalgia when recalling the long, late and always stimulating discussions about everything from postmodernism to the correct proportion of Scottish whisky to Drambuie in a Rusty Nail (cocktail) with my eternal friends and close colleagues Andy Hammond, Davinia Hoggarth and Zakia Shiraz. I'm not sure if we ever finally did find out what freedom is, but we came pretty close and certainly identified some serious contenders. On the subject of friendship and freedom, Laura Schmidli deserves a special mention – although geographically far away I have always felt an especial affinity and closeness to you, and your putting up with my long work-/life-stressed whining in late-night discussions, often related to the writing of this book, has lifted my spirits on countless occasions. Thanks also to the kindness and companionship of Chris Clarke, Louise Walker, James Malcolm and all the other members of my PhD cohort who helped make the narcissistic angst of doctoral study more bearable. Finally, thank you James Brassett, and Linda Åhäll (the best office-mate anyone could have).

Since leaving Warwick I have been fortunate enough to have entered a department, American Studies at the University of Hull, which is equally encouraging in its support for young scholars and their research. Especial thanks to my colleagues David Eldridge, Jo Metcalf, Jenel Virden, John Osborne, Barnaby Haran and Sylvia Tynan who make Hull American Studies such a communal and supportive environment to work in. Thanks also to my new Hull friends Jason Burkinshaw, Cecilia Brioni, Imogen Bloomfield, Fruela Fernandez, Martin Nickson and Riccardo Orlandi who have kept me sane and grounded the past few years and made moving to a strange city a wonderful experience. Special thanks also to James Zborowski who read an early chapter draft and has provided frequent intellectual advice and guidance.

I am forever grateful to my family, especially my mum, dad and brother for their encouragement and support throughout my life. Thanks also to my wonderful girlfriend Sally who is surely the most patient person on the planet having put up with my book-related moaning for several years now – offering only kindness, encouragement and affection in response.

I would like to thank all the archivists, librarians, scholars and interviewees who made the research process so enjoyable and educative – you offer an invaluable service. The Margaret Herrick Library and its entire fantastic staff at the Academy of Motion Picture Arts and Sciences warrant a special mention for letting me use their reading-room as a second-home for two summers running. They are a truly world-class research facility thanks in no small part to the wonderful team of people they have working there. Thank you Edinburgh University Press (EUP) for taking a punt on me and getting me into print. In particular my editors at EUP, Gillian Leslie and Richard Strachan, have been wonderful, and extremely patient as I've dragged my feet a few times getting this over the line.

Last but not least, I would like to thank my closest colleagues and most influential mentors throughout the period of writing this book, Chris Moran and Richard Aldrich. Chris, along with friendship and the useful diversions of mini-golf and discussions as to the relative merits and weaknesses of Arsenal FC, you have also effectively performed the role of a second supervisor throughout my PhD and into my early career as an academic. It was through long conversations with you about secrecy and intelligence that many of the ideas for this book emerged. Thank you for all your help over the last few years, and indeed for your mentorship since first teaching me as a first year undergraduate.

Finally, thank you Richard Aldrich. Words seem hopelessly insufficient as a form of repayment for the enormous debt of gratitude that I owe you. Mentor, supervisor, patron, friend, father figure, colleague and collaborator – you have been all these things to me and always in a manner that has left me humbled. Despite your success and experience you have always conducted yourself around your junior colleagues and supervisees with a humility and grace that is befitting of someone who has reached the top of their profession and attained the respect of their peers. You are a supervisor who cares deeply about the lives and futures of your students, and you bend over backwards for them. I hope that if I could take one thing away from the experience of being supervised by you, it would be that care and devotion you have shown to helping others around you. In this increasingly competitive world of professional scholarship, such generosity is a rare virtue, but one that is surely vital for the furtherance of our profession.

INTRODUCTION

> *If official secrecy had a devastating impact on American history, its impact on Americans' understanding of that history was a collateral disaster.*[1]
> Richard Gid Powers, introduction to
> Senator Daniel Patrick Moynihan, *Secrecy: The American Experience*

13 Rue Madeleine, a 1947 semi-documentary that commemorates the sacrifice and courage of the Central Intelligence Agency's (CIA's) wartime predecessor, the Office of Strategic Services (OSS), opens with a shot of the US National Archives Building on Pennsylvania Avenue. The building's location, at the heart of the nation's capital on the Washington Mall, amidst so many iconic monuments to American democracy, is no accident. Like the Washington or Lincoln Memorial, it is a depository of historical experience that binds up the nation. In its inner-sanctum, as audiences then and now would know, the United States of America's founding documents, including the Constitution and the Declaration of Independence, are housed. After the establishing shot the camera slowly tilts from top to bottom, surveying the archive's columnar neo-classical facade – a common architectural feature of America's monuments that evokes a sense of both history and authority. Finally, it comes to rest on a statue in the forecourt of the archive called Future. On Future's plinth, the inscription reads: 'What is Past is Prologue'. At this point we hear the booming voice of an omniscient narrator – an oratory style borrowed from the newsreels of the time that was also a defining feature of the semi-documentary format:

IN SECRECY'S SHADOW

Yes, here in the National Archives in Washington, DC, past is prologue. For this is the final resting place of the histories and records of tens of thousands of illustrious Americans. World War II has come to a victorious conclusion. And now new names and new records are being added to the list. For the nation and the world are for the first time learning of silent and significant deeds performed in foreign lands by a legion of anonymous men and women, the Army of Secret Intelligence.[2]

Figure I.1   *13 Rue Madeleine* (1947) opens with a scene celebrating the centrality of the US National Archives as the central depository of the nation's past.
Source: Henry Hathaway, Twentieth Century-Fox, 1947.

INTRODUCTION

The combined effect of the images and the dialogue is clear: America's past, even the very recent past of its secret wartime intelligence activities, is transparent and accessible to the American people. All they had to do is look in the nation's official historical depository, and an authoritative vision of those 'silent and significant deeds', now no-longer silent, would be plain for all to see.

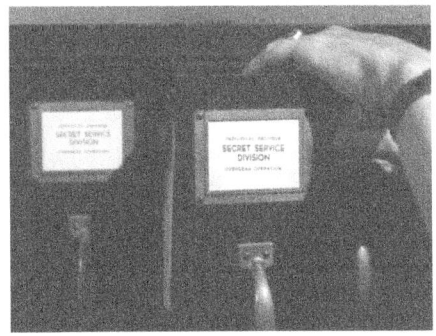

Figure I.2   Records of America's secret Second World War intelligence activities are safely filed within the official record. *Source: 13 Rue Madeleine*, Henry Hathaway, Twentieth Century-Fox, 1947.

3

Just under half a century later, in the dénouement to Oliver Stone's conspiracy thriller *JFK* (1991), a near-perfect inversion of *13 Rue Madeleine*'s opening scene takes place. As a teary-eyed Kevin Costner, playing New Orleans District Attorney Jim Garrison, addresses the jury with his closing argument on defendant Clay Shaw's culpability for the death of President Kennedy, it is as though Shaw is no longer on trial, but the American historical record itself:

> All these documents are yours – the people's property. You pay for them! But because the government considers you children who might be too disturbed or distressed to face this reality, or because you might possibly lynch those involved, you cannot see these documents for another seventy-five years! I'm in my early forties, so I'll have shuffled off this mortal coil by then, but I'm already telling my eight-year-old son to keep himself physically fit, so that one glorious September morning, in the year 2038, he can walk into the National Archives and find out what the CIA and the FBI [Federal Bureau of Investigation] knew! They might even push it back then. Hell it may become a generational affair – with questions passed down father to son, mother to daughter. But someday, somewhere, someone may find out the damn truth. We better, we better or we might just as well build ourselves another government ... The truth is the most important value we have, because if the truth does not endure, if the government murders truth, if we cannot respect the hearts of these people, then this is not the country in which I was born in and it is certainly not the country that I want to die in.[3]

As the credits roll soon after this impassioned plea, the same inscription from Future's plinth appears: 'What is Past is Prologue'. The implication of the proverb in both *JFK* and *13 Rue Madeleine* is the same: the politics of the present should be guided via a judicious reading of the nation's past. However, each conceives our relationship to that past in entirely different ways. In *Rue Madeleine*, an authoritative and unified vision of America's past is directly accessible to its citizens via that hallowed temple of national memory: the national archives. In *JFK*, however, that 'final resting place of the histories and records of tens of thousands of illustrious Americans' is sullied by the debilitating effects of classification upon the authority of the national historical record.

The forty-five years that separates these films witnessed the meteoric rise of the American national security state. The attendant expansion of US government secrecy had a corrosive effect upon that unified and authoritative vision of America's past that is presented in *Rue Madeleine*. In the second half of the twentieth century secrecy figured as history's aporia – problematising the 'official story' of the past by revealing the dubious status of its empirical foundations in the partially concealed and even actively distorted archives of the

INTRODUCTION

Figure I.3   Oliver Stone places American history on trial in *JFK* (1991). Kevin Costner plays New Orleans District Attorney Jim Garrison who personifies the collapse of public trust in American government since the Second World War. *Source:* Oliver Stone, Warner Brothers, 1991.

state. By so destabilising the foundations of national memory, secrecy rendered a fundamental transformation in the American people's relationship to their past that is apparent in the difference between these two scenes.

This book is about that transformation. It traces the formation and breakdown of the consensus vision of American history that was forged in the embers of the Second World War and then melded out of shape by the rise of government secrecy and the national security state that followed. The timeframe of this transformation was actually much shorter than the forty-five years between *Rue Madeleine* and *JFK*. Rather, it took place in the few short decades after the Second World War that culminated in the nadir of public trust in government in the wake of President Kennedy's death, the Vietnam War, Watergate and the repeated revelations of CIA and FBI misdeeds in 1975. Stone's *JFK* is the heir to the culture of suspicion set in motion by these events. Moreover, it is a culture that continues to define our current age; public trust in government has never fully recovered from these seminal moments that, as Don DeLillo put it, 'broke the back of the American century'.[4]

The idea that American culture grew increasingly sceptical of US government institutions in this period – especially its intelligence service – and consequently of the 'official story' of America's past, should come as no surprise to those familiar with post-war US history. The breakdown of the liberal consensus, as this process is sometimes known, is so well-studied that it is now almost an axiom of post-war periodisation whereby 1950s conformity and consensus gave way to the increasing fracture and dissent of the long 1960s.[5] In this respect, the story of this book is a fairly conventional one, although it seems wise at this juncture to acknowledge the critics of such a simplistically reductive

5

view of American culture and society as defined by these neat periodisations.[6] Americans, if such a people exist, did not simply go from the white-picket fence to the barricades, from the grey flannel suit to technicolour tie-dye. But, if polls are to be believed, something quite fundamental did change en masse in this period that, as this book argues, transformed Hollywood's representation of American intelligence specifically, and American culture more generally: American citizens stopped trusting their government.[7]

Unsurprisingly, this breakdown of public trust decisively shaped the way in which many Americans viewed their secret intelligence agencies, especially the CIA. As a consequence, cultural portrayals of the Agency at any given time offer a kind of oblique bellwether of a much broader socio-cultural phenomenon that fundamentally transformed the American people's relationship with their government. During the 1950s, for example, when American faith in government was at an all-time high, the media adopted a broadly deferential attitude towards the CIA. By the end of the 1960s, however, when that fragile consensus of the previous era began to crack, popular portrayals of the Agency were often either irreverent or outright sceptical, and the CIA became a lightning-rod for wider public anxieties regarding secrecy and the excesses of US foreign policy.

The CIA is therefore an emblematic institution. It resonates in the American imagination for reasons more abstract and ideational in nature than its bricks-and-mortar 'reality'. This is not to say that the CIA as public myth bears no relation to its documented reality. On the contrary, it is to argue that to try to understand the implications of those activities through narrow empirical terms alone is to ignore the profound moral, cultural and ideological questions that they often provoke. In the United States those questions are especially provocative because they often touch upon and occasionally threaten ideas considered fundamental to the American creed: secrecy threatens core American ideals of openness and accountability; espionage and surveillance violate the right to privacy and individual civil liberties, as do repressive tactics, including torture and assassination; last but not least the Agency's role in bolstering executive authority threatens the constitutional division of powers and the checks and balances it affords.

Out of all of these more abstract ideas that the CIA's public profile has come to emblematise, secrecy has had by far the most profound implications for American culture, and Americans' understanding of their history. As Timothy Melley put it, during the Cold War the CIA became 'a symbol of public unknowing'.[8] Its fictional representation in the post-war period offered a kind of barometer at any given moment of public anxieties about secrecy and its impact upon 'factual' discourses or authoritative forms of knowledge. As the American public became more cognisant of official duplicity, Hollywood responded with increasing scepticism towards the idea, presented in the opening sequence of *13 Rue Madeleine*, that it was possible to construct an authentic and authoritative vision of American intelligence through official sources and government cooperation. Those resplendent columns of the national archives on Pennsylvania Avenue, which in the opening shots of *Rue Madeleine* evoked the centrality and authority of the official record to the nation's past, were by the 1970s a symbol of deception.

This journey from naïve credulity to a deep and abiding scepticism of the official record, and indeed all forms of authoritative knowledge, was a gradual process that went through several stages. Those stages are more easily perceptible when looking at the formal evolution of post-war spy cinema, or the changes in its generic structure, than at the level of content. During the timespan of this study, from the Second World War to the 1970s, there were four major forms by which Hollywood represented America's secret government bureaucracies:

1. The Semi-documentary Melodrama (1945–58)
2. Ironic/'Camp' Romance (1959–66)
3. Tragic Realism (1966–72)
4. The Conspiracy Thriller (1973–9)

These dates are inexact and intended merely as guidelines, suggesting the emergence and the peak of each narrative form's popularity. Moreover, the relatively finite periods shown above do not account for the lasting influence of many of these forms. The latter three categories in particular continue to influence the narrative structure of spy thrillers to this date. The Jason Bourne franchise, for example, was, for all intents and purposes, a post-9/11 revamp of the 1970s conspiracy thriller format. The romance of the James Bond format continues to be popular today, although the series has adopted a more 'realist' inflection in recent years. Even the semi-documentary, by far the most antiquated of these forms – with its unreconstructed paeans to the patriotism and dutiful sacrifice of the OSS and FBI appearing quaint from the vantage of our more sceptical conspiracy-theory-saturated post-Watergate world – were influential upon the development of the docudrama. From this perspective, *JFK*, with its fusion of documentary footage and fictional reconstructions, has more in common with *13 Rue Madeleine* than the opening vignette of this introduction may have you think.

These caveats aside, this formal evolution of post-war spy cinema through these four types progressed along a discernible vector that mirrored and sometimes influenced the widening credibility gap between citizens and their government. As the exponential growth of US government secrecy caused people in increasing numbers to stop trusting their government, Hollywood began to question, with growing irreverence, the 'official story', and the idea, as presented in the opening sequence of *13 Rue Madeleine*, of the state as the arbiter of historical authenticity. This had profound consequences. Socially and politically, the erosion of the official story's epistemic authority helped facilitate the collapse of the post-war liberal consensus; an age of relative harmony and conformity, particularly where matters of American foreign policy were concerned, gave way to discord and dissent. Culturally, as Melley argues, government secrecy, and the attendant public scepticism towards consensus history and the 'official story' that it provoked, was the handmaiden of postmodernity, whose defining feature was the destabilisation of all forms of authoritative knowledge.[9]

So let us now briefly trace this evolution of the representation of American secrecy and espionage in Hollywood cinema – from the credulous faith in the official story, and the state as the arbiter of historical authenticity, in the immediate aftermath of the Second World War, to the postmodern incredulity of later decades.[10] The opening scene of *13 Rue Madeleine* perfectly encapsulates the governing principles of the semi-documentary, the first of our four forms of post-war spy thriller. These were films that purported to be meticulously researched and historically accurate dramatisations of real events. To bolster their realism they used location shooting and chiaroscuro lighting and often blended newsreel segments in with dramatic reconstructions. They also borrowed the booming voice of an omniscient narrator from the newsreel. Louis de Rochemont, the producer behind *13 Rue Madeleine*, often dubbed the 'father of the docudrama', made his name as a producer of the *March of Time* newsreel series before the war, and was hired by Twentieth Century-Fox's Darryl F. Zanuck in order to bring the techniques of newsreel documentary making to Hollywood features. But the most prized form of authentication for the semi-documentary filmmakers came in the form of official or quasi-official endorsements of their stories. J. Edgar Hoover of the FBI leant his signature to a number of semi-documentary productions, and OSS chief William Donovan did likewise, although he withdrew his support for *13 Rue Madeleine* halfway through the film's production for reasons that are revealed later in the book.

The semi-documentary's spirited patriotism and wholehearted acceptance of official narratives of US intelligence activities may appear almost comically naïve to the modern viewer – although contemporary films and television series made with the cooperation of the CIA, like *Zero Dark Thirty* (2012), are not so different from their early Cold War predecessors. Yet for filmmakers in the immediate post-war period there were a number of good reasons to privilege the US government's perspective. Some of those reasons were responses to repressive or censorious tendencies within early Cold War Hollywood cinema. This was the era of the House Un-American Activities Committee (HUAC), of course, where official endorsement provided welcome protection from McCarthyite charges of political subversion. Hollywood's industry censor, the Production Code Administration (PCA), also required filmmakers to seek approval from government agencies and individual employees before representing them. And finally American tort law, which prior to the landmark *The New York Times Co. v. Sullivan* (1964) ruling was far stricter in its defence of libel and slander plaintiffs, discouraged studio lawyers from permitting unendorsed representations of living public figures.

That said, the semi-documentary was not born entirely out of political expediency. Rather, it was a form that was earnestly developed by people like Louis de Rochemont and Twentieth Century-Fox studio mogul Darryl F. Zanuck who believed in the power and responsibility of the cinema to document reality. This was a belief born out of their experiences of the Second World War. Having witnessed young men die, 'even had them die in my arms', as Zanuck recalled, and having filmed something of the horrors of war for the American public, filmmakers returned to civilian life with the conviction that the cinema should educate as much as it should entertain.[11] Moreover, war elevated the epistemic authority of cinema as a medium, and documentary films in particular. Chapter 1 of this book explores the impact of the Second World War upon the cinema, and cinema upon the conduct of war, through a history of John Ford's OSS Field Photographic Unit (FPU), a group of more than 300 Hollywood filmmakers and technicians who produced training, reconnaissance and propaganda films and whose work, it is argued here, had a profound impact upon the development of both war and cinema.

Hollywood's close relationship with the OSS did not simply end with the conclusion of the war, or even after Truman's dissolution of the OSS in October 1945. Following Truman's decision, OSS chief General William Donovan campaigned vigorously for the establishment of a permanent peacetime central intelligence agency. Chapter 2 documents how Hollywood played a vital role in this campaign by producing a series of films, made with the cooperation and assistance of Donovan and numerous other OSS veterans, that celebrated the OSS's wartime achievements while at the same time advocating for its permanent successor. These films, in particular *13 Rue Madeleine*, spoke with a new authority that the war had granted them and proclaimed themselves as realistic semi-documentary renderings of the OSS's wartime activities. As already discussed, the semi-documentary's claims to authenticity were usually based upon their access to government officials and advisors, who sometimes officially endorsed the films.

In the context of the Second World War's immediate aftermath, the semi-documentary's faith in the official record was understandable. As Scott Lucas puts it, during the war 'the [American] public was conditioned to the illusion of the US government as helpful provider of news'.[12] Many of those who worked on the post-war OSS films had helped make that news, either working directly for government propaganda agencies or in cooperation with them.

Moreover, the films that government propaganda agencies made during the war, including Ford's OSS Field Photographic Unit, were so powerful, and vividly real, that audiences had little reason to doubt their veracity.[13] The OSS-produced concentration camp films, for example, proved so compelling at the Nuremberg trials that they effectively sealed the fate of the Nazi defendants, condemning many of them to the gallows. Nobody could contest the authority of those shocking images of human cruelty and suffering at Auschwitz or Dachau, even if they were, ultimately, OSS propaganda films, cut together to achieve a certain effect, and shown at just the right moment in the trial for maximum impact. Propaganda need not always be untrue. Moreover, all documentaries whether endorsed by government or not, are in some sense political – advocating a certain narrative, idea or argument. As wartime production chief of the Office of War Information's (OWI) overseas Bureau of Motion Pictures, Phillip Dunne, put it: 'In the broadest sense the documentary is always, therefore, an instrument of propaganda.'[14]

But the semi-documentary's reliance upon government endorsement, buttressed by the requirements of the PCA and studio lawyers, posed a worrying question for filmmakers: What happens when the agency you are attempting to represent refuses to endorse your production? This in fact occurred during the production of *13 Rue Madeleine*. William Donovan, who was initially enthusiastic about the film, pulled his support halfway through in an abrasive letter to de Rochemont that called into question the accuracy of his picture. With most of the film already shot, de Rochemont and co-producer Darryl F. Zanuck scrambled to reshoot scenes and obfuscate the identity of the Agency they were representing by re-christening them '077', a move that provoked scathing rebukes by some reviewers in the press. In this instance it proved mildly bothersome and embarrassing for de Rochemont and Zanuck, but what happens if a government agency with a particular passion for anonymity, an agency like the newly formed CIA, established in the National Security Act of 1947, simply refused, as a matter of course, to engage with filmmakers or even allow them to acknowledge their existence? The answer is that for the first decade of their existence, during a period often described by intelligence historians as the 'Golden Age' of CIA covert action, the CIA were almost entirely absent from Hollywood cinema and American popular culture more generally.[15] Indeed the subject of American covert intervention in world affairs was almost a complete taboo in the American media. As one television executive put it in 1955: 'Officially, our government has no foreign espionage system in peacetime. Therefore, it is important in our stories that when X goes to a foreign country, it must not be for the purpose of official or unofficial espionage.'[16] Chapter 3 examines this period of CIA anonymity in Hollywood during an age of consensus when the American media, including the film industry, proved too meek to question America's mushrooming covert operations.

INTRODUCTION

The first film to explicitly mention the CIA was Alfred Hitchcock's *North by Northwest* (1959). Not coincidentally, it was also the first of a new breed of spy thriller: the tongue-in-cheek romantic adventure format, epitomised by the James Bond films, which debuted a few years later and were deeply influenced by Hitchcock's classic caper. These films were altogether different from their austere semi-documentary predecessors. They were light-hearted, self-effacing and sexy, and featured colourful and exotic locales all shot in colour using high-production values that brought audiences into cinemas for a spot of vicarious tourism in droves. Perhaps most significantly for the development of the representation of American espionage onscreen, they rejected and often explicitly mocked the semi-documentaries' claims to authenticity via their cooperation with government. 'This film has not been made with the consent or cooperation of The Federal Board of Regulations (F.B.R.) or The Central Enquiries Agency (C.E.A.)', reads the opening text of 1967 'camp' countercultural classic *The President's Analyst*, sardonically mocking the semi-documentaries' reliance on such statements, '[a]ny resemblance to persons living or dead is purely coincidental, and so forth and so on'.[17] Chapter 4 examines the emergence of this irreverence within the 'camp' spy cinema and television of the 1960s that rejected the idea of authenticity and instead celebrated artifice. Although few of these were decidedly political, for example they rarely offered radical critiques of the CIA and US Cold War foreign policy and often they deliberately avoided mention of the Cold War altogether, their departure from the semi-documentaries' state-sourced method of historical representation was important. It marked a decisive cleavage away from consensus history and towards the epistemological scepticism of postmodernity. In the process, by breaking with state-sourced representation, it helped lay the foundations for the more politically charged scepticism in the conspiracy cinema of the 1970s.

The third form of spy cinema – realism – receives scant attention in this book. This is not because I deem it unimportant. Indeed, aesthetically speaking, some of the most powerful works of literature and film during the Cold War, like John Le Carré's 1963 novel *The Spy Who Came in from the Cold*, and its 1965 cinematic adaptation by British director Martin Ritt, are archetypes of this form. But in Hollywood cinema at least, the form failed to make its mark. Films like the aforementioned *The Spy Who Came in from the Cold*, or *The IPCRESS File*, to give two of the most well-known examples, were British films with British cast and crew. Yes the former did well in America, at least as well as a downcast realist British spy drama can be expected to do, but it never came close to supplanting the James Bond imagery of espionage. Perhaps, as numerous scholars have suggested, the cultural phenomenon of the realist spy thriller made most sense in Britain, a nation struggling to come to terms with the collapse of its empire, and where the Cambridge Spies scandals had shattered the James Bond image of the British intelligence establishment as being populated by dashing young heterosexuals whose service to queen and country was almost as unimpeachable as their virility.[18]

An earlier draft of this book included a chapter on Alfred Hitchcock's late career. Inspired by the Cambridge Spies stories filtering back from his homeland, Hitchcock set about attempting to undo his own influence with *North by Northwest*, a format that the Bond films had emulated and then stretched to cartoonish proportions. Hitchcock's late-career trilogy of Cold War spy thrillers, *Torn Curtain* (1966), *Topaz* (1970) and the unmade *The Short Night*, were rare examples of the realist format crossing the Atlantic and being applied as a means of representing American, rather than British, intelligence. Significantly, however, Hitchcock was British, and these films were inspired by British headlines, even though they featured American agents. While *Torn Curtain* was a box-office hit, the highest-grossing film of Hitchcock's career in fact, this was likely more to do with the film's stars, Paul Newman and Julie Andrews, who were imposed on Hitchcock by the studio, as was the film's upbeat conclusion that contrasted starkly with the director's increasingly bleak vision of espionage, and compromised the film's intended realist aesthetic.[19] Both *Torn Curtain* and *Topaz* were critical failures, and are usually regarded by Hitchcock scholars as symptomatic of the great director's artistic decline in his twilight years. Although Hitchcock's aim was to introduce the spy realism that was then flourishing in the country of his birth to his adopted homeland, he failed. The American public of the 1960s simply wasn't interested in such downcast narratives that declared, in the paradigmatic line from his unmade final espionage feature, *The Short Night*: 'Spying and espionage. Everybody suffers from it. The gains are vague and abstract. And the losses are all personal.'[20]

By the mid-1970s, however, the American public was ready for a more cynical vision of American secrecy and espionage, one that lacked the tongue-in-cheek humour of the romantic narratives of the previous decade. The reasons for this are obvious: with the tragedy of the Vietnam War still unfolding, revelation piled upon revelation of government secrecy and deception filtered into the public domain. From the publication of the Pentagon Papers in 1971, which demonstrated that four successive US government administrations had deceived the public about their intentions in Vietnam, to Watergate, which leaked out slowly and by accretion, and finally the barrage of revelations of CIA and FBI misdeeds throughout the course of 1975 that rocked the US intelligence community and led to the establishment of numerous Congressional and Presidential enquiries, the early to mid-1970s was a period of time in which the idea that the American government often acts conspiratorially was not a fiction, but all too real.

With the emergence of the conspiracy thrillers in the 1970s, examined in the final chapter of this book, Hollywood's journey away from state-sourced realism, incredulously rejected by the 'camp' cinema of the 1960s, had come full circle. Theirs was a realism of sorts, with low-key lighting, naturalistic sound, claustrophobic atmospheres and location shooting that continued the legacy of film noir, but it was a miasmatic kind of realism that bespoke a sense that things were not as they seemed. It was a mise en scène that, according to Alan Pakula, perhaps the most significant architect of the form, 'while seeming real and unstylised would nonetheless have a sense of the surreal about it.'[21] The purpose, as Pakula later clarified in a handwritten note, was to articulate the juxtaposition in American life between 'THE APPEARANCE OF OPENNESS and THE REALITY OF SECRECY'.[22] Thus, when Pakula's *The Parallax View* begins and ends with a blue-ribbon commission – redolent of the Warren Commission – officially declaring that no conspiracy was behind the assassinations featured in the film, the uncanny slow zoom and eerie soundtrack undercut the authority of the committee's assertions. In Pakula's celluloid world, and the many conspiracy thrillers of the 1970s that his films helped inspire, there is a pervasive sense that truth, and the august official institutions that had previously administered it, has been subverted. The fault for this erosion of epistemological certainties was invariably shadowy government or corporate institutions, and occasionally explicitly the CIA itself.

This, in essence, is the outline story of this book: evolution, or devolution perhaps, from the epistemological stability and political conservatism that came with *13 Rue Madeleine*'s unimpeachable faith in the validity of the official record, to the postmodern paranoia that emerged in tandem with the secret state's expansion. But before I proceed to tell this story in much greater depth, and immerse the reader more fully in the bramble thicket of interweaving narratives and specific documents that comprises the chaotic raw material of history, a materiality that at times may obfuscate the simplicity of my overarching narrative, and whose entropy it is the historian's duty to attempt to invert, I would like to conclude this introduction, if the reader's patience will permit me, with a few observations on theory and method. Those less patient with cultural and historiographic theory may wish to skip ahead now to the opening chapter, for it has not been my intention to write an explicitly theoretical work; sorting through the bramble thicket has been task enough. That said it would be disingenuous to ignore the guiding theoretical observations that have helped me to see a way through that thicket, and have provided frameworks for approaching a medium – Hollywood spy cinema – that the more stalwart defenders of orthodox historiography may still dismiss as bunk.[23]

My theoretical concerns have focused almost entirely, for obvious reasons, on the relationship between fiction and fact. It is a bottomless domain, long the preserve of literary theorists and, since the pioneering work of historical theorists like Hayden White, a question of fundamental importance for contemporary historiography as well. My interest in White's work, among others, is born out of desire to depart from the straightforward dichotomy that intelligence historians have typically drawn between fact and fiction by adopting a 'mythbusting' approach.[24] There is, of course, not enough space here to do justice to the vastness and the intricacies of the debates that surround this question of realism. But perhaps those interested in similar questions may wish to follow the inadequately few lines of enquiry that time and space will permit me to provide.

The jumping-off point, or the first principle that has guided this study almost from the moment of its inception, is that simply debunking fiction as misleading and historically inaccurate offers a poor interpretative yield for the historian.[25] For fiction can be historically useful and enlightening for reasons other than the historical details it chooses to get right or wrong. Moreover, as White has persuasively argued, the historian has much more in common with the novelist – deploying the same narrative techniques – than they may like to concede.[26] As Robert Rosenstone has argued, extending White's project into an analysis of the relationship between history and film specifically, the historian's traditionally suspicious attitude towards visual representations of the past belies a lack of self-reflection about the fictional origins of many of the techniques of their own craft.[27]

The two most common alternatives to the epistemological brinksmanship that characterises the mythbusting approach are either the exploration of how life has imitated art, or vice versa. There are numerous examples in this book where either of these approaches may bear interesting fruit. Lending credence to the former, a number of fictional texts examined in this book have proved strangely prescient in their vision of the CIA. Graham Greene's *The Quiet American*, for example, first published in 1955 and then bowdlerised a few years later by Joseph Mankiewicz who adapted it to the screen, seemed to foresee the consequences of America and the CIA's increasing intervention in Vietnam more than a decade before the US obligingly fulfilled his tragic prophesy. His next novel, *Our Man in Havana* (1958), was likewise prognostic in its depiction of Batista's cruel but decaying regime, as well as for its depiction of the British intelligence establishment, long before the details of the Cambridge Spies story were fully known to the public, which for many appeared to confirm Greene's perception of them as an elitist and twittishly ineffectual class of self-serving patricians more interested in preserving their own reputation and circling the wagons in times of crisis or just routine incompetence than in the preservation of national security.

Fiction has not just proved eerily prophetic at times, but has also influenced the real world of espionage. Explaining the folly that led to the Bay of Pigs, former CIA Director William Colby wrote:

INTRODUCTION

> [E]ver since the glory days of the OSS ... the Agency had enjoyed a reputation with the public at large not a whit less than golden. After all, we were the derring-do boys who parachuted behind enemy lines ... matching fire with fire in an endless round of thrilling adventures like those of the scenarios in James Bond films.[28]

President Kennedy, who authorised the Cuban invasion, was likewise an avid-Bond reader, and numerous intelligence historians have suggested that his romantic vision of espionage, in part inspired by his love of spy fiction, helped sway his belief in the infallibility of the CIA – at least until the men were on the beach. The Bay of Pigs offers an important lesson in the real dangers that mythologies, when they are believed, can pose. Recognising the power that the right kind of mythologising can play in helping them navigate the will of the American people, the US Congress and the President, the CIA and its predecessor the OSS carefully encouraged positive visions of their work, whether true or not. As CIA apostate Victor Marchetti put it:

> A good part of the CIA's power position is dependent upon its careful mythologizing and glorification of the exploits of the clandestine profession ... the selling of the intelligence business is designed to have us admire it as some sort of mysterious, often magical, profession capable of accomplishing terribly difficult, if not miraculous, deeds. Like most myths, the intrigues and successes of the CIA over the years have been more imaginary than real. What is real, unfortunately, is the willingness of both the public and adherents of the cult to believe the fictions that permeate the intelligence business.[29]

Today the CIA's engagement with Hollywood is more frequent and extensive than at any point in its history. As Tricia Jenkins has documented in her study of the contemporary relationship between the Agency and Hollywood, since the mid-1990s the CIA has worked in close cooperation with a number of productions to rectify their tarnished popular image.[30] Perhaps most controversially, Republican members of the House attacked the CIA for sharing classified material on the killing of Bin Laden with the producers of *Zero Dark Thirty* (2012) – the accusations led to the formation of a Senate panel to investigate the charges.[31] Equally controversial was the film's apparent justification of the CIA's use of torture in the war on terror, which Senator John McCain, a victim of torture during the Vietnam War, condemned as 'grossly inaccurate'.[32] The significance that the CIA now places upon managing public perceptions – both real and fictional, including those put about by Hollywood – is testament to the continued influence art has had upon life.

The second common historical approach to fiction, often the preferred method of the cultural historian, is the study of the past *through* fiction by gauging the impact of life upon art. As my brief chapter outline has already indicated, clearly events and ideas such as the Second World War, the Cold War liberal consensus, the Bay of Pigs, Watergate and Vietnam had profound implications for spy fiction in the post-war period. It would be counter-productive for the historian to attempt to view cultural texts in isolation from these major historical developments. But pure historicism will only take us so far in understanding the historical significance of spy fiction.

The problem with both of these approaches, of art imitating life or life imitating art, is not that they are necessarily misleading. Indeed both yield insightful interpretations. The problem, rather, is that while they show a greater deference towards fiction, and see greater historical value in it than the mythbusting approach, both still implicitly maintain a dichotomy between fact and fiction. Both adopt a linear billiard-ball notion of causality whereby fictional texts and historical events are deemed essentially separate entities that may from time to time impact upon one another, even dramatically, but are always, in the end, apart. Such an understanding frequently provokes chicken-and-egg debates about the relationship between the cultural, the historical and the political that will likely continue in perpetuity. Was the CIA a product of dominant cultural myths about espionage or the cause of them? General Donovan's post-war publicity campaign certainly made use of these myths by arguing, successfully, for the establishment of a permanent peacetime central intelligence agency. But then again many of the post-war OSS films that bolstered his campaign simply recycled old espionage tropes that predated the OSS. Then again those tropes were themselves a product of First World War jingoism and romantic notions of British imperial adventure, especially during the Great Game, which itself was largely constructed by fiction, which itself was influenced by . . . When does myth end and history begin? We could go on asking ourselves this question, spinning in circles, for many pages. We could trace the question of the relationship between spy fiction and spy fact all the way back to Homer's *Iliad* and the shadow warfare magic of the Trojan War and still not feel entirely content with the answer such endless genealogies would bring.

To avoid this constant chasing of our tail, what is needed is an understanding of causality that recognises the complex interrelationship between fact and fiction, or what Ann Douglas has described as 'synchronicity when it comes to sorting out the relations between . . . economics, politics, and culture'.[33] Fredric Jameson, borrowing Louis Althusser's concept of 'structural causality' in his interpretation of literary narratives as socially symbolic acts, provides just such an understanding. Jameson, a Marxist, who nevertheless wishes to complicate the vulgar Marxists' conception of the economic base's deterministic relationship to the ideological superstructure – that culture is merely a symptom of the mode of production – argues that what he calls 'totality',

INTRODUCTION

or history writ large, is nothing more than the sum of its parts. As Robert Paul Resch explains:

> According to ... *structural causality*, relations between elements of the whole are not exterior to the whole, as is the case with transitive causality, nor are they expressions of its immanent principle, as with expressive causality. Instead, the whole is nothing less than the reciprocal effectivities of its elements, at the same time as these elements are determined by the whole, that is, by their interrelationship with all the other elements within the whole. The cause of the effects is the 'complex organization of the whole' while the latter is precisely 'the sum of the effects and their interrelationships.'[34]

According to this understanding, the analytic categories of culture, politics, economics and society that comprise the rich tapestry of history are not discreet components that operate autonomously, but an interwoven part of the same complex ecosystem. Just as a marine biologist can learn something about the health of a reef system by studying the behaviour of a single species that inhabits it, so too can the historian learn something about the past, in all its rich variety, by examining a fictional text. Or, more pertinently, just as the CIA cannot be understood independently from the development of US Cold War foreign policy, and vice versa, neither can the 'real' CIA and its place and meaning within American history be understood without examining its representation in fiction. For Jameson, one key implication of this approach is the periodisation of history.[35] For when meta-historical change occurs, when one epoch replaces another, it is only because the same transformations are happening, synchronically, across the entire ecosystem of the past. Thus when we observe structural transformations in fiction, we are also simultaneously observing political, social and economic changes as well: this, in essence, is what Jameson means when he says that narrative performs socially symbolic acts.[36]

The structural transformation of Hollywood spy cinema from the Second World War to the 1970s is thus indicative, although not straightforwardly so, of other wider transformation in American culture, politics and society. Driving these transformations – whether we seek to understand the emergence of the conspiracy thriller in the 1970s, or the historical contingencies that led to Watergate, or the widening credibility gap between citizens and the American Government – were secrecy and official deception. Secrecy, like a mysterious bacteria suddenly appearing on a fragile reef, infected every aspect of American history during the Cold War. The paranoia that accompanied it was not just the domain of crackpots on the fringes, as Richard Hofstadter would have it, but of presidents, filmmakers, novelists, religious preachers, military planners, intelligence agencies, whole governments, revolutionaries, soldiers, sailors ... 'This is the age of conspiracy,' wrote Don DeLillo, 'the age of connections, links, secret relationships.'[37] DeLillo also tells us that it is an age in which the CIA functions as 'America's myth', taking on 'shapes and appearances, embodying whatever we need at a given time to know ourselves or unburden ourselves'.[38]

It is this age that has replaced that stable world of fixed truths and political certainties that pervades the opening scene of *13 Rue Madeleine*. And it is an age that we still inhabit to this day. For this reason, I hope that you will find this story of the transformation of Hollywood's vision of American espionage from the Second World War to the 1970s instructive, whether you are a historian, a filmmaker, a conspiracy theorist or a spy. For the one thing that this story may teach us, is that history, that 'noble cause' that once bound up the nation, is only ever as credible as our faith in the veracity of the documentary record.[39] The moment that we began to view *13 Rue Madeleine*'s paean to the National Archives with scepticism was the moment that everything began to change.

Notes

1. Richard Gid Powers' introduction to Daniel Patrick Moynihan, *Secrecy: The American Experience* (New Haven: Yale University Press, 1999), p. 17.
2. *13 Rue Madeleine* (Henry Hathaway, Twentieth Century-Fox, 1947).
3. *JFK* (Oliver Stone, Warner Brothers, 1991).
4. Don DeLillo, *Libra* (London: Penguin Modern Classics, 2006), p. 181.
5. See, for example, Tom Engelhardt, *The End of Victory Culture: Cold War America and the Disillusioning of a Generation* (New York: Basic Books, 1996); Rick Perlstein, *Nixonland: The Rise of a President and the Fracturing of America* (New York: Scribner, 2008); Geoffrey Hodgson, *America in Our Time: From World War II to Nixon: What Happened and Why* (Princeton: Princeton University Press, 2005); Iwan W. Morgan, *Beyond the Liberal Consensus: A Political History of the United States since 1965* (London: Palgrave Macmillan, 1994); Daniel T. Rogers, *Age of Fracture* (Cambridge, MA: Harvard University Press, 2012).
6. See, for example, Arthur Marwick's discussion of the problems of periodisation in his introduction to Arthur Marwick, *The Sixties: Social and Cultural Transformation in Britain, France, Italy and the United States, 1958–74* (Oxford: Oxford University Press, 1999). See also John Patrick Diggins' excellent history of the 1950s that problematises the reductive idea that it was simply a decade of social conformity and political conservatism: John Patrick Diggins, *The Proud Decades: America in War and Peace, 1941–1960* (New York: W. W. Norton and Company, 1989).
7. For a detailed statistical analysis of the breakdown of public trust in American Government in the second half of the twentieth century, see 'Public Trust in Government: 1958–2014', Pew Research Center US Politics and Policy, available online at <http://www.people-press.org/2014/11/13/public-trust-in-government>, accessed 30 March 2015.
8. Timothy Melley, *The Covert Sphere: Secrecy, Fiction, and the National Security State* (Ithaca: Cornell University Press, 2012), p. 35.

9. Melley, *The Covert Sphere*.
10. Lyotard famously defined postmodernism as 'incredulity toward metanarratives'. See Jean-François Lyotard, *The Postmodern Condition: A Report on Knowledge* (Manchester: Manchester University Press, 1984), xxiv.
11. Zanuck cited in George F. Custen, *Twentieth Century's Fox: Darryl F. Zanuck and the Culture of Hollywood* (New York: Basic Books, 1998), p. 265.
12. Lucas, Scott, *Freedom's War: The American Crusade against the Soviet Union* (New York: New York University Press, 1999), p. 11.
13. A notable exception to this is Josephine MacNab's objections to Ford's *The Battle of Midway*. I begin the first chapter with the issues she raised in a letter to the director.
14. Phillip Dunne, 'The Documentary and Hollywood', *Hollywood Quarterly*, 1:2 (January, 1946), p. 167.
15. See, for example, Rhodri Jeffreys-Jones, *Cloak and Doller: A History of American Secret Intelligence* (New Haven: Yale University Press, 2002), pp. 154–78; David Rudgers, 'The Origins of Covert Action', *Journal of Contemporary History*, 35:2 (April 2000), pp. 249–62.
16. Maurice Unger to Eddie Davis, 3 November 1955, Ziv Entertainment Collection, Man Called X Correspondence File, Wisconsin State Historical Society (Hereafter WSHS), Madison.
17. *The President's Analyst* (Theodore J. Flicker, Paramount, 1967).
18. See Simon Willmetts and Christopher Moran, 'Filming Treachery: British Cinema and Television's Fascination with the Cambridge Five', *The Journal of British Cinema and Television*, 10:1 (January 2013), pp. 49–70.
19. Lesley L. Coffin, *Hitchcock's Stars: Alfred Hitchcock and the Hollywood Studio System* (Lanham: Rowman and Littlefield, 2014), p. 175.
20. David Freeman, *The Last Days of Alfred Hitchcock: A Memoir Featuring the Entire Screenplay of 'Alfred Hitchcock's The Short Night'* (Woodstock: The Overlook Press, 1984), p. 174.
21. 'It Could Only Be A Movie', Says Alan Pakula About his Suspense Film, 'The Parallax View', Alan Pakula Papers, Folder 363 'Publicity', AMPAS, Beverly Hills.
22. 'Handwritten Notes', 21 February 1973, Alan Pakula Papers, Folder 373 'Story Notes', AMPAS, Beverly Hills; emphasis in original.
23. See Simon Willmetts, 'Reconceiving Realism: Intelligence Historians and the Fact/Fiction Dichotomy', in Christopher Moran and Christopher J. Murphy (eds), *Intelligence Studies in Britain and the US: Historiography since 1945* (Edinburgh: Edinburgh University Press, 2013a), pp. 146–71.
24. See, for example, Nicholas Dujmovic, '"Hollywood, Don't You Go Disrepectin My Culture": *The Good Shepherd* versus Real CIA History', *Intelligence and National Security: Special Issue on Spying in Film and Fiction*, 23:1 (February 2008), pp. 25–41; Frederick P. Hitz, *The Great Game: The Myths and Reality of Espionage* (New York: Vintage Press, 2005); Stan A. Taylor, 'Introduction: Spying in Film and Fiction', *Intelligence and National Security: Special Issue on Spying in Film and Fiction*, 23:1 (2008), p. 1; David Stafford, *The Silent Game: The Real World of Imaginary Spies* (London: Viking Press, 1989); Amy Zegart, 'Cloaks, Daggers, and Ivory Towers: Why Academics Don't Study U.S. Intelligence', in Loch Johnson (ed.), *Strategic Intelligence: Understanding the Hidden Side of Government*, volume one (Westport: Praeger Publishers, 2006), pp. 21–32.
25. I have outlined my objections to the 'mythbusting' approach to spy fiction more fully in Willmetts, 'Reconceiving Realism'.
26. Hayden White, *Tropics of Discourse: Essays in Cultural Criticism* (Baltimore:

Johns Hopkins University Press, 1978); Hayden White, *Metahistory: The Historical Imagination in the Nineteenth Century* (Baltimore: Johns Hopkins University Press, 1973); Hayden White, *The Content of the Form: Narrative Discourse and Historical Representation* paperback edition (London: Johns Hopkins University Press, 1990). Other theorists that have looked at the relationship between fiction, narrative and history that have influenced this study include: Frederic Jameson, *The Political Unconscious: Narrative as a Socially Symbolic Act* (Ithaca: Cornell University Press, 1981); Frank Ankersmit, *History and Tropology: The Rise and Fall of Metaphor* (Berkeley: University of California Press, 1994); Linda Hutcheon, *A Poetics of Postmodernism: History, Theory, Fiction* (London: Routledge, 1988); Paul Ricoeur, *Time and Narrative*, three volumes (Chicago: University of Chicago Press, 1984, 1985, 1988); Dominick LaCapra, *History and Criticism* (Ithaca: Cornell University Press, 1985).

27. Robert Rosenstone, *Visions of the Past: The Challenge of Film to Our Idea of History* (Boston: Harvard University Press, 1995). Other significant works that explore the relationship between film and history include: Robert Rosenstone, 'History in Images/History in Words: Reflections on the Possibility of Really Putting History onto Film', *American Historical Review*, 93:5 (1988), pp. 1,173–85; Robert Rosenstone, *History on Film/Film on History* (London: Longman Pearson, 2006); George Custen, *Bio/Pics: How Hollywood Constructed Public History* (New Brunswick: Rutgers University Press, 1992); David Eldridge, *Hollywood's History Films* (London: I.B. Tauris, 2006); Marc Ferro, *Cinema and History*, trans. Naomi Greene (Detroit: Wayne State University Press, 1988); Peter C. Rollins (ed.), *The Columbia Companion to American History on Film* (New York: Columbia University Press, 2005); Bob Sklar, 'Does Film History Need a Crisis?', *Cinema Journal*, 44:1 (autumn 2004), pp. 134–8; Jennifer E. Smyth, *Reconstructing American Historical Cinema from Cimarron to Citizen Kane* (Lexington: University Press of Kentucky, 2006); Jennifer E. Smyth (ed.), *Hollywood and the American Historical Film*, (London, Palgrave Macmillan, 2011); Warren Susman, 'Film and History: Artifact and Experience', *Film and History*, 15:2 (May 1985), pp. 26–36; Hayden White, 'Historiography and Historiophoty', *American Historical Review*, 93:5 (1988), pp. 1,193–9; Robert Brent Toplin, *Reel History: In Defense of Hollywood* (Lawrence: University Press of Kansas, 2002); Robert Burgoyne, *Film Nation: Hollywood Looks at U.S. History*, second revised edition (Minneapolis: University of Minnesota Press, 2010).
28. William Colby and Peter Forbath, *Honorable Men: My Life in the CIA* (New York: Simon and Schuster, 1978), p. 180.
29. Victor Marchetti and John D. Marks, *The CIA and the Cult of Intelligence* (New York: Coronet Books, 1974), pp. 35–6.
30. Tricia Jenkins, *The CIA in Hollywood: How the Agency Shapes Film and Television* (Austin: University of Texas Press, 2012).
31. Mark Hosenball, 'Senate Panel to Examine CIA Contacts with "Zero Dark Thirty" Filmmakers', *Reuters*, 2 January 2013. Available online at http://www.reuters.com/article/2013/01/03/us-usa-ciafilm-idUSBRE90200420130103, accessed 28 July 2015.
32. McCain cited in Xan Brooks, 'John McCain Criticises *Zero Dark Thirty's* Depiction of Torture', *The Guardian*, 20 December 2012. Available online at http://www.theguardian.com/film/2012/dec/20/john-mccain-zero-dark-thirty, accessed 28 July 2015.
33. Ann Douglas, 'Periodizing the American Century: Modernism, Postmodernism and Postcolonialism in the Cold War Context', *Modernism/Modernity*, 5:3 (September 1998), p. 75; emphasis in the original.

34. Robert Paul Resch, *Althusser and the Renewal of Marxist Social Theory* (Berkeley: University of California Press, 1992), p. 50.
35. Fredric Jameson, 'Periodizing the 60s', *Social Text*, 9:10 (1984), pp. 178–209.
36. Fredric Jameson, *The Political Unconscious*.
37. Don DeLillo, *Running Dog*, vintage reissue edition (New York: Vintage, 1989), p. 111.
38. Don DeLillo, *The Names* (New York: Knopf, 1982), p. 317.
39. Peter Novick, That Noble Dream: The 'Objectivity Question' and the American Historical Profession (Cambridge: Cambridge University Press, 1988).

1. THE FACTS OF WAR: CINEMATIC INTELLIGENCE AND THE OFFICE OF STRATEGIC SERVICES

I think I saw the European war as a newsreel war, only taking place on the silver square above my head, its visual conventions decided by the resources and limits of the war cameraman, as I would now put it, though even my 10-year-old eyes could sense the difference between an authentic newsreel and one filmed on manoeuvres. The real, whether war or peace, was something you saw filmed in newsreel.

J. G. Ballard, *Miracles of Life: An Autobiography*

On a late summer afternoon in mid-September 1942, Mrs Josephine MacNab took the subway from her home on Riverside Drive in the Upper West Side to New York's Grand Central Terminal. Walking the remaining few blocks to the Trans-Lux theatre on Lexington and 52nd Street, her thoughts turned to the war in the Pacific. The experiences she conjured were starkly real, familiar to any cinemagoer of the twentieth century: the tense disembarkation from an LCC landing craft, the chilling whine of a Japanese bombing raid, the distant stare of an American Marine gazing out at the expansive Pacific. Although she had never personally experienced any of this, she had a good idea of how it may seem. She had seen many of these images before in the newsreels. These prosthetic memories were not lived experiences, but they were, in a certain sense, no less real in their immediacy.[1] Had she attempted the same feat of psychic empathy only twenty-five years previously, imagining the American trenches in Cambrai or the Somme, the grainy mental-reel before her would have seemed far less real – lacking the visual credibility of the vivid Technicolor images of the British and American landing at Bone, or the Battle of the Coral Sea.[2]

Josephine passed over a quarter to the ticket seller for the showing of newsreels that afternoon. Only newsreels and travelogues were shown at the Trans-Lux theatre, satisfying a growing public demand for documentary features, particularly news of war.[3] At this particular performance, Josephine saw 'photographs taken of the Commando Raid on the coast of Norway, the terrific punishment taken by the Chinese in a bombing by the Japanese and a showing of a film depicting the intensive training our boys are undergoing'. Sitting before these pictures, Josephine was at once 'struck with the stark realism of these films' – they were unlike anything American audiences had ever witnessed before.[4] It is easy to forget, from the vantage of today's media-saturated world, where we have become desensitised to the power of the image, how compelling such footage must have been. The cinema was a livelier place in those days. Feelings of extreme physical discomfort were not uncommon reactions to the most vivid images presented, and theatre brawls and riots in response to particularly controversial subjects were not unheard of. Moreover, by the 1940s the newsreel was unquestionably one of the most influential sources of information for the American public:

> At its height, in the United States alone, the American newsreel was seen weekly by at least 40 million people, and throughout the world by more than 200 million. For many people, especially the illiterate, it was a principal source of news until the coming of television, providing the imagery with which to perceive and conceive the nature of political and military events, distant geographic locales, technological innovation, and foreign people and cultures.[5]

The final showing that afternoon was an eighteen-minute documentary report of the decisive Battle of Midway. The legendary Hollywood director John Ford had shot the film. Shortly before America's entry into the war, Ford had hastily assembled a group of Hollywood filmmakers and technicians to form what would become the OSS's Field Photographic Unit (FPU), tasked with the production of motion pictures for the purposes of propaganda, intelligence collection, reconnaissance, training and historical documentation. Ford's assignment at Midway was the first time he or any of his unit would film combat.

The story of how he made *The Battle of Midway* (1942), which would later win the Academy Award for best documentary feature, is among the most heroic tales of Hollywood lore: along with his assistant cameraman Jack Mackenzie Jr, Ford climbed atop a powerhouse 'on the narrow, triangular sliver of land called Eastern Island'.[6] Although not as conspicuous as the infamous Cunningham Combat Camera, a mobile 35 mm camera developed

IN SECRECY'S SHADOW

by the FPU in 1945 that injudiciously resembled a machine gun, his 16 mm handheld pointed directly at the oncoming Japanese planes coupled with his exposed position made him '[a]n obvious and clear target'. As OSS-chief William J. Donovan noted in his report of the battle: 'the power house was repeatedly strafed'.[7] During the raid, a Japanese bomb narrowly missed Ford and Mackenzie by about twenty feet and threw showers of debris at them. Ford was knocked unconscious by a piece of flying concrete and wounded by metal shrapnel buried in his arm.[8] Had the bomb landed just a few feet closer, or had Ford sat slightly to the left, the world would have been deprived of such masterpieces of post-war cinema as *She Wore a Yellow Ribbon* (1949), *Rio Grande* (1950), *The Searchers* (1956) and *The Last Hurrah* (1958).

Ford and Mackenzie prudently climbed down from the powerhouse and continued to film, managing to capture some of the most vivid images of war

Figure 1.1 The Cunningham Combat Camera was introduced late in the war in 1945. Mark Armistead, an officer in Ford's FPU, recalled that the Cunningham Combat Camera was 'probably the lousiest camera ever made. The thing would never run. It would buckle. It looked like a machine gun and if you're in combat and you're pointing something that looks like a machine-gun people take a dim view of that.' FPU officer Robert Parrish recalled an incident in his autobiography where he was asked by Ford to shoot a photographic report of the old State Department building next to the White House with the camera. After a few minutes of filming, the sight of the Cunningham camera mounted on a tripod with a 'ray-gun' like zoom lens attached and pointed directly at the White House provoked a Marine sergeant to order his troops to take up combat positions and train their rifles on Parrish. The sergeant had Parrish arrested and he later received a court-martial for the incident. *Source:* Imperial War Museum, London, UK.[9]

that the American public had ever seen: 'spectacular color footage of a burning hangar, antiaircraft guns defending the island, and sailors and marines dashing around in the midst of raging black smoke and flames, trying to dodge the strafing'.[10] Josephine could not help but be impressed by these images. Earlier that week, during a screening at New York's Radio City Music Hall, 'people screamed and wept and had to be helped out of the theater by ushers'.[11] Josephine thanked Ford for the 'superbly photographed' images, for which 'the American public owe you a deep sense of gratitude'. But, amidst the trawl of factual programming on offer at the Trans-Lux that day something was amiss in this particular feature. In spite of the narrator's soothing reassurance that 'Yes – this really happened', set to the sound of the Star-Spangled Banner playing over images of the American flag being raised, the illusion of reality was lost on Josephine: 'why, oh why', she complained to Ford

> should [*the*] 'Hollywood touch' have been added to something that spoke so eloquently for itself and which gave stark living reality a touch of unreality, by so deliberating [*sic*] 'setting a stage', with a voice reminding us that behind a glorious sunset lurks something ominous; and then the feminine voice, in a highly unpleasant tone, interpolating about a certain boy, his sister and his mother and the completely uncalled for comment about getting the boys to the hospital![12]

The scenes that Josephine took particular issue with featured Jane Darwell's sentimental narration, intended to speak for the 'Mothers of America', introducing domestic scenes of young recruit Bill Kinney's father, sister and mother, 'just like the rest of us mothers in Springfield or any other American town'. As Kinney's B-17 takes off, Darwell cries out, 'Good luck! God bless you, son!' Later, over scenes of a bombed-out hospital, Darwell's syrupy voice urges: 'Get those boys to the hospital, please do! Quickly! Get them to clean cots and cool sheets. Give them doctors and medicine, a nurse's soft hands.'[13] John Ford biographer Joseph McBride argues that the narration had the desired effect of 'putting the average American or Briton into the film, which describes Midway as "our outpost – your front yard".'[14] The film's editor, Robert Parrish, however, was less convinced. Presaging Josephine's reaction, he thought the scenes 'just corny ... maudlin', and told Ford as much.[15] Ford, however, was undeterred. The accolades he had accrued in the immediate pre-war years for such films as *Stagecoach* (1939), *The Grapes of Wrath* (1939) and *How Green Was My Valley* (1941) were due to his characteristic fusion of melodrama with a realist aesthetic that closely resembled the cinematography of famed depression-era documentary filmmaker Pare Lorentz.[16] For Ford, like many of the documentarians who came of age under the auspices of US government or military service during the Second World War, realism was an instrument that lent credibility to their storytelling, but the stories – at least those that were intended for public consumption – remained essentially the same.

Ford left Midway for Hollywood on 14 June, stopping briefly in Hawaii on the way. In Honolulu he handed the eight canisters of footage to Parrish. Concerned that interference from military brass would prevent the film's release, Ford instructed Parrish to edit the top-secret footage in Hollywood and then hide it at his mother's house and await further instruction.[17] Parrish asked Ford whether he wanted the film cut as a 'straight documentary or a propaganda film'.[18] Ford replied, 'What's a propaganda film?' – taking umbrage at the very suggestion. 'Well, I mean,' Parrish carefully rephrased, 'is it for the public or for the OSS?' Ford sonorously replied, 'It's for the mothers of America. It's to let them know that we're in a war, and that we've been getting the shit kicked out of us for five months, and now we're starting to hit back.'[19]

In spite of Ford's redress, Parrish's question was a legitimate one. Much of the film shot by the FPU was not intended for public consumption and was, on the face of it, 'strictly utilitarian documentary footage, with little or no attempt at aesthetic shaping'.[20] As McBride put it:

> [U]nlike propaganda films aimed at least in part at civilian audiences, such as the *Why We Fight* series or Ford's own *The Battle of Midway*, most Field Photo films tended to be less emotional than analytical, offering hard-boiled presentations for professionals who did not need preaching or soft-soaping. Some of the films were not even edited but simply reels of raw footage from the field.[21]

It is unlikely, of course, that such an unrefined cinematic treatment of war, without narrative structure or explication, would garner mass appeal. Moreover, out of respect for operational secrecy, or simply the families of the deceased, uncensored and unedited footage of war was never appropriate for the Trans-Lux screen. Yet it was precisely this 'preaching or soft-soaping' that had irked Josephine. 'Is the American public considered incapable of imagining for themselves, inso far [*sic*] as their own is concerned?' she asked Ford. 'I had a real sense of being "talked down at" – of having to have my pill sugarcoated! Perhaps this seemed the more so because these pictures were shown with other films whose impact was felt because of the lack of just this.'[22]

Back in Hollywood, Ford had screenwriter Dudley Nichols, who had worked with him on *Stagecoach* (1939), and MGM producer James Kevin McGuinness hastily assemble a script for *Midway*. He asked Twentieth Century-Fox composer Alfred Newman to score the film, which included the 'Red River Valley' accordion track from Ford's adaptation of Steinbeck's dust-bowl epic *The Grapes of Wrath* (1939). Scouring his rolodex, he asked Jane

Figure 1.2 John Ford poses with film stock at Midway. *Source:* John Ford Mss, Lilly Library, Indiana.

Darwell and Henry Fonda, who had starred in *The Grapes of Wrath*, alongside Donald Crisp and Irving Pichel, who featured in Ford's last film before he went on active duty, *How Green Was My Valley* (1941), to narrate the film, lending it that Hollywood 'touch of unreality' about which Josephine had so indignantly complained.

Hollywood trickery did, however, win over one particularly influential plaudit. Fearing that bureaucratic infighting between the various services would prevent the film's release, Ford took the completed picture straight to the White House. Shortly before screening the film for President Roosevelt, Ford handed Parrish a short piece of footage that contained a close-up of his OSS colleague at Midway, James Roosevelt, the President's oldest son. Parrish quickly edited the scene into the film, and filled a gap in the soundtrack so that the narrator introduces 'Major Roosevelt'.[23] In the White House screening room the President was joined by his wife Eleanor; 'members of the Joint Chiefs of Staff; presidential press aide Stephen Early; and FDR's chief of staff, Admiral William Leahy, a vigorous opponent of Donovan and the OSS'.[24] As

Parrish recalled, the President talked throughout the screening. He would say, '[O]h that's a B-17 and that's a ...'[25] Then, when the image of his son came onscreen, the entire room fell silent. 'When the lights came up, Mrs. Roosevelt was crying. The president turned to Admiral Leahy and said, "I want every mother in America to see this picture."'[26]

Josephine, however, whose son had not been in the picture, remained unmoved by Ford's trickery. She had chosen the Trans-Lux newsreel theatre because she sought authenticity not showmanship. She didn't want to be preached to, 'talked down at' or have the realities of war 'soft-soaped'. She wanted information, direct and unmediated information about the realities now faced by thousands of young Americans. She understood the power and potentiality of the moving image to convey, perhaps more than any other medium, something of those realities, despite Hollywood's renowned capacity for fabrication. Like Ford she was suspicious of propaganda. She expected the cinema to resemble an OSS briefing room, with the screen presenting the objective facts of war. Put another way, as she sat amidst the dimmed lights of the Trans-Lux that day, she had become an intelligence consumer. And like millions of Americans, from the 'Mothers of America' to the Joint Chiefs of Staff, Josephine regarded the cinema as perhaps the most significant, and certainly the most authentic purveyor of that intelligence.

From the moment that Hollywood filmmakers sought to present the 'objective facts of war' through a vivid documentary aesthetic that was still shockingly new to wartime audiences, the consumption of cinematic intelligence became a collective experience that bound American civilian, political and military life. What drove this shared desire for intelligence at every level of American society was an awakened psychological impulse that war had wrought to understand and even to experience something of the realities of war, out of empathy for the soldiers fighting on the front, or out of political, tactical and strategic necessity. '[T]he cruelty and violence of war have taught us to respect – almost to make a cult of – actual facts', wrote André Bazin in 1946.

> The taste for ... documentary news, combined with that for the cinema, reflects nothing if not modern man's will to be there, his need to observe history-in-the-making, not only because of political evolution but also because of the evolution as well as irremediable intermingling of the technological means of communication and destruction.[27]

The coming of war had elevated the epistemic authority of cinema to a position of pre-eminence among the informational mediums. The OSS and the military understood this, and invested heavily in the cinematic collection and presentation of intelligence during the war. But with greater authority came greater expectations of the medium. For the first time cinemagoers like

Josephine viewed the screen as a window of truth on to the world. Hollywood, ever responsive to its audiences, was for the most part happy to oblige, but it did so by applying its well-honed techniques of fictional storytelling to the raw materials of documentary combat footage.

Truth, as the Office of War Information (OWI) put it, was a 'strategy'.[28] Documentary realism served not only the cause of accurate reporting, but the United States as well. This chapter tells the story of a moment in time when Hollywood's 'strategy of truth' and the objectives of the United States Government were aligned. The decades that followed the end of the Second World War would witness the gradual erosion of this consensus, due in no small part to the activities of the Central Intelligence Agency and the expansion of US Government secrecy that accompanied them. But at the moment when documentary realism first entered mainstream Hollywood cinema, the 'official story' of the United States Government was regarded with deference as authoritative.

The documentary aesthetic in Hollywood cinema and America's first centralised foreign intelligence agency were born of the same need to comprehend the world. It was no coincidence then that the greatest concentration of Hollywood filmmakers in any of the wartime services was under John Ford's command in the OSS. But, to adapt a philosophical axiom of postcolonial studies, this will to knowledge was shaped and driven by politics and power, and with the United States's desire to comprehend the world came an implicit desire to intervene. The wartime 'passion for the real' would fundamentally transform the aesthetic, political and ontological underpinnings of Hollywood cinema from a medium that had been committed to isolationism, fantasy and the idea that cinema's task was purely to entertain, into a politically engaged and interventionist cinema underpinned by a faith in the potentiality of film to accurately document reality.[29] But it had also brought to an end an age of cinematic innocence in which, like the nickelodeons and vaudeville theatres of old, the moving image was conceived purely as an object of escapism, fantasy and amusement:

> Since motion pictures can play a vital role in waking up America to the things that are being faced by our boys – let's have what they are doing unadulterated, and not give one the feeling that we are witnessing a studio or rehearsed performance. I am sure that we can take it seated comfortably in a motion picture theatre chair, if the boys can take it 'out there'.
>
> It is my opinion that your role is a tremendously important one, and it is for this reason that I have taken the liberty of bringing my own personal thinking to your attention – for whatever it might be worth!
> Sincerely yours,
> (Mrs.) Josephine MacNab

John Ford's Navy

Ford's idea for the creation of a military unit of Hollywood filmmakers and technicians likely took shape over long conversations in the 1930s with his friend Merian C. Cooper aboard his 106-feet ketch, the *Araner*, while they performed semi-official spying missions on the Japanese for the US Naval Reserve (USNR) off the coast of the Baja peninsula. The two had first met in 1934 when Cooper, the recently appointed head of production at RKO – following the success of his film *King Kong* the previous year – brought Ford to the studio to direct a remake of the British First World War drama, *The Lost Patrol*. The film's martial themes of gallantry, toughness and camaraderie united the pair. Ford never served in the First World War, but he wished he had. 'Evidently feeling ashamed that he had stayed in Hollywood making Westerns while others died in battle, Ford created a phony war record for himself and maintained the legend of his World War I service for the rest of his life.'[30]

Cooper, by contrast, had considerable military experience. Like OSS chief General 'Wild Bill' Donovan who had led the legendary 'Fighting 69th' into

Figure 1.3 John Ford with members of his photographic unit aboard his yacht, *Araner*. *Source:* John Ford Mss, Lilly Library, Indiana.

battle during the First World War, he was a war hero. After dropping out of naval college, he joined the Georgia National Guard in 1916 and participated in General 'Black Jack' Pershing's Mexican border raids against Pancho Villa.[31] He served as a pilot during the First World War and received a Distinguished Service Cross for heroism after he was shot down over the Argonne Forest. His recommendation for the medal by Commanding Officer Lewis T. Turnbull provides the story of his valour:

> In the course of a bombing mission on Dun-sur-Meuse on September 26th 1918, the formation was attacked, far behind the German lines and at an altitude of 15000 feet by a formation of enemy scout planes three times the size of our own formation. In the course of the fight which followed, five of the seven planes of our formation were shot down. In attempting to protect a plane below the formation, Lieut. Cooper took a very exposed position, against overwhelming odds, and by skilfully manoeuvring his plane he enabled his observer, Lieut. Edmund C. Leonard, to bring down one enemy aircraft and assist in bringing down another. Lieut. Cooper held this position until his Observer was severely wounded and his motor burst into flames. The plane then started down out of control. Thinking his Observer dead, Lieut. Cooper climbed from his cockpit, intending to jump from the plane. Upon seeing that his Observer was still alive, Lieut. Cooper showed great courage and determination, despite the flames in the cockpit, climbed back and succeeded in cutting off the gas supply to the motor and managed to extinguish the flames. In doing so, Lieut. Cooper was severely burned on the hands and face. Despite the fact that his hands were practically useless as a result of the burns, and the great pain he suffered, he succeeded in gaining control of the plane and brought it down without further injury to himself or his Observer.[32]

This story could only be told months later, after the signing of the Armistice and following Cooper's release from a German prison camp. On the day of the crash, the US Army had pronounced him killed in action, and his certificate of death dated 26 September 1918 can still be found in his personal papers.[33]

Cooper's military contacts and experience of organising experimental volunteer units during the Polish–Soviet War (where his plane was again shot down over enemy lines!), leant credence to Ford's novel ideas on the practical application of Hollywood expertise for military and intelligence-gathering purposes. Befitting their reputation as renegades within the tightly controlled Hollywood studio system, Ford and Cooper didn't wait for permission from senior military brass to begin organising their unit. In 1939 Ford began recruiting approximately 300 'highly trained technicians' from the major studios to serve in a volunteer unit that was affectionately dubbed 'John Ford's

Figure 1.4 Use of the viewfinder in photography is illustrated by Lt Gregg Toland, USNR, as he conducts a class for a special photographic unit of the Naval Reserve undergoing training in the use of modern picture and still cameras at Hollywood. *Source:* John Ford Mss, Lilly Library, Indiana.

Navy'.[34] In April 1940, Ford's unit was officially recognised as the Naval Reserve Photographic Section of the Eleventh Naval District headquartered in San Diego.

The group met every 'Tuesday night from eight to midnight' on Twentieth Century's studio lot. Studio boss Darryl F. Zanuck, who would later join the US Army Signal Corps and serve alongside Ford's unit filming the allies' North African invasion, gave them permission. The unit drilled on the Fox soundstages using 'weapons from the Fox prop department and uniforms borrowed from the Western Costume Company'.[35] Camera equipment was borrowed from a company called Fax Dean whose employee Mark Armistead had volunteered for Ford's unit and film stock was gathered from Fox's short ends.[36] The unit took 'supplemental classes on Monday and Wednesday evenings at other locations, including the Los Angeles Naval Reserve Armory'.[37]

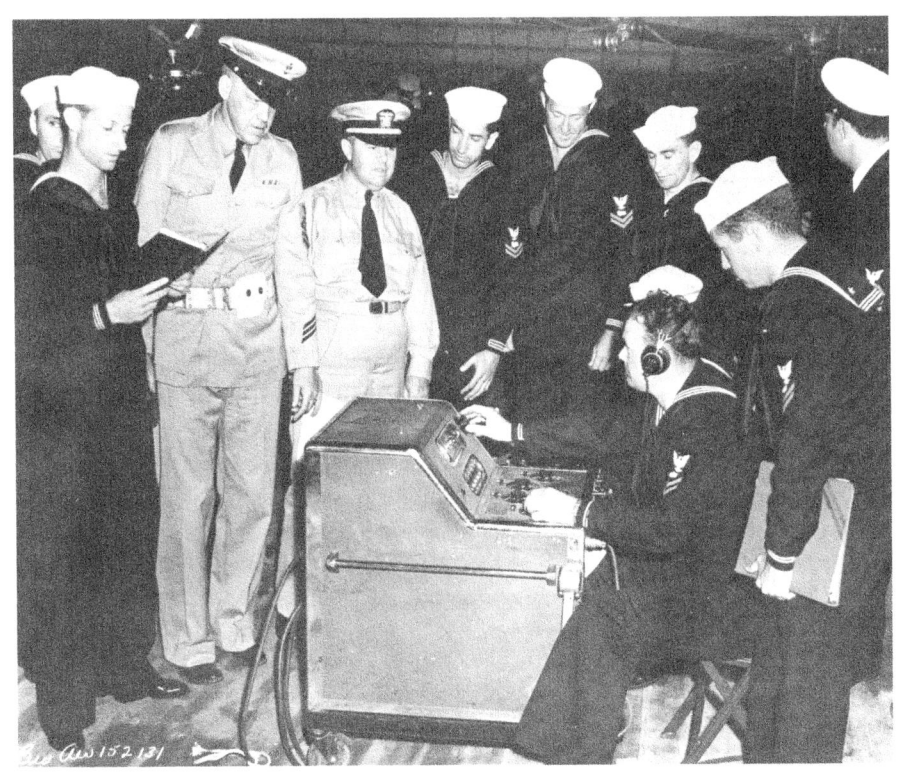

Figure 1.5 In addition to their training as still and motion picture cameramen, members of the special photographic unit of the Naval Reserve learn to handle intricate sound equipment at the Twentieth Century-Fox studios in Los Angeles. Officiating are Chief J. Pennick (left) and Lt. Comdr. E. H. Hansen. *Source:* John Ford Mss, Lilly Library, Indiana.

Gregg Toland, Ford's cinematographer on *The Grapes of Wrath*, who won acclaim a few years later for his use of deep-focus in Orson Welles's *Citizen Kane* (1941), provided camera instruction (see Figure 1.4). Alongside Toland, Ford's soundman, Edmund H. Hansen, trained the recruits in the use of sound equipment (see Figure 1.5). 'Military Indoctrination' was taught by Ford; Jack Pennick, an actor and ex-marine who served as Ford's drillmaster; Ben Grotsky, a fast-talking navy veteran from Brooklyn whose rudimentary grasp of spelling and punctuation was more than made up for by his uncanny ability to resource almost anything: from a camera crew in Hollywood, to three trucks of rationed coal in liberated Paris, at a moment's notice; and Lieutenant Commander Alfred J. 'Jack' Bolton, who acted as a 'liaison between Hollywood and the Navy.'[38] Other notable recruits included 'cameramen Joseph H. August, Sid Hickox, John Fulton, Alfred Gilks, and Harold Rosson;

editors Otho Lovering and Robert Parrish; special effects technician E. R. 'Ray' Kellogg' and Frank 'Spig' Wead, 'a retired navy flier who had turned to scriptwriting after breaking his neck falling down the stairs in his home in 1927'.[39]

Weaponising Cinema

Over the summer of 1940, Ford and Cooper enlisted the help of the Office of Naval Intelligence's Ellis Zacharias and Lieutenant Colonel John W. Thomason in their attempts to get their unit recognised as part of regular naval operations. Cooper made regular trips to Washington, DC between June and September to promote the unit among senior navy officials, including Vice Admiral Herbert F. Leary, later commander of the US fleet in the Pacific and Rear Admiral Robert L. Ghormley, acting chief of naval operations.[40] During this period, they honed their case for a 'Naval Photographic Organization' drawing up a proposal that they drafted and redrafted several times over the course of the summer.

The final draft, signed by Ford, Cooper, Edmund Hansen, Jack Bolton and Frank Wead, reads like a manifesto for the value of cinema as a practical tool for military and intelligence purposes. While the majority in Hollywood still regarded cinema's role in society as purely for entertainment, Nazi Germany, as the proposal frequently points out, understood the power of cinema as a tool of persuasion and its potential as a means of military perception:

> It is obvious that German forces have provided themselves with adequate personnel and material, and that their experimentation to improve methods of photography and transmission is vigorously pushed. Even the scanty footage of film that Germany has released indicates beyond all doubt that the German leaders consider photography to be a vital weapon and an integral part of their land and sea forces.[41]

The use of film by the Nazis for propaganda purposes is well documented.[42] 'A Nazi boast' Ford's proposal noted, is that in 'World War One, the conquest of Romania required the operations of two armies at a cost of thousands of lives. In World War Two, Romania was conquered by a motion picture, BLITZKREIG [sic] IN POLAND.' Less studied, however, is the Nazis' direct military application of film to the battlefield: 'It is said', noted Ford and his colleagues, that 'virtually every Nazi aircraft and motorized unit is equipped with an automatic motion picture camera; other units, including every naval craft, are provided with cameramen'. Although the proposal was written more than a year before the US was officially at war with Nazi Germany, the subtext was clear: war with Germany was coming, and America could ill-afford to lag behind their future foe in the vital military application of cinematic technology.

But in an optimistic rallying cry, and with a nod to the supremacy of the American cinema, the authors noted that 'the Germans have never been as good in the use of such devices as this nation; they have not been so inventive and it is believed when proper principles are laid down we can rapidly outstrip them technically'.[43]

With this aim in mind, the proposal identified three core applications of cinema in military operations: 'training', 'morale' and 'combat intelligence'. Conforming to the theory of Paul Virilio, that the development of an increasingly automated 'logistics of perception' is both a central and inevitable aspect of military development, what is apparent in the proposal's elaborations upon all three of these areas is the authors' faith in the objective capacity of cinema to achieve a superior means of perception to written reports or human observation.[44] Film, in their opinion, by providing what Virilio refers to as 'the sight machine' – a mechanised and autonomous means of military perception – circumvented the deficiencies of human subjectivity: poor eyesight, fallible memory, slow or inadequate communication, vital loss of detail, lack of awareness or in some cases even outright fabrication. Film, with its ontological status as a material facsimile of reality, as André Bazin upheld, was the *only* medium that could communicate a detailed, authentic and, crucially, 'objective' intelligence picture. Or so the pioneers of film as a documentary medium, like Ford and Cooper, believed.

In the first area, 'training', for example, the authors noted the use of film in the improvement of landing procedures and flight-deck operations aboard the US's first aircraft carrier, the *Langley*. Each landing was filmed and meticulously studied. 'It was found that verbal reports from pilots and observers on the flight deck of successful approaches, landings, and crashes, often differed in vital detail from what study of the motion picture film revealed.'[45] Morale or propaganda films must be presented 'factually' the authors stressed, underlining the word for further emphasis. A realistic presentation of the United States' naval strength would provide 'a psychological life to the whole nation'.[46] The use of film for 'combat intelligence' is provided the greatest attention in the proposal. Film could allow for a more accurate, rapidly communicated and easily consumable intelligence picture of ongoing operations. With the arrival of television, which the authors identified as a vital area for research and development, a continuous and near-instantaneous stream of visual intelligence could be provided for commanders overseeing the field:

> In the battle of Jutland, for example, if Beatty and Jellico had received from aircraft televised information of the German fleet . . . how different would the deployment have been! And how differently, with *sureness* and *precision* based on *knowledge*, would Jellico have handled the British Grand Fleet! The camera at a time like this may prove the cause of a

complete and *decisive action, rather than an inconclusive one*, an action so complete that it may end a war immediately.

If motion picture film of the different phases of the daylight action of Jutland had been available for study *immediately* upon its conclusion, tactical errors would have been discovered which could never be repeated again; an *immediate* intelligence plan based on *sure, rather than uncertain knowledge*, would have been laid out for the night's action which followed . . . The *whole picture* would have been presented to the Commander in Chief with *impressive* and *dramatic accuracy*. (emphases mine).

The words that I have italicised in this passage are revealing. First, they indicate the authors' epistemological faith in cinema's capacity for verisimilitude – providing a more totalising and authentic field of perception for military commanders. Second, they demonstrate what Virilio has described as cinema's 'imposture of immediacy' upon modern warfare: the collapsing of space and time in the theatre of operations into a seamless stream of automated and actionable images of the shifting topography of the battlefield. Taken together, they denote the vital co-development of cinematic and military technologies as Virilio traces in *War and Cinema*, a relationship that would impact not only the military and the motion picture industry, but perception itself. Ford, Cooper and their cosignatories were visionaries of a new form of warfare that was yet to be realised – warfare in which, as Virilio put it, 'the supply of images would become the equivalent of an ammunition supply', and the automated 'sight machine', made possible by the cinema, would begin to determine military tactics and strategy over and above direct human perception.[47]

Hollywood's Intelligence Archive

The Navy declined Ford and Cooper's proposal, but it was eventually taken up, in more or less the same form, by William Donovan's Office of Strategic Services (OSS) who realised the value of cinematic intelligence to his agency. But, first, Donovan was confronted with a more pressing concern. President Roosevelt had signed the Office of the Coordinator of Information (COI) – that would later become the OSS – into law on 11 July 1941 in an effort to coordinate the various activities of America's numerous propaganda and intelligence agencies. But the near unprecedented nature of a centralised foreign intelligence agency in the United States meant that America was woefully ill-informed about the nations and conflicts with which they would soon be embroiled. They lacked even the most basic reconnaissance on the various fronts in Europe, North Africa and the Pacific. Although some cartographic information would have been available to them, American military planners needed to *see* what these terrains looked like in order to adequately visualise the various tactical and strategic imperatives. Moreover, the sheer volume of information required for the colossal undertaking of planning America's entry into a war that raged across several continents necessitated a highly efficient means of communication that could effectively relay and condense such vast quantities of information. The visual medium was the only form capable of achieving this.[48] The old cliché that a picture tells a thousand words was, in this instance, regarded with life or death importance.

But Donovan had no photographic archive to which he could turn. Or at least, no such archive existed in government. And so it was to Hollywood that Donovan turned, whose pictorial archives of the requisite locales were undoubtedly unmatched by anything the government could provide. In particular, it was the newsreels, travelogues and documentary films, shot around the world for more than two decades, which would prove most valuable. In a certain sense then, before the establishment of the COI, Hollywood had been America's most active foreign intelligence agency.

On 20 December 1941, the COI employed the documentary newsreel producer, *March of Time*'s Richard de Rochemont, on a non-compensatory basis as a consultant to the Research and Analysis Branch.[49] De Rochemont's brother and fellow *March of Time* producer Louis features heavily later in our story as he went to work after the war campaigning and later working for the CIA.

Upon arriving at the COI, Richard de Rochemont was asked by the head of the COI's Visual Presentation Branch (VPB), Colonel Atherton Richards, to look into establishing a Pictorial Records Section (PRS) of the Reports Division for use in the visual presentation of intelligence.[50] 'When COI first started' an associate of de Rochemont's from *March of Time*'s parent company Time-Life informed him, its

> main job, outside of counter-propaganda news and broadcasts, was the compilation of information for President Roosevelt from the reports of MID (Military Intelligence Division), ONI (Office of Naval Intelligence) and FBI. Even the digests of these reports made a tremendous amount of reading. So, Donovan and his aides started developing the visual process of presenting information . . . this included films, maps, charts and similar visual methods. This is the division that Richards heads.[51]

Richards was a Hawaiian pineapple magnate who had been 'impressed by the visual pyrotechnics of industrial designers he had seen at the New York World's Fair'.[52] Inspired, Richards asked Merian C. Cooper to help him create a War Situation Room in the White House, redolent of Kubrick's masterful *Dr. Strangelove* set. Richards' and Cooper's war room was to be 'outfitted with

Figure 1.6 Richard de Rochemont, photographed on 15 June 1945.
Source: Baltimore Sun Photographic Archives.

the latest electrical, mechanical and photographic gadgetry; and dominated by an immense illuminated globe on which could be projected everything from weather fronts to the disposition of land, air and naval forces'.[53] It was just the kind of eccentric scheme that would appeal to Donovan. The idea was eventually shot down by a covetous Joint Chiefs of Staff, only after they had their own headquarters equipped with two such rooms. But Richards' concept of visual presentation remained intact and was embraced wholeheartedly by Donovan and the COI. Indeed Donovan 'allocated a remarkable 24.9 percent of his first annual budget toward the design of visual presentations'.[54]

The Pictorial Records Section of the Visual Presentation Branch, as envisaged by Richards and de Rochemont, would 'aim to provide a continuous supply of existing motion picture film and photographs, drawn entirely from existing stocks and libraries, for the use of the Coordinator in visual presentations'.[55] The scheme would require significant investment, as 'such an operation should not be set up on a small scale since to be effective it must be comprehensive'.[56] Using the laboratory currently under construction for Ford's Photographic Unit in the south building of the Department of Agriculture, the section would copy and develop an enormous amount of film – estimated at more than 150,000 feet per week – requiring a staff of sixty-nine, or forty, depending on the budget allowed.[57]

The activity of the section would be divided into two separate functions. First, was to provide motion picture 'intelligence reports' conveying 'information for military intelligence officers or commanders having special interest in particular regions. For this purpose, such films must be extremely detailed.' The second was for use 'in visual presentations where the same amount of detail is not needed and where the discussion of a particular region becomes a small part of the discussion of a general strategic problem'. Although the two functions 'do not hang together very well within the framework of visual presentation', films collected or edited for the first function, 'could be used in part after re-editing' for the second.[58]

Surveying the film industry's ready-made intelligence archive, Richard de Rochemont filed a report for Richards that listed a panoply of possible sources, most of which would be taken from the footage shot by that previously inconsequential movement of Hollywood documentarians. Loyal to his own craft, de Rochemont listed the newsreels and travelogues as the best place to start. 'The companies which produce newsreels (Paramount, Twentieth Century Fox, M.G.M., R.K.O. Pathé and Universal) have sent their cameramen all over the world and by exchange agreements have received documentary film from foreign companies.' For obvious reasons, the travelogues most appealed to de Rochemont. M.G.M's *Fitzpatrick Travel Talks*, for example:

> must have literally millions of feet of negative, cut and uncut, which might be of use. Twentieth Century Fox has produced a series called The Magic Carpet of Movietone, which started in 1928, and has continued ever since. Pathé once put out the Van Beuren Travelogue series. Universal, Columbia, Warner Brothers, all have descriptive film in their vaults.[59]

Another useful stock of material from the major studios' libraries was the film shot for the purposes of back projection. Actors would be filmed in front of pre-shot scenes, often taken from around the world, which was projected on to translucent paper. 'For instance,' de Rochemont noted, 'Fox had their cameramen in Europe and North Africa for a period of nearly a year. United Artists made background material in Italy for use in their film "Dodsworth". Hundreds of examples could be given of this sort of activity.'

Not content with material shot by the major studios alone, de Rochemont expanded his survey to include 'professional and amateur explorers' like Father Hubbard who 'has made an enormous amount of film on Alaska alongside other 'scientists', 'naturalists' and 'traveller-explorers such as Julian Bryan, Andre La Varre, Armand Denis, Andre Roosevelt' and 'Mr. and Mrs. Martin Johnson . . .' Although their films lacked the production quality for wide distribution, their content, if 'properly interpreted, would be of considerable aid to anyone making a study of strategic areas'.

Alongside these professional or semi-professional explorers, 'the ordinary American tourist, who, in the past twenty years, has penetrated almost every part of the globe and has very often taken with him a 16mm motion picture camera', could provide a further wealth of material. De Rochemont suggested tracking these tourists down via the Kodak Eastman Company – who could ask each amateur photographer to fill out a government questionnaire detailing where and what they have filmed. 'The most promising answers to the questionnaire would be investigated and it is reasonable to suppose that there would be complete cooperation on the part of the average citizen contacted in this way.' More easily obtainable than these privately owned films were the films shot by various US Government departments, particularly during the New Deal, which sponsored a number of documentary filmmakers, as well as American universities that had extensive film units such as Harvard and the University of Minnesota.

The film industries of Britain, Canada, Australia and India were also worth consulting. The film-quota systems in place in many of these countries, often denigrated by film historians as the source of the cheaply produced 'quota-quickies', was in this instance a great asset for de Rochemont's intelligence-gathering operation. Many of the theatres in these countries filled quotas with 'film of a newsreel or documentary nature, this being the easiest for small filmmakers to produce. It is rare that these films are of sufficient theatrical merit to be exported, but copies of them may be obtained through propaganda ministries, tourist bureaus and consulates.' The British Ministry of Information had already conducted some research into this material, and would more than likely be happy to cooperate with the COI. In particular, the 'very large and comparatively unknown' Indian film industry, alongside the Egyptian Misr Film Company, could provide documentary and travelogue films covering vital strategic areas in Asia and the Middle East.[60]

The survey presented a colossal task. Even ignoring the much larger stock of still-photography taken by travellers armed with Kodak and Leica cameras, the collection and analysis of this enormous amount of material would take months, if not years, to process, and a sizeable staff to research, analyse, edit and archive all the material. By February 1942 a skeleton staff was in place at the Apex Building in Washington, DC managed by the editor for the Pictorial Records Section, Edward Warren, and supported by film-industry experts such as Dan Gillmour, Fred Abbott, Ralph Warren, A. Seymour Houghton and Lois Jacoby.[61] Studios were contacted and notices were placed in amateur film magazines asking filmmakers to advise the COI of any film made outside of the United States.[62] Unsurprisingly, the new division was swamped with material from enthusiastic cineastes. Persistent requests were made for additional staff, particularly librarians, required to index and archive the sheer volume of information flooding in. Field researchers were given extensive training by military personnel on the type of material required from the files of film companies and the stocks of amateur filmmakers. Researchers were then sent to various regions of the United States and asked to collect and collate relevant material – rigorous selectivity had to be maintained at all times to prevent the Washington office from being overwhelmed.[63]

A staff dedicated to the medium of still photography also collected images. Each still photography field researcher was given a 'priority list' of subjects on which to collect. This, of course, posed a significant security risk. If field researchers suddenly began to prioritise, for example, the Normandy coastline, the US military's strategic priorities would be easy for the enemy to glean. As a precaution, researchers were to keep the priority list strictly confidential, and it would be 'concealed from persons owning still photos or movie film by the device of having the researcher express an interest in all kinds of subject matter, keeping to himself the kinds of subject matter in which he is actually interested'.[64]

Once the film associated with a given priority arrived in Washington, it was to be viewed by COI editors and military personnel who would copy useful segments and then edit them together

> into a documentary film on the subject in question . . . At this point, a complete documentary film consisting of all material on Region 'X' will be ready for presentation to interested persons. This film can be duplicated any number of times for distribution and exhibition at any point in the world where a 35mm. projector is available.[65]

Unavoidably, in spite of these careful attempts at pre-selection and indexing, the new office received far more material than they could ever process. The problem became so acute by 1943 that the then chief of the Pictorial Records Section, John F. Langan, invented an entirely new film-indexing system known as the aperture card – that mounted a chip of microfilm on a punched card for identification purposes. Langan patented the idea after the war and sold it on to Atherton Richards and OSS chief of Intelligence in Europe, and, later, CIA director during the Reagan administration, William Casey. Richards and Casey made a small fortune selling the technology to the US military in the early 1950s.[66]

The Pictorial Records Section realised, to an unprecedented extent, the immense strategic and even tactical value of film for intelligence purposes. In turn it changed the nature of intelligence itself by reinforcing and sometimes replacing written reports with the power of the visual medium. If Paul Virilio's technological determinism in *The Logistics of Perception* is to be believed, then such an event was perhaps inevitable – the push towards an ever-broader field of vision that is increasingly automated, necessitated the inclusion of cinema in the toolkit of intelligence agencies. But such a view ignores the contingencies upon which this unique relationship between Hollywood and the COI/OSS existed. The COI sought out Hollywood because they had no choice. America's distaste for intelligence in its isolationist period meant that no equivalent of Hollywood's archive of visual material on key strategic areas existed in government. It is no coincidence that nearly a quarter of the COI's first annual budget was spent on visual presentation. Before the shadow warfare for which the OSS is now most famous, Donovan's intelligence agency's chief asset was arguably its utilisation of film for intelligence-gathering and presentation purposes. But if Donovan was to gather contemporary cinematic intelligence, he needed his own filmmaking outfit. Fortunately, he had one ready-made, in Ford and Cooper's Field Photographic Unit.

Wild Bill Donovan and the Origins of the OSS Field Photographic Unit

In a nostalgic letter to his former OSS colleague, Otto C. Doering, written a few years before his death, Merian C. Cooper boasted that it was he who had supplied General Donovan with the idea of establishing America's first central intelligence agency. The two dined together from time to time at New York's 21 Club, and on one such occasion Cooper recalled telling Donovan about how the Polish had divided their intelligence activities into 'offensive' and 'defensive' sections. 'The Offensive Intelligence – which the United States has never had – we are sure going to need if we fight either the Germans or the Japanese. It is the toughest racket I know in war', he told Donovan. 'It means working inside enemy country, and was filled in Poland and Russia with all kinds of assassins, saboteurs, agent provocateurs . . . If you want a risky business and you really want to see war like Americans have never seen it, this is it.'[67] Although almost certainly an exaggeration, Cooper's work for the Visual Presentation Unit made him present at the birth of America's fledgling foreign intelligence and espionage community.[68] According to McBride, 'Cooper used his influence with Donovan to smooth Ford's way into the COI', and persuaded Donovan to promote Ford to Commander so that he carried the appropriate level of prestige required to run a major component of the newly formed intelligence agency.[69]

With the benefit of hindsight, Donovan's organisation appears the likeliest of hosts for Ford's wartime photographic unit. To start with, there was Donovan himself, who seemed an almost perfect embodiment of the characteristics that Ford most admired. First, he was a war hero, one of the most decorated soldiers of the First World War due to his courageous leadership of the Fighting 69th. Like Cooper, he had also served under 'Black Jack' Pershing in the raids against Pancho Villa. Although it is unlikely that Donovan and Cooper knew each other from that time, it would certainly have provided a choice icebreaker: fuelling dinnertime reminiscences at the 21 Club of gallant cavalry charges across the Sonoran Plain. Second, like Ford, Donovan was a proud Irish-American. Leader of the 'Fighting Irish Brigade', whose grandfather had been associated with the Fenians (a secret Irish revolutionary society) his Irish heritage, as his biographer Anthony Cave Brown writes, 'was undoubtedly important in the shaping of WJD's political attitudes, for in his dealings with the British during World War II he was to display, occasionally, a Fenian

Figure 1.7 Head of OSS, William 'Wild Bill' Donovan. *Source:* United States National Archives, College Park, Maryland.

stubbornness and, more frequently, dislike of the institutions of the British Empire'.[70] In spite of his intermittent recalcitrance, like Ford he was a committed interventionist, believing increasingly as the 1930s wore on that war with Germany was inevitable. In the run up to Pearl Harbor, he became one of the most stalwart proponents of American support for the British among President Roosevelt's inner circle. Knowing this, and realising his influence and status, the British eagerly courted him during his visits to Europe in the months prior to Pearl Harbor.

Donovan was also a fan of the motion pictures, as his later financial backing of Ford and Cooper's post-war production company, Argosy Pictures, attested to. Although Frances Stonor Saunders – in her landmark study of the CIA's covert patronage of culture during the Cold War – suggests that Donovan's support for Argosy may have served a more instrumental purpose in allowing intelligence agencies (or former intelligence agencies) 'to suggest themes for Hollywood audiences', Donovan's motivations were more likely benign, wishing to support two loyal OSS veterans in an industry he admired.[71] That said, like his great rival, J. Edgar Hoover, Donovan certainly understood the immense public relations value of keeping Hollywood on close terms. In August 1939, on his way to a hunting trip in the Yukon, he worked with scriptwriter Norman Reilly Raine who sat with him on the long train ride from Chicago to Seattle discussing his treatment of *The Fighting 69th*.[72] Based on Donovan's exploits during the First World War, the film starred James Cagney and George Brent (who played Donovan), and was produced by Warner Brothers whose increasingly oppositional stance towards Nazi Germany had 'inspired the studio to look backward for themes to remind viewers about the importance of vigilance and solidarity'.[73] At a time when Donovan was beginning to campaign vocally for the US to take a more actively interventionist stance, it certainly did not hurt to have a Hollywood motion picture released that celebrated his wartime heroism and drew implicit allusions to the present European crisis. As Chapter 2 of this book documents, after the war, and following the disbandment of the OSS, Donovan again enlisted the support of Hollywood filmmakers to both celebrate the legacy of his organisation's wartime service, and to advocate for the establishment of a permanent peacetime central intelligence agency. Although Ford himself was not involved in the post-war OSS film cycle, Donovan no doubt understood the immense publicity value of having more than 300 Hollywood filmmakers and technicians on his staff.

Unlike the navy brass who had declined Ford's proposal, Donovan was committed to unorthodox approaches to war. 'Donovan may be included in the list of wizards', wrote Anthony Cave Brown, 'good and bad, who shaped the theory of warfare in the second half of the twentieth century'.[74] This theory included methods, like covert action, espionage and psychological operations that had hitherto been regarded as unseemly by American officials.[75] As one of FDR's cabinet advisors put it, Donovan was a man who was 'afraid of nobody and nothing, least of all a new concept'.[76] Ford's new concept of cinematic intelligence, with its emphasis on propaganda and combat intelligence, included precisely the kinds of novel techniques that Donovan encouraged.

Donovan's unconventional approach to warfare was provisioned by a recruitment strategy, which, unlike the navy, thought nothing of enlisting hundreds of Hollywood filmmakers and technicians with little or no military experience. The OSS's roster included everyone from merchant bankers; business people and lawyers (Donovan was a lawyer by profession); to Frankfurt School intellectuals Herbert Marcuse and Franz Neumann; history professors like Arthur Schlesinger Jr, who later become one of the intellectual godfathers of the postwar liberal consensus and would serve in the Kennedy administration; economists like Walt Rostow, leading thinker in modernisation theory, advocate for American intervention in Vietnam and special assistant for National Security Affairs to President Johnson; and who could forget Moe Berg, the OSS's very own major league baseball catcher who played for the Boston Red Sox before joining the OSS as a special operations officer in 1943?[77] Donovan's desire to attract 'the best and the brightest' entailed a recruitment strategy, much criticised in the press, that focused much of its attention upon elite Ivy League universities, especially Yale, and members of the upper echelons of American society. As a consequence the press gave them the unofficial moniker of 'Oh So Social', giving the impression that Donovan's outfit was more of an elite country club for the beau monde of East Coast society that were keen to avoid being drafted into more strenuous, or life-threatening wartime service. As Washington Columnist Drew Pearson described it:

> If you should by chance wander in the labyrinth of the OSS you'd behold ex-polo players, millionaires, Russian princes, society gambol boys, scientists and dilettante detectives. All of them are now at the OSS, where they used to be allocated between New York, Palm Beach, Long Island, Newport and other meccas frequented by the blue-bloods of democracy. And the girls! The prettiest, best-born, snappiest girls who used to graduate from debutantedom to boredom now bend their blonde and brunette locks, or their colorful hats, over work in the OSS, the super-ultra-intelligence-counter-espionage outfit that is headed by brilliant 'Wild Bill' Donovan.[78]

Ford's motivations for joining OSS belied this widely held popular prejudice of Donovan's outfit as a country club for the well-heeled. Ford was a patriot, and wished to serve his country. Likely motivated by the guilt he felt for not enlisting in the First World War, he sought out military action, and took a substantial cut in his salary in order to do so. He was almost killed in the line of duty on more than one occasion. Twelve members of the FPU would lose their lives during the war and many more were wounded. Although this was a proportionately lower casualty rate than frontline combat units, it demonstrates, nevertheless, that shooting combat footage, especially when equipped with mobile cameras that resembled machine-guns, was often a dangerous and at times fatal business.

December 7th: Scripting an Intelligence Failure

Throughout the war, the FPU utilised their training in documentary filmmaking to deliver on all three areas of Ford and Cooper's 1940 proposal: Training, Morale and Combat Intelligence. Much of the surviving record of their work falls into the first category, including such 'nuts-and-bolts training films' as '*OSS Basic Military Training, Blind Bombing, Ground to Air Transfer, The 8-Man Fol-Boat, The E 2-Man Fol-Boat, Nylon Rubber Boat, Suspended Runway, A Report on Airborne Rockets Prepared by the Joint Committee on New Weapons and Equipment of the Joint Chiefs of Staff*' and so on.[79] Such functional titles leant themselves to a utilitarian style of filmmaking with an economy of expression learnt from the newsreels and the pre-war documentarians. Indeed one of Ford's first acts within COI was to have newsreel director Bonney Powell, from Fox Movietone, come and give a training session on 'straight newsreel coverage as contrasted with production work'.[80] These basic training films certainly contained little of the soft-soaping or sugar-coating that Josephine MacNab disliked in *Midway*.

Only two of the films OSS produced, *Midway* and *December 7th*, were released as features for public consumption, although much of the combat footage they shot was edited and reused by the newsreels and as well as for Frank Capra's *Why We Fight* propaganda series. *December 7th* documented the Japanese attack on Pearl Harbor and its aftermath. It blended documentary footage and staged reenactments – a technique borrowed from *The March of Time*. An early synopsis for the film, then titled *The Story of Pearl Harbor: An Epic in American History*, begins with a foreword emphasising their belief in the primacy of film as a documentary and historical medium: 'It [Pearl Harbor] is a story of such surpassing importance to all Americans that it should be told for future generations, not by the written and by the spoken word alone, but graphically – by means of the motion picture.' From the very outset of America's entry into the Second World War film had achieved a position of preeminence among the reportorial mediums.

In January 1942 the Secretary of the navy, Frank Knox, approached the COI requesting that Ford, Toland and 'the best talent available' produce a 'complete motion picture factual presentation of the attack upon Pearl Harbor'. Hearing news of the film, Secretary of War Henry Stimson wrote separately to Donovan offering the War Department's involvement in the production.[81] Ford, who had promised Gregg Toland a turn at directing, sent his cinematographer to Hawaii to make the picture. Perhaps naïvely, Ford presumed Toland's picture would be a short, uncontroversial newsreel presentation of the events. What he got instead was an incendiary 'feature-length hodge-podge of documentary and dramatization' that accused the military of a vital lack of preparedness in the run up to the attack and cast them as 'blind to the spying by much of the Japanese-American population of Hawaii'.[82] It was, as McBride notes, 'the most controversial film made by Ford's unit during the war'.[83]

Pearl Harbor was a debacle for all concerned, but by all accounts it was the US Navy who felt most sensitive about the implication that they were caught off-guard. It was their base that was bombed, virtually undefended, and it was they who at that time had the most developed intelligence capacity within the US Government. By the time the film went into production, Admiral Husband E. Kimmel, commander-in-chief of the Pacific Fleet, had already been forced into retirement following the report of the Roberts Commission in January 1942. In this context, Toland's maladroit handling of the subject antagonised the navy's already-inflamed sensitivity over the issue of culpability for Pearl Harbor still further. Unsurprisingly, the film fell afoul of military brass and was shelved. Eventually, Ford negotiated a compromise, and had Bob Parrish recut 'a severely truncated and far milder version'.[84] The film would not be released until 1943, when it was shown to US war workers as part of its Industrial Incentive Program. Like *Midway*, it won the Academy Award for Best Documentary.

The edited version of the film broadly follows the three-part structure of Toland's original. It begins with tranquil scenes of unwitting Hawaiian civilians going about their daily lives before the tragic interruption of the Japanese sneak attack. The story then depicts a heroic American fight back, against the odds, when facing the second wave of Japanese bombers. Finally, the film ends on a melancholic coda: the weary but hopeful survivors are shown memorialising the fallen, and vowing to learn the lessons of their ill-preparedness so that another Pearl Harbor could never occur. Although less damning of the navy than Toland's longer version, it still retains an air of criticism driven home amidst the combat sequences when the narrator comments upon the Japanese fallen as 'grim telltale evidence that the list of dead Japs might have been larger, and the list of our casualties smaller, had we been sufficiently on alert'. As a former navy man himself, Ford was more sensitive than Toland to the possible offence that such a line may cause. But he was also perhaps still a little peeved by the navy's refusal to take on his unit. Moreover, Donovan also maintained a lingering animosity towards the navy who had failed to share their MAGIC intercepts of Japanese cables in the

Figure 1.8 US Navy planes and a hangar burning at the Ford Island Naval Air Station's seaplane base, during or immediately after the Japanese air raid on Pearl Harbor, Hawaii (USA), on 7 December 1941. *Source:* Wikimedia Commons.

run-up to Pearl Harbor. As Anthony Cave Brown suggests in his biography of Donovan, the navy's obstructionism may well have prevented Donovan from predicting the attack. [85] Although Ford made Toland's film more palatable for the high command, it did not entirely mask the widely shared view in OSS that Pearl Harbor was a foreseeable tragedy brought about by the failings of military intelligence.

The most extensive cuts to Toland's version are made to the first half of the film: the opening 38 minutes are almost entirely lost from the released picture. The section in question features a lengthy dialogue on the loyalty of Japanese-Americans between Uncle Sam, played by Walter Huston, and Mr C (Uncle Sam's conscience), played by Henry Davenport. Although Uncle Sam advocates an idealistic vision of an inclusive multicultural American society where Japanese-Americans are loyal citizens, he is continually rebuffed as naïve by the cool realism of Mr C, who claims in a regrettable tone to be 'merely relaying the facts'. Mr C notes, more than once, the presence of 157,000 Japanese-Americans who disingenuously assert their loyalty to America while maintaining a separate cultural, religious and ethnic identity defined by Shintoism, which, as the film tells us, 'preaches honor of the ancestors, thereby keeping alive the fires of nationalism and preserving a racial and social bond with the unbroken and divinely descended imperial dynasty. To be a Shintoist,' it unequivocally concludes, 'is to be a Japanese. This is not, nor can it be, a matter of choice. It is a duty.' Belabouring the point, the film shows a number of ordinary Japanese-American citizens passing secrets to the Japanese Embassy. As if it still wasn't clear by the end of the conversation whose perspective Toland favours, Mr C leaves Uncle Sam as he nods off to sleep dreaming nightmare images of the Japanese-American presence intercut with stock newsreel footage of the fascist menace in Germany and Japan and ending with an image of Hitler, thus cementing the link between Japanese-Americans and the Nazi peril.

Xenophobic in the extreme, Ford and Parrish rightfully cut these sequences that cast aspersions on the loyalty of an entire demographic of the American people. Although the American Government's policy of Japanese-American internment during the war acted out these aspersions, it still needed to maintain the elaborate fiction that this policy was motivated by specific security concerns rather than racial prejudice. As such the Office of War Information (OWI) actively discouraged filmmakers, often unsuccessfully, from producing blatantly racist denunciations of Japanese-Americans.[86] Ford likely removed these sequences with the OWI's edicts in mind; however, his opposition to the sequence was based primarily upon aesthetic grounds. The framing device of well-known Hollywood stars acting out a dialogue between Uncle Sam and his conscience smacked of unreality, violating the realist principles that Ford had laid down in his original proposal for the unit. The staged combat sequences, too, particularly when compared to the starkly real footage of Ford's *Midway*, with its shaky camera reacting to flying debris and explosions, appear unconvincing and were 'viewed as an embarrassment at the time by people within the government who knew the difference between genuine combat footage and a Hollywood facsimile'.[87]

Ford's appraisal of Toland's version was confirmed by his close friend and scriptwriter Kevin McGuinness: 'The best general observation I can make in relation to Greg's picture', wrote McGuinness, 'is that, in the nature of present events, the U.S. Navy can deal only in facts. In its relation to the public, it can only report with the motion picture camera. It must not editorialize, or fictionalize.' Anticipating Josephine MacNab's response to Ford's own *Midway*, which McGuinness worked on, he warned that 'if the public suspects any fiction in a picture supposedly factual, it will question everything on the screen. The resultant loss in faith will do more harm than many pictures can outweigh in good.' McGuinness agreed with Ford's decision to remove the Uncle Sam scenes: 'They're pure fiction', he wrote, 'and as such don't belong in a report.' He also commended Ford's discretion in steering clear of the question of the Japanese in Hawaii – 'there is no final determination of their loyalty or disloyalty which enables you to say they were or were not Fifth Columnists. Probably they were both, but saying so is confusing.'[88]

Aside from the issues of authenticity, McGuinness also emphasised, with political astuteness, that the story should emphasise the navy's comeback – 'the hero is the repair job' he told Ford.

> I'd crowd in every interesting foot of the salvage operations I could and finish off with a burst of glory when the battle wagons put to sea again. I'd embroider the finish with wipes and quick dissolves showing whatever stirring shots there are of the Navy at sea and finish it with the biggest shots I had of task forces in operation.[89]

Ford's film indeed finishes on a similarly resurgent note, pledging retribution for the Japanese attacks. McBride claims that Ford's willingness to publicly criticise the navy by leaving in snippets of Toland's stark denunciation of their ill-preparedness may well have been motivated by a lingering resentment at the navy for not accepting his organisation as part of the regular service.[90] Yet the classical comic structure of the final film, leading from turmoil to progress, allowed Ford to have his cake and eat it – maintaining limited criticisms of the navy while still celebrating its heroism in the face of adversity and its vital significance to the war effort.

Although Ford exorcised the most conspicuous examples of fictionalisation in Toland's picture, the consciously dramatic approach to factual filmmaking left an impression on Ford. The elegiac scenes after the Japanese attack in Toland's film, in which the voice of dead soldiers introduce domestic scenes of their parents and loved ones, are almost identical to similar scenes in *Midway*. Moreover, the funeral scene that follows, set to a melancholic men's chorus of *My Country Tis of Thee*, was indiscriminately plagiarised by Ford in the final sequence of *Midway*. When writer-producer of *December 7th*, Samuel Engel, saw *Midway* with Toland, he apparently leapt out of his chair screaming, 'The sonofabitch stole our scenes! That's exactly what we have in our picture, the stuff we told him about in Pearl Harbor!'[91] McBride explains away the episode as Ford's cunning way of upbraiding the insubordinate Toland and Engel who had ignored his instructions to make a straightforward and inoffensive newsreel feature.[92]

The inclusion of the scripted elegiac scenes in *December 7th*, and there appropriation by Ford for *Midway*, marked an important aesthetic departure from the training and technical films that were the mainstay of the FPU's production and not intended for public consumption. The use of such overtly fictionalising techniques to tell these 'true stories' reflected the peculiar provenance of the FPU filmmakers who were schooled in the techniques of Hollywood storytelling and ever-sensitive to their audience whom they still deemed desirous of such 'soft-soaping' that Josephine MacNab so decried. But the resort to a heavy measure of fiction in their documentary report of Pearl Harbor was also born out of necessity. Reconstructed scenes replaced actual footage of the attacks and their aftermath – although this was in large part because almost no footage of the actual attacks existed. The crafted tripartite narrative of the shock attack followed by a heroic fight-back followed by the melancholic coda was needed to excavate meaning from the event for audiences still struggling to come to terms with America's sudden entry into the war. Finally, it was necessary to fictionalise or refashion the raw materials of actuality to appease the US Government and the American military, especially the Navy.

Ford's FPU may well have been committed to what the Office of War Information termed its 'strategy of truth', and by doing so helped advance the epistemic authority of film as a medium and documentary cinema in particular. But they were also always fully aware that the documentary was a form of storytelling just like any other, requiring narrative strategies and fictional devices just like a fictional feature film. The ease with which Ford's brigade of Hollywood filmmakers applied the same Hollywood techniques to non-fictional filmmaking demonstrated that the key distinction between the documentary and the fictional feature was not fundamentally about the reality or unreality of the subject. Rather, the distinction resided in a gap between the inherently political nature of documentary films vis-à-vis the traditional disavowal of politics in Hollywood fictional features. As screenwriter and wartime chief of production of the OWI's overseas Motion Picture Bureau, Phillip Dunne, put it:

> [The documentary] may deal in fantasy or fact. It may or may not possess a plot. But most documentaries have one thing in common, each springs from a definite need; each is conceived as an idea-weapon to strike a blow for whatever cause the originator has in mind. In the broadest sense the documentary is almost always, therefore, an instrument of propaganda. And in this we can make the first major distinction between the documentary and entertainment media.[93]

Zanuck, Ford and the Filming of the North African Invasion

On 12 November 1942, Ford landed in Algiers, where he was due to help film Operation Torch, the allied invasion of North Africa. He was greeted by his former boss at Twentieth Century-Fox, the legendary Hollywood mogul: Darryl F. Zanuck. 'Can't I *ever* get away from you?', Ford asked. 'I'll bet a dollar to a doughnut that if I ever go to Heaven, you'll be waiting at the door for me with a sign reading "Produced by Darryl F. Zanuck."'[94] Spurred by

Figure 1.9 Twentieth Century-Fox studio boss Darryl F. Zanuck, who served in the US Army Signal Corps during the Second World War and oversaw the filming of the Allies' North African invasion. *Source:* Wikimedia Commons.

Ford's enlistment, Zanuck joined the US Army Signal Corps in January 1941 as a reserve lieutenant before being made a colonel a year later and placed on active service. Like Ford, Zanuck was recruited by the military for his filmmaking experience, producing combat and training films for the army.

On 29 April 1942 Zanuck was granted a leave of absence from Fox and was sent to England to observe the allied training programme. Zanuck requested that his weekly salary of $5,000 be suspended while on active service, but this was not confirmed until August that year when the board of directors met. In effect, Zanuck had drawn his salary for four months while on active service and also continued to receive dividends for his shares in Fox. This would precipitate the greatest scandal of his career when he was investigated for corruption and profiteering upon his return to civilian life in 1943 by Senator Truman's War Investigation Committee. He was also investigated by the Army Inspector General for showing alleged favouritism to Fox in his role as head of the Research Council of the Academy of Motion Pictures Arts and Sciences, which, among other things, acted as a liaison between the film industry and the armed services.[95] Although Zanuck took the brunt of the Senate Committee's criticism, Ford's activities were also investigated. This prompted Ford to begin documenting his activities in OSS more meticulously, including a Field Photo War Diary of the North African Invasion written by cameraman Robert Johannes.[96]

Ford and thirty-two members of his unit were temporarily assigned to Zanuck in North Africa to help shoot '16mm color footage of the invasion for newsreels and a War Department documentary'.[97] In total, Zanuck commanded twelve combat camera teams in the field, led by Ford, Anatole Litvak, director of the landmark semi-documentary, *Confessions of a Nazi Spy* (1939), the first explicit condemnation of Nazi Germany by a Hollywood film, and Albert Klein, a lieutenant in the Army Pictorial Service (APS).[98]

Ray Kellogg along with Chief Photographer Lloyd Goldstein were the first to reach North Africa, accompanying Major-General Terry Allen's First Infantry Division. They went ashore at Arzeu 'with the first assault wave at 0130 hours on the morning of 8 November 1942'.[99] For the next few days Kellogg and Goldstein covered the allied invasion, photographing everything of military significance: troops scrambling ashore from their Higgins boats, dogfights overhead, fires started by bombing and artillery and the warehouses and docks in the port once they were reached. Kellogg and Goldstein continued across the North Algerian shore with the First Infantry Division to Oran, where they entered the city on a tank, dodging sniper fire while filming 'the harbor and docks and some damaged sections of the city'.[100]

Ford arrived in Algiers a few days later and set up headquarters there. After waiting until 16 November for the First Infantry to arrive from Oran, Ford, Pennick and Johannes accompanied Kellogg and Goldstein in a British LCT, tasked with filming the Division's activities in the early stages of the Tunisian campaign. They landed at Dellys the following day, where they filmed the camouflaging of tanks in town, and the unloading of crew, weapons and equipment. They left Dellys that night and arrived early the next morning in Bone, where an air raid was underway. Emerging unscathed from German strafing, the group rapidly continued their march east, crossing the Tunisian border in the late afternoon. The terrain in North-Eastern Algeria 'is a succession of hills and valleys, and one would have no warning of the approach of German planes until they came over the crest of a nearby hill. Then they would zoom down into the valley, strafe and bomb, and disappear over the next hill'. During a refuelling stop near Souk el Arba, 'all hell broke loose' when they were spotted by a group of Messerschmitt overhead. Fortunately, no damage was done, and they bivouacked their tanks for the night 'in sagebrush on the plains and dug foxholes for ourselves'.

A few days later, just outside Beja, Johannes filmed a Junker-88 coming down in flames after a Spitfire shot it out of the sky. Seeing that the bombardier had bailed out, Johannes, Pennick and Ford jumped into a jeep 'and raced across ditches and gullies' to pick him up. Emotionally exhausted, their prisoner begged them to let him see his crew one last time, who were his best friends, but when they arrived at the wreckage, 'his pals were beyond recognition'. Against his objections, they shot pictures of his captor alongside the wreckage and his deceased colleagues. In the meantime a French soldier arrived and threatened to execute their German prisoner. The OSS film crew, who handed

Figure 1.10 OSS Field Photographic Officer Ray Kellogg (1905–76) shoots film footage from his perch on the tail of a German plane shot down near Bizerte, Tunisia, in November 1942 during the allied invasion of North Africa. *Source:* Getty Images.

over the bombardier to an American intelligence officer for questioning, prevented him from doing so.

At Oued Zarga, 50 miles from Tunis, they handed over their 2,000 feet of film of the first phase of the North African invasion to an Army signal corps officer who forwarded it to the APS in London. It had been agreed that all OSS footage would pass through army censors before being distributed. Colour stock was used throughout on Zanuck's orders, who 'believed the ideal climactic conditions in Africa would warrant the use of colored motion picture film. Thus the camera crews were equipped with 16mm cameras and kodachrome film; approximately 16 to 20 thousand feet of film was shot daily.'[101]

Along with its use in newsreels as well as for internal military tactical and strategic purposes, the film was cut together by Zanuck into a feature-length documentary, *At the Front in North Africa with the US Army* (1943).[102] The film contained the now-standard Timespeak narration (borrowed from the *March of Time*) and included striking colour footage of troop movements, aerial bombardments and combat footage, including a tank battle at Terbourba. Yet the critical reaction to the film was mostly negative. First there was the issue of Zanuck's own posturing, featuring footage of himself 'wearing a helmet and a .45 pistol, and a scene in which he fires a tommy gun at a German airplane. Zanuck was ridiculed in the press as a "Hollywood colonel," a strutting peacock who seemed to be trying to win the war single-handedly.'[103] But as Joseph McBride documents, perhaps the greatest store of criticism was levelled, ironically, at the film's lack of pyrotechnics, sluggish pace and dull realism:

> Released on February 25, 1943, the sluggishly paced documentary fails to offer much sense of the overall invasion; most of the running time is consumed with shots of convoys of troops and equipment moving through nondescript desert landscapes. The army officially viewed Zanuck's material with a 'lack of enthusiasm.' Capra considered it dismayingly weak by comparison with *Desert Victory*, the 1943 British Ministry of Information documentary on the African campaign against Rommel, which supplements its impressive battle footage with liberal use of night battle scenes staged in a studio. 'I don't suppose our war scenes will look as savage and realistic as those we usually make on our back lot, but then you can't have everything,' Zanuck admitted to General Olmstead after filming was completed in December.[104]

Ford's *Midway* and Zanuck's film of the African invasion had encountered two sides of the public's increasing demand for realism. The first, articulated by Josephine MacNab, demanded the excision of overt Hollywood fakery; the second decried the lacklustre composition of undramatised reality. Realism, it seemed, would have to fall somewhere in between verisimilitude and imagination.

In spite of the negative reception of his film, the experience of war confirmed Zanuck's predilection for realistic filmmaking. Soon after his return to studio life in the summer of 1943, Zanuck addressed an audience of Hollywood luminaries as the keynote speaker for the film seminar of the Writers' Congress hosted by University of California, Los Angeles (UCLA). In attendance were the author, critic and Nobel laureate Thomas Mann, Paramount studio executive Y. Frank Freeman, producer Dore Schary, social scientists Robert Merton and Paul Lazarsfeld and the actor and president of the Screen Actors Guild, James Cagney.[105] Although he lacked his fabled mallet that he liked to blithely swing while conducting studio meetings at Fox, Zanuck addressed this rather incongruous mélange with his customary air of unbreachable authority. Invoking Matthew Arnold, he laid out his vision of the American cinema committed to a realist aesthetic and an ideology of liberal interventionism:

> We have radiated sweetness and light since the advent of pictures, and we have carefully refrained from even remote contact with the grim and pressing realities before us in the world ... We must forge ahead. We're in danger of being left, like so many of our isolationists, with the ground out from under us. We've got to move into new ground, break new trails. In short, we must play our part in the solution of the problems that torture the world. We must begin to deal realistically in film with the causes of wars and panics, with social upheavals and depression, with starvation and want and injustice and barbarism under whatever guise.[106]

For much of the rest of his career Zanuck worked tirelessly to put these principles into practice. In 1944 he produced a biopic of Woodrow Wilson, extolling the late President's brand of liberal internationalism. The same year he approached Ford with a script based on Republican Presidential candidate and staunch anti-isolationist Wendell Wilkie's book *One World*.[107] Ford declined, and the picture was never made, but Zanuck's liberal commitment to contemporary social and political issues, particularly the direction of US foreign policy, remained unperturbed. After the war, he was a major architect of the semi-documentary cycle, bringing Louis de Rochemont to his studio from *March of Time* to make docudramas that, among other things, celebrated the legacy of OSS and called for the establishment of a peacetime foreign intelligence agency. We shall return to this in the following chapter. Above all, Zanuck had come to realise that realism and liberalism were intimately wedded, and that cinema would have a profound role to play in the establishment of the post-war new world order, defined by America's conscious entry as the dominant power on the world stage. But before this could occur, the story of the Second World War, and its unequivocally Manichean construction of American good against Nazi evil, had to be indelibly prescribed. This task would fall, in no small part, to John Ford's OSS Field Photographic Unit, in their final act before being disbanded.

The Authority of Cinema at the Nuremberg Trials

Ford and his unit documented numerous other combat operations before the end of the war. Perhaps most noteworthy was their footage of the D-Day invasion that saw a number of FPU officers, including Ford, risk their lives in the service of their wartime filmmaking by going ashore at Normandy.[108] But it was their work after peace was declared in Europe, compiling footage for the Nazi war crimes tribunals at Nuremberg, which arguably left the most lasting legacy upon international relations and the public's memory of the war.

In the summer of 1945, Ford's unit was asked to compile motion picture evidence of Nazi atrocities to support the prosecution of war criminals at the Nuremberg trials. It was to be the first time in history that film would be presented as evidence at a trial.[109] That cinematic evidence was deemed permissible at the tribunal demonstrated how far the documentary aesthetic had come in convincing the public, and its lawyers, of film's capacity for verisimilitude. In the pre-war age of cinema as 'pure entertainment', it is almost unthinkable that a film, produced, directed, written and edited by a team of Hollywood filmmakers, could be regarded as authentic testimony forming a core pillar of the indictment against the accused in the most significant trial of the twentieth century.[110]

'One potential difficulty of film as a piece of trial evidence', writes legal historian Michael Salter, 'is that it does not depict the war crimes of specific defendants... In one sense, it represented "hearsay evidence" that could, in principle, have been excluded under rules of evidence that apply within domestic criminal trials.'[111] Film was deemed necessary at Nuremberg for three important reasons. First, the sheer scale of the Nazi atrocities, and the evidence of their occurrence, could not be communicated to the court efficiently and effectively by any means other than the visual medium. Just as the strategic planning of this vast global war had required filmic and graphic presentation via the work of the OSS's Visual Presentation Branch and the FPU, so too did its final judgement. A single film could give a sense of the Nazi death camp horrors more quickly, powerfully and arguably more authentically than a thousand witness testimonies. As US Prosecutor Thomas Dodds put it when introducing the *Nazi Concentration Camps* film at the trial, he cautioned that it was 'by no means the entire proof which the prosecution will offer', but that it represented 'in a brief and unforgettable form an explanation of what the words "concentration camp" imply'.[112]

Second, the monstrous extremities of Nazi war crimes may inspire incredulity towards any other form of testimony. As legal scholar Lawrence Douglas writes, 'The Nazis themselves had recognized that the incredible nature of their atrocities would cast long shadows of doubt upon any allegedly eye-witness reports.' Citing Primo Levi, Douglas notes the recollection of concentration camp inmates of 'the frequent taunt from their captors that should they survive, their stories would not be believed: "and even if some proof should remain and some of you survive, people will say that the events you describe are too monstrous to be believed: they will say that they are exaggerations of Allied propaganda and will believe us, who will deny everything, and not you."'[113] Even today, the OSS films are still invoked as incontrovertible refutations of Holocaust-denial. The perceived authenticity of film leant unparalleled credulity to the enormity of the prosecution's claims.[114]

The final, more controversial, but nevertheless well-documented reason for the use of film at Nuremberg was so that the Allies could dramatise Nazi guilt, and stage their condemnation to the world through a carefully managed media event. As both Zanuck and Ford had learnt, in order to convince, the authenticity of documentary cinema had to be matched by its sensational presentation in dramatic form. None of the OSS's wartime documentaries would prove more sensational, more dramatic, than the films produced for the Nuremberg trial.

Ford himself played little role in the tribunals. After D-Day he reluctantly returned to civilian life to make the propaganda film, *They Were Expendable* (1945). During its production a scaffold fell on him and broke his leg, rendering him incapacitated when OSS work for the trials began in earnest. In his stead Ford sent Ray Kellogg, who was accompanied by Robert Parrish, Bud Schulberg, Bob Webb, Joe Zigman, Lieutenant English and acclaimed director George Stevens from the US Army Signal Corps. The team was officially assigned to trial counsel 'James Donovan's "special projects" sub-division of the US prosecution'.[115] Donovan had served in OSS and worked closely with its successor during the Cold War.[116] Supreme Court Justice and former Attorney General Robert H. Jackson led the prosecution. According to Robert Parrish, the OSS team were handed the list of indictments and told to 'find some film wherever you can that will match the points of the indictment.'[117] The four counts of the indictments were:

1. Common Plan or Conspiracy
2. Crimes against the Peace
3. War Crimes
4. Crimes against Humanity

The first count established that the perpetration of crimes against the peace, war crimes and crimes against humanity were intentional and intrinsic to Nazi dogma. It focused in particular on the Nazi party's pre-war establishment of totalitarian control over all aspects of German society, from the indoctrination of the youth to the eradication of all political opposition, and the establishment of the Führer as the supreme leader. It summarised the party's aggressive conspiracy to overthrow the Treaty of Versailles and Germany's consequent expansion into Austria, Czechoslovakia and Poland in pre-war Europe. Finally, it detailed how the Nazi policies of 'Lebensraum' and the creation of a 'master race' constituted a conspiracy that inexorably led to the following three counts.[118]

The second count indicted the defendants for participating 'in the planning, preparation, initiation, and waging of wars of aggression, which were also wars in violation of international treaties, agreements, and assurances'.[119] The third count, war crimes, included the Nazis' murder, torture and acts of brutality against occupied civilian populations, the use of civilians as slave labour, the killing of civilian hostages, the plunder of private and public property, the exaction of collective penalties, the wanton destruction of cities, towns and villages not justified by military necessity, the conscription of civilian labour, the forcing of civilians of occupied territories to swear allegiance to a hostile power and the 'Germanization' of those populations.[120] The final count, the case for which relied heavily upon the OSS's cinematic evidence, dealt with the holocaust, among other acts of mass extermination and repression by the Nazis.

The FPU gathered much of its footage for the trial from teams of filmmakers sent to film the horrific scenes encountered by the allies upon liberating the Nazi concentration camps. Material was also gathered from German propaganda films, such as Leni Riefenstahl's *Triumph of the Will*, which was reverse-engineered to show an alternative narrative of the Nazi's nefarious designs. Riefenstahl was arrested by FPU officer Budd Schulberg at her chalet in Kitzbühel, Austria, who set her to work identifying Nazi war criminals featured in the captured German footage. They also captured Heinrich Hoffmann, Hitler's personal photographer, and had him catalogue all of his still files for the prosecution. Hoffmann's son-in-law, Baldur von Schirach, former leader of the Hitler Youth, was one of the defendants at Nuremberg. Kellogg took unconcealed glee in running footage of Schirach in the adjoining room to Hoffman, which made the latter wince and ask if his son-in-law was being properly cared for. 'Hoffman is a dirty old bastard', Kellogg told Ford, 'with a dirty greasy vest.'[121]

The team also recycled German propaganda footage of Judge Freisler's vitriolic prosecution of the 20 July bomb plotters at the People's Court. 'Imagine eleven hours of film with [Freisler] screaming all the way through it', Kellogg told Ford. 'Defendant Field Marshal Witzleben was pathetic. They had given him an old civilian suit many sizes too large and no belt, every time he used his hands to blow his nose or wipe off the sweat his pants would fall down. It was diabolical ridicule in the extreme.'[122] Each time a defendant attempted to speak the judge

Figure 1.11   22 November 1945: Hitler's photographer Heinrich Hoffmann (1885–1957) inspecting evidence during the Nuremberg War Crimes Trial. *Source:* Getty Images.

would interject screaming 'SCHWEIN!' recalled Parrish.[123] When the Panzer General Hoepner appeared before the court, the judge remarked, '[Y]ou remind me of an animal . . . a pig, I believe!' The General was then asked what animal he thought he had acted like during the plot, to which he replied '"a Jackass . . . because I was stupid." The judge broke in and screamed "That's where you are wrong . . . a donkey is an animal of character, you are not! Therefore you are a pig!"'[124] Kellogg and Parrish recut the footage into the film *Nazi Supreme Court Trial of the Anti-Hitler Plot*, providing a powerful illustration of the Nuremberg tribunal's juxtaposing principles of justice and the rule of law. Another film produced by the team, *That Justice Be Done*, reinforced this message.

Other footage proved harder to come by. OSS officers scoured liberated Europe for footage that would support the indictments. Dan Kiley, a member of OSS Visual Presentation Branch, compared them to touring G-Men like Edward G. Robinson in *Confessions of a Nazi Spy*.[125] James Donovan went to Paris 'in his ultimately successful efforts to track down film evidence of SS concentration camp guards beating and otherwise maltreating their inmates'.[126] Stuart

Schulberg, Budd Schulberg's younger brother, located a piece of film in the Berlin apartment of SS Officer Arthur Nebe showing the experimental gassing of inmates using a car exhaust pipe on the outskirts of Mogilev.[127] The film of the 20 July bomb plotters' trial was sourced by Parrish, Kellogg and Budd Schulberg from a covetous major in the Russian Army stationed in Berlin. After days of wooing him and plying him with vodka and dinner at their Wannsee house, the deadlock was finally broken when the officer learnt that John Ford was their commanding officer. 'You mean John Ford the movie director?', asked the major with boyish excitement. 'Yes . . . he's our boss, he's our commander,' they replied. 'John Ford is the commander you work for! I've written two books about him!' the Russian officer blurted out excitedly. The next day he backed up a truck behind Wansee and unloaded all of the film.[128]

The courtroom was redesigned by Dan Kiley from the Visual Presentation Branch to maximise the impact of the films upon the court, the defendants and the gathered media. Projection facilities were installed, a large screen was set up and space had to be cleared for newsreel camera crews and the gathered press. All this had to be incorporated without 'turning the entire proceedings into a "media spectacle", which would risk trivializing both the gravity of the proceedings and the important issues at stake'.[129] Kiley's brief stated simply that 'there should be no allowance in design and layout for purely decorative, propagandistic, or journalistic purposes'.[130] As a result, a booth was installed for the press behind a glass screen from which they could view the proceedings without interrupting the trial. The verbal exchanges were 'piped in' via a specially installed sound system.[131] Legal historian Michael Salter notes that the media presence caused friction between Justice Jackson's 'rather more legalistic agenda' and 'the OSS's attempts to apply its familiar tactics of media manipulation and psychological warfare'.[132] Ultimately, however, Jackson acquiesced, understanding that media coverage was vital to the success of 'his ambitious goal of creating a historic precedent designed to re-assert the rule of law' in the conduct of international relations.[133]

Among other concessions to the media savvy OSS, Jackson expedited the trials of lesser war criminals at Nuremberg to placate 'media criticism of undue delay'.[134] He also appointed Gordon Dean as press spokesman to 'handle all contacts with press, radio, or other communications and supervise any activities directed to the public information'.[135] Although Salter stresses the importance of Dean in stage-managing the event, Kellogg would privately complain of his ineptitude, claiming that it was only after Kellogg interceded that the army overturned their initial policy of prohibiting photography at the trial.[136] After the war, the veteran documentarian Pare Lorentz produced a film covering the events of the trials taken from FPU and Army Signal Corps footage, but it was suppressed by the military on the grounds that it would impede American public support for German reconstruction.[137]

Figure 1.12 The OSS installed a screen in the Nuremberg courtroom (see left) in order to show the films they produced for the trials. The screen occupies a prominent position in the courtroom in order for the films to achieve maximum effect, however, the OSS team who helped redesign the courtroom were also conscious of the need to maintain the dignity of the proceedings; they placed the screen to the side of the judges to not interfere with the core deliberations and built a separate room for watching journalists where the court's proceedings were piped in via an intercom system they had installed. *Source:* Getty Images.

But perhaps Jackson's greatest compromise was in re-sequencing the order of the trial in order to dramatise the impact of the *Nazi Concentration Camps* film. If the film had been introduced to the court on a strictly procedural basis, it would have been shown much later in the trial as one of the key pieces of evidence in support of the fourth count, crimes against humanity. Instead the film was shown early, in order to 'meet the perceived need to add drama, emotion, and excitement' according to OSS official Bernard Maltzer.[138] Prior to the screening, the prosecution's case progressed with the monotonous 'recitation of documentary evidence'.[139] Some of the less remorseful defendants treated the proceedings with disdain. Immediately prior to the film's screening on 29 November 1945, Göring, Ribbentrop and Hess laughed and joked over

CINEMATIC INTELLIGENCE AND THE OSS

Figure 1.13 Nuremberg Trial defendants in their dock, circa 1945–6. The OSS had foot lamps installed beneath them so that their faces could be lit during the screening of the concentration camp film in order for the court and the world's watching media to gauge their reactions. *Source:* Getty Images.

the reading of 'Göring's telephone conversation with Ribbentrop on the day of Hitler's triumphant entry into Vienna, describing the whole thing as a lark, with birds twittering, etc'.[140] The screening of the film was designed in part to sabotage their haughty air by confronting them with the visual reality of their barbarous crimes. 'I can hardly wait until we hit them with the Concentration Camps' film', wrote Kellogg, as he hastily cut it together.[141] Spotlights were installed to highlight the defendants' reaction to the film. As the court lights dimmed, only their faces remained illuminated, for all to see.

The film opens with signed affidavits from George Stevens (who made liberation films for the Army Signal Corps) and Kellogg, attesting to its authenticity and the accuracy of the narration. Kellogg's statement, sworn to John Ford a few days earlier, states that the film was cut from 80,000 feet of footage, all of which was of a similar nature. The hour-long documentary that followed contained the most horrific images of human suffering and cruelty ever witnessed on film. A camp at Leipzig is introduced with the story of 200 political prisoners who were burned alive by twelve SS men and a Gestapo agent in a wooden structure in the camp. The charred corpses of those who fled the flames are shown on the film, their bodies contorted, almost lifelike, into agonising postures still gasping for life before they were gunned down or electrocuted if they made it as far as the barbed wire fence. At Penig, the living skeletons of teenage girls are shown. The film then follows the rescue of the stricken survivors by the 6th Army Division supervised by the Red Cross. The film notes how German staff at the nearby air force hospital are forced to help those whom they had formerly persecuted. Surviving young women are seen smiling – the narrator notes that this may be the first time they were able to do so in years. At Ohrdruf, a woodshed layered with corpses is shown. The liberating troops survey the scene with expressions of disbelief – a sentiment mirrored by the film's audience in the Nuremberg courtroom.

General Eisenhower tells American congressmen invited to visit the camps that the barbarous treatment received by the inmates is almost unbelievable. 'I want you to see for yourselves and be the spokesmen for the United States.' The film cuts to footage of more corpses, strewn randomly across the ground, which signals the Nazis' callous indifference towards human life. The charred remains of several cremated inmates are then shown. Prominent Nazi party members and a German medical major are confronted by the barbarous consequences of their ideology on a forced tour of the camp. They are hustled inside a woodshed piled with corpses, and read a list of the crimes carried out at Ohrdruf next to the crematory. They exhibit no emotion, the narrator tells us, and all deny knowledge of activities inside the camp.

At Hadamar, a Nazi institution under the guise of an insane-asylum, dubbed 'The House of Shudders' by locals, is shown. In the region of 35,000 Poles, Russians and Germans were taken there and executed mainly for political and religious reasons. The infirm survivors are examined by a major from the American War Crimes Commission. From the graveyard 20,000 bodies are exhumed. The remaining 15,000 were murdered in the gas chamber and cremated. At Breendonck, former inmates reenact the medieval torture scenes common in the camp: beatings with a barbed wire stick, restrained prisoners hit repeatedly with a cosh, a man is tied in chains that are gradually tightened with a tourniquet, a thumb-screw is demonstrated on a maid and a Belgian shows how his crotch was ripped open. Prisoners display their scars to the cameras from beatings and cigarette burns. At a camp near Hannover, inmates weep as they receive bread and soup for the first time in recent memory. The deaths continue even after the liberation of the camps. At Arnstadt German civilians are forced to dig up the bodies of the deceased for the second time. Before the liberation, we are told, they had exhumed the bodies and moved them away from the town to get rid of the stench.

At Buchenwald, local Weimar townspeople are given an enforced tour of the camp. They are shown walking to the camp in orderly file, many smiling or with relaxed expressions, as if on a pleasant outing. As they enter the camp, they are greeted by a macabre display of exhibitions laid out on a table. They are shown a lampshade made from human skin for an SS officer's wife. Parchments of human skin used as canvasses for obscene paintings are also shown alongside two human heads shrunk to one-fifth of their original size. The camera tracks the changing expressions of the townspeople, from nonchalance, to disbelief, to abject horror.

At Dachau, the narrator notes that prisoners came from across Europe, including 1,600 surviving priests of numerous denominations. An orderly row of prison clothes is shown hanging outside the gas chamber. The narrator explains with chilling matter-of-factness that the prisoners removed their clothes in the belief that they were going to take a shower. The word 'Brausbad' (shower-bath) is printed above the chamber door. Inside are dummy showerheads, masking the gas pipes. Behind the chamber the camera records the engineer room, with its intake and outtake pipes, pressure valves and push button panels – testaments to the banality of evil everywhere on display. The camera cuts to a canister of cyanide powder – routinely administered to the unwitting condemned.

At Belsen, the captured SS guards are ordered to clear the camp. They are shown tossing the emaciated corpses into a pit. There are so many bodies that articulated ploughs are brought in to clear the dead. The camera pans slowly across the deceased, coming to rest on the victims' faces – their anguished expressions are death masks of the incomprehensible cruelty and agony incurred at the camps. Robert Parrish described a similar scene, not used in the final film, in an interview with Dan Ford:

> [T]wo men come over ... and they take the body of a baby and they throw it sort of to the camera and it slides down a wooden thing into a lion pit – where there are other bodies – there must have been 500 bodies – and this particular shot – when they throw this body down, the camera follows it and goes past it because it gets caught on a nail and the camera comes back to it – and the fella up there takes a long poll and he pokes it and it slides down and the camera follows it down ... It was the first time I'd seen the kind of film that you can see now on Buchenwald ... How would you do that kind of thing ... how would you allow yourself to be ... Well ... I have no answer.[142]

Describing the scenes, the disembodied narrator maintains notes of Von Voorhis's unadorned Timespeak authority. It does not equivocate. Not that the images would allow it to. But it does so in a subdued way, melancholic, with an air of disbelief at the scale of the human tragedy unfolding, twenty-four frames per second. The narrator was no longer driving the story as in the *March of Time* newsreels. As James Donovan put it when introducing the film to the court, '[T]hese motion pictures speak for themselves.'[143] But the filmmakers took care to cross-reference their images with other mediums of testimony, as if by way of acknowledgement that the veracity of cinematic evidence may well be doubted. Along with the signed affidavits that begin and end the presentation, the film makes constant reference to written evidence: at Hadamar, for example, the film notes the discovery of a meticulously kept record book filled with thousands of death certificates. During the scenes from Buchenwald, the narrator takes care to reinforce the 'pictorial evidence of almost unprecedented crimes perpetrated by the Nazis' with 'the story in written form . . . contained in the official report of the Prisoner of War and Displaced Persons Division of the United States Group Control Council'.

Oral testimony is also given to camera. The commanding officer from the regiment of the Royal Artillery describes the rescue operation at Belsen: 'When we came here, conditions were indescribable . . . None of us are likely to forget what the Germans have done here.' At the same camp a camp doctor and former inmate are interviewed. She is noticeably healthier than the living skeletons that surround her, lending credence to the extreme nature of her descriptions. She describes the effects of starvation, and the bouts of typhoid and other diseases that ensued. She gives examples of the medical experiments performed on prisoners at the camp: 20 cm^3 of Benzedrine was intravenously injected into some of the inmates, many of whom did not survive. Sterilisations and other gynaecological experiments were performed on nineteen-year-old girls. Some of the men grew so hungry that they ate pieces of human liver and heart to stay alive.

At Mauthausen, the filmmakers were confronted by their doppelganger, Lt Jack Taylor, OSS officer from Hollywood, California, who had been interned at the camp after a failed mission behind enemy lines in October 1944. He tells the camera how he was arrested by the Gestapo and severely beaten. Even though he was in uniform, he was treated as a non-prisoner of war and sent to Mauthausen. 'Two American officers at least have been executed here', he tells the camera, holding an insignia from one, and the dog-tags of another, again demonstrating the filmmakers' keen awareness of the need to reinforce their claims through forms of testimony and evidence other than the moving image. Taylor is asked how many ways people were killed in the camp: 'Five or six ways,' he replies, 'by gas, by shooting, by beating, that is beating with clubs, ah, by exposure, that is standing out in the snow, naked, for 48 hours and having cold water put on them, thrown on them in the middle of winter, starvation, dogs, and pushing over a hundred-foot cliff. This,' he assures the viewer 'this is all true, has been seen and is now being recorded.' Taylor's biography as an American spy from Hollywood, California, may well have inspired incredulity from extreme sceptics of American propaganda techniques. But as Michael Salter writes, his testimony 'has a particular authenticity and resonance'.[144] Before he delivers his damning account he reassures his audience, in a measured tone, '[B]elieve it or not, this is the first time I have ever been in the movies.'

As the court lights went up, the defendants stayed seated 'as if turned to stone'. They were slow to rise when the judges 'filed out in disgusted silence'.[145] The film had achieved its desired effect upon the defendants. As they sat watching it, their faces spot-lit in sharp relief to the darkened courtroom, many must have felt the noose tighten around their necks. Hjalmar Schacht, who broke with the Nazi regime in 1938 after Kristallnacht and who was interned at Dachau, turned his back on the screen. Hans Fritzsche, who had already seen part of the film, turned white at the opening scenes featuring the prisoners fleeing the burning barn. Hans Frank, the so-called 'Butcher of Poland', broke into tears on a number of occasions, and was heard muttering 'Horrible, Horrible'. Fritz Sauckel broke into tears, mopped his brow and shuddered at the images of the Buchenwald crematorium. Wilhelm Keitel removed his headphones. Rudolf Hess, who was taken prisoner by the British after flying to Scotland in 1941 to negotiate peace, glared at the screen 'looking like a ghoul with sunken eyes'. Von Neurath bowed his head, Ribbentrop closed his eyes, Speer looked melancholic and swallowed hard and Von Papen sat with his head bowed and hand over his brow, staring at his feet. The defence attorneys muttered 'for God's sake – terrible', and the film made some uncomfortable with being in the same room as their defendants. Only Göhring and Julius Streicher, the editor of the anti-Semitic paper *Der Stürmer*, appeared relatively unfazed, although the former's conceit from earlier that day had visibly evaporated.

The defendants' stunned reactions lasted into the evening. Dr Gustave Gilbert, an American psychologist at the trial, went to talk to the prisoners in their cells immediately after the screening of the film. 'No power in heaven or earth will erase this shame from my country! – not in generations not in centuries!' Fritzsche told them. 'To think we lived like kings and believed in that beast!' was Hans Frank's surmise. 'How can they accuse me of knowing such things?' asked Naval Commander Karl Dönitz. 'They ask me why I didn't go to Himmler to check on the concentration camps. Why that's preposterous! He would have kicked me out as I would have kicked him out if he came to investigate the navy!' Sauckel was visibly distressed when Gilbert entered his cell. When they asked about the film, 'He stretched out his fingers and cried, wild-eyed, "I'd choke myself with these hands if I thought I had the slightest thing to do with those murders! It is a shame! It is a disgrace for us and for our children – and our children's children!"' Von Papen, when asked why he had not watched the film, admitted, 'I didn't want to see Germany's shame.' Even Göring was perturbed, but in an unremorseful way – 'It was such a good afternoon too', he told Gilbert, 'until they showed that film. They were reading my telephone conversations on the Austrian affair, and everybody was laughing with me. And then they showed that awful film, and it just spoiled everything.'[146]

The film made its intended impact on the American press as well. The 'Horror Films' hit the headlines across the nation.[147] It represented the FPU's final cinematic statement to the world before being officially disbanded along with the OSS. After Nuremberg, nobody could doubt, as they had done before the war, the power of film as a documentary medium. Never before had film been used at a trial in this way, and arguably never before had it had such a profound impact upon its audience. Although the filmmakers took care throughout to cross-reference their claims from written sources, oral testimony and collected artefacts, the pictures really did speak for themselves. These images of death-house horror continue to be used to this day as incontrovertible evidence of the Nazis' crimes and have contributed significantly to the construction of public memory of the Holocaust. Other than Julius Streicher, and a few committed Holocaust-deniers, few would challenge the authenticity of the film. It had achieved what no written document or oral testimony could ever achieve, in giving us a sense, as Thomas Dodds put it, of 'what the words "concentration camp" imply'.[148] It was the ultimate example of the newfound epistemic supremacy of film as witness to the cruel and shocking barbarity of the real.

And yet, as Robert Parrish, who edited the camp films, well knew, the realism on display at the trials was as much an invention, staged for the cameras, as any of the other propaganda films the FPU had produced. 'The film was very effective at the trial', Parrish reflected, 'but I also know that you can fake up anything – film is terribly malleable – and it can be dishonest or honest, and just because you have a picture of somebody saying something it doesn't even mean that they ever said it.'[149] Of course Parrish was not seeking to deny that the events they filmed had taken place. Rather, his unease was directed at the prominent role that cinema's emotive language had come to play, in an otherwise legalistic affair. The affective power of documentary cinema may well have its place, but in a court of law it at least deserved some cross-examination. 'When I said films can make you think what you want to be thought', Parrish continued, '... we found a piece of film ... about Göhring – because he was the man who was supposed to have said "bomb Poland" – of course there's no such film.' So instead they cut together a film with an image of Göhring, and then a shot against the sky, and then newsreel footage of the invasion of Poland. It presented the desired effect, but it was just that, an effect.[150]

This exploitation of montage could never have been achieved through any other medium. All the films shown at Nuremberg were constructed in this way. Although the filmmakers who entered the camps and cut the horrific footage of their liberation together could never doubt the culpability of those who their films condemned to the gallows, some nevertheless maintained a lingering unease about the use of such a powerfully emotive and 'malleable' medium as the principal basis upon which their convictions were sealed. The continual references in the films to written and material evidence of the Nazis' crimes was symptomatic of that unease – as if to say that film should not shoulder the burden alone. But such a cinematic war required a cinematic conclusion. The magnitude of the Nazis' crimes coupled with the new epistemic authority that the war had rendered unto film meant that only the cinema could bring home something of the reality of the Holocaust to the Nuremberg audience. If the extreme cruelty of the Holocaust placed it, as Robert Braun put it, on 'the limits of representation', only film could come anywhere close to reaching those limits.[151] As Lawrence Douglas put it:

> The filmic witness could offer pictures where speech failed; it could produce visual knowledge of atrocities that resisted summary in the words of eyewitness testimonials. Such a view echoed an understanding that both saw documentary film as capable of offering a more complete and transparent window upon the 'real', and anticipated the crisis of representation that has come to characterize efforts to find an idiom capable of capturing the Holocaust's central horror.[152]

But despite the irrefutable credibility of the concentration camp films shown at Nuremberg, they were still propaganda films – produced by a US Government intelligence agency and designed by a team of Hollywood filmmakers for maximum emotive impact upon the courtroom and the world's watching media. During the Second World War, as Scott Lucas has written, 'the public was conditioned to the illusion of the US Government as helpful provider of news'.[153] So too was Hollywood, whose newfound taste for documentary realism became one of the principal conduits of government propaganda dressed as news. Such propaganda may have disguised itself at Nuremberg in the illusion of what André Bazin has described as our perhaps naïve faith in cinema's unique capacity for objectivity, but such scepticism ignores the power with which wartime documentaries communicated the real, despite their provenance. Josephine MacNab was right: film did play a 'vital role in waking up America to the things that are being faced by our boys', and by the Jews, the Gypsies, the homosexuals, the Prisoners of War (POWs) and all of the persecuted who met their end at Auschwitz, Dachau or any of the other Nazi death camps whose horror placed them almost beyond the bounds of human imagination.

The war transformed the American cinema from a domain of fantasy and escapism, of 'pure entertainment', to a place where millions of Americans regularly sought to encounter the real. The OSS FPU played a significant role in facilitating that transformation. But just as war had transformed the cinema, cinema had transformed war. Stock film footage found in Hollywood archives provided a visual impression of the battlefield for military planners. Training films produced by the FPU provided detailed technical advice to new recruits. Flown reconnaissance missions provided the American military planners with a more detailed picture of the global terrain than ever before. If Paul Virilio is correct in his assertion that the technological development of what he terms 'the logistics of perception', or the ways and means by which we *see* the battlefield, has a fundamentally transformative effect upon the conduct and morality of war, then the cinematic intelligence work of the OSS may just have been its most significant contribution to the history of warfare. Neither cinema nor war could ever be viewed the same again.

Notes

1. Alison Landsberg, *Prosthetic Memory: The Transformation of American Remembrance in the Age of Mass Culture* (New York: Columbia University Press, 2004).
2. The first motion picture footage of combat was taken during the Spanish–American War of 1898. It was not until the Second World War, however, that motion pictures began to achieve pre-eminence as a reportorial medium. This was due to the technological development of cinema, in particular the arrival of sound, colour and more mobile equipment that produced far more authentic motion picture records of war. The cinema of the 1940s also boasted huge audiences, making cinema, and in particular the newsreels, quite probably the most widely consumed news format of the period.
3. Raymond Fielding, *The American Newsreel, 1911–1967* (Norman: Oklahoma University Press, 1972), p. 202.
4. Josephine MacNab to Commander John Ford, 21 September 1942, John Ford Mss, Box 1, Correspondence File August–September 1941, Lilly Library.
5. Raymond Fielding, *The March of Time, 1935–1951* (New York: Oxford University Press, 1978), p. 4.
6. Joseph McBride, *John Ford: A Life* (New York: Faber and Faber, 2003), p. 335. For an evocatively written account of John Ford's contribution to the war effort, along with the service of William Wyler, John Huston, Frank Capra and George Stevens see Mark Harris, *Five Came Back: A Story of Hollywood and the Second World War* (New York: Penguin, 2014).
7. William J. Donovan in McBride, *John Ford*.
8. John Ford medical history report card signed by Lieutenant Commander Frederick S. Foote, (MC) USNR, US Naval Air Station, Midway Island, 4 June 1942, John Ford Mss, Box 1, Correspondence File June–July 1942, Lilly Library, University of Indiana, Bloomington.
9. Mark Armistead, an officer in Ford's FPU, recalled that the Cunningham Combat Camera was 'probably the lousiest camera ever made. The thing would never run. It would buckle. It looked like a machine gun and if you're in combat and you're pointing something that looks like a machine-gun people take a dim view of that.' Mark Armistead Interview with Dan Ford, John Ford Audio Tapes, Tape 1: Mark Armistead, Series VII, Lilly Library, University of Indiana, Bloomington. For

Robert Parrish's account of the incident while filming the old State Department building see Robert Parrish, *Growing Up in Hollywood* (St Albans: Triad Paperbacks, 1976), pp. 157–60. For more on the Cunningham Combat Camera see Barry Salt, 'Film Style and Technology in the Forties', *Film Quarterly*, 31:1 (1977), pp. 46–57; Ray Zone, 'Vintage Instruments', *American Cinematographer*, 84:1 (2003), p. 104.
10. McBride, *John Ford*, p. 336.
11. McBride, *John Ford*, p. 364.
12. Josephine MacNab to Commander John Ford, 21 September 1942, John Ford Mss, Box 1, Correspondence File August–September 1941, Lilly Library, University of Indiana, Bloomington.
13. *The Battle of Midway* (John Ford, United States Government, 1942). Available online at 'The Internet Archive', https://archive.org/details/BattleOfMidway.
14. McBride, *John Ford*, p. 363.
15. Robert Parrish Interview with Dan Ford, John Ford Mss, Series VII – Interview Tape 70, Lilly Library, University of Indiana, Bloomington.
16. For a discussion of the influence of Pare Lorentz's influence on Ford's *The Grapes of Wrath*, see Vivian C. Sobchack, '*The Grapes of Wrath* (1940): Thematic Emphasis through Visual Style', *American Quarterly*, 31:5 (winter 1976), pp. 596–615.
17. In an interview with Dan Ford, Robert Parrish explained that the film 'was classified because it was the first time radar had been photographed – and Ford also knew that if you showed that there'd be a big drama about it – we masked it out – we put a big black thing over it – the first time that had been done and of course it intrigued everybody'. Robert Parrish Interview with Dan Ford, John Ford Mss, Series VII – Interview Tape 70, Lilly Library, University of Indiana, Bloomington.
18. McBride, *John Ford*, p. 362.
19. Parrish, *Growing Up in Hollywood*, p. 144.
20. McBride, *John Ford*, p. 349.
21. Ibid., pp. 349–50.
22. Josephine MacNab to Commander John Ford, 21 September 1942, John Ford Mss, Box 1, Correspondence File August – September 1941, Lilly Library, University of Indiana, Bloomington.
23. Robert Parrish Interview with Dan Ford, John Ford Mss, Series VII – Interview Tape 70, Lilly Library, University of Indiana, Bloomington.
24. McBride, *John Ford*, p. 363.
25. Robert Parrish Interview with Dan Ford, John Ford Mss, Series VII – Interview Tape 70, Lilly Library, University of Indiana, Bloomington.
26. McBride, *John Ford*, p. 363.
27. André Bazin, 'On Why We Fight: History, Documentation, and the Newsreel (1946)', trans. and ed. Bert Cardullo, reprinted in *Film and History: An Interdisciplinary Journal of Film and Television Studies*, 31:1 (2001), pp. 60–2.
28. See Clayton Koppes and Gregory Black, *Hollywood Goes to War: How Politics, Profits, and Propaganda Shaped World War II Movies* (Berkeley: The Free Press, 1987), p. 56.
29. The phrase 'passion for the real' was famously used by the philosopher Alan Badiou to describe what he regarded as one of the defining features of the twentieth century. See Alan Badiou, *The Century*, trans. Alberto Toscano (New York: Polity Press, 2007).
30. McBride, *John Ford*, p. 98.
31. Rosalie Schwartz, *Flying Down to Rio: Hollywood, Tourists, and Yankee Clippers* (College Station: A&M University Press, 2004), p. 272.

32. Commanding Officer First Lieutenant Lewis T. Turnbull, 20th Aero Squadron to Headquarters, 8 December 1918, Merrian C. Cooper MSS, Box 6 Folder 2, Harold B. Lee Library, Brigham Young University, Provo.
33. Merian C. Cooper US Army Certificate of Death, 26 September 1918, Merian C. Cooper MSS, Box 33 Folder 15, Brigham Young University, Provo.
34. Letter to Chief of Naval Personnel from John Ford, 12 September 1944, John Ford mss, Box 1, Correspondence File 1939, Lilly Library; see also McBride, *John Ford*, pp. 319–21.
35. McBride, *John Ford*, p. 321.
36. Interview with Mark Armistead, John Ford Audio Tapes, Tape 1: Mark Armistead, Series VII, Lilly Library, University of Indiana, Bloomington; Interview with Robert Parrish, John Ford Audio Tapes, Tape 70: Robert Parrish, Series VII, Lilly Library, University of Indiana, Bloomington.
37. McBride, *John Ford*, p. 321.
38. McBride, *John Ford*, p. 320.
39. McBride, pp. 321, 180.
40. Merian Cooper to Admiral Leary, 9 July 1940, Merian C. Cooper MSS, Box 4 Folder 7, Brigham Young University, Provo, Harold B. Lee Library; Merian Cooper to Rear Admiral Robert L. Ghormley, 8 July 1940, Merian C. Cooper MSS, Box 33 Folder 15, Harold B. Lee Library, Brigham Young University, Provo.
41. Proposed Naval and Photographic Organization, undated, Merian C. Cooper MSS, Box 4 Folder 7, Harold B. Lee Library, Brigham Young University, Provo.
42. See, for example, Eric Rentschler, *The Ministry of Illusion: Nazi Cinema and Its Afterlife* (New Haven: Yale University Press, 1996); Susan Tegel, *Nazis and the Cinema* (London: Bloomsbury Continuum, 2007).
43. Proposed Naval and Photographic Organization, undated, Merian C. Cooper MSS, Box 4 Folder 7, Harold B. Lee Library, Brigham Young University, Provo.
44. Paul Virilio, *War and Cinema: The Logistics of Perception* (London: Verso, 2009).
45. Proposed Naval and Photographic Organization, undated, Merian C. Cooper MSS, Box 4 Folder 7, Harold B. Lee Library, Brigham Young University, Provo, p. 5.
46. Ibid., p. 6.
47. Paul Virilio, *War and Cinema: The Logistics of Perception* (London: Verso, 2009).
48. Barry Katz, 'The Arts of War: "Visual Presentation" and National Intelligence', *Design Issues*, 12:2 (summer 1996), pp. 3–21.
49. Report on Richard de Rochemont's record of service in response to inquiry, 6 January 1954, Richard de Rochemont MSS, Box 12, CIA File, American Heritage Center, University of Wyoming, Laramie (hereafter AHCW).
50. Richard de Rochemont to Lieutenant Frank Spencer, 6 January 1942, Richard de Rochemont MSS, Box 12, CIA File, AHCW.
51. Allen Dibble to Richard de Rochemont, 2 January 1942, Richard de Rochemont MSS, Box 155, OSS File, AHCW.
52. Katz, 'The Arts of War', p. 5.
53. Ibid., pp. 5–6.
54. Ibid., p. 5.
55. Project for Pictorial Records Section Reports Division of Visual Presentation Branch, undated, Richard de Rochemont MSS, Box 12, CIA File, AHCW.
56. Richard de Rochemont to Atherton Richards, 6 January 1942, Richard de Rochemont MSS, Box 12, CIA File, AHCW.
57. Project for Pictorial Records Section Reports Division of Visual Presentation Branch, undated, Richard de Rochemont MSS, Box 12, CIA File, AHCW.

58. Richard de Rochemont to Atherton Richards, 6 January 1942, Richard de Rochemont MSS, Box 12, CIA File, AHCW.
59. 'Survey of Available Material', undated, Richard de Rochemont MSS, Box 155, OSS File, AHCW.
60. Ibid.
61. Memorandum from Visual Presentation Branch, 20 February 1942, Richard de Rochemont MSS, Box 12, CIA File, AHCW.
62. Unsigned letter to Atherton Richards, 13 February 1942, Richard de Rochemont MSS, Box 12, CIA File, AHCW.
63. Dan Gillmor to Atherton Richards – Progress Report on Pictorial Records Section, 21 February 1942, Richard de Rochemont MSS, Box 12, CIA File, AHCW.
64. Ibid.
65. Ibid.
66. Susan A. Cady, 'Microfilm Technology and Information Systems' in Mary Bowden, Trudi Hahn and Robert Williams (eds), *Proceedings of the 1998 Conferences on the History and Heritage of Science Information Systems* (Melford, NJ: Information Today ASIS Monograph Series, 1999), pp. 182–4.
67. Merian Cooper to Otto C. Doering, 10 May 1971, Merian C. Cooper MSS, Box 33 Folder 14, Harold B. Lee Library, Brigham Young University, Provo.
68. As almost every biography of Donovan and history of the OSS attests, it was his trips to Europe in 1940 and 1941 where he encountered several senior British intelligence officials that proved decisive in persuading him of America's need for a centralized civilian intelligence agency. See, for example, Anthony Cave Brown, *The Last Hero: Wild Bill Donovan* (London: Times Books, 1982); Richard Dunlop, *Donovan: America's Master Spy* (New York: Skyhorse Publishing, 2014); Douglas Waller, *Wild Bill Donovan: The Spymaster Who Created the OSS and Modern American Espionage* (New York: Simon and Schuster, 2012).
69. McBride, *John Ford*, p. 338.
70. Brown, *Donovan*, p. 16.
71. Frances Stonor Saunders, *Who Paid the Piper: The CIA and the Cultural Cold War* (London: Granta, 1999), p. 286.
72. Brown, *Donovan*, p. 134.
73. Michael E. Birdwell, *Celluloid Soldiers: Warner Brothers' Campaign against Nazism* (New York: New York University Press, 2001), p. 80; for more on Donovan's involvement with the production of *The Fighting 69th* see David Welky, *The Moguls and the Dictators: Hollywood and the Coming of World War II* (Baltimore: Johns Hopkins University Press, 2008), p. 183.
74. Brown, *Donovan*, p. 12.
75. Ibid., p. 436.
76. Ibid., p. 300.
77. For more on the role of Frankfurt School intellectuals in OSS see Barry Katz, *Foreign Intelligence: Research and Analysis in the Office of Strategic Services, 1942–1945* (Cambridge, MA: Harvard University Press, 2013). On Moe Berg see Nicholas Dawidoff, *The Catcher Was a Spy: The Mysterious Life of Moe Berg* (New York: Vintage, 2011). For more on OSS recruitment of academics during the war, including Arthur Schlesinger Jr and Walt Rostow, see Robin Winks, *Cloak and Gown: Scholars in America's Secret War* (London: The Harvill Press, 1987).
78. Drew Pearson cited in Brown, *Donovan*, p. 301.
79. McBride, *John Ford*, p. 350.
80. Lieutenant Commander Bonney Powell (USNR) to Commander John Ford, 28 November 1941, John Ford MSS, Correspondence File November–December 1941, Lilly Library, University of Indiana, Bloomington.

81. Henry Stimson to William J. Donovan, 3 February 1942, John Ford MSS, Correspondence File February–May 1942, Lilly Library, University of Indiana, Bloomington.
82. McBride, *John Ford*, pp. 354–5.
83. McBride, *John Ford*, p. 354.
84. McBride, *John Ford*, p. 354.
85. Cave Brown, *Donovan*, pp. 196–200.
86. Koppes and Black, *Hollywood Goes to War*, pp. 248–77.
87. McBride, *John Ford*, pp. 383–4.
88. James Kevin McGuinness to John Ford, 24 March 1943, John Ford MSS, Correspondence File January–March 1943, Lilly Library, University of Indiana, Bloomington.
89. James Kevin McGuinness to John Ford, 24 March 1943, John Ford MSS, Correspondence File January–March 1943, Lilly Library, University of Indiana, Bloomington.
90. McBride, *John Ford*, p. 354.
91. Robert Parrish, *Hollywood Doesn't Live Here Anymore* (Boston: Little, Brown and Company, 1988), p. 19.
92. Ibid.
93. Phillip Dunne, 'The Documentary and Hollywood', *Hollywood Quarterly*, 1:2 (January 1946), p. 167.
94. Darryl F. Zanuck, *Tunis Expedition* (New York: Random House, 1943), p. 64.
95. George F. Custen, *Twentieth Century's Fox: Darryl F. Zanuck and the Culture of Hollywood* (New York: Basic Books, 1998), pp. 258–9.
96. McBride, *John Ford*, p. 380.
97. McBride, *John Ford*, p. 376.
98. Ibid.
99. Robert Johannes, 'African Invasion', Field Photo War Diary Vol. 6, John Ford MSS, Correspondence File June–September 1945, Lilly Library, University of Indiana, Bloomington.
100. Ibid.
101. Ibid.
102. *At the Front in North Africa with the US Army* (Darryl F. Zanuck, United States Government, 1943). Available online at https://archive.org/details/AttheFrontinNorthAfricawiththeU.S.Army.
103. McBride, *John Ford*, p. 378.
104. Ibid.
105. Ibid, p. 272.
106. Darryl F. Zanuck, 'Do Writers Know Hollywood?: The Message Cannot Overwhelm the Technique', *The Saturday Review*, 30 October 1943, p. 12.
107. Custen, *Twentieth Century's Fox*, p. 270.
108. John Ford to Secretariat, Report of the Officer Returning from the Field, 9 September 1944, John Ford MSS, Correspondence File September–December 1944, Lilly Library, University of Indiana, Bloomington.
109. Christian Delage, *Caught on Camera: Film in the Courtroom from the Nuremberg Trials to the Khmer Rouge*, trans Ralph Schoolcraft and Mary Byrd Kelly (Philadelphia: University of Pennsylvania Press, 2013).
110. For a discussion of the way in which the Second World War transformed Hollywood's general tendency to regard cinema as 'pure entertainment', see Clayton Koppes and Gregory Black, *Hollywood Goes to War: How Politics, Profits, and Propaganda Shaped World War II Movies* (Berkeley: The Free Press, 1987), pp. 1–16.

111. Michael Salter, *Nazi War Crimes: US Intelligence and Selective Prosecution at Nuremberg: Controversies Regarding the Role of the Office of Strategic Services* (Abingdon: Routledge, 2007), p. 266.
112. Thomas Dodds cited in Ibid., pp. 264–5.
113. Lawrence Douglas, pp. 'Film as Witness: Screening *Nazi Concentration Camps* before the Nuremberg Tribunal', *Yale Law Journal*, 105 (1994), pp. 450–1. Douglas is citing Primo Levi, *The Drowned and the Saved*, trans. R. Rosenthal (New York: Vintage, 1989), pp. 11–12.
114. Prior to writing this, it never occurred to me that I would be so directly confronted with what I perceive as the reductionist claim, often made, that postmodern relativism excuses Holocaust deniers. To this denunciation I offer the following reply: the 'postmodern' theories that have inspired my approach, if they can be called that, in particular those of Jameson, Foucault, Barthes and White who challenge the idea that linguistic or indeed visual representation provide transparent windows on to the past, do not seek to deny the existence of incontrovertible historical facts. Such claims can be found nowhere in their work, and those who take issue with their theories on this basis do so misguidedly. Holocaust deniers are not postmodernists: they are counterfactualists who seek to establish an alternative view of history, which they regard as all too real. In this sense the techniques of postmodern theory are more likely to disparage their debased understanding of the past than they are to support their claims. No right-minded scholar, postmodern or not, would ever seek to deny the barbarous reality of the Nazis' crimes. Where postmodernists may differ, or perhaps not, is that the incontrovertible facts of these crimes, or any historical facts, can be presented in different ways, with different ideological and political implications. The fact that the Nazis committed near-incomprehensible crimes does not mean that the Allies didn't stand to benefit, or were not able to exploit these facts after the war, to their advantage. To invoke the decidedly un-postmodern Winston Churchill, history is written by the victors, even if their victory was, by any standard, just and right.
115. Salter, *Nazi War Crimes*, p. 260.
116. Phillip J. Bigger, *Negotiator: The Life and Career of James B. Donovan* (Crenbury: Associated University Presses, 2006).
117. Robert Parrish Interview with Dan Ford, John Ford Mss, Series VII – Interview Tape 70, Lilly Library, University of Indiana, Bloomington.
118. 'The Avalon Project: Documents in Law, History and Diplomacy', *Yale Law School*, http://avalon.law.yale.edu/imt/count1.asp, accessed 31 March 2015.
119. 'The Avalon Project: Documents in Law, History and Diplomacy', *Yale Law School*, http://avalon.law.yale.edu/imt/count2.asp, accessed 31 March 2015.
120. 'The Avalon Project: Documents in Law, History and Diplomacy', *Yale Law School*, http://avalon.law.yale.edu/imt/count3.asp, accessed 31 March 2015.
121. Raymond Kellogg to John Ford, 20 November 1945, John Ford MSS, Correspondence File October–November 1945, Lilly Library, University of Indiana, Bloomington.
122. Raymond Kellogg to John Ford, 20 November 1945, John Ford MSS, Correspondence File October–November 1945, Lilly Library, University of Indiana, Bloomington.
123. Robert Parrish Interview with Dan Ford, John Ford Mss, Series VII – Interview Tape 70, Lilly Library, University of Indiana, Bloomington.
124. Raymond Kellogg to John Ford, 20 November 1945, John Ford MSS, Correspondence File October–November 1945, Lilly Library, University of Indiana, Bloomington.
125. Dan Kiley cited in Salter, *Nazi War Crimes*, p. 258.

126. Ibid., p. 267.
127. 'Nuremberg: Its Lessons for Today', http://www.nurembergfilm.org/films_within_film.shtml, accessed 31 March 2015.
128. Robert Parrish Interview with Dan Ford, John Ford Mss, Series VII – Interview Tape 70, Lilly Library, University of Indiana, Bloomington.
129. Salter, *Nazi War Crimes*, pp. 255–6.
130. Cited in Katz, 'The Arts of War', p. 18.
131. Salter, *Nazi War Crimes*, p. 256.
132. Ibid., p. 257.
133. Ibid., p. 255.
134. Ibid., p. 256.
135. Ibid., p. 257.
136. Raymond Kellogg to John Ford, 20 November 1945, John Ford MSS, Correspondence File October-November 1945, Lilly Library, University of Indiana, Bloomington.
137. 'Nuremberg: Its Lessons for Today', http://www.nurembergfilm.org/suppression.shtml, accessed 31 March 2015.
138. Bernard Maltzer, cited in Salter, *Nazi War Crimes*, p. 263.
139. Ibid., p. 267.
140. Dr G. M. Gilbert's *Nuremberg Diary* cited in Ibid., p. 270.
141. Raymond Kellogg to John Ford, 20 November 1945, John Ford MSS, Correspondence File October–November 1945, Lilly Library, University of Indiana, Bloomington.
142. Robert Parrish Interview with Dan Ford, John Ford Mss, Series VII – Interview Tape 70, Lilly Library, University of Indiana, Bloomington.
143. James Donovan cited in Salter, *Nazi War Crimes*, p. 262.
144. Ibid., pp. 267–8.
145. Airey Neave cited in Ibid., p. 272.
146. The reactions of the defendants are taken from the diaries of Dr Gustave Gilbert and Dr Henry Kellerman, cited in Ibid., pp. 270–5.
147. Ibid., p. 276.
148. Thomas Dodds cited in Ibid., pp. 264–5.
149. Robert Parrish Interview with Dan Ford, John Ford Mss, Series VII – Interview Tape 70, Lilly Library, University of Indiana, Bloomington.
150. Ibid.
151. Robert Braun, 'The Holocaust and the Problems of Historical Representation', *History and Theory*, 33:2 (May 1994), p. 182.
152. Lawrence Douglas, 'Film as Witness', pp. 451–2.
153. Scott Lucas, *Freedom's War: The American Crusade against the Soviet Union* (New York: New York University Press, 1999), p. 11.

2. 'WHAT IS PAST IS PROLOGUE': HOLLYWOOD'S HISTORY OF THE OSS AND THE ESTABLISHMENT OF THE CIA

You can't fight facts nor can you make fiction serve the purpose of facts.
Darryl F. Zanuck to Louis de Rochemont, January 1947

On 1 October 1945, the OSS was officially disbanded. Some of its vestige components, such as the Research and Analysis (R&A) Branch and Secret Intelligence (SI) were reassigned to the State Department and the Department of War's newly created Strategic Services Unit (SSU). Others, like the FPU officers at Nuremberg, were left to finish their special assignments. But for all intents and purposes, America's first experiment with a centralised intelligence and special operations agency was over. It was a necessary wartime evil, rendered unnecessary by the coming of peace. Or so, for the time being, it seemed.

Just over two weeks later, General Donovan established a 'Motion Pictures Committee', to provide technical assistance to Hollywood filmmakers seeking to portray the OSS's wartime activities. Thus began in earnest his public relations campaign for the establishment of a permanent peacetime central intelligence agency. Although waged across several mediums, Hollywood cinema was vital to Donovan's campaign.[1] 'In the battle for mass opinion in the Cold War,' writes Tony Shaw, 'few weapons were more powerful than the cinema.'[2] Moreover, few were more effective in glamourising the traditionally disreputable profession of spying and espionage to a suspicious American public than the filmmakers and stars who had already managed to significantly elevate the public's opinion of one American intelligence agency, the

FBI, in the previous decade.[3] In the two intervening years between the dissolution of the OSS and the establishment of the CIA from October 1945 to September 1947, three major Hollywood motion pictures were released that celebrated the OSS's wartime achievements and made the case for a permanent peacetime CIA. These were, consecutively, Paramount's *O.S.S.* (1946), Warner Brothers'/United States Pictures' *Cloak and Dagger* (1946), and Twentieth Century-Fox's *13 Rue Madeleine* (1947). If, as intelligence historian Bradley F. Smith writes, the 'O.S.S. was more influential in its impact on people's ideas and imagination than its practical wartime achievements', then it was Hollywood's post-war commemoration of those achievements in these films that helped animate, perhaps more than any other medium, the public imagination in favour of the establishment of the CIA in the National Security Act of 1947.[4]

It would not be the last time that such a public debate over the virtue and necessity of American intelligence would be waged, but at no other time would the stakes be higher. America stood at a crossroads: could it return to business-as-usual isolationism and risk another Pearl Harbor, or should it accede that in a post-Hiroshima age, the threat of nuclear annihilation made engagement with, and knowledge of, the outside world indispensable to the nation's continued survival? The onset of the Cold War would eventually answer that question, ending irrevocably what C. Vann Woodward described as 'America's long history of free security'; from 1947 to the present day America's intelligence and national security apparatus expanded almost inexorably.[5] But, for a brief moment in time, when the evaluations of the war and the ramifications of the peace were yet undetermined, the establishment of the CIA appeared far from inevitable.

The debate revolved around two competing lessons from the war, both of which were, in part, a legacy of John Ford's OSS Field Photographic Unit. The first, which Donovan hoped to impart, was espoused in the FPU's cinematic treatment of Pearl Harbor: America had been caught sleeping, and the creation of effective intelligence was the vital remedy. The second, poignantly reinforced by the films presented at Nuremberg, preached the values of liberal democracy in opposition to the savage cruelties of the Nazi regime that were perpetrated in no small part by a powerful secret bureaucracy. When Donovan's proposal for a post-war intelligence service was leaked to the press in February 1945, up went the charge, later echoed by President Truman, that plans for the creation of an 'American Gestapo' were afoot.[6] To counter these fears, Donovan sought, paradoxically, to establish both a romantic past and a realist future for a peacetime CIA – stressing the derring-do nobility of the OSS's wartime achievements while also emphasising the necessary evil of its succession to prevent another, potentially atomic, surprise attack.

Hollywood Enlists in General Donovan's Campaign for a Permanent Peacetime Intelligence Agency

Donovan's campaign, whether told through the press, radio or Hollywood cinema, rested upon the determination of OSS veterans to tell their story. Many felt aggrieved at the 'Oh-So-Social' connotations that their wartime outfit still evoked. Major Andy Rogers, for example, 'a big blond Texan who served in Yugoslavia, Greece, and northern Italy', complained that when he told people he was in the OSS, he could tell 'they thought I'd spent the war going to Washington cocktail parties'.[7] As Stewart Alsop and Thomas Braden recalled in their 1946 history of the OSS, itself a product of Donovan's publicity drive, Major Rogers' experience 'summed up the gripe of many an OSS soldier' who wondered whether their achievements needed to be 'quite so secret'.[8]

To this day it is a common maxim among intelligence officers that their failures are publicised while their successes are often kept secret. But when Donovan caught wind of Truman's plans to disband his agency, the intelligence officer's characteristic reticence soon gave way to a torrent of disclosure. 'As the hostilities came to an end', recalled OSS veteran Roger Hall, 'General Donovan began to have some well-founded fears about the continued existence of his baby ... Something drastic had to be done ... He and his advisors talked it over, the eventual decision being, "Bring it out in the open, lift the cloak and show what the dagger has done."'[9]

On 13 September 1945, Donovan authorised all current and former OSS personnel to verbally disclose details of their activities to their family and friends. He also began establishing procedures to allow officers to publish their accounts.[10] It was a little late in coming – the previous month Allen Dulles, the future CIA chief, had already leaked the story of Operation Sunrise, one of the OSS's great success stories of the Second World War that led to the premature surrender of German forces in Italy, to the *Saturday Evening Post*. Donovan also established the Reports Declassification Section (RDS), which spearheaded his public relations (PR) offensive. The RDS was led by Commander John Shaheen, a public relations man from Chicago who before serving in the OSS had directed the Republican Party's publicity machine. Shaheen furnished a revolving door of interested journalists, filmmakers and former veterans with previously classified materials. He recruited 'a staff of journalists, authors, photographers, and motion picture and radio men, which he proceeded to shake well with a highly competent mixture of public relations and promotion experts'.[11] Roger Hall, who worked for the section, provides a description of the heady atmosphere of public disclosure in the RDS in the immediate post-war period:

> When the section was ready to produce, the security lid which had been so tightly locked down on everything the O.S.S. had done since

its inception was lifted. The story was told through every information medium short of skywriting.

Most of it went out one of two ways: it was either written in our offices and released to the press, or the writers came in, were given access to material, and then wrote stories which had to be cleared by the section. Whenever possible, pictures were furnished to illustrate copy. Which is where I came in. My assignment entailed seeing all the hitherto top-secret O.S.S. motion pictures and deciding what could be clipped out and used for still shots in newspapers and magazine articles.

'Deadline Johnny' Shaheen ran the place as though it were straight out of *The Front Page*. The O.S.S. story was the hottest thing in the news picture; the public was eating it up and howling for more. Our offices swarmed with newsmen, magazine men, newsreel men, radio men, syndicated columnists, and free lancers, all crying for material and pictures.[12]

Shaheen also sat on Donovan's Motion Picture Committee. He was joined by Allen Dulles; Edward Buxton, the former assistant director of OSS and major investor in John Ford's post-war production company, Argosy Pictures; David Bruce, head of the OSS office in London who Merian Cooper had introduced to Donovan before the war; and Colonel Russell J. Forgan, a senior OSS officer and close confidant of Donovan's.[13] The committee liaised with the studios, feeding them heroic stories from former veterans, recently declassified materials from the RDS and stock footage taken from the films of the FPU. In addition they helped foster links between filmmakers and returning OSS veterans who relished the opportunity of extending the glamour of their wartime service by returning to Hollywood as peacetime technical advisors.

The studios had a short window of opportunity. By the end of 1945, all OSS records would be transferred to the War Department, who, on 28 December 1945, would impose a blackout on the material.[14] In the months leading up to this blanket classification, Twentieth Century-Fox, Paramount and Warner Brothers, who all released films about OSS the following year, worked tirelessly to secure the documentary basis for their semi-documentary features. Louis de Rochemont, for example, having left *March of Time* to work for Zanuck at Fox, sent ex-OSS officer Lt. Michael Carroll on a scouting trip a week prior to the War Department's blackout. He returned from Washington with details of key locations, including the Operations Group headquarters in the so-called 'Q-Building', the Congressional Country Club and OSS's headquarters in London at 70 Grosvenor Street. He also obtained copies of an OSS research and development book and an 'Intelligence Manual' that included descriptions, pictures and dimensions of various gadgets, guns and mines among other intriguing examples of OSS field equipment.[15]

Historian James Deutsch argues that Hollywood never gained access to classified OSS files because they were in the War Department's possession.[16] But he ignores the chaotic nature of their transferral. For one thing, many key operational details had already been released to filmmakers and members of the press via the work of the RDS before the War Department got their hands on them. For another, materials were often sourced through unofficial channels, or donated by former officers who held on to their wartime spy memorabilia. Former FPU officer William Radar, for example, approached de Rochemont with a short film that he had brought with him to the West Coast, which featured 'training and briefing of our special agents, and their actual infiltration behind enemy lines'.[17] Even Donovan, perhaps wishing to remain in control of the post-war narrative of his organisation, kept microfilms of his OSS files, which he later handed over to his biographer Anthony Cave Brown.[18] Moreover, while neither the OSS Motion Picture Committee nor the RDS were technically authorised to declassify OSS files, they did place pressure on the War Department to release documents. Shaheen, for example, arranged a screening in Washington of the classified film *S.I. in Action* for representatives of all the studios. The film contained footage of OSS officers parachuting into France behind enemy lines – a scenario that was dramatised by all the post-war OSS films.[19]

Whatever the extent of the studios' access to OSS files, in a certain sense they didn't need it. Hollywood was already awash with tales from former members of Ford's unit, among other filmmakers who had served across Donovan's organisation. These filmmaker-spies wanted their story to be told – and who better to tell it than the industry that first schooled them in the techniques of cinematic intelligence gathering! Twentieth Century-Fox's roster, for example, whose soundstages Ford had used to drill his unit before the war, included, among others, Ray Kellogg, set to return from Nuremberg to work in the special effects department; Sol Halprin, head of Fox camera department who built the FPU laboratories in Washington; Jim Mitchell, publicity stills man who served behind enemy lines in Asia; and Bert Leeds, who also served in Ford's unit filming in the European theatre of operations for war diary purposes.[20]

In a memo to Zanuck, Leeds detailed the OSS's principal functions and wartime activities touching on sabotage, psychological warfare, subversive activities, supply of resistance groups and special missions. He also sketched out the OSS training regimen of 'radio, photography, map reading, unarmed combat, sharpshooting in virtual darkness, disguise and every type of demolition – from "burning pencils" to the exacting use of quantities of plastic to destroy bridges and dams'. He also informed Zanuck that vast quantities of footage of OSS operations were available – some of which was in his possession – that could be of use for research purposes. Giving examples of numerous wartime operations that could be transferred to the silver screen Leeds concluded that 'O.S.S. operations could be developed into a great motion picture', adding that Ray Kellogg had informed him prior to his departure from Washington that 'General Donovan will be happy to lend full cooperation in the making of a film on this subject; especially to yourself and this studio'.[21]

Alongside the resident OSS veterans, tens of former spies flocked to Hollywood offering their services in exchange for a relatively handsome consultancy fee and the opportunity to work, if only temporarily, in a profession whose glamour was perhaps only matched by their former careers as espionage agents. Captain Richard Phenix (an auspicious name given his expressed desire to see OSS rise from its ashes), for example, approached de Rochemont with an impressive curriculum vitae of his activities that included various positions as a cryptographic officer in which he claimed he was privy to '90% of the traffic from the underground on the Continent and elsewhere' making him 'intimately familiar with not only the entire Communications network, which was the nerve system for ALL OSS operations, but with the work of all branches of OSS'. Providing his reasons for 'so immodestly offering my services', Phenix wrote:

> I would be gratified to be a part of the motion picture industry for a short time; but my major reason, I think, is that I am so intensely enthusiastic about the work OSS has done, and feel so strongly that such an agency should be maintained along the same lines as the 400 year old British Intelligence.[22]

Phenix placed only one condition on the provision of his support to the production: he wanted his anonymity to be maintained. '[It is] entirely possible that I shall be attached to OSS – or its peacetime counterpart – again, and my usefulness might well be impaired if I were ever publicly connected with the organization.'[23]

The studios regarded documentary authenticity as vital to the success of their OSS pictures. The public appetite for realism had been piqued by the newsreels and propaganda features during the war that John Ford's OSS FPU had helped produce. Now the studios sought to bring some of the authenticity of the newsreels to their feature-film productions by fusing melodrama with a documentary aesthetic in a form pioneered by de Rochemont, first at *March of Time* and then at Twentieth Century-Fox, which became known as the 'semi-documentary'. Along with in-depth research, the use of location shooting, 'Timespeak' newsreel narration and the fusion of documentary and reenacted footage, one of the key identifying characteristics of the semi-documentary was the use of government, or in the case of the OSS, former government employees as technical advisors. The semi-documentaries celebrated their alliances with the state, a hangover from the wartime cooperation and consensus that existed between Hollywood and the US Government. Indeed the consent of, and sometimes endorsement by, the requisite government bureaucracy – often the FBI in the first decade of the Cold War whose director, J. Edgar Hoover, remained as publicity-savvy as ever and continued to co-opt Hollywood (and Louis de Rochemont in particular) in order to promote his bureau – was heralded as the gold-standard of authentication.

Thus, the use of former OSS files and former officers as technical advisors became a key component in each of the films' marketing strategies that sought to appeal to the American public's newfound penchant for realism. Paramount, for example, proudly proclaimed to the press that '[t]hirty or more real-life bemedalled heroes of the O.S.S. have actively contributed to the realism of the picture as technical advisors or bit players or in both functions'.[24] As a result certain key members of Donovan's former staff became hot-property in Hollywood, and a bidding war ensued for their services. Despite this fierce competition between the studios, a sense of wartime camaraderie persisted among the veterans. George Skouras, President of United Artist Theatres and self-appointed coordinator of the OSS veterans in Hollywood, hosted a dinner at Perino's where 'champagne flowed and toasts resounded' for 'all the OSS specialists and executives associated with the OSS productions'.[25]

Although in the coming months the productions they created would do their best to debunk their former organisation's 'Oh-So-Social' stigma, amidst this new atmosphere of disclosure, the return to civilian life for this particular group of former espionage agents was almost as glamorous and privileged as their detractors imagined. The going rate for a technical advisor at the time was a maximum of $200 a week.[26] Many who worked on the films, however, secured a much higher rate of pay. John Shaheen, for example, eagerly sought by both Paramount and Fox, reached an agreement with Paramount after Fox bulked at his $750-a-week asking price.[27] Shaheen brought with him to Paramount a team of 'eighteen specialist, most of them former O.S.S. men, some of whom played small parts in the film', who assisted in overseeing the authenticity of the picture. His team included Raphael Beugnon, former OSS officer and native of Paris, who won a Distinguished Service Cross for single-handedly blowing up a bridge near to the French capital; Major Robert Cordell, who trained almost all the O.S.S. paratroopers; Fred Voltz, who helped General MacArthur's escape from the Philippines; Frederick Wauch, who served for OSS in Ceylon, India, Burma and China; Rene Dussaq, an Argentinian-born operative who made more than 160 parachute jumps winning the Distinguished Service Cross, Croix de Guerre with Palm and a recommendation for the Silver Star in the process; and Frank Pullman, native of Los Angeles, who flew dangerous B-17 night missions for the OSS in Southern France and was equally as decorated as the rest of the group.[28]

After losing out on Shaheen, a disappointed but undeterred Louis de

Rochemont had to make do with Mike Carroll; Otto C. Doering, Donovan's Executive Officer, a close friend of Merian Cooper, Argosy investor, and investigator at the Nuremberg trials; Major Rees; and Peter Ortiz, another key Donovan aide and Argosy investor who turned actor and appeared in John Ford's Argosy-produced *Rio Grande*. Warner Brothers' *Cloak and Dagger* took its title from Corey Ford and Alistair MacBain's insider-history first serialised by *Collier's* in 1945 and published the following year by Random House. Former operative Michael Burke and OSS documentarian Andries Deinum provided further technical assistance to director Fritz Lang.

Competition among the studios to be the first to provide an authentic representation of America's first central intelligence agency provided a comfortable return to civilian life for dozens of former OSS officers. Between them, Paramount, Fox and Warner Brothers had amassed the largest concentration of former government agents working in Hollywood in the history of the American motion picture industry.

Figure 2.1   Alan Ladd and Geraldine Fitzgerald star in *O.S.S.* (1946). The film was made with the blessing of former OSS chief William Donovan and received technical assistance from several former OSS officers. *Source*: Paramount Pictures/Margaret Herrick Library.

O.S.S. (1946)

Paramount was the first to release its film. O.S.S. opened in New York on 26 May 1946.[29] Irving Pichel, who had provided some of the narration for Ford's Midway documentary, directed the film. The following year, Pichel fell victim to the House Un-American Activities Committee's notorious inquisition into Hollywood. He was blacklisted and fled the United States, remaining in exile until the very end of his life. *Cloak and Dagger* scriptwriters Ring Lardner and Albert Maltz, who were part of the infamous 'Hollywood Ten', were likewise later persecuted by HUAC. Although OSS was certainly a hotbed of liberal internationalism – of a Wilsonian stripe – and even welcomed Marxist intellectuals into its fold, communists would have taken little comfort from a film that was intended in part to assist Donovan's campaign to establish the CIA. There was very little that was 'Un-American' about these films; indeed each wrapped themselves in the flag, and the OSS with it – attempting to normalise the idea that America could lie, deceive, sabotage and spy, just like the phantom communists in Hollywood that HUAC sought to purge. Yet in doing so, the film also sought to redefine Americanism. Pre-war notions of American innocence, openness and naivety, as contrasted by European sophistication, decadence and deception, were replaced by a new realism that was alert to the dangers of the post-war world and America's inescapable entanglement with it. The casting of the fresh-faced Alan Ladd (who was not without his hardboiled credentials) as new OSS recruit agent John Martin, emphasised this national right of passage from prelapsarian innocence – born out of isolationism and republican virtue – to the requisite sophistication of an interventionist age. This point, and the urgency of its implications, is expressed most explicitly in the film by an OSS instructor as he meets his new recruits for the first time:

> We can't waste too much time with you. We're late. Four hundred years. That's how long ago the other major powers started their OSS. We've only got months, to build the first central intelligence agency in our history. A world-wide organization that'll beat the enemy at its own game. It's not your kind of game. You don't know each other. You're here under assumed names, but you're all average decent Americans. And Americans aren't brought up to fight the way the enemy fights. We can learn to become intelligence agents and saboteurs, if we have to. But we're too sentimental, too trusting, too easy-going, and what's worse, too self-centered . . . Forget everything you've ever been told about fair play and sportsmanship.[30]

A near-identical sermon with the same utilitarian logic is delivered in a near-identical scenario by the OSS instructor in Fox's *13 Rue Madeleine*:

> You're going to have a lot to remember and a couple of things to forget. Now the average American is a good sport, plays by the rules. But this war is no game, and no secret agent is a hero or a good sport. That is, no living agent. You're going to be taught to kill, to cheat, to rob, to lie. And everything you learn is moving you to one objective, just one, that's all: the success of your mission. Fair play, that's out. Years of decency and honest living, forget all about them. Or turn in your suits. Because the enemy can forget – and has.[31]

Both scenes get to the heart of General Donovan's attempts to disabuse his opponents of their 'American Gestapo' sloganism. If espionage was deemed 'Un-American', then perhaps it was because such antiquated notions of Americanism were no longer compatible with the geo-political realities confronting America after the intelligence failure at Pearl Harbor, and the looming spectre of atomic annihilation with the onset of the Cold War. Indeed, the rapid expansion of CIA espionage and covert action from 1947 onwards was frequently justified in official circles, and to the public, in the same relativist and consequentialist terms. The 1954 Doolittle Report, for example, advocated the expansion of CIA activities with strikingly similar language and logic to the two aforementioned scenes:

> If the United States is to survive, long-standing American concepts of 'fair play' must be reconsidered. We must develop effective espionage and counterespionage services and must learn to subvert, sabotage and destroy our enemies by more clever, more sophisticated and more effective methods than those used against us. It may become necessary that the American people be made acquainted with, understand and support this fundamentally repugnant philosophy.[32]

This new ends-justifies-the-means 'Americanism' promoted by Donovan after the war was embodied in the hard-boiled heroes of the OSS film-cycle: the tough yet ultimately virtuous Alan Ladd as John Martin in *O.S.S.*, or the screen-gangster turned incorruptible G-Man, James Cagney, who played the central protagonist in *13 Rue Madeleine*.

Starring alongside Ladd in *O.S.S.* was Geraldine Fitzgerald as the equally tenacious Elaine Dupree. The film's sexual politics were self-consciously progressive for its time. At the start of the film Martin questions whether a woman can perform such difficult and dangerous work. 'Stop worrying about my sex,' Dupree upbraids him, 'treat me like any other member of the team' – 'some of the most successful spies in history have been women', the commanding officer adds. As part of his publicity campaign, Donovan was keen to inform the public that women had just as much of a vital role to play. The memoir of OSS agent Elizabeth MacDonald, for example, published in 1947 as *Undercover*

Girl, included a two-page introduction from Donovan attesting to the vital work women performed for the OSS during the war, although he added that MacDonald was relatively unique as 'only a small percentage' of women went on operations behind enemy lines.[33] Yet the idea of female agents still seemed incredible to some. Miss Kay Lindsay, for example, from Norfolk, Virginia, wrote to the now-defunct OSS in August 1946 asking for clarification on the issue after watching Paramount's film:

> Dear Sirs: I have just seen the moving picture 'O.S.S.', and a great argument developed afterwards as to the actual truth of the picture. The men claim that no women have ever been exposed to such circumstances and dangers as Miss Fitzgerald was in the movie. They claim the movie was all 'Hollywood', in other words – very unreal. I would appreciate any information that you could give me on this subject. It would help to settle an argument with my husband-to-be! Thanking you very much. I remain Sincerely, yours, Miss Kay Lindsay.[34]

The War Department, who received Miss Lindsay's letter, settled the argument with this reply:

> The motion picture 'O.S.S.' is purely a commercial production, although, like the numerous books and articles about the subject, is generally factual as to the way things happened ... The files are replete with instances of outstanding bravery and notable accomplishments on the part of women who were associated in the work. It is safe to say that there were many cases equal to and possibly more outstanding than that depicted in the motion picture.[35]

The film's plot sees Dupree, Martin and two other new OSS recruits parachute into France to make contact with the French resistance to help sabotage German railway routes in the build-up to D-Day. In one of the central action sequences, Martin rescues Dupree from an explosion planted on a Nazi train. Aggravated by her assignation as the rescued damsel in distress, and dutifully committed to the war effort, Dupree reproaches Martin for coming back for her and potentially threatening the success of the entire mission – 'Never come back for me again', she tells him. Her wish is granted. At the film's conclusion the two are sent on one final mission of the utmost importance. They are asked to make contact with another OSS agent who knows the whereabouts of German panzer divisions lying in wait for the allied advance. While Martin is attempting to make radio contact, the Gestapo arrests Dupree. Torn between making radio contact and potentially saving thousands of lives, or rescuing Dupree, Martin chooses the greater good. When we first meet Dupree at the beginning of the film she speaks with great adulation of Joan of Arc. The symbolism of this by the end of the film is clear. Dupree knows her fate. She must go to her death as a martyr, for the liberation of France and the defeat of Nazi tyranny.

Dupree's death marks the culmination of a series of sacrifices that do their best to overturn the 'Oh So Social' moniker. The film continually stresses the courage, dedication and sacrifice of America's spies while also emphasising the dangerous and vital nature of their work. In one scene the OSS chief, presumably modelled on Donovan, reminds his commander of the 'large part we can play in the key French campaign'. This message is reinforced throughout the film by cuts to the wider military campaign, introducing the D-Day landings, for example, after a successful OSS sabotage operation, or the final scene where Martin and his commander discuss the sacrifice of their unit while a victorious American brigade rolls past. Repeatedly the OSS are shown to be a vital component in the allies' success in the European invasion – confirming OSS historian Bradley Smith's argument that the OSS's near-mythical reputation is more a product of post-war exaggeration than an accurate reflection of its genuine contributions to the war effort. In reality, as Smith explains, although OSS operatives certainly performed dangerous missions in occupied Europe, their role was subordinate to the British Special Operations Executive (SOE), and further subordinated to the massive combined military operations.[36]

Although Paramount's marketing campaign heralded *O.S.S.*'s authenticity, the film was less of a documentary than a melodrama, and played to the conventions of the spy thriller – perhaps reflecting the inclinations of its scriptwriter, Richard Maibaum, who later wrote the James Bond screenplays. Still, certain hallmarks of the documentary aesthetic remained. Most notably, the film opens with a signed statement from General Donovan, attesting that '[w]hile the characters in this motion picture are fictitious, the story is based on a composite of actual incidents'. Donovan's note echoes Ray Kellog's signed affidavit at the start of *The Concentration Camp* film at Nuremberg. The need to swear upon some sort of higher authority than the intrinsic content of the film itself remained. *O.S.S.* was the only film that would gain Donovan's explicit approval in this way. James Deutsch speculates that Donovan may have wished to repay Paramount for providing the OSS with currency during the war to finance operations in Finland and Sweden under the aegis of Paramount executive Stanton Griffis who served in OSS as a special agent in Finland.[37] There may well be some truth in this, but the extent of OSS relations with employees from all of the major studios, particularly Ford and Zanuck's Twentieth Century-Fox, attenuates this idea somewhat. Perhaps a more likely explanation was the influence of Shaheen, and the timing of the film's release. As discussed later in this chapter, Donovan seemed to recoil from his initial burst of candidness as his publicity campaign wore on and the establishment of the CIA appeared increasingly likely.

Perhaps the most authentic scenes in the film, likely pruned from FPU films and the recollections of Shaheen and the numerous other OSS veterans on hand at the studio, are the training sequences near the beginning. The montage featured fresh recruits learning to operate their radios and other vital pieces of equipment while also being introduced to key tradecraft such as losing an enemy tail and always being alert to alternative escape routes. *The New York Times* commented that the brief scenes had 'the factual credibility of a documentary', although it regarded the film's overall plausibility as 'questionable'.[38] The realism of another scene, which featured a close-up of a wire-recorder, was deemed so authentic by the War Department that it aroused the ire of former OSS officers now in the SSU, who suggested that the offending scene be deleted.[39] Overall though, as numerous reviews identified, the film owed more to the conventions of melodrama than the documentary aesthetic pioneered in-part by Ford's OSS FPU. While it brandished its authenticity through Donovan's signed foreword and the accompanying publicity that boasted of the numerous OSS officers who advised on the picture, it was commended more for its tight script and the performances of Ladd and Fitzgerald than for its genuine insights into OSS's wartime activities. Nevertheless, realistic or not, it was a clear public relations coup for Donovan and his film committee. It celebrated, as the *New York Times* review put it, 'the myriad exploits of that brave and largely unsung corps of daring young men and women who did so much to sap the enemy's strength and prepare him for the final kill.'[40] In place of the 'Oh-So-Social' and 'American Gestapo' tags of old, new myths about the OSS were starting to take shape, myths crafted by the same Hollywood studios who had supplied so many of Donovan's wartime recruits.

CLOAK AND DAGGER (1946)

Warner Brothers were the next to release their OSS picture; Fritz Lang's *Cloak and Dagger* opened in New York on 4 October 1946.[41] Lang, a German with Jewish ancestry, fled Nazi persecution in 1934. Before entering into exile he was a leading light of German expressionism, perhaps most famous for his caliginous dystopia *Metropolis* (1927), and his murder thriller and noir precursor *M* (1931). But he was also a pioneer of spy cinema. His *Spione* (1928) and *Dr. Mabuse* virtually invented the genre on film. From the femme fatale to the evil and often-ethnicised villain, or from the underground lair to the gadgets and elaborate chases Lang brought many of the stock conventions of spy cinema to the screen. Lang doubtless regarded *Cloak and Dagger* as a continuation of this tradition. Despite its claims to authenticity, it did not disappoint in offering many of these now-tired tropes that he had brought into existence: 'they loaded the whole thing down with the baldest and most familiar of spy-thriller clichés' wrote a disappointed Bosley Crowther in *The New York Times*.

Figure 2.2 Fritz Lang's *Cloak and Dagger* (1946) starring Gary Cooper as OSS agent Alvah Jesper. Lang was deeply frustrated by the interference of producer Milton Sperling who significantly altered the ending of the film. *Source:* United States Pictures/Academy of Motion Picture Arts and Sciences, Beverly Hills, California.

'In telling the melodramatic story of a young American atomic scientist who penetrates Italy, via Switzerland, during the war to scout the Nazis' work,' he continued, 'they have tossed in a Mata Hari, a mysterious character with a thick black beard, any number of beetling German agents and a lovely Italian partisan. And of course, it is the last who helps the hero achieve success after a fly-by-night passage of romancing and a blistering gun duel by his side.'[42]

The finished picture may not have comprised a classic addition to the Lang oeuvre, but in fairness to the director, it was a compromised piece, with much of his original vision left on the cutting room floor by producer Milton Sperling, whom the fractious Lang had managed to aggravate throughout the production. Moreover, the characterisation of *Cloak and Dagger* as a simple, even trite, genre film overlooks the sinuous and oftentimes politically and historically fascinating path via which the final screenplay eventually emerged.

Today *Cloak and Dagger* is perhaps best remembered by film historians for the unusually high number of soon-to-be blacklisted writers working on the production. Member of the Hollywood Ten, Alvah Bessie, and fellow future blacklistee, Ben Maddow, wrote the initial treatment but went uncredited as the final film bore almost no resemblance to it. Ring Lardner and Albert Maltz, who wrote the final versions of the script, also fell victim to HUAC as members of the Hollywood Ten. Andries Deinum, one of the technical advisors on the project, was hounded out of Hollywood in 1955 after refusing to cooperate with HUAC.[43] Lang was also investigated by the US Government, owing to his anti-fascist popular front politicking in the previous decade. Although he never appeared before HUAC, the FBI maintained a file on him since 1939. Lang believed himself blacklisted, but, as David Kalat notes, 'it is doubtful he ever was; his horrible reputation in Hollywood provided excuse enough for producers to avoid his company'.[44] Ironically, at the same time as he was being investigated for his left-wing sympathies, critics attacked him for expressing fascist tendencies, associating German Expressionism 'and his misanthropic depictions of human events' as evidence of a proto-Nazi style.[45] '"I hate Hitler – I hate Stalin – I hate all dictatorships!" Lang said in his defense.' His

Figure 2.3 Film director Fritz Lang photographed in 1969. Lang made his name as one of the key members of the German expressionist movement with films like *Metropolis* (1927) and *M* (1931). Lang, who had Jewish ancestry, fled Nazi persecution in 1934 for Hollywood. He was notoriously cantankerous on set, which caused serious problems with the cast and crew of *Cloak and Dagger*. Source: Wikimedia Commons.

experience echoed that of many of HUAC's victims, including his *Cloak and Dagger* scriptwriters, whose communist sympathies were largely contingent upon their pre-war and wartime opposition to fascism rather than a doctrinal commitment to the conspiratorial overthrow of the United States Government.

In the summer of 1946 J. Edgar Hoover asked for an update from the FBI's Los Angeles office on communist propaganda activities in Hollywood. Convinced that communists had infiltrated the American motion picture industry, Hoover scolded his LA lieutenant Richard Hood after three months with no reply. 'Feeling the heat', writes John Sbardellati in his history of the FBI in Hollywood, 'the Los Angeles office quickly issued a report listing eighteen pictures possibly contaminated with left-wing messages'. Included in the list was *Cloak and Dagger*. There was no evidence to suggest that any of these films, *Cloak and Dagger* included, were part of a communist plot, but what they all 'had in common was the simple fact that Communists and suspected fellow travellers were part of their cast and crew'.[46]

In their incendiary and often grossly exaggerated history of leftist influence and activism in Hollywood, Ronald and Allis Radosh cite *Cloak and Dagger* as a key example of a film that venerated HUAC's suspicions of the communists' infiltration of the American film industry. Claiming that the film was 'in effect an all-Communist and fellow-traveler production', they argue that it offered a 'propaganda barrage' that echoed 'the Soviet line'.[47] Of course the reality of the film's politics, as well as the earlier screen treatment written by Bessie and Maddow, was far more nuanced. Marxist undercurrents in all the screenplay drafts as well as the final film, if they existed at all, were subtle, and usually more in keeping with Hollywood's Capraesque concern for the common man than the tenants of *Das Kapital*.

Let us take, for example, Bessie and Maddow's early treatment of *Cloak and Dagger* that includes some autobiographical elements from their past involvement in popular front politics. Its barely detectable theme of class solidarity cannot be seen in isolation from the treatment's overriding political message, namely, its patriotic endorsement of the OSS's wartime contribution and its advocacy for its peacetime successor. In 1938 Bessie joined the Abraham Lincoln Brigade to fight for the Republicans in the Spanish Civil War. He joined the American Communist Party thereafter and became a film reviewer for the left-wing magazine *The New Masses*. During the war he wrote anti-fascist films for Warner Brothers such as *Northern Pursuit* (1943), *Objective Burma* (1945) and *Hotel Berlin* (1945).[48] One of the central characters in the *Cloak and Dagger* treatment is clearly autobiographical. Army Private Roy Brown is recruited by OSS for his experience as 'an American guerrilla fighter behind the fascist lines in Spain'.[49] In the final scene of the unfinished treatment, Brown is joined by Spanish Republican exiles in a fatal attempt to capture the Gestapo headquarters in France.

Bessie's cowriter, Ben Maddow, was part of the left-wing 1930s American documentary movement. In 1942 he co-wrote the screenplay for *Native Land*, a landmark semi-documentary narrated by Paul Robeson that depicted civil rights violations and the repression of the trade union movement documented by the La Follette Committee in 1938. Maddow was another wartime documentarian, serving in the Air Force Motion Picture Unit.[50] In spite of their left-wing credentials, the pair's combined experience of guerrilla warfare and documentary filmmaking made them uniquely qualified to pen an authentic treatment of the OSS's 'shadow warriors'.

The plot of the treatment was much closer to Paramount's *O.S.S.* and Fox's *13 Rue Madeleine* than the finished *Cloak and Dagger*. Whereas the completed picture stars G-Man Gary Cooper as an atomic physicist turned OSS-agent, arguably reinforcing perceptions of the OSS as elitist, Bessie and Maddow's treatment echoed the other OSS films' emphasis on espionage as the occupation of the common man, dispelling the 'Oh-So-Social' slur and seeking to overturn traditional conceptions of spying as 'Un-American'. The treatment begins with an exchange between William Donovan and President Roosevelt in which the general is asked to establish a 'world-wide counter-espionage system that will be independent of military and naval intelligence, and the FBI as well'. Donovan was originally tipped to play himself in the picture.[51] As Donovan leaves the President's office his aide asks him: 'Where are you going to find these people. Spies. Thieves. Murderers. Saboteurs?" Donovan gestures outside his car window at the thousands of people rushing to work: 'There they are,' he says. 'The ordinary people. Those are our spies, our saboteurs, our murderers.'

The scene then dissolves to an establishing shot of a crowded mid-Western American football stadium. Out of this prototypical American scene is formed Donovan's espionage agency (Donovan was a former college football star, as was the film's technical advisor Michael Burke). The camera pinpoints Donovan's aide seated in the stands. After the game, he follows the coach and the players into the dressing room. 'The football coach – Lou Cameron – is sketching out a play to his men on a blackboard. The diagrams he makes have a strangely military aspect to them', the treatment continues. 'Cameron is a typical American product. Tall, weather-beaten, he was an all-American end in his earlier days, not so long ago. Now he is the outstanding football strategist of the time. His reputation is nation-wide, and he is an innovator.'

Cameron is recruited to the OSS, and the following sequence traces his 'journey from the Midwest to the secret OSS', learning his tradecraft at a country farmhouse near Washington where Cameron is joined by 'the other OSS men who have been selected from the average, but exceptional, cross-section of America'. The rag-tag brigade include Spanish Civil War veteran Roy Brown and Professor of Art History William Prentiss. Their transformation into an intrepid special operations unit helped establish a formula familiar to us today through Robert Aldrich's *The Dirty Dozen* (1967), similarly focusing on the recruitment and training of a wily OSS unit. The format's most recent airing is in George Clooney's *The Monuments Men* (2014), which likewise traces its generic lineage back to the 1946 OSS semi-documentary melodrama cycle. As with *O.S.S., 13 Rue Madeleine* and the aforementioned updated incarnations of the genre, Bessie and Maddow's treatment then suggests a training montage – a right of passage from ordinary American citizens to experts 'in all the black arts of subversion'. The scene is a metaphor for the United States' transition from naïve isolationism to the utilitarian political realism of an interventionist age – an age that necessitated an effective espionage and counter-espionage agency. In the *Dirty Dozen*, of course, the recruits hardly begin as innocents, perhaps owing to the political climate in 1967 in which few Americans any longer regarded their nation, or indeed its denizens, as political innocents. The remainder of Bessie and Maddow's treatment follows the same formula as *O.S.S.* and *Rue Madeleine*: the new recruits are assigned a dangerous mission that sees them parachute behind enemy lines into occupied France to seek out local resistance forces who help them locate and destroy a secret Nazi factory.

The treatment does provide a few faint allusions to the writers' Marxist past by emphasising the role of class-consciousness in the overthrow of the Nazis. The OSS agents make contact with the French underground in the 'working-class section' of Marseilles and obtain information on the secret Nazi plant via a peasant informant who observes military vehicles while working in the fields. The final clue is provided by local children whose 'fathers are former factory workers' enslaved by the Germans and returned to France to work in the plant. These faint dialectics may have been detectable to the paranoid eyes of HUAC and the FBI in the climate of anti-communist hysteria that was to come, but the treatment's strand of egalitarianism was hardly incendiary – 'the main political position it [*Cloak and Dagger*] supports', writes Keith Brooker in his *Film and the American Left* research guide, 'is good old-fashioned American patriotism.'[52] The same could be said of Bessie and Maddow's early treatment.

Ironically, the film's egalitarian patriotism was exactly what was needed to help temper McCarthyite attacks against America's fledgling intelligence community. Hollywood and Donovan's determination to dispel notions of OSS elitism would become all the more important in the increasingly populist atmosphere of post-war America, exploited by anti-communists like J. Edgar Hoover, Richard Nixon and Joseph McCarthy to attack blue-blooded East Coast communists like Alger Hiss. Once established the CIA never quite managed to rid themselves of their elitist image, partially due to their Ivy-League focused recruitment strategy, which may in part explain Senator McCarthy's later suspicion of the newly formed agency. But in this dawning age of anti-communist paranoia in which, as Richard Hofstadter put it, populist 'status anxieties' produced ostracising contests over who and what was 'American', the post-war work of a significant proportion of the Hollywood Ten that proclaimed the inherent patriotism of America's first central intelligence agency, was useful indeed.[53] Although foreign espionage and subversion would soon once again be regarded as the sole preserve of America's enemies – this time the communists-within – it was helpful for a time at least that Hollywood spies were not just cruel or insouciant Nazis, or the Godless and effeminate Robert Walker in *My Son John* (1952), but 'weather-beaten' 'All-American' Football coaches like Lou Cameron.[54]

Cloak and Dagger was produced and financed by Milton Sperling, a former scriptwriter turned independent producer. Like John Ford, and so many of those involved in the post-war OSS productions, Sperling gained experience making documentaries on active service with the Marine Corps. Upon return to civilian life, he founded his production company, United States Pictures, which was closely affiliated with Warner Brothers due to Sperling's marriage to Harry Warner's daughter Betty.[55] *Cloak and Dagger* was the fledgling company's first production.

Sperling bought the screen rights to Corey Ford and Alistair MacBain's early insider OSS history in the autumn of 1945, seeking to lend the production a patina of authenticity. The book came with General Donovan's stamp of approval, explaining in the foreword, somewhat paradoxically, that 'it is only fair to the men of O.S.S.', who knew their heroism may never be known, that their story should be told to the American people.[56] The completed film likewise failed to register the irony of venerating OSS secrecy while at the same time publicising those same secrets: 'I'm in OSS', Colonel Walsh tells the central protagonist Professor Alvah Jesper. 'Never heard of us?' he continues. 'Well that's fine; we're not supposed to get any publicity.'[57] The two then casually discuss atomic secrets with little regard for the protocols of secrecy. Thus the film establishes one of the central dichotomies of the semi-documentary spy cycle: the inherent contradiction between official secrecy and the publicity generated by the films' claims, echoed by studio marketing departments, to offer an authentic history of secret intelligence. The 1946 OSS films maintained this contradiction without irony, but it was a contradiction that was to eventually prove the undoing of the semi-documentary cycle, when the gap between secrecy and publicity, or government classification and the ideal of an accessible national past, became all too obvious for critics and audiences alike.

Donovan was delighted to hear of Ford and MacBain's deal with Sperling. On the very same day as OSS's formal dissolution he wrote to them offering his enthusiastic support for the motion picture. In turn, they kept him abreast of all developments on the project, including sending him script drafts. Donovan also gave his permission for the producer 'to portray me in the opening scene of the proposed picture', but asked for the opportunity 'to review this section of the script personally'.[58] Ford and MacBain's original treatment followed the now-familiar pattern of narrating the recruitment, training and parachuting into danger behind enemy lines by 'average everyday Americans who successfully outmaneuvered and outwitted the centuries-old spy rings of Europe and Asia'.[59] While their book leant the film its credibility, it was more a series of vignettes than a sustained narrative. 'Sperling had bought a title', explained technical advisor Michael Burke, 'the book had no beginning, middle, and end'.[60] The treatment did, however, identify 'the project known as "McGregor" . . . in which an OSS team subverts the Italian High Command and manoeuvres the mass-surrender of the Italian Navy'.[61] Burke had taken part in the McGregor mission, and so the former college football star and future president of the New York Yankees was signed as a technical advisor to provide the central details of the plot.[62]

Led by John Shaheen, Operation McGregor saw a team of OSS agents sneak ashore in Sicily to persuade an Italian Admiral to defect. The admiral's brother, a New York journalist named Marcello Girosi, accompanied the unit. Their wider ambition was to attempt to convince the Italian Navy to surrender their fleet to the allies. According to OSS historian Patrick K. O'Donnell, 'the mission turned out to be a bit of a farce, since nobody bothered to inform the McGregor team that the Italian navy had already agreed in secret to surrender to the British at Malta'. Nevertheless, some good was salvaged from the mission, 'including the capture of a key Italian scientist'.[63] In the film, Burke's story is given a Cold War twist, with atomic physicist Professor Alvah Jesper, played by Gary Cooper, going ashore in Italy to persuade fellow Italian nuclear physicist to defect to the allies. It was this kernel of success, divorced from the wider ambiguities or even outright failings of the mission, that provided the spirited story of OSS that Donovan, his small army of technical advisers in Hollywood, and the filmmakers themselves, sought. It was upon this selective, exaggerated and partially fictionalised basis that the myth of covert action as infallibly effective emerged. It was a myth that would help sustain the CIA and its burgeoning covert activities for the first two decades of its existence.[64]

The Dutch-born documentary filmmaker and OSS veteran Andries Deinum joined Burke, Ford and MacBain at Paramount to complete the advisory team. Deinum's fluency in German and his appreciation for German culture made him one of the few confidants of the notoriously cantankerous Fritz Lang. Deinum and Burke 'became frequent dinner guests at Lang's house'.[65] In his biography of Lang, Patrick McGilligan relates an episode in which the two rehearsed one of the central set pieces of the film, a fight scene between Jesper and a fascist agent (one of the few scenes noted by reviewers), with 'close-ups of clutching, clawing hands' and 'Gina, the film's female lead, tossing in kicks and punches from the sidelines . . .' According to McGilligan, Lang loved this type of scene, which he had shot numerous times before, but sought a fresh way to stage it. 'After dinner, Burke and Dienum (sic), these two graduates of the OSS, rolled around on the floor for what seemed like hours, Dienum (sic) remembered, acting out variations of weaponless struggle. The director hovered over them, 'making a square with his fingers,' in Dienum's (sic) words, 'to get the shots.'"[66] During shooting, Lang repeated the performance on his lead actor Gary Cooper, with his two technical advisors nodding appreciatively from the sidelines at his 'throttling technique.'[67]

Lang's otherwise prickly demeanour incited a number of problems during the production. To start with he banned Milton Sperling from the set, and excluded him from story conferences. Determined to be the first to release an OSS motion picture, Sperling placed a number of budgetary and time constraints on Lang, which McGilligan suggests is a key explanation for the unimaginative character of the finished picture. In this context, Lang's irascible attitude may well be forgiven as part of the customary struggle for creative autonomy between director and producer. But he also extended his ire to his cast and crew. Lilli Palmer, Cooper's co-star who was imposed on Lang by Sperling, was singled out especially for Lang's abuse. Palmer was greeted each day on set by a combination of barbed remarks, condescension and outright vitriol from her director. Things came to a head when Palmer walked off set after an especially excoriating torrent of abuse. In solidarity, the crew joined her. The walkout lasted three days, only to be resolved by an agreement from Lang that 'a special representative of the management would sit by the camera to ensure a 'suitable' working atmosphere.'[68] When shooting resumed, 'a gray-haired man in a slouch hat' sat next to the camera, sometimes dozing, overseeing Palmer's remaining scenes.[69] Lang affected a cordial demeanor towards his lead actress for the remainder of the shoot, but the atmosphere was filled with tension until the final take.

Lang's frosty attitude towards his cast, crew and producer may have emboldened Sperling to carry out what Lang regarded as an unforgivable defilement. The original ending of the film, scrapped by Sperling, saw Jesper return for one final assignment to destroy a Nazi atom-bomb factory hidden underneath a brewery in Bavaria. By the time he gets there, however, it's too late – the Nazis have fled 'to one of the so-called neutral countries. Spain – or to Argentina...' and they have taken their atom-bomb factory with them.[70] The scene would have provided the most direct evocation of Donovan's dire warnings of a future atomic Pearl Harbor. Predicting a repeat of the interwar years, a contemptuous dying German scientist, Dr Krauss, tells Jesper:

> You've won the war. You will be hard on us – for a while. Soon, as usual, you will weaken – when we tell the world about our starving people – our undernourished children. You are soft. You will demobilize your armies. In six months your highly efficient secret service will be no more. You do

not approve of such security measures. You will talk yourselves to sleep. Yes, time is Germany's friend and we know how to wait and work. We will carry on for we know how to learn from past mistakes.[71]

Seeking reassurance, Jesper nervously asks his OSS comrade, 'What Dr. Krauss said – about forgetting and giving up our vigilance – that was just bluster[?]' The officer looks despondent, shaking his head. 'I didn't tell you before – didn't want to discourage you – but OSS is folding up. Orders have come through to cut down the European staff.' His words grow bitter. 'A few months from now after it's over in Japan, there won't be any OSS. Some folks think it's easy to whip up such a highly specialized organization when the emergency arises – a little emergency like a war." Jesper stares in disbelief, 'almost with horror. "But there won't be any time – the next time!"' The final shot is of Jesper, 'with stricken, worried eyes' as 'he walks slowly to the stairs – a man who senses possible defeat for mankind through misuse of the new scientific era that lies ahead'.[72]

The scene was shot at great expense in Bronson Canyon, where Lang had an imitation bomb factory built for his great climax. 'Planes flew overhead, paratroopers dropped from the skies, the bomb factory blew up for the cameras', writes McGilligan, 'adding thousands upon thousands of dollars in budget costs'.[73] It is not entirely clear why Sperling would allow such an expensive scene to be shot, only to remove it from the final version. McGilligan suggests that Sperling cut it for reasons of historical authenticity: 'Milton Sperling, Michael Burke, Andries Dienum, Willy Ley, and another adviser on the picture – a scientist from Los Alamos – all tried to talk Lang out of the scene on the principle that nothing of that sort had transpired during the war.'[74] But it would have been unusual indeed for a Hollywood producer to allow historical accuracy to get in the way of a good story. Lang himself, 'only interested in authenticity when it served his purposes, was adamant. He wanted to make a statement against war and weapons of mass destruction.'[75] As he told Peter Bogdanovich in a later interview, '*this* was why I wanted to make the picture'. Defending the premise of the finale, Lang gave the example of the Nazi heavy water factory in Norway destroyed by Allied saboteurs – made famous by Anthony Mann's *The Heroes of Telemark* (1965), released shortly before Lang gave the interview.[76] Even the concept of a continued Nazi atomic threat from 'a so-called neutral' country like Argentina was not too far-fetched for Hollywood. The same year as *Cloak and Dagger* came out saw the release of Alfred Hitchcock's *Notorious* (1946) – its plot centred on the McGuffin of a cache of uranium ore stored in the wine cellar of a post-war Nazi spy ring operating out of Brazil. In a certain sense Hitchcock's *Notorious* could almost be read as a sequel to Lang's *Cloak and Dagger*, the master of the spy genre picking up where its originator had left off, marking the passing of the baton from one of Hitchcock's great mentors in the art of German expressionism, to Lang's most esteemed apprentice.

There is no evidence in the production files to suggest that the scene was cut for ideological reasons, but certainly its effect was to decimate Lang's intended apocalyptic anti-nuclear message. In his history of atomic bomb cinema, Jerome Shapiro claims that it was only after the Soviets detonated their atomic bomb in August 1949, ending the United States' nuclear monopoly, that Hollywood began 'to produce a great number of bomb films, and only then do we begin to see images of America truly at risk or under attack'.[77] Few films in this period, Shapiro argues, exploited the apocalyptic Cold War visions of nuclear destruction visited upon American cities. For Shapiro, most of the films that did feature the bomb in the first five years of its existence reinforced the illusion that America could retain the secret of atomic power and perpetuate its nuclear monopoly.

In its intended form, *Cloak and Dagger* would have confounded both of these tendencies that Shapiro identifies in Hollywood's initial reaction to the bomb – rubbishing the naïve idea that America could maintain its nuclear monopoly and offering instead a Promethean vision of the apocalyptic ends to which science had been put. Only the briefest glimmer of this intended moral remains in the film: holding an apple in his hand, Jesper delivers the following sermon to Colonel Walsh near the beginning of the picture:

> In a few years maybe we'll be able to break up the atomic structure of this apple. When we do that, it will become a bomb. The energy in this one little apple could pulverize this university, this whole town. Its fine hospitals, its libraries, its wonderful medical school, to say nothing of all the people in it. But we still wouldn't be able to make one little apple. We're running ahead of ourselves. Society isn't ready for atomic energy. I'm scared stiff. For the first time thousands of allied scientists are working to make what? A bomb! But who was willing to finance science before the war to wipe out tuberculosis? And when are we going to be given a billion dollars to wipe out cancer? I tell you we could do it one year![78]

In his seminal study of the impact of the bomb upon American culture and society, Paul Boyer notes that public attitudes towards science in the wake of Hiroshima were initially divided. While some, like President Truman, heralded the bomb as 'the greatest achievement of organized science in history', and 'a clear-cut indication of what can be accomplished by our universities, industry, and Government working together', others, like Pastor Harry Emerson Fosdick, regarded the event as 'the most colossal breakdown of optimism in history'.[79] 'The high hopes built on these scientific achievements', the 'normally cheerful' Fosdick surmised, 'have crashed to the ground as man has proved to be so insane, so corrupt, that the more power you give him the more he will destroy himself ... The flash of the atomic bomb lights all that up with frightening clarity ... We are Frankensteins, who have created a technological civilization that in the hands of sin can literally exterminate us.'[80] J. Robert Oppenheimer, one of the chief architects of the bomb, would become perhaps the most influential atomic Cassandra (as with the Greek myth, Oppenheimer's prophesies of destruction were soon cursed to be ignored after an investigation by HUAC). 'We have made a thing, a most terrible weapon', Oppenheimer told a meeting of the American Philosophical Society in January 1946, 'a thing that by all the standards of the world we grew up in is an evil thing. And by so doing ... we have raised again the question of whether science is good for man'.[81]

This divided opinion on the implications of the bomb, from Truman's optimism of a new scientific age, to Oppenheimer's Promethean foreboding, is reflected in two remarkably different screenplay drafts of *Cloak and Dagger*'s deleted final scene. In the earlier temporary shooting script, dated 4 March 1946, when the OSS team realises the Nazi bomb factory has been moved, the following exchange occurs between Jesper (Jessup in this version) and his fellow OSS officer Cronin:

CRONIN:
...
Peace? There's no peace! We've won this war and a new one starts. It's year one of the Atomic Age, and God have mercy on us all!

JESSUP:
(in a sudden shout)
No! I'm not afraid. It's the year one of a new age – okay, then. I believe in people! I believe in science! In spite of wars and pestilence and poverty and death – man moves forward. I believe it.

He swings around. CAMERA HOLDS on his face as he walks toward the entrance.

JESSUP:
(continuing)
I want the sunshine. I want sun on my face. We'll find this plant. We'll control this new thing. We'll give man the energy to make over his sick world.

In the final shot, replete with philosophical symbolism, Jessup walks out of the cave where the Nazi factory was hidden, 'the sun strikes his face' and, staring up at the sky, he whispers, 'I believe in the Ginas. I believe in future!'[82]

In the final script, written only a few days later, the supreme optimism of Jesper's/Jessup's closing sermon is entirely reversed. Moreover, the added few words in Cronin's dialogue gives the lie to the idea that America can maintain its nuclear monopoly, a sentiment that was largely responsible for the initial optimism about the bomb:

CRONIN:
... (with an ironic chuckle)
Our secret! Our ultra, hush-hush, absolutely exclusive, super-protected top secret! Peace? There's no peace! It's year one of the Atomic Age, and God have mercy on us all!

JESPER:
God have mercy on us is we're fools.
God have mercy on us if we think we can <u>keep</u> science a secret!
God have mercy on us if we think we can wage other wars without destroying ourselves.

As Jesper leaves the cave in this final version, the sense of optimism from the previous version is gone. Staring wistfully at the sky, a sky out of which future atomic bombs might rain down, Jesper looks forward to reuniting with Gina and returning home. In this version, however, Jesper contemplates the future with 'a deep breath', sighing forlornly for the fate of humankind.

These two remarkably different endings reflect American society's initial uncertainty towards the bomb. It was an uncertainty characterised, as Paul Boyer argues, by an inability to fully comprehend its apocalyptic implications. The final version of the script, with its foreboding vision, surely reflected Lang's intentions. Indeed it is this version that he quotes, almost verbatim after more than two decades, in his interview with Bogdanovich. It also would have been more in keeping with the nightmarish character of Lang's oeuvre, which may have satisfied the auteur critics at least, helping to salvage an otherwise unremarkable film. Although lacking in authenticity, at least in its depiction of the Nazi's atomic capacity, the apocalyptic image of inevitable nuclear proliferation would have served Donovan and the former-OSS's purposes – bringing home to the American public in the starkest of terms, the perilous consequences of dissolving America's first central intelligence agency.

By removing Lang's climax, and ending on an optimistic note, Sperling reduced the film to an assemblage of stock clichés of the romantic spy genre. If Sperling had indeed acted out of concern for the film's authenticity, then the irony was that the cut was to have the opposite effect: 'fast and slick entertainment', Bosley Crowther labelled it, which forewent the 'realm of realities' in favour of 'the baldest and most familiar of spy-thriller clichés'.[83] Other reviewers echoed Crowther's faint praise: 'a workmanlike job' wrote one critic, while another criticised Lang's inability 'to maintain the high melodramatic note on which "Cloak and Dagger" opens' – a feat that would have surely been obtained if the original ending had remained.[84] For almost all of the reviewers, it seems, while the film provided slick entertainment, like Paramount's *O.S.S.* it failed to deliver on the promise of realism made by the studios' marketing departments. For all the technical advisors both of these films employed, the critics, and the American public, were still left wanting for something that smacked of the authenticity of the documentary films that they had seen, and that the OSS had helped to produce, during the war. If anyone could satisfy that demand for realism, it was the *March of Time* producer and so-called father of the semi-documentary technique: Louis de Rochemont.

13 RUE MADELEINE (1947)

Seeking to deliver upon his homecoming pledge from military service to bring 'the grim and pressing realities before us in the world' to the American cinema, Zanuck brought *March of Time* producer Louis de Rochemont to Twentieth Century-Fox in 1944 to produce documentary and semi-documentary features.[85] Along with his brother Richard, who had helped OSS ascertain Hollywood footage for their Visual Presentation Branch during

Figure 2.4   James Cagney as OSS agent Bob Sharkey in Louis de Rochemont's 1947 semi-documentary *13 Rue Madeleine* (1947). *Source:* Henry Hathaway, Twentieth Century-Fox, 1947.

the war (see pp. 37–41), Louis de Rochemont pioneered the unique blend of factual documentary reportage with fictional storytelling and staged reënactments that became the hallmark of the modern documentary and docudramatic formats. Unlike other newsreel services, which were released twice weekly as segmented nine- or ten-minute shorts, the *March of Time*'s monthly features dealt with a limited number of subjects, later focusing on a single topic or event in each episode, and ran as long as twenty minutes. The greater length and depth afforded to each topical issue germinated a more structured, ideational, narrative-driven discursive style more in keeping with most contemporary understandings of the documentary form. Before the war, the *March of Time* films were the *only* regular documentary 'features' shown to mainstream Hollywood audiences. *March of Time* profoundly influenced the emergence of the documentary aesthetic in Hollywood cinema. As Raymond Fielding put it:

> Until the coming of the *March of Time*, there was no documentary film movement in the United States in so far as the mass theatrical audience was concerned . . . It was the *March of Time* alone which successfully introduced and established the documentary format for film audiences in the United States.[86]

De Rochemont brought numerous *March of Time* techniques with him to Fox and injected them into their melodramatic feature-film output. Some, like Westbrook Von Voorhis's unmistakable booming 'Timespeak' narration, as well as the incorporation of newsreel segments into docudramatic features, had already been deployed before and during the war in films like *Confessions of a Nazi Spy* (1939) and, with a greater sense of irony, in *Citizen Kane* (1941). Extensive location shooting, in-depth historical research and, most importantly, the direct cooperation and often endorsement by US Government officials and agencies who would testify to the film's authenticity were likewise key characteristics of de Rochemont's filmmaking style at Fox. Later, de Rochemont became known as 'the father of the semi-documentary'.

In 1945 de Rochemont produced *The House on 92nd Street* in cooperation with J. Edgar Hoover and the FBI. It celebrated the Bureau's wartime counterintelligence work. De Rochemont had worked with Hoover previously on two *March of Time* films, *Men of the F.B.I.* (1941) and *F.B.I. Front* (1942). Delighted with the publicity that these films provided, Hoover wrote to de Rochemont in 1942 telling him: 'We of the FBI obviously are extremely proud of the manner in which you have portrayed our activities' and in a handwritten post-script he signed off – 'It is grand to have such a friend as you.'[87] A month later, in November 1942, Hoover awarded de Rochemont the FBI's

Distinguished Service Cross, explaining, 'I hope it will always serve as a constant memento of our feelings toward you.'[88]

As a result of his close relationship with Hoover, de Rochemont was afforded unprecedented access to the FBI's files during the production of *The House on 92nd Street*. One recurring reference in the files to the mysterious 'Secret Process 97' intrigued him.[89] In the manner of a true Hitchcockian McGuffin, de Rochemont was able to construct the picture around this device without actually knowing what it was.[90] In the wake of Hiroshima, the FBI informed de Rochemont that, amazingly, much of the information pertaining to *The House on 92nd Street* involved Nazi attempts to recover details of the atomic bomb. An article in *The New York Times* claimed that de Rochemont could be counted among 'those who for many months were in close touch with one of the war's top secrets and never knew it until the story of the atomic bomb was released'.[91] The revelation led the studio to include a foreword that stated the film offered a true representation of the FBI's attempts to protect the atomic bomb and other war secrets. News of de Rochemont's insider knowledge also reached Colonel Parkinson who had served as an army intelligence G-2 officer at the Tennessee bomb plant. Having read an article about the film by Hollywood gossip columnist Louella Parsons, Parkinson began 'stirring up quite a mess in the War Department against the picture's release'.[92] Although the War Department had no official jurisdiction over the film, Hoover was keen to get their approval so as to avoid any unwanted criticism of his disclosures.

De Rochemont had unwittingly produced the first ever atomic bomb picture. *The House on 92nd Street* opened to critical acclaim, with reviewers particularly impressed by the atomic-bomb angle, giving credence to the film's claim of documentary realism: 'With the end of World War II we are due for many exciting "now it can be told" stories', exclaimed one enthusiastic reviewer, 'but this is the most spine-tingling of all because the atomic bomb was America's top priority secret'.[93] The success he achieved with *The House on 92nd Street* did not end de Rochemont's interest in the FBI. His relationship with Hoover would lead to the production of a number of other short and full-length features such as *Walk East on Beacon* in 1952, but for the subject of his next semi-documentary feature, de Rochemont turned to Hoover's great wartime rival: the Office of Strategic Services.[94]

De Rochemont met William Donovan at the St Regis Hotel in New York during *The House on 92nd Street*'s run at the Roxy in late September 1945. George Skouras, Donovan's man in Hollywood, arranged the meeting. Perhaps aware of de Rochemont's relationship with Hoover, Donovan 'made a very good case for an independent intelligence unit and told why it should not be handed over to F.B.I.'.[95] After discussing the inner workings of the OSS in some detail, the two agreed to cooperate on the basis of promoting a future permanent intelligence agency. A few days later, de Rochemont met Donovan's

Figure 2.5   Louis de Rochemont made his name as the producer of the *March of Time* newsreel service. During the war he was brought to Twentieth Century-Fox to by Darryl F. Zanuck to help make realistic semi-documentary features. *Source:* American Heritage Center, Laramie, Wyoming.

film liaison committee. 'The discussions were very general but the committee stressed their desire to see the picture authentic and away from "cloak and dagger" stuff.' De Rochemont reassured the committee that he intended to make the picture factual like *92nd Street*, 'but it had to be a good movie as well . . . a very factual picture of O.S.S. Operations could be made but it would receive very little circulation, but a picture that was semi-factual and exciting dramatic entertainment would be seen by millions', he told them. While audiences were demanding realism in increasing numbers, purely factual documentaries remained commercially unviable, even after the wartime newsreels and propaganda features had piqued public interest in the form. The committee acknowledged that 'we would have to dramatize and fictionalize' in order to repeat the success of *92nd Street*, which they agreed was 'wonderful publicity for J. Edgar Hoover and the F.B.I.'.[96] While the committee raised concerns about the historical authenticity of the OSS pictures, their priority was to gain maximum publicity for their cause. Like Fritz Lang, the former OSS appeared only interested in authenticity when it suited their purposes.[97]

13 Rue Madeleine took shape in late November/early December 1945. Fox scriptwriter Sy Bartlett, who had just returned from a colourful wartime career with the Army Pictorial Services and then later as an intelligence officer for Eighth Bomber Command, joined de Rochemont's long-time collaborator, John Monks, to write a second outline. The first, co-written by Monks and former Donovan aide John Stuart Martin, was rejected because it bore too close of a resemblance to the *Cloak and Dagger* story. With a few significant amendments and additions, Bartlett and Monks' outline was more or less adopted in its entirety for the final picture: Bob Sharkey, played by G-Man

James Cagney, is an OSS instructor who sends a team of agents into occupied France. One of these agents, Bill O'Connell (whose real name is Wilhelm Kuncel), is a German double agent. Aware of his real identity, Donovan and Sharkey furnish him with misinformation about the Allies' planned invasion of Europe. Unfortunately, the elaborate double cross fails when Kuncel learns that he is being set up. Knowing the identities and whereabouts of his fellow OSS operatives in Europe, Kuncel poses a grave threat to his colleagues. With no time to train up other agents, Sharkey agrees to parachute into Europe to apprehend Kuncel and get his agents out. It was a courageous, but nevertheless rash decision – Sharkey is one of the few intelligence officers to know exact details of the planned D-Day landings. The Gestapo apprehend him and torture him for information. Realising the severe implications for the Allies' invasion plans should Sharkey talk, headquarters in Washington authorise an air-strike on the Gestapo headquarters in France – at 13 Rue Madeleine. Sharkey is martyred for the wider cause, and on this bittersweet note, the film ends with a final refrain dedicated to the silent sacrifices made by so many American intelligence agents who helped secure allied victory during the war. [98]

Zanuck foresaw the potential for controversy almost immediately: 'There is one thing that we must make very clear to the audience, otherwise we are in serious trouble,' he told de Rochemont and the screenwriters. 'We plant early in the story that Donovan and Sharkey know that they have a spy in the organization, and we must then and there explain to the audience why they permit the Nazi spy to continue to work with them,' Zanuck continued. 'Otherwise the audience will think they are idiots. This point must be expressed on at least two occasions. In this connection, it must be explained by Sharkey, or someone, that obviously the Nazi spy has been put in the OSS organization only to be used once to pull off one big, gigantic double-cross.'[99] Four days after Zanuck raised this concern, Bartlett and Monks returned a revised outline to Zanuck with extra explanatory attention given to the early scene in which we discover that O'Connell is a double agent. '[T]he Nazi agent will take back with him an important piece of misinformation which will be worthy of the gamble they've taken with him', the revised outline carefully explains, taking care to underline the word 'misinformation', so the purpose of the plot device could not be missed.[100]

Lieutenant Mike Carroll, one of the technical advisors on the film, reiterated Zanuck's concern with the central plot device upon seeing the script, and also raised a further thorny issue: the climactic scenes in which Sharkey parachutes into occupied Europe and is captured and tortured by the Gestapo were completely unrealistic and constituted a significant failure on the part of the OSS – why would Donovan jeopardise the entire Allied invasion plans by agreeing to send an agent to Europe who knew of the exact operational details of the planned D-Day landings? Zanuck, however, commended the dramatic impact of Sharkey's capture and martyrdom, which set the film apart from the clichéd romance narratives of the film's competitors. Although later drafts emphasise that Sharkey had no choice but to parachute into Europe, the plot-line remained. It was a decision that may just have proved fatal for the production's up-until-then cosy relationship with Donovan.

De Rochemont showed Donovan the outline, including the controversial plot elements on 27 December 1945.[101] The producer later recalled that Donovan received the outline favourably and gave it his tacit approval. He must have been fairly confident at this stage that Donovan would endorse the finished product because the script drafts thereafter contain extended depictions of Donovan himself – that would be impossible to include without the former OSS chief's support. De Rochemont had also long proposed the inclusion of *March of Time* footage of Donovan to be edited into the finished production – an inclusion that would require Donovan's signed approval.[102] On 1 March 1946, de Rochemont encountered the first obstacle in the hitherto harmonious relationship with the former OSS. Colonel Russell Forgan, a close confidant of Donovan's and a member of his film committee, sent a letter to de Rochemont and Donovan that included strident criticism of the authenticity of the picture. To begin with, he dismissed the idea of one man being able to singly accomplish so much as 'utterly ridiculous'. His protestations on this basis were perhaps a little unfair, or at least disproportionate. *Rue Madeleine* was no more or less 'ridiculous' in its use of a conventional romantic plot of individual heroism than the other OSS films in production that had Donovan's full-support. Indeed *Cloak and Dagger* and *O.S.S.* (the latter received Donovan's signed approval) were arguably far guiltier in their deployment of stock tropes and melodramatic clichés from the espionage genre.

Perhaps more seriously, however, Forgan concurred with Mike Carroll, describing the idea of any individual with knowledge of Overlord being sent to France prior to D-Day as 'completely implausible.'[103] De Rochemont tried to reassure Forgan that the script would emphasise that 'it is not yet the eve of D-Day' and that the initial mission was to 'obtain information' that would 'enable the allied air forces to destroy the V-2 bombing dump', which was 'the major menace to Eisenhower's invasion'.[104] The controversy of depicting a German OSS agent could be resolved, thought de Rochemont, by inserting a few lines about why he was allowed to enter OSS in the first place and who discovered him there. De Rochemont proposed that perhaps the British or the F.B.I. had tipped off the OSS.[105] By including the British, de Rochemont was also addressing another of Forgan's criticisms – that the British SOE had been given no credit for their meticulous selection of sabotage targets.[106] De Rochemont also promised that he would do his best to rectify any elements of '"unrealism"'. 'There will not be, I trust, any major and ridiculous inaccuracies', but, '... this is Hollywood,' he reminded Forgan, 'and, in obeisance to local tradition, no doubt our picture will not (to my regret) avoid entirely certain creative license. It must be remembered that our production does not purport factually to depict OSS war activities. It is not, in a narrow sense, a "documentary" any more than was "House on 92nd Street" and probably less so.'[107] Donovan absorbed Forgan's criticisms but continued to offer his support to the production. De Rochemont met Donovan for a final time in May 1946. Having read the latest script drafts that still included the offending elements of 'unrealism' to which Forgan objected, the General gave his full verbal approval and, according to de Rochemont, 'seemed willing to cooperate ... in any way'.[108]

The next major obstacle to their story came, predictably, from Joseph Breen's Production Code Administration (PCA), Hollywood's pious industry censor since the early 1930s. Along with the PCA's customary censorship of tasteless biblical references, undue violence and explicit sexuality, Breen was especially concerned with actions that could be imitated by criminals, asking Fox to remove scenes illustrating items such as the 'Spring Cosh' and the manufacture of a Molotov Cocktail.[109] He also instructed Fox to 'rewrite Sharkey's line, "You're going to be taught to kill – to cheat, to rob – to lie", in such a manner as to get away from the direct inference that an officer of the United States is teaching immorality'. Breen and the PCA stood here in direct opposition to one of the central moral and political premises of Donovan's publicity campaign and Hollywood's articulation of it – namely, the consequentialist moral relativism implied within the realist argument that America could no longer afford to be naïve in intelligence matters in a world increasingly populated by hostile nations more than prepared to employ devious means in order to achieve their foreign policy aims. 'Perhaps a line to the effect that the enemy teaches killing, cheating, robbing and lying, and it is his job to teach the new-comers how to cope with such an enemy,' suggested Breen, 'can obviate such an objection'.[110] More worryingly, Breen opposed the film's denouement on similar grounds, requesting that they rewrite the scene 'in such a way as to escape having the flavor that the United States fliers are going to deliberately kill their own agent'.

Upon receipt of the PCA's objections, Jason Joy, who preceded Breen at the PCA before moving to Fox to work as their liaison officer with the censors, immediately telephoned the PCA to dispute the requested changes, claiming that they would 'rob the story of all its authenticity and believability'.[111] Zanuck and de Rochemont stood fast against Breen – most of the offending scenes remain relatively intact in the final production, as does the utilitarian logic that justifies Sharkey's martyrdom. In any case, Fox knew their relationship with the PCA could be repaired – by now it was almost standard industry practice for directors and producers to see how far they could transgress the provisions of the code. The relationship with Donovan and the former-OSS, however, would prove far more fragile.

The first serious doubts that their film would receive official sanction came at about the time of Donovan's third and final meeting with de Rochemont in May 1946, when the General verbally approved the script. Damaging rumours had been circulating in Washington, DC that de Rochemont had 'cut corners' and circumvented the War Department's classification of all OSS records through his personal contacts in the FBI as well as Donovan's former agency. The rumours, which were likely true given the degree of research conducted for the production as well as the extensive network of former OSS agents coming forward with information and material to share with the producers, had made Washington increasingly wary of de Rochemont's ability to sidestep official control and many considered him to 'have used devious means infringing upon or interfering with the duties of Fox's Washington liaison office'.[112] At the very least, de Rochemont feared it would delay official sanction of their production.

On his part, Zanuck had long recommended the abandonment of any explicit reference to Donovan and the OSS, fearing the spectre of a Congressional enquiry into OSS activity that may well cause an about-face from Donovan and his initial agreement to support the production. Zanuck asked de Rochemont to consider the possibility of 'substituting Army Intelligence – G2 – in place of O.S.S.' in case of any objections that Donovan may pose. 'You will recall', wrote Zanuck, 'that when I originally suggested this many months ago I had the feeling that O.S.S. was in for a ride and that we would get no official or military support'.[113] Ultimately, however, both de Rochemont and Zanuck concluded that removing OSS from the picture would damage the integrity of the well-researched training and recruiting scenes, which de Rochemont had invested so much energy and faith in.[114] Nevertheless, sensing a change in Donovan's attitude and perhaps wary of Forgan's objections, Zanuck gave de Rochemont explicit instructions to keep the screenplay away from the eyes of Donovan's committee.[115]

On 4 June 1946, Zanuck and de Rochemont's fears began to be realised when Donovan demanded to see the shooting script and informed them that he would not provide them with signed permission to use newsreel footage of him until he had seen the first cut of the film. De Rochemont, however, put this down to Donovan's disappointment with Paramount's *O.S.S.* and felt confident that the General would see the comparative virtue of their production with all its *March of Time* authenticity. Sometime around 1 July, de Rochemont received a telephone call from Colonel Doering, of Donovan's film committee, asking to discuss Forgan's objections to the screenplay. Growing increasingly alarmed, de Rochemont sought reassurance, and received it from John Shaheen who told him that he considered *13 Rue Madeleine* 'a good story and expressed the opinion that the General would like it and approve it'.[116] Then, on 3 July, in a short, strident, letter from Donovan, came confirmation of Zanuck and de Rochemont's worst fears:

> I have gone over the script very carefully. I understand that some of your people have said that since OSS is dissolved they are entitled to write any kind of a story they wish. I would like to remind you that I set up the Committee in order to aid various companies which desire to write a script on OSS . . .
>
> The picture is a phony. With all the excellent authentic material which we have sought to make available to you it seems absurd that your company would persist in making a picture that not only lacks reality but plausibility.
>
> It is impossible for me to approve of the representations made in the script that this is authentic, or even a typical, story of OSS operations, and it would clearly be unfair to OSS agents who voluntarily jeopardised their lives to engage in valuable clandestine operations to couple their names and experiences with the events pictures in the script.
>
> I concur entirely with the criticisms of Messrs Forgan and Doering (attached).[117]

What are we to make of this sudden, although by no means unexpected, about-face from Donovan? We may, perhaps, take his letter at face value, and presume that the inaccuracies of the picture, and in particular Forgan's objections, had compelled the General to withdraw his support. Yet the creative liberties of *Rue Madeleine* were hardly worse than *O.S.S.* or *Cloak and Dagger*. Indeed both were severely criticised in the press for their historical infidelities – and yet Donovan saw no reason to react in either instance, even offering his signed approval for the former. Perhaps then it was the specific plot details – the story of the German double agent in OSS or Sharkey's reckless decision to parachute into Europe despite his knowledge of Overlord. Mike Carroll, the technical advisor on *Rue Madeleine*, called around his OSS contacts for further details, but nobody seemed to 'know if the General based his objections on a specific scene or on the general "German-spy-within-OSS" theme'.[118] George Skouras expressed his surprise at Donovan's objections and reassured Fox that he would surely change his mind once he saw the completed picture.[119] Zanuck felt the same way, as he reassured de Rochemont:

> I think . . . we are completely in the clear. As a matter of fact we did far more than could be expected of us. I don't know of what more we could have done to make our story more authentic. After all we are in the business of producing entertainment and I think we are all to be complimented on the efficient manner in which we endeavored to treat a worthwhile organization . . . I am more than ever certain that either General Donovan has been misinformed as to the content of our script or

the people who have read the script for him are not accustomed to visualizing a finished picture from a scenario.[120]

If the film's inaccuracies were indeed the cause of Donovan's decision, they do not explain the timing of his rebuke. As de Rochemont asked Zanuck and Jason Joy, why did he not reject the plot on the basis of the numerous outlines and treatments he was sent, all of which contained the offending elements that gave the producers cause for caution?[121] Donovan was still offering his tacit support as late as May 1946, and nobody within his film committee, Forgan aside, gave any indication of disapproval prior to Donovan's 3 July letter. Perhaps it simply took time for the inferences of the plot to sink in, and the cumulative effect of Forgan's objections, coupled with Donovan finally seeing the completed script, are explanation enough. In truth we will never know what exactly motivated his decision. But it seems reasonable to assume that had the film been released six months previously, when Donovan's publicity campaign was in full swing, then the General would have found it very difficult to forego the opportunity of a film that, even with the problematic plot elements, provided a celebratory narrative of the OSS in such an influential medium. With the Central Intelligence Group (CIG) established in January 1946 and swiftly emerging as a legitimate successor to the OSS, it is perhaps worth speculating that by the summer of 1946, Donovan simply no longer needed the publicity – his campaign had already succeeded in part. The writing, it seemed, was almost on the wall, the fate of America's post-war intelligence bureaucracy soon to be sealed in the National Security Act of 1947, and the last thing Donovan needed was a sensationalised Hollywood production by a producer who had already raised eyebrows within the War Department.

America had found that its new OSS, and with it Donovan's unprecedented openness, always a means to an end, came swiftly to a close. It marked the end of a long and fruitful relationship between Hollywood and America's first central intelligence agency – a relationship born on the soundstages of Twentieth Century-Fox with the creation of John Ford's Field Photographic Unit more than half a decade previously, and ending at that very same studio in the summer of 1946. In the intervening years Hollywood's documentarians had provided the OSS with a new means of intelligence collection, analysis and presentation – a logistics of visual perception that would fundamentally alter the way in which war was perceived – both on the planning tables of the War Department and for cinema audiences, like Josephine MacNab in the Trans-Lux theatre, who witnessed realistic footage of war for the first time. They had produced raw intelligence, strategic planning reports, training films and propaganda. They had documented the North African invasion, provided one of the first assessments of the attack on Pearl Harbor and they could, without exaggeration, take a significant proportion of the credit for bringing the Nazi war criminals to justice at the Nuremberg trials. In turn, this relationship provided the documentary aesthetic with a veracity and moral authority that would have been unthinkable in pre-war Hollywood, with its general aversion to factual or political filmmaking. It had also satisfied the American public's growing demand, throughout the war, for greater realism in their motion pictures. It was an impulse that would continue into the post-war years with the semi-documentary cycle of films, many of which celebrated American intelligence, particularly the wartime activities of the OSS and its beltway rival, the FBI.

Yet it was always a relationship that could not last. Hollywood and American intelligence, in spite of Donovan's post-war publicity campaign, ultimately sat at opposite ends of the continuum between secrecy and publicity. Once Donovan's publicity campaign came to an end with the creation of the CIA, the commitment to secrecy was restored and the bright lights of Hollywood celebrity were the last thing the CIA sought, or needed. The CIA would not call upon Hollywood again for almost fifty years. At the end of the Cold War, when people once again questioned the need for American intelligence, the CIA sought out the publicity of the American film industry, and history, as ever, would be repeated.[122]

Back at Fox, Zanuck sprang swiftly into action. He had Hathaway reshoot all the scenes containing references to the OSS so that Donovan's organisation was no longer explicitly identifiable. Charles Gibson, who played Donovan in the film, was rechristened as 'Walter Abel', and Zanuck told Hathaway to dress him 'in an army uniform with the rank of a full colonel or brigadier general and a couple of service ribbons from World War One. Therefore', Zanuck continued, 'we will leave the door wide open as to what branch of the government we are representing and at this time Donovan's men were not in uniform and the audience can be left to decide for themselves whether we are representing army, G-2 or OSS or Army Special Service Division'.[123] Zanuck still held out hope that Donovan would change his mind and, at least, with it shot this way, it was still possible to identify the unit as OSS to audiences. But Donovan did not change his mind. As such, the OSS of the film were renamed '077' – a wafer-thin veil.

Of course, audiences and critics knew who the film was about – no amount of obfuscation could change that, especially given the foregoing publicity for the film. A 'tough and brilliant tribute to the Office of Strategic Services' concluded Harold Barnes of the *New York Herald Tribune*, without even a second-thought of who the '077' moniker was intended for.[124] '[E]ven though we did not mention OSS in 13 RUE MADELEINE', wrote Zanuck, 'the newspaper critics recognized immediately that it was OSS. You can't fight facts nor can you make fiction serve the purpose of facts.'[125] Many reviewers agreed with Barnes' positive assessment – 'realistic, absorbing and free from superficial romance', concluded another reviewer.[126] By avoiding the romantic clichés of Paramount and Milton Sperling's OSS productions, the Sharkey plotline, with its tragic conclusion, had evidently pleased critics despite irking certain sections of Donovan's film committee. Yet not all of the reviews were positive. Perhaps most influentially, Bosley Crowther's scathing review in *The New York Times* astutely cut to the heart of the producers' quarrel with Donovan and its ramifications for the film's documentary claims:

> In the light of the many fancy stories of the wartime activities of the O.S.S. – you know, the 'cloak and dagger' boys who worked behind the enemy lines – it seems rather odd that any movie pretending to recount such derring-do should have to dissemble in naming the organization involved. Yet apparently the reckless producers of '13 Rue Madeleine' were compelled to the ultimate precaution by their own inventiveness. Thus it is, in this brisk and bristling picture ... that an outfit called 'Secret Intelligence,' not O.S.S., does the fancy stuff through a unit tagged '0–77' – a feeble and wistful disguise.[127]

Zanuck was furious. 'Somebody ought to write Mr. Crowther and let him know the facts', he vented to de Rochemont. 'He should certainly be told that General Donovan begged to have his name put on the picture and that Donovan realized that he made a mistake in objecting to the original script.' In any case, 'movie fans apparently do not read the Times', Zanuck sardonically concluded. 'The box office attendance on 13 RUE MADELEINE are [sic] clear-cut factual and I might add documentary representations of the above theory.'[128]

Zanuck's last remark, although laced with sarcasm and written in a fit of pique, was revealing. Hollywood had never relied upon government endorsement for its box-office success – if anything the opposite was true. And although realism was in increasing demand during and immediately after the Second World War, it was an effect that was achieved more through narrative strategies, in particular the eschewing of romance, and aesthetic touches such as the use of location shooting, the Timespeak narration and noir-inspired claustrophobic camera angles and chiaroscuro lighting. None of this was dependent upon government support – and none of it was necessarily a product of extensive research in the National Archives as was so proudly proclaimed in *Rue Madeleine*'s opening sequence. Moreover 'in obeisance to local tradition', as de Rochemont put it, none of the other OSS pictures released the previous year were, in the end, premised upon verisimilitude. Their melodramatic frameworks and use of stock characters and generic narrative structures obfuscated the real-life origins of their stories almost beyond recognition. In this sense, it is tempting to conclude that the support of Donovan's film committee, and the numerous former-OSS technical advisors who worked on all three pictures, provided little more than window dressing, lending the productions a patina of authenticity that could be exploited by the studios' marketing departments.

But the relationship between Hollywood and OSS, and its subsequent breakdown, was important in terms of Hollywood's representation of American intelligence in one crucial respect, articulated by Crowther in his review of *Rue Madeleine*: without the OSS's, and later CIA's support, the object of representation began to disappear from view. Although it was obvious in *Rue Madeleine* who '077' was supposed to be, in later spy films this was rarely the case – the CIA disappeared from view at precisely the moment when increasing scrutiny and direct representation of its organisation and its activities was most needed. It would take twelve years, from the Agency's establishment in 1947, for the letters 'C-I-A' to even be uttered in a major Hollywood motion picture – Alfred Hitchcock's *North by Northwest*. And even then, as the (presumably) CIA-chief 'The Professor' replies with a shrug to Roger Thornhill when asked if he is a CIA agent: 'FBI, CIA – we're all in the same alphabet soup'.[129]

But like the OSS, the CIA was too distinctive, too unique in the American experience, for it to be submerged from view amidst the bureaucratic soup forever. It would take a new form of representation, one entirely opposed to the documentary or semi-documentary aesthetic, and one that, not coincidentally, partly originated with Hitchcock's *North by Northwest*, for the CIA to begin appearing onscreen. By the time it did, the CIA had already lost control of its narrative. By turning his back on Hollywood, Donovan set a precedent that the CIA would continue – a precedent that would eventually lead to the creation of a fictional counter-narrative of the Agency, entirely divorced from the firm bonds of cooperation laid down by John Ford between Hollywood and America's first central intelligence agency. History abhors a vacuum, and if Donovan or the CIA were not prepared to help fill it, then somebody else would. It was just that it could no longer hold true, as the opening to *13 Rue Madeleine* put it, that the National Archives were 'the final resting place of the histories and records' of America's secret intelligence. Instead, authors and filmmakers would need to go elsewhere to find their stories of American intrigue. The US Government could only be regarded by Hollywood as the arbiter of historical authenticity so long as it proffered the stories and records upon which a shared national past could be based. By abdicating that responsibility, and pulling the drawbridge on its secret activities shut, the state sowed the seeds of the more critical voices that would emerge in Hollywood, and elsewhere, in later decades.

Notes

1. For more on Donovan's relationship with the media and his post-war campaign for the establishment of the CIA see Larry Valero, '"We Need Our New OSS, Our New General Donovan, Now ...": The Public Discourse over American Intelligence, 1944–53', *Intelligence and National Security*, 18:1 (2003), pp. 91–118.
2. Tony Shaw, *Hollywood's Cold War* (Edinburgh: Edinburgh University Press, 2007), p. 1.
3. See John Sbardellati, *J. Edgar Hoover Goes to the Movies: The FBI and the Origins of Hollywood's Cold War* (Ithaca: Cornell University Press, 2012) and Richard Gid Powers, *G-Men: Hoover's FBI in American Popular Culture* (Carbondale: Southern Illinois University Press, 1983).
4. Bradley F. Smith, *The Shadow Warriors: O.S.S. and the Origins of the C.I.A.* (London: André Deutsch, 1983), p. 414.
5. Comer Vann Woodward, 'The Age of Reinterpretation', *American Historical Review*, 66:1 (October 1960), p. 2.
6. Thomas F. Troy, *Donovan and the CIA: A History of the Establishment of the Central Intelligence Agency* (Frederick: University Publication of America, 1996), p. 259.
7. Major Andy Rogers cited in Stewart Alsop and Thomas Braden, *Sub Rosa: The O.S.S. and American Espionage* (New York: Reynal and Hitchcock, 1946), p. 232.
8. Ibid.
9. Roger Hall, *You're Stepping on My Cloak and Dagger* (London: William Kimber and Co., 1958), pp. 201–2.
10. Smith, *The Shadow Warriors*, p. 407.
11. Hall, *You're Stepping on My Cloak and Dagger*, p. 202.
12. Ibid, p. 202.
13. 'Motion Pictures of OSS Activities', 19 October 1945, Louis de Rochemont Collection, 5716, Box 7 Folder 5, American Heritage Center, University of Wyoming, Laramie (hereafter AHCW).
14. Louis de Rochemont to Ray Klune, 18 December 1945, Louis de Rochemont Collection, 5716, Box 7 Folder 5, AHCW.
15. Mike Carroll to Louis de Rochemont, 19 December 1945, Louis de Rochemont Collection, 5716, Box 7 Folder 5, AHCW.
16. James Deutsch, '"I Was a Hollywood Agent": Cinematic Representations of the Office of Strategic Services in 1946', *Intelligence and National Security*, 13:2 (1998), p. 87. Deutsch contests the arguments of James Robert Parish and Michael Pitts who argue that filmmakers *did* grant access to the files. See James Robert Parish and Michael R. Pitts, *The Great Spy Pictures* (Metuchen: Scarecrow Press, 1974), p. 358.
17. William Rader to Louis de Rochemont, 4 December 1945, Louis de Rochemont Collections, 5716, Box 7 Folder 5, AHCW.
18. Anthony Cave Brown, *The Last Hero: Wild Bill Donovan* (London: Times Books, 1982).
19. Louis de Rochemont to Mr F. D. Langton, 14 November 1945, Louis de Rochemont Collection, 5716, Box 7 Folder 5, AHCW; Louis de Rochemont to John Monks and Sy Bartlett, 14 November 1945, Louis de Rochemont Collection, 5716, Box 7 Folder 5, AHCW.
20. 'Five 20th-Fox Employees to Aid "O.S.S." Advisors', *Hollywood Reporter*, 30 April 1946.

21. Bert Leeds to Darryl F. Zanuck, 18 October 1945, Louis de Rochemont Collections, 5716, Box 5 Folder 7, AHCW.
22. Captain Richard Phenix to Louis de Rochemont, 12 December 1945, Louis de Rochemont Collections, 5716, Box 7 Folder 5, AHCW.
23. Ibid.
24. OSS Clipping file cited in Deutsch, '"I Was a Hollywood Agent"', p. 89.
25. 'Cloak and Dagger Publicity Material', Cloak and Dagger Production Files, Folder 15, Warner Brothers Archive, University of Southern California, Los Angeles.
26. Joe Moskowitz to Jason Joy, 29 October 1945, Louis de Rochemont Collections, 5716, Box 7, Folder 5, AHCW.
27. Louis de Rochemont to Lew Schreiber, 5 November 1945, Louis de Rochemont Collections, 5716, Box 7 Folder 5, AHCW.
28. 'Paramount's 'O.S.S.' Guided by O.S.S. Men' in Paramount Press Sheets 1945–6, Group A5, Margaret Herrick Library, Academy of Motion Pictures Arts and Sciences, Beverly Hill (Hereafter AMPAS).
29. Deutch, '"I Was a Hollywood Agent"', p. 89.
30. *O.S.S.* (Irving Pichel, Paramount Pictures, 1946).
31. *13 Rue Madeleine* (Henry Hathaway, Twentieth Century-Fox, 1947). James Deutsch also compares these two scenes in his article. See Deutsch, '"I Was a Hollywood Agent"', pp. 94–5.
32. 'Report on the Activities of the Central Intelligence Agency' by Special Panel of Consultants Chaired by Lieutenant General James Doolittle, September 1954. Available online at http://www.foia.cia.gov/sites/default/files/document_conversions/45/doolittle_report.pdf, accessed 31 March 2015.
33. Elizabeth MacDonald, *Undercover Girl* (New York: Macmillan, 1947). MacDonald, whose married name was McIntosh, joined the CIA and worked as a career spy for much of her life. Upon retirement she published a history of women in the OSS; see Elizabeth P. McIntosh, *Sisterhood of Spies: The Women of the OSS* (Annapolis: Naval Institute Press, 2009).
34. Kay Lindsay cited in Deutsch, '"I Was a Hollywood Agent"', p. 90.
35. Ibid., p. 91.
36. Smith, *Shadow Warriors*, pp. 252–3.
37. Deutsch, '"I Was a Hollywood Agent"', p. 89. Details of this operation appear in Richard Harris Smith, *OSS: The Secret History of America's First Central Intelligence Agency* (Berkeley: University of California Press, 1972), pp. 15, 199.
38. Bosley Crowther, 'The Screen: "O.S.S." War Spy Thriller, with Alan Ladd, Miss Fitzgerald in Leading Roles, Makes its Appearance at the Gotham', *The New York Times*, 27 May 1946.
39. Deutsch, '"I Was a Hollywood Agent"', p. 90.
40. Bosley Crowther, 'The Screen: "O.S.S." War Spy Thriller, with Alan Ladd, Miss Fitzgerald in Leading Roles, Makes its Appearance at the Gotham', *The New York Times*, 27 May 1946.
41. *Cloak and Dagger* (Fritz Lang, United States Pictures/Warner Brothers, 1946).
42. Bosley Crowther, 'The Screen: "Cloak and Dagger," with Gary Cooper and Lilli Palmer, New Actress from England, in the Lead Roles, Arrives at Strand', *The New York Times*, 5 October 1946.
43. Heather Oriana Petrocalli, *Portland's 'Refugee from Occupied Hollywood': Andries Deinum, his Center for the Moving Image, and Film Education in the United States*, Master's Thesis, Portland State University, Department of History. Available online at http://pdxscholar.library.pdx.edu/open_access_etds/608, accessed 27 February 2014.

44. David Kalat, *The Strange Case of Dr. Mabuse: A Study of the Twelve Films and Five Novels* (New York: McFarland and Company, 2005), p. 102.
45. Ibid.
46. John Sbardellati, *J. Edgar Hoover Goes to the Movies: The FBI and the Origins of Hollywood's Cold War* (Ithaca: Cornell University Press, 2012), p. 98.
47. Ronald Radosh and Allis Radosh, *Red Star over Hollywood: The Film Conlony's Long Romance with the Left* (New York: Encounter Books, 2006), pp. 87–8.
48. Burt A. Folkart, 'Alvah Bessie, Blacklisted By Studies, Dies', *Los Angeles Times*, 24 July 1985.
49. Alvah Bessie and Ben Madow, *Cloak and Dagger Treatment*, undated, Cloak and Dagger Production Files, Folder 3, Warner Brothers Archive.
50. Dick Vosburgh, 'Obituary: Ben Maddow', *The Independent*, 14 October 1992.
51. Edwin Schallert, 'Gen. Donovan Will Play "Cloak and Dagger" Role', *Los Angeles Times*, 30 November 1945.
52. Keith Brooker, *Film and the American Left: A Research Guide* (Westport: Greenwood Publishing Group, 1999), p. 139.
53. Richard Hofstadter, *The Paranoid Style in American Politics and Other Essays* (New York: Random House, [1964] 2008); David S. Brown, *Richard Hofstadter: An Intellectual Biography* (Chicago: University of Chicago Press, 2006); John Fousek, *To Lead the Free World: American Nationalism and the Cultural Roots of the Cold War* (Chapel Hill: University of North Carolina Press, 2000).
54. Treachery and homosexuality were often equated with anti-communists in this era, leading to the persecution of many gays or alleged gays in government known as 'the lavender scare'. By contrast, American patriotism and what Michael Kackman calls 'the ideal citizen type', were usually associated with traditional notions of heteronormative masculinity. See Robert D. Dean, *Imperial Brotherhood: Gender and the Making of Cold War Foreign Policy* (Amherst: University of Massachusetts Press, 2003); Robert J. Corber, *In the Name of National Security: Hitchcock, Homophobia and the Political Construction of Gender in Postwar America* (Durham, NC: Duke University Press, 1993); Alan Nadel, *Containment Culture: American Narratives, Postmodernism and the Atomic Age* (Durham, NC: Duke University Press, 1995); Michael Kackman, *Citizen Spy: Television, Espionage, and Cold War Culture* (Minneapolis: University of Minnesota Press, 2005).
55. Patrick McGilligan, *Fritz Lang: The Nature of the Beast* (Minneapolis: University of Minnesota Press, 2013), p. 332.
56. Corey Ford and Alistair MacBain, 'Cloak and Dagger', *Collier's*, 6 October 1945; 'U.S. Pictures Sets "Cloak and Dagger"', *Hollywood Reporter*, 3 October 1945; Corey Ford and Alistair MacBain, *Cloak and Dagger: The Secret Story of OSS* (New York: Random House, 1946).
57. *O.S.S.* (Irving Pichel, Paramount Pictures, 1946).
58. William Donovan to Corey Ford, 1 October 1945, Cloak and Dagger Collection, Box 1, Folder 2, Warner Brothers Archive.
59. 'A Suggested Screen Treatment Based on the Colliers' Serial 'Cloak and Dagger' By Lieutenant Colonel Carey Ford and Major Alistair Macbain, Cloak and Dagger Collection, Box 1, Folder 2, Warner Brothers Archive.
60. Michael Burke, *Outrageous Good Fortune* (New York: Little, Brown and Company, 1984), p. 59.
61. A suggested Screen Treatment Based on the Colliers' Serial 'Cloak and Dagger' By Lieutenant Colonel Carey Ford and Major Alistair Macbain, Cloak and Dagger Collection, Box 1, Folder 2, Warner Brothers Archive.
62. Burke, *Outrageous Good Fortune*; 'Obituary of Michael Burke, 70; Spy, Ex-N.Y. Yankees President', *Los Angeles Times*, 7 February 1987.

63. Patrick K. O'Donnell, *Operatives, Spies and Saboteurs: The Unknown Story of the Men and Women of World War II's OSS* (New York: Free Press, 2004), p. 55.
64. For more on the self-sustaining mythologisation of CIA covert action during the 1950s see Smith, *Shadow Warriors*, pp. 390–420; Rhodri Jeffreys-Jones, *The CIA and American Democracy*, third edition (New Haven: Yale University Press, 2003), pp. 81–99; Douglas Little, 'Mission Impossible: The CIA and the Cult of Covert Action in the Middle East', *Diplomatic History*, 28:5 (2004), pp. 663–701; Simon Willmetts, 'The Burgeoning Fissures of Dissent: Allen Dulles and the Selling of the CIA in the Aftermath of the Bay of Pigs', *History: The Journal of the Historical Association*, 100:340 (April 2015a), pp. 167–88.
65. McGilligan, *Fritz Lang*, p. 334.
66. Ibid.
67. 'Lang Strives for Reality: Director is Unique for Mastery of Violence, Tense Action in Films', *Morning Telegraph*, 29 October 1946.
68. McGilligan, *Fritz Lang*, p. 338.
69. Ibid.
70. Final Shooting Script Part 1, 7 March 1946, Cloak and Dagger Collection, Box 1, Folder 12, Warner Brothers Archive, p. 105.
71. Outline of Cloak and Dagger, 8 November 1945, Cloak and Dagger Collection, Box 1, Folder 8, Warner Brothers Archive, p. 51.
72. Ibid, p. 52.
73. McGilligan, *Fritz Lang*, p. 339.
74. Ibid, p. 339. David Kalat provides a similar account: 'Sperling felt that the audience knew the Nazis had no nuclear capacity, and the ending would be laughable . . .' Kalat, *The Strange Case of Dr. Mabuse*, p. 101.
75. McGilligan, *Frtiz Lang*, p. 339.
76. Peter Bogdanovich, *Fritz Lang in America* (London: Studio Vista Limited, 1967), p. 70; emphasis in original.
77. Jerome F. Shapiro, *Atomic Bomb Cinema* (London: Routledge, 2002), pp. 58–9.
78. *Cloak and Dagger* (Fritz Lang, United States Pictures/Warner Brothers, 1946).
79. Truman and Fosdick cited in Paul Boyer, *By the Bomb's Early Light: American Thought and Culture at the Dawn of the Atomic Age* (Chapel Hill: The University of North Carolina Press, 1994), pp. 266–71.
80. Ibid., p. 71.
81. Oppenheimer cited in Boyer, p. 273. See also Kai Bird, *American Prometheus: The Triumph and Tragedy of J. Robert Oppenheimer* (New York: Atlantic Books, 2009).
82. *Cloak and Dagger* Temporary Script, 4 March 1946, Cloak and Dagger Collection, Box 1, Folder 11, Warner Brothers Archive, p. 122.
83. Bosley Crowther, 'The Screen: "Cloak and Dagger," with Gary Cooper and Lilli Palmer, New Actress from England, in the Lead Roles, Arrives at Strand', *The New York Times*, 5 October 1946.
84. 'Cloak and Dagger', *Independent Film Journal*, 14 September 1946; '"Cloak and Dagger" Story of OSS Agent Has Excitement', *Film Bulletin*, 14 September 1946.
85. Darryl F. Zanuck, 'Do Writers Know Hollywood?: The Message Cannot Overwhelm the Technique', *The Saturday Review*, 30 October 1943, p. 12.
86. Raymond Fielding, *The March of Time, 1935–1951* (New York: Oxford University Press, 1978), p. 73.
87. J. Edgar Hoover to Louis de Rochemont, 11 September 1942, Louis de Rochemont Collection, 5716, Box 4 Folder 8, AHCW.
88. J. Edgar Hoover to Louis de Rochemont, 17 November 1942, Louis de Rochemont Collection, 5716, Box 4 Folder 1, AHCW.

89. Barry Lyndon and Charles Booth to Louis de Rochemont, 19 August 1944, Louis de Rochemont Collection, 5716, Box 15 Folder 11, AHCW.
90. A MacGuffin is an object of desire at the centre of a plot, which all the central characters seek. In a number of interviews throughout his career, Hitchcock noted that the actual nature or specific identification of the MacGuffin was unimportant. Rather, the import of the MacGuffin is its effect upon the characters that desire it: its role as the motive force of their actions throughout the narrative of a film or novel. In this sense, the true nature of the MacGuffin, as with 'secret process 97', need not be identified to the audience at all. Quentin Tarantino's *Pulp Fiction*, for example, masterfully exploited this idea of the MacGuffin by having the central characters locate a mysterious briefcase, the contents of which is never revealed to the audience.
91. Thomas M. Pryor, 'By Way of Report; Checking Up on U.S. Movies Abroad – A Note on the Atom Secret – Other Items', *The New York Times*, 12 August 1945.
92. Colonel Jason S. Joy to Darryl F. Zanuck, 16 August 1945, Louis de Rochemont Collection, 5716, Box 15 Folder 11, AHCW.
93. Harrison Carroll, 'House on 92nd St. Is Greatest Spy Picture', *Herald Express*, 19 October 1945.
94. For more on de Rochemont's relationship with the FBI, see Shaw, *Hollywood's Cold War*, pp. 53–8.
95. Louis de Rochemont to Colonel Jason S. Joy, 12 July 1946, Louis de Rochemont Collections, 5716, Box 7 Folder 7, AHCW.
96. Ibid.
97. McGilligan, *Frtiz Lang*, p. 339.
98. John Monks Jr and Sy Bartlett, 'O.S.S. Story Outline', 5 December 1945, '13 Rue Madeleine File', University of Southern California Cinematic Arts Library (USC-CA), Los Angeles.
99. Ibid.
100. John Monks Jr and Sy Bartlett, '"32 Rue Madeleine" Revised Story Outline', 12 December 1945, '13 Rue Madeleine File', University of Southern California Cinematic Arts Library (USC-CA), Los Angeles.
101. Louis de Rochemont to Colonel Jason S. Joy, 12 July 1946, Louis de Rochemont Collections, 5716, Box 7 Folder 7, AHCW.
102. Louis de Rochemont to Darryl F. Zanuck, 4 June 1946, Louis de Rochemont Collections, 5716, Box 7 Folder 6, AHCW.
103. Colonel Russell J. Forgan to General William Donovan, 1 March 1946, 'Russell J. Forgan Papers', 73089-8.36, Box 1, The Hoover Institute, Stanford.
104. Louis de Rochemont to Darryl F. Zanuck, 2 June 1946, Louis de Rochemont Collections, 5716, Box 7 Folder 6, AHCW.
105. Ibid.
106. Colonel Russell J. Forgan to General William Donovan, 1 March 1946, 'Russell J. Forgan Papers', 73089-8.36, Box 1, The Hoover Institute, Stanford.
107. Colonel Russell J. Forgan to William Casey, 19 March 1946, 'Russell J. Forgan Papers', 73089-8.36, Box 1, The Hoover Institute, Stanford.
108. Louis de Rochemont to Colonel Jason S. Joy, 12 July 1946, Louis de Rochemont Collections, 5716, Box 7 Folder 7, AHCW.
109. Joseph I. Breen to Colonel Jason S. Joy, 12 April 1946, Louis de Rochemont Collections, 5716, Box 7 Folder 6, AHCW.
110. Ibid.
111. Colonel Jason S. Joy to Louis de Rochemont, 15 April 1946, Louis de Rochemont Collections, 5716, Box 7 Folder 6, AHCW.
112. Louis de Rochemont to Darryl F. Zanuck, 23 May 1946, Louis de Rochemont Collections, 5716, Box 7 Folder 6, AHCW.

113. Darryl F. Zanuck to Louis de Rochemont, 14 February 1946, Louis de Rochemont Collections, 5716, Box 7 Folder 6, AHCW.
114. Darryl F. Zanuck to Louis de Rochemont, 15 February 1945, Louis de Rochemont Collections, 5716, Box 7 Folder 6, AHCW.
115. Louis de Rochemont to Colonel Jason S. Joy, 12 July 1946, Louis de Rochemont Collections, 5716, Box 7 Folder 7, AHCW.
116. Louis de Rochemont to Colonel Jason S. Joy, 12 July 1946, Louis de Rochemont Collections, 5716, Box 7 Folder 7, AHCW.
117. General William Donovan to Louis de Rochemont, 3 July 1946, 'Russell J. Forgan Papers', 73089-8.36, Box 1, The Hoover Institute, Stanford.
118. Mike Carroll to Louis de Rochemont, 29 July 1946, Louis de Rochemont Collections, 5716, Box 5 Folder 8, AHCW.
119. Darryl F. Zanuck to Henry Hathaway, 9 July 1946, Louis de Rochemont Collections, 5716, Box 7 Folder 6, AHCW.
120. Darryl F. Zanuck to Louis de Rochemont, 12 July 1946, Louis de Rochemont Collections, 5716, Box 7 Folder 6, AHCW.
121. Louis de Rochemont to Colonel Jason S. Joy, 12 July 1946, Louis de Rochemont Collections, 5716, Box 7 Folder 7, AHCW.
122. Tricia Jenkins, *The CIA in Hollywood: How the Agency Shapes Film and Television* (Austin: University of Texas Press, 2012), pp. 32–72.
123. Darryl F. Zanuck to Henry Hathaway, 9 July 1946, Louis de Rochemont Collections, 5716, Box 7 Folder 6, AHCW.
124. Howard Barnes, 'On the Screen', *New York Herald Tribune*, 16 January 1947.
125. Darryl F. Zanuck to Louis de Rochemont, 16 January 1947, Louis de Rochemont Collections, 5716, Box 5 Folder 8, AHCW.
126. Wand Hale, '"13 Rue Madeleine" is Thrilling OSS Drama', *Daily News*, 16 January 1947.
127. Bosley Crowther, 'The Screen', *The New York Times*, 16 January 1947.
128. Darryl F. Zanuck to Louis de Rochemont, 16 January 1947, Louis de Rochemont Collections, 5716, Box 5 Folder 8, AHCW.
129. *North by Northwest* (Alfred Hitchcock, MGM, 1959).

3. QUIET AMERICANS: THE CIA AND HOLLYWOOD IN THE EARLY COLD WAR

BARTHOLEMEW: Do you know what C.I.A. is Mrs. Lambert?
REGGIE: I don't suppose it's an airline, is it?

(Charade, 1963)[1]

If the historical record was comprised solely of Hollywood movies, one could be forgiven for thinking that the CIA did not exist for the first decade of the Cold War. From its creation in the National Security Act of 1947 up to an all-too-fleeting reference in Hitchcock's *North by Northwest* in 1959, buried amidst an 'alphabet soup' of other US intelligence agencies, the CIA existed without even a dim flicker of explicit recognition from the silver screen. It was not that the Agency went entirely unnoticed by the American public. Although certainly, relative to today, where the Agency features in American culture like a Leviathan – a metastasising cultural hieroglyph for all that is malignant with American foreign policy – it kept a remarkably low profile. Yet the image of the CIA that did make it, on occasion, into the public domain – an image that is, which the CIA endorsed – was a long way from the narratives of romance, action and intrigue that Hollywood had traditionally created.

On 3 August 1953, *Time Magazine* ran its cover story on Allen Dulles, who would become the CIA's longest-standing and most charismatic spy-chief. The image on the cover perfectly evoked the iconoclastic purpose of the article within, which sought to point out the difference, at least as Allen Dulles and *Time Magazine* saw it, between the myth and reality of America's first peacetime centralised foreign intelligence agency. In the background was the archetypal sleuth, with dagger pulled and cloak drawn to conceal the bottom half of his face. Beneath his brimmed black hat gazed a single uncovered eye, leering with nefarious intent. In the foreground, in sharp relief, was the instantly recognisable profile of Allen Dulles, puffing on his trademark pipe. His placid smile and neatly trimmed grey moustache and hair were reassuringly avuncular – giving a sense of a man at ease with the world, and his profession. His slightly skewed bowtie, along with his dated rimless oval spectacles, lent him a professorial air. Indeed, it was no coincidence that *North by Northwest*'s CIA chief, played by Leo G. Carroll who would later reprise the same role in *The Man from U.N.C.L.E.*, was named only 'The Professor'. It is doubtful that a more trustworthy face existed in America. It evoked qualities that stood in opposition to everything that the cloaked sleuth behind him represented: openness, contemplation, intelligence, trustworthiness and somebody who was unflappably reasonable. It was a far cry from the prevailing public image of the Agency today, or the anxieties over the creation of an 'American Gestapo' that had existed only a few years previously.

The cover story within, appositely titled *The Man with the Innocent Air*, began with an epigraph from Sun Tzu: 'What enables the wise sovereign and good general to strike and conquer, and achieve things beyond the reach of ordinary men, is foreknowledge.' The opening paragraphs immediately contemporise Sun Tzu's timeless wisdom by extending Donovan's now-axiomatic argument that permanent peacetime intelligence was necessary to avoid a future atomic Pearl Harbor: the stakes, as the article pointed out, were higher than at any other point in history. 'Allen Dulles has the most important mission in the long, sordid, heroic and colorful history of the intelligence services', it explained. 'This scholarly, hearty, pipe-smoking lawyer' was the only man, as Churchill had once described Admiral Jellicoe, 'who could lose the war in an afternoon.'

Tzu's quote also served another purpose: it gave this essentially modern bureaucratic institution an ancient and venerable heritage. In July 1946 Donovan had suggested to Dulles 'that they spread the story that because George Washington employed some irregular means of warfare, the Father of the Country had been a pioneer in the use of O.S.S.-type operations'.[2] His aim was to counteract the widespread notion that intelligence was an aberration of the modern world that had little in common with American traditions. This was to become a standard public relations ploy of the CIA – used to this day.[3] Future Director of Central Intelligence (DCI) William Casey, for example, another OSS veteran who had earlier followed Donovan's suggestion by writing a history of the American Revolution emphasising Washington's use of spies, proudly announced to a Senate committee in 1983: 'I claim that my first predecessor as Director of Central Intelligence was . . . George Washington, who appointed himself.'[4] With similar intent, the *Time* article made historical

Figure 3.1 Allen Dulles, the longest-serving Director of Central Intelligence (from 1953 to 1961), was often portrayed in the American media during his tenure as a genial pipe-smoking contemplative leader. His image inspired numerous Hollywood spy chiefs, perhaps most famously Leo G. Carrol's role as 'The Professor' in *North by Northwest* and Alexander Waverley in hit television show *The Man from U.N.C.L.E. Source:* Wikimedia Commons.

parallels between the CIA and everything from biblical references to Joshua sending spies into Jericho; the use of espionage networks in ancient China, where, as the article explains 'military intelligence became . . . a respected art'; through Sir Francis Walsingham's espionage network in Elizabethan England; to more modern, but no less mythical examples such as Mata Hari in the First World War. As historian Bernard Porter has argued, this long and continual narrative of intelligence, which claims that 'every state and every government has resorted to it, since the dawn of time', implicitly supposes that 'espionage is both necessary and "natural"'.[5]

By contrast, the modern CIA, so the article explained, resembled 'nothing so much as a research foundation' – a kind of university campus with an expressed focus on foreign relations. Unlike the diabolical sleuth behind Dulles on the cover, it consisted of experts 'on Lower Slobbovian economic history', or lawyers 'or the archaeologist who is trained to draw conclusions from incomplete and obscure evidence'. These experts and intellectuals, men and women who quietly interpret and contemplate the world rather than attempting to change it, led by their scholarly chief who wouldn't look out of place in elbow patches behind a Yale lectern, vastly outnumbered, so the article claimed, 'spies, agents or cloak & dagger men'.[6]

But there was something missing from this story, something, which a bolder American film industry, unrestrained by McCarthyite attacks from the House Un-American Activities Committee, the ever-watchful eye of Joseph Breen at the Production Code Administration or studio lawyers who advised against any unauthorised depiction of government agents or institutions, may perhaps have wanted to tell. Just over two weeks after *Time* ran the feature, the CIA, encouraged and aided by the British, overthrew the democratically elected Iranian Government, and its progressive leader who had proposed the nationalisation of the British-controlled Iranian oil-fields: Mohammad Mosaddegh. It was one CIA-backed coup among many, in an era that intelligence historians have defined as the 'Golden Age' of covert action.[7] *Time Magazine* did not report the CIA's involvement in this event.

During the first decade and a half of its existence, the CIA, among other things, helped to limit communist influence in the 1948 Italian elections; assisted British MI-6 in their attempt to overthrow the Albanian communist government; funded the Filipino counter-insurgency campaign against the Hukbalahap; provided covert patronage to artists, writers, musicians and, indeed, filmmakers, in what has retrospectively been termed the CIA's 'Cultural Cold War'; ousted the democratically elected Mohammad Mosaddegh in the 1953 Iranian coup; ousted the democratically elected Jacobo Árbenz in the 1954 Guatemalan coup; launched operations against the Sukarno Government in Indonesia; and would repeatedly, almost obsessively, attempt to either kill or overthrow Castro in Cuba – an obsession that would eventually prove the undoing of this so-called 'Golden Age' of impunity, in April 1961, on the beaches at the Bay of Pigs.

Significantly, all of these stories, with the exception of that last fateful debacle in Cuba, went almost entirely unnoticed by the American press. In a survey of *Time Magazine*'s extensive coverage of the ousting of Mosaddegh, for example, John Foran reveals that the CIA were afforded only one oblique reference, which itself was not an admission of the CIA's involvement in the coup.[8] The same magazine that had described the CIA as a kind of 'research foundation', failed to report, only a few weeks later, an operation that significantly confounded this view. A year later, during the CIA-backed Guatemalan coup, Dulles helped suppress *The New York Times* journalist Sydney Gruson, who he believed was sympathetic to the Arbenz regime.[9]

There were a few exceptions that proved this rule of media reticence towards CIA covert activities in the early Cold War. Most noteworthy were a series of articles written by Richard and Gladys Harkness in the *Saturday Evening Post* in the autumn of 1954 that revealed, for the first time, CIA involvement in Guatemala and Iran. These were a far cry, however, from the muckraking exposés that excoriated the CIA for the excesses of its covert activities two decades later. Rather, they were part of a coordinated and timely public relations offensive by Allen Dulles in response to the increasingly vocal calls led by Senator Mike Mansfield for the creation of a watchdog committee to oversee CIA activities. The articles were, as David Shamus McCarthy writes, 'propaganda masquerading as journalism' that propagated the CIA's line that the Arbenz and Mosaddegh governments were beholden to a vast Soviet-directed conspiracy to spread communism across the globe.[10] Echoing the obsequious tone of the *Time Magazine* story, they described Dulles as 'a tough-minded, hardheaded, steel spring of a man with an aptitude and zest for matching wits with an unseen foe'.[11]

But apart from these coordinated slivers of light into the murky world of covert operations, the CIA's 'golden age' of intervention for the most part escaped public attention. Cloaked in near-total secrecy, the assumptions and convictions that undergirded the Agency's burgeoning covert action activities were left unchecked. 'The system', as novelist Don DeLillo later characterised it, 'would perpetuate itself in all its curious and obsessive webbings, its equivocations and patient riddles and levels of delusional thought, at least until the men were on the beach ... After the Bay of Pigs, nothing was the same.'[12]

Covert action was the great unmentionable of the CIA's early history. So much so, that the Agency's founding charter in the National Security Act of 1947 makes no explicit reference to it. Instead, it included the capacious provision that the CIA may 'perform such other functions and duties' as 'the National Security Council may from time to time direct'.[13] It was fortunate that the Agency's two most significant architects, William Donovan and Allen Dulles, were lawyers by training. For in time the CIA would interpret this clause broadly to encompass all aspects of its cloak-and-dagger activities. 'Taken out of context and without knowledge of history', cautioned General Counsel Lawrence Houston in a letter to Admiral Hillenkoetter, the first Director of Central Intelligence, 'these sections could bear almost unlimited interpretation, provided the service performed could be shown to be of benefit to an intelligence agency or related to national intelligence'.[14] Clark Clifford, a lawyer serving in the Truman administration who supervised the drafting of the Act, recalled that covert action was not explicitly mentioned 'because we felt it would be injurious to our national interest to advertise the fact that we might engage in such activities'.[15]

In spite of, or rather because of, this lack of explicit mandate, CIA covert operations grew exponentially in this period, almost entirely unchecked by official or unofficial mechanisms of accountability. Without the prying eyes of the American media, who from the 1960s onwards would prove the only consistent and credible oversight mechanism for America's mushrooming intelligence and covert operations activities, an intoxicating self-confidence emerged within the CIA and policymaking circles, in the near-wholesale appropriateness and applicability of covert action as a panacea for Cold War contestations. 'They got caught up in a spirit of compelling action', as DeLillo put it.[16] This was in part a legacy of Donovan and the OSS, and indeed Hollywood's commemoration of that legacy. 'Whether myth or not', writes OSS historian Bradley Smith, 'the O.S.S. claim to independent shadow warfare prowess strengthened Washington's belief that it could retain superpower status cheaply and helped lead the United States into making its central intelligence agency into something that it hoped could produce shadow warfare magic'. This effort, Smith concludes, 'to prop up America's position by heavy reliance on shadow warfare rested on sand'. As CIA officer David Atlee Phillips observed in a postmortem of the Bay of Pigs in 1961: 'secret shenanigans couldn't do what armies are supposed to do'.[17] But it was only with the failure at the Bay of Pigs, and the sensational headlines that it inspired, that this lesson began to sink in. Before then, there were very few outside of the CIA willing to review their near-messianic faith in covert operations with a critical eye.

In his withering post-Cold War indictment of excessive US Government secrecy, Senator Daniel Patrick Moynihan argued that many of the excesses and failures of US Cold War foreign policy could be explained by a lack of transparency and accountability.[18] Left to develop in a vacuum, without the robust deliberative processes that characterise a healthy democratic society, the failings of secret policies and institutions, like the numerous unaccountable covert operations conducted by the CIA during the early Cold War, were compounded by being left unchallenged. The successes, on the other hand, were taken as *post hoc ergo propter hoc* justification for the expansion of covert operations and their indiscriminate application. The CIA had succeeded, in operational terms at least, in Italy, Iran and Guatemala, so why wouldn't it succeed again on the beaches of Cuba? Never mind the localised conditions and contingencies of those insurgencies, let alone questions of morality and success considered within the wider, more normative, temporality of the long-term consequences of these actions for American foreign relations and prestige.

It would of course be an over-inflation of the significance of this book's subject to claim that Hollywood alone could have performed the requisite oversight in this period that may have tempered the hubris that led to the Cuban debacle. Oversight comes in many forms, both official (Congress, Supreme Court, official commissions and so forth) and unofficial (media, popular culture, activism and so on). Yet Hollywood's attitude towards the CIA in this period, marked by a deference to secrecy so complete that they failed to make even a single reference to the CIA or its activities for the first decade of its existence, is surely emblematic of a wider deference among the American media in the 1950s towards the birth and development of the US national security state, and the proliferation of US Government secrecy that accompanied it. History is comprised as much by silences and ellipses as it is by the fullness of the historical record. Nowhere is this truer than in the history of secret institutions. This chapter seeks to examine and explain one of those silences. For a while Hollywood turned its back on American espionage while the CIA's covert operations quietly expanded. These two phenomena were intimately connected.

Cherishing Anonymity:
Hollywood and the CIA in the Early Cold War

CIA historian Rhodri Jeffreys-Jones has argued that perhaps Allen Dulles' most significant achievement as Director of Central Intelligence (DCI), 'was that until April 1961 he kept America on his side'.[19] This was doubtless true, but it was not through openness, or public engagement – *Time Magazine* exposés aside. Rather, in a complete inversion of Donovan's post-war public relations campaign, Dulles, and his immediate predecessors as DCI, kept America onside by remaining reticent in the face of public or media enquiry, particularly when the question of covert action was raised. In 1955, for example, he denied a request from Donovan that OSS memoirist Peter Tompkins be allowed assistance and access to wartime files.[20] Similarly, when Polish defector Pawel Monat attempted to publish his memoir, Dulles had its publication delayed for a year 'for non-security reasons'.[21] Although the CIA had used public spokespeople since May 1951, engagement with the media had been very limited. Indeed, as an internal history of their public relations department put it: 'often as much time was spent deflecting media enquiries with the standard "no comment", as answering them'.[22]

Of course there was no shortage of Hollywood enquiries during this period from film and television producers seeking the kind of endorsement and authorisation that Donovan's former OSS had once provided. In the summer of 1951, for example, vice-president of Cavalier Productions Eugene B. Rodney wrote to his friend DCI Walter Bedell Smith asking permission to make a film about the CIA. Smith's polite response was that 'we [the C.I.A.] deliberately cherish anonymity as an aid to effectiveness in this trade', and therefore 'we would be extremely reluctant to have CIA identified in the film'.[23] A similar request from Paramount earlier that year for assistance with their film *My Favorite Spy*, was met with a far less courteous refusal: in a handwritten note at the bottom of a CIA memorandum discussing the film, it is described as 'a lousy picture' that 'makes no reference to CIA' and in consequence 'no further action' was to be taken.[24] The following year, Warner Brothers hit a nerve with the publicity-shy Agency when they requested assistance with a contemporary spy picture. They were told in a mildly threatening tone that the CIA 'would not only be unable to afford such guidance but that we would take every step to discourage the production of a picture which purported to represent current US espionage'.[25]

Occasionally, the CIA were slightly more cooperative, but not without significant reservations. In June 1958, for example, an appointment was 'tentatively made' with Paramount's George Seaton, working on an early version of *The Counterfeit Traitor*. But the CIA officer who arranged the meeting was rebuked for doing so, claiming in his defence that he 'would not have done even this much except that [Paramount] seemed importunate'.[26] More tangible support was afforded to MGM in 1953: they were given access to an unclassified version of a film about the American Flyers. Yet even this relatively minor assistance sparked controversy when Deputy Assistant to the Secretary of Defense, William Godel, exaggerated the relationship in a meeting at the Pentagon. 'I was told yesterday' wrote Tracy Barnes who was then working under Frank Wisner for the CIA's covert action outfit, the Directorate of Plans, 'that you made a remark substantially as follows: "Tracey Barnes' outfit has MGM people making a movie out on the West Coast . . ." . . . We are not having MGM make a film . . . We have merely made available, for possible use, some material which might be included to advantage in MGM's own film.'[27]

Hollywood's relationship with the FBI during this same period could not have been more different. Hoover and his agents developed their already-close ties to Hollywood to make the FBI agent the archetypal hero of the post-war anti-communist crusade. In films like Louis de Rochemont's *Walk East on Beacon* (1952), and *The FBI Story* (1959), and in television series like Ziv Entertainment's *I Led Three Lives*, based on the life of the FBI's star informant, Herbert Philbrick, the FBI agent came to represent what Michael Kackman has described as the 'ideal citizen type' – a morally irreproachable, authoritative, white, male, heteronormative figure of 'appropriate' American citizenship battling Godless communism or the un-American subversive forces of the 'enemy within'.[28] Not only did Hoover work closely with filmmakers to craft a certain image of his organisation, but he also implemented a kind of censorship over depictions he did not like – Darryl F. Zanuck and Samuel Fuller, for example, were forced to remove all references to the FBI in *Pick Up on South Street* (1953) after they aroused the ire of the Bureau's director.[29] Indeed his presence in Hollywood was so ineluctable, that when Alfred Hitchcock attempted to make *Notorious* (1946) without the Bureau's permission, he was told by the Production Code Administration 'that the industry has a kind of "gentleman's agreement" with Mr. J. Edgar Hoover, wherein we have practically obligated ourselves to submit to him, for his consideration and approval, stories which involve the activities of the Federal Bureau of Investigation'.[30]

Figure 3.2 J. Edgar Hoover maintained close ties to Hollywood throughout his tenure as head of the FBI (1935–72). Unlike the CIA, the FBI worked closely with filmmakers to carefully craft their public image and mystique. *Source:* Wikimedia Commons.

The combination of the CIA's passion for anonymity, with Hoover and the FBI's penchant for publicity, highlighted American counter-espionage at home while entirely ignoring America's own covert activities abroad. 'Officially our government has no foreign espionage system in peacetime' declared one television executive of Ziv Entertainment, the same company that had produced the FBI series *I Led Three Lives*, and 'therefore, it is important in our stories that when X goes to a foreign country, it must not be for the purpose of official or unofficial espionage'.[31]

In fact *The Man Called X*, the Ziv TV show under discussion by this executive, was perhaps the closest Americans came in the 1950s to witnessing US covert action onscreen. Agent 'X' was dispatched each week to a different exotic locale, including some strangely prescient 'hotspots' like Nicaragua, Honduras, Iran and Vietnam. One episode was even set around the events of the Iranian coup – although its focus, ironically, was the malevolent designs of the Kremlin rather than scheming CIA agents. Yet in spite of the international character of 'X's' assignments, as Michael Kackman points out, the Ziv producers were very careful to present 'X' as an invited guest of whichever troubled nation appeared in the week's episode rather than an invading CIA agent. In this way, the show presented 'X' as an extension of the spirit of the Truman doctrine – 'to support free peoples who are resisting attempted subjugation'. 'X' was a welcome guest, assisting in democracy promotion, rather than a covert operative plotting the overthrow of a democratically elected government.[32]

Coupled with the frequent appearance of the FBI in the films and TV shows of the decade, the effect of the CIA's absence was to create the impression that invasive spying and espionage were the sole-preserve of the Soviet Union and its agents in America, not American agents abroad. Just as it was before the Second World War, espionage returned to its traditional designation as a wholly 'Un-American' activity.

But what explains this near total compliance by the American media, and particularly the American film industry, to the wishes of the American intelligence community? Why didn't they just make films about the CIA anyway, with or without their permission, or provide representations of the FBI free from the interference of the Bureau itself? This question seems all the more pertinent given the often negative depiction of both agencies in Hollywood movies in the decades that followed.

The simplest answer would indulge in periodisation of the crudest kind, an argument so familiar that it feels almost embarrassing to rehearse it here: the fifties was an era of conformity and consensus, particularly among the mainstream media, while the sixties witnessed the shattering of that consensus and the emergence of numerous radically critical voices – especially where the CIA and US Foreign Policy was concerned. This was, after all, an era before the combined events of the Kennedy Assassination, Vietnam and Watergate broke the back of the 'American Century' and inspired a new generation of journalists like Seymour Hersh and Woodward and Bernstein, or filmmakers like Sydney Pollack and Oliver Stone, who very much defined themselves in opposition to the prevailing logic of US Foreign Policy.

Actually, in reference to Hollywood, such a periodisation is rooted in some basic historical truths, albeit still lacking in nuance as a singular explanation. This was, of course, even up until the end of the 1950s, a period of American film history haunted by the House Un-American Activities Committee (HUAC). Although many of the red-baiting films that are often regarded as synonymous with the politics of Hollywood in this period were produced begrudgingly – in response to HUAC, and on shoestring budgets with little hope of ever turning a profit – that is not to say that it wasn't a period that saw many of the more critical voices in the industry silenced and others dissuaded from taking on controversial political themes.[33] The 'popular front' politics of the 1930s that had inspired John Ford to make *The Grapes of Wrath* and others in the film industry to deal with social problems and oppose fascism in Europe had all but dissipated by the 1950s.[34] Hollywood was always a reluctant mouthpiece for McCarthyism, but criticism of the basic logic of US Cold War ideology and the institutions that put it into practice was almost entirely unheard of. It would have been bold, if not totally impossible, to produce a film representing the US

Government, or one of its institutions, without, at least, obtaining their tacit consent – and even more unthinkable if it were a critical depiction.

On its own, however, such an explanation tends to over-emphasise the external political climate while overlooking practices, mechanisms and institutions that were particular to the film industry – many of which long predated HUAC and McCarthyism. The least coercive or indeed positively affirmative of these was the lasting presence of the documentary or semi-documentary aesthetic, which coveted government endorsement and celebrated the state as the arbiter of historical authenticity.

Andrew Sarris once described the semi-documentary as 'a passing fancy of the American cinema'.[35] For an auteurist like Sarris, perhaps, the semi-documentary produced little of aesthetic note – certainly nothing that would appear in the coveted lists and canons that are the lifeblood of auteurist criticism (although *Citizen Kane* is undoubtedly influenced by, or at least at times is consciously parodying, the semi-documentary aesthetic). But it is surely not without significance that up until the end of the 1950s, the semi-documentary, with its reliance upon government endorsement, was the *only* form in which contemporary American Government institutions and officials found themselves 'realistically' rendered in both cinema and television. The FBI, for example, appeared in semi-documentary television shows like *I Led 3 Lives* and films like *I Was a Communist for the FBI* (1951), Louis de Rochemont's *Walk East on Beacon* (1952) and Mervyn LeRoy's *The FBI Story* (1959). Ziv Entertainment, the production company behind *The Man Called X*, produced numerous semi-documentary espionage television series in the period, including *Behind Closed Doors*, which was based upon the files of John Ford's old boss in Naval Intelligence before he joined OSS, Ellis Zacharias, who introduced each week's episode and thereby leant the show credibility.[36]

All of these semi-documentary espionage films and television shows continued the legacy of filmmakers like John Ford and Louis de Rochemont who had pioneered the documentary aesthetic in the service of the American war effort. Like de Rochemont's *The House on 92nd Street* and *13 Rue Madeleine*, they told their stories through the booming declarative cadences of their Von Voorhis-esque 'Timespeak' omniscient narrators. And like those films also, they continued to celebrate the state as the arbiter of historical authenticity, wearing their endorsements – 'This film was made with the cooperation of the FBI' – as a badge of pride and as testament to their credibility.

There were no semi-documentaries that were made about the CIA during this period, although, as is discussed at the end of this chapter, some producers did try. For the Agency knew that as long as the semi-documentary remained the only form by which American filmmakers and television producers could directly represent their activities onscreen, they could control the narrative about those activities. As it turned out, their decision to 'deliberately cherish anonymity', as Bedell Smith put it, kept their activities off-screen for the majority of the decade. But it would also lead to them relinquishing control of their popular narrative when a new form of representation emerged in the following decade that parodied and opposed the representational constriction of the semi-documentary, particularly its reliance upon government endorsement that increasingly lacked credibility as the Cold War wore on.[37]

Reinforcing the aesthetic choices of filmmakers was the censorious hand of the Production Code Administration (PCA), which virtually ruled out the possibility of any film being made about a government department without their prior approval – thereby helping to sustain the semi-documentary format in this period. Since the early 1930s, the PCA required filmmakers to consult governments, both American or foreign, when representing any public institutions or individuals. In the 1950s the CIA did not need 'to take every step to discourage' productions that sought to represent their activities, because the PCA did it for them – or at least required filmmakers to seek the CIA's endorsement – endorsements that, as we have seen, were entirely unforthcoming. As late as the mid-1960s, when some unlicensed representations of the Agency had already begun to appear, the PCA continued to try to censor critical portrayals.

The makers of *John Goldfarb, Please Come Home* (1965), for example, a screwball comedy based loosely on the Gary Powers incident of May 1960, were severely reprimanded by the Code for their depiction of the CIA, among other branches of the US Government: 'If the portrayal of . . . the head of the C.I.A., should appear to be abusive or offensive in any way in the finished picture, this would be a clear cut Code violation and, in addition, an important matter of industry policy', they were told.[38] By this time, however, the authority of the Code had evidently waned after years of increasing sex, violence and political satire onscreen; *Goldfarb*'s producers left their offensive portrayal in – the C.I.A. chief, named 'Heinous Overreach', spends the majority of the film mumbling and blubbing into the side of a sofa. Perhaps a hangover from the *Bay of Pigs*, he and his organisation are portrayed as farcically incompetent. Significantly, it wasn't the CIA or the PCA that hindered or prevented the film's release, but the University of Notre Dame, who sued the producers in 1964 for the film's defamatory depiction of their American football team, delaying the film's release by a year. In fact, of all the victims of the film's portrayals, the CIA and Notre Dame likely had the least grounds for offence: the film's sexual and racial politics appear almost deliberately offensive – portraying an infantilised Arab sheikh lasciviously chasing around his harem in various oversized gold-plated children's toys. As Jack Shaheen, who has written a comprehensive study of Hollywood's racist portrayals of Arabic culture writes, although Notre Dame deemed the lampoon insensitive enough to have their day in court, 'No Arabs . . . attempted to sue the producers for the gross caricatures and mocking of Islam'.[39]

Figure 3.3 *John Goldfarb, Please Come Home!* (1965) was a screwball comedy based loosely on the Gary Powers incident. It featured a Director of Central Intelligence called 'Heinous Overreach'. The film's release was delayed after the University of Notre Dame sued the producers for its depiction of their football team. *Source:* Parker-Orchard Productions/ Chicago Tribune Photographic Archive.

This brings us to our final, more specific explanation for Hollywood's relative failure to produce unlicensed representations of the CIA until the end of the 1950s: defamation law. In 1964 the US Supreme Court ruled in *The New York Times* v. *Sullivan* case that the First Amendment prohibited a public official from recovering damages for allegedly false statements relating to his official conduct unless the plaintiff could prove that the defendant acted with actual malice, that is with actual knowledge that the statement was false or with reckless disregard as to its truth.[40] Subsequent cases extended this rule to all 'public figures', not just public officials.[41] This represented a monumental change in the law and resulted in far greater freedom to criticise public figures in the US than in virtually any other country in the world. Prior to these rulings, US defamation law was similar to English law, which remains among the most favourable in the world to libel claimants.

The impact of these rulings upon Hollywood's representation of US Government institutions was profound. With legal constraints lifted, the onus was no longer on studios to seek official endorsement or support for their representation of American public officials and institutions. For example, when the producers of the 1976 adaptation of Woodward and Bernstein's *All the President's Men* sought legal assurances for their representation of public officials in the film, they were informed that since *The New York Times* v. *Sullivan*, 'public figures are generally held to have no right of privacy ... this is particularly true where the matter is one of general public interest, such as the Watergate matter we are dealing with here'.[42] Similarly, in 1995, when former CIA Director Richard Helms learnt of a particularly sinister depiction of him in Oliver Stone's biopic – *Nixon*, his lawyers wrote to Stone threatening legal action if the scene was not removed from the final cut. In response, Stone's lawyers cited *The New York Times* v. *Sullivan*, reminding Helms that since he was a public figure, Stone and the filmmakers were entitled to represent him as they saw fit so long as no malice was deliberately intended. In the end the scene, which features a particularly ominous encounter between Helms and Nixon, with the former reciting Yeats' 'Second Coming' while circling Nixon in predatory fashion with black eyes lending him a satanic presence, was indeed cut from the feature. Stone later claimed it was for creative reasons, but it seems unlikely given the dramatic power of the scene that can be found on the DVD extras and on YouTube, and is quite possibly the most sinister depiction of a DCI ever filmed.[43] In any case, the films of Oliver Stone, often criticised for their historical 'creativity', particularly in their depiction of public officials and institutions, would not have been possible without the *The New York Times* v. *Sullivan* ruling.

It is perhaps no coincidence then that the first explicit representations of the CIA in films like *Charade* (1963), *Operation C.I.A.* (1965), *The President's Analyst* (1967) and James Bond's CIA companion – Felix Leiter, directly correlated with this liberalisation of US defamation law. Up until the mid-1960s, however, studio legal departments were careful to avoid any direct mention of CIA officials in screenplays, and indeed any mention of the CIA at all.[44] Even Louis de Rochemont, who had done so much to propagate positive cinematic depictions of America's intelligence agencies, was frustrated in his attempts to represent the CIA in *Man on a String* (1960) through fear of legal repercussions:

> We couldn't get permission from any government bureau to use in our picture, [sic] the fact that we were conducting espionage against the Soviets. So we had to form our own bureau in the thing. We called it the CBI, the Central Bureau of Intelligence, instead of CIA. But we were not allowed to do it. It's against the law to impersonate an agency.[45]

Given the level of caution taken by Hollywood legal departments during the early history of the CIA, the Agency's policy of non-cooperation with

Hollywood amounted not merely to the abeyance of 'official' CIA motion pictures but all pictures featuring the CIA. With government approval required to satisfy the fears of legal departments, the ball remained firmly within the CIA's court, who knew that, unlike today, their refusal to engage with filmmakers would not result in a litany of unapproved films about them. Indeed knowing that the law provided them with protection from unsolicited representations of their activities, the Agency even made requests to studio lawyers to ensure that all explicit references to the CIA were removed from scripts.[46] Knowing that the CIA were invariably uncooperative, Hollywood legal departments in turn often simply avoided the potential need to contact the Agency by instructing filmmakers to use fictional institutions. In this sense, the Hollywood legal departments acted as a form of industry self-censorship – filtering out potentially libelous material before films went into production.

A significant example of this form of industry censorship occurred during the production of Alfred Hitchcock's well-known spy film, *North by Northwest* (1959). In early screenplay drafts of the film, the CIA is explicitly referenced in a number of scenes. Moreover, one of the early working titles for the film was 'The C.I.A. Story'.[47] In fact, a fleeting reference is made to the CIA in the final picture during the airport scene in an exchange between the central protagonist Roger Thornhill, and the CIA chief, who is referred to in the film as 'The Professor':[48]

>   Thornhill: You're police, aren't you? Or is it F.B.I.?
>   Professor: F.B.I. C.I.A. O.N.I. We're all in the same alphabet soup.[49]

Remarkably, this was the first explicit mention of the CIA in a major Hollywood production coming more than a decade after the Agency's creation. Yet by burying the mention of the CIA amidst the alphabet soup of other intelligence agencies, the Professor's employers are deliberately obfuscated. This strategy of representation was no accident. Indeed this line in the script was, in part, written for Hitchcock by MGM's legal department who informed the director to change the dialogue to add the initials of other federal agencies as follows:

>   The dialogue in the script now reads:
>   Thornhill: You're police, aren't you? Or is it F.B.I.?
>   Professor: F.B.I. C.I.A. We're all in the same alphabet soup.
>
>   It is suggested it be changed to read:
>   Thornhill: You're police, aren't you? Or is it F.B.I.?
>   Professor: F.B.I., C.I.A., O.N.I., C.I.C., M.I., A-2. We're all in the same alphabet soup.

R. Monta
P.S. You don't have to use the initials of all six organizations mentioned above. If you were to use only four of them it would do, the idea being to avoid identifying our characters with any given one of those institutions.[50]

In another such script alteration, Hitchcock reshot the conference-room scene in order to replace a sign reading 'Central Intelligence Agency' with a partially concealed flat brass plate, half in and half out of the picture (see Figure 3.4).[51]

As these alterations reveal, studio legal departments who preferred not to approach the CIA, advised filmmakers, through strategies of obfuscation, to avoid any clear and direct representation of the CIA itself. In this manner studio legal departments effectively functioned as a form of censorship upon the representation of American Government. Thus it was not until the liberalisation of defamation law in the 1960s that the CIA began to appear onscreen as anything more than a pseudonym or composite of various American intelligence organisations. Prior to the 1964 Supreme Court ruling in *The New York Times* v. *Sullivan*, defamation law empowered the state rather than the media. The significance of this case in effectively reversing this position cannot be overstated in any consideration of the changing political landscape in Hollywood during the 1960s and its ability to offer direct and controversial representations of the US Government.

Taken together, these aforementioned explanations for Hollywood's political timidity and compliance with the US Government – a reactionary political climate, the lasting influence of the semi-documentary aesthetic and the legacy of cooperation between the industry and government from the Second World War, the influence of the PCA, and a stringent legal environment for

Figure 3.4   Partially concealed plaque from *North by Northwest* (1959). Hitchcock was asked to reshoot the scene that originally contained a plaque reading 'Central Intelligence Agency'. *Source:* Alfred Hitchcock, MGM, 1959.

the representation of public officials – tend to suggest a system of largely self-imposed censorship over Hollywood's representation of government institutions and officials. In other words, the CIA did not need to directly interfere and censor depictions of US covert action because filmmakers and studios were already disciplined into avoiding unlicensed representation. However, simply because the CIA could rely upon a compliant film industry does not mean that it did not, on occasion, interfere with it, or utilise it for its own purposes. Indeed if anything the temptation would be stronger, particularly when it came to utilising cultural means to combat the Soviet Union in the abstract battlefields of culture and ideology. Hollywood had proudly gone to work for the OSS to combat fascism, and it is more than likely that many would have done the same for the CIA against the Soviet Union, which was, by the 1950s, being equated with Nazism.[52] Just because Hollywood was not making movies *about* the CIA does not mean that they weren't making them *for* them. It is this question of the extent of the CIA–Hollywood relationship in fighting the so-called 'cultural cold war' that this chapter will now briefly consider.

Figure 3.5 Allen Dulles (right) with Eric Johnston (left), President of the Motion Picture Association of America, and James A. Mulvey (centre), President of the Society of Independent Motion Picture Producers. *Source*: ACME Telephoto/Baltimore Sun Photographic Archives.

Dangerous Liaisons: The CIA in Hollywood

One way in which the American film industry maintained regular contact with the CIA was through its official representatives in Washington. The PCA was overseen by the Motion Picture Producers and Distributors of America (MPPDA), later renamed the Motion Pictures Association of America (MPAA). The MPPDA was established to advance the interests of the American motion picture industry, in particular through lobbying in Washington. The MPPDA's head from 1945 to 1963 was Eric Johnston, who maintained a close relationship with Allen Dulles and the CIA – keeping them informed of major developments in the film industry that may be of relevance as well as reporting on meetings with key Soviet officials and, indeed, Khrushchev himself.[53] Jack Valenti, who took over the MPPDA's reins from Johnston in 1963, continued to have close contact with numerous DCIs. There is nothing that is particularly surprising or revelatory about this. Indeed it was, in part, Johnston and Valenti's job to have friends in high places, and to represent the American film industry to those friends. It is hardly surprising that Allen Dulles and numerous future DCIs can be counted among them. What is perhaps slightly more controversial is the question over whether the CIA's influence in Hollywood stretched much beyond this official, or semi-official, point of contact with the MPPDA.

In her landmark book on the CIA's clandestine sponsorship of various cultural fronts and institutions during the Cold War, Frances Stonor Saunders identifies a consortium of major motion picture producers that included all the heads of the major studios, who were willing to assist the CIA as well as C. D. Jackson and the Psychological Strategy Board, in their Cold War schemes. Citing a single entry in C. D. Jackson's log journal, she also argues that the CIA devised what they referred to as their 'Hollywood formula' in this period, which sought to utilise the major studies to secure positive depictions of American society in-keeping with their propaganda objectives.[54] But her main piece of evidence in support of these quite sensational claims, are a series of 'movie reports' sent to the CIA suggesting various script-changes to promote a more wholesome and inclusive image of American society. In particular, the reports suggested countering Soviet propaganda claims of the systemic racism of American society by inserting black actors into key scenes in films like the Dean Martin and Jerry Lewis comedy *The Caddy* (1953). Saunders, however, wrongly attributes those reports to CIA officer Carleton Alsop.[55] As the work of film historian David Eldridge has shown, the actual author of the reports, which were indeed sent to the CIA, was Paramount's head of domestic and foreign censorship, Luigi Luraschi.[56]

What this suggests, in contrast to Saunders' vision of the CIA as a 'puppet-master' that secretly controlled many of America's major culture industries during the Cold War, including Hollywood, is an atmosphere of cooperation in which patriotic citizens regularly volunteered information and suggested ideas to the Agency without solicitation. This would be more in keeping with the tradition of cooperation between Hollywood and the OSS during the war, as well as Hoover's FBI. This wartime generation of filmmakers still comprised numerous former OSS officers or others who had performed intelligence work for various services during the war. Those former OSS filmmakers still working in the industry doubtless knew people, on an informal basis, who continued their intelligence careers by joining the CIA. The memories and the friendships did not just fade-away, and in this context it is hardly surprising that Saunders lists filmmakers like Zanuck and Harry and Jack Warner as members of the CIA's 'Hollywood consortium'. They were likely friends with numerous CIA officials anyway, and certainly sympathetic to their mission, having witnessed the birth of America's centralised foreign intelligence and espionage apparatus during the war. Moreover, in the 1950s the CIA was not imbued by popular culture with the same sinister undertones as today. Many liberal artists, writers and filmmakers, people like Peter Matthiessen who established the literary magazine the *Paris Review* with CIA assistance, regarded working for the CIA as 'honorable government service' that offered them the opportunity to travel and write.[57]

This emphasis on cooperation as opposed to coercion is closer in spirit to the arguments of Cold War and CIA historians like Scott Lucas, Hugh Wilford and Helen Laville who argue, in contrast to Saunders, that the CIA's 'Cultural Cold War' operated through what they term 'state-private networks' – a willing collaboration of the often fluid boundaries between private citizens and the state.[58] As with Hollywood's representation of the CIA itself, filmmakers were more than happy to serve their country and assist the CIA, often volunteering information and even proposing plots without solicitation. If the CIA wanted to call upon Hollywood, for whatever reason, they undoubtedly could have. Whether or how frequently they did, however, is a question that is yet unanswered.

One already well-documented example is their covert sponsorship of the animated adaptation of George Orwell's *Animal Farm*. After purchasing the screen rights to both *Animal Farm* and *1984* from Orwell's widow, Sonia Blair, the CIA recruited none other than Louis de Rochemont to produce the film. He in turn hired the British animation studio Halas and Batchelor to make the picture. Orwell's novel was already anti-Soviet, and specifically anti-Stalin in its politics. But it also contained an implicit critique of capitalism as well, or at least all forms of authoritarianism: whether communist, capitalist or fascist. This is reinforced at the end of the novel when the despotic pigs, led by their Stalinist leader Napoleon, sit down at the table drinking and gambling with the humans they had initially overthrown. The 'creatures outside looked from pig to man, and from man to pig, and from pig to man again; but already it was impossible to say which was which'.[59] As Tony Shaw puts it in his chapter

IN SECRECY'S SHADOW

Figure 3.6 The CIA sponsored the 1954 animated adaptation of George Orwell's *Animal Farm*. A number of changes were made to Orwell's original book. Leader of the animal uprising Napoleon, whose character is intended to resemble Stalin, is pictured here. *Source:* John Halas and Joy Batchelor, Halas and Batchelor, 1956.

on the CIA's animated adaptation of *Animal Farm*, 'Orwell's suggestion is that there is no difference between old tyrannies and new, between capitalist exploiters and communist ones.'[60] In the film, significantly, the ending is changed so that the pigs dine alone. Moreover, perhaps owing as much to that much-maligned 'Hollywood-touch' than the ideological predilections of the film's sponsors, the animals stage a final heroic overthrow of Napoleon – ending the film on a far more optimistic note. There were other more subtle changes, too, which have been documented extensively elsewhere, all of which served to heighten Orwell's critique of Stalinism, and diminish his more universal critique of the excesses of both sides of the Cold War.[61]

If this fairly well-known example demonstrates that the CIA were willing to and did utilise Hollywood from time to time, it is also remarkable that it stands as *the only* credible example of its kind, in a period littered with examples of the CIA's covert patronage of the arts. There may have been others, still classified or yet to be unearthed in the archives. *Argo* (2012), the recent

Academy Award winning adaptation of Antonio Mendez's account of the CIA's rescue operation of American diplomats during the 1979 Iranian hostage crisis, popularised at least one other example of the CIA's enlistment of the film industry in a covert action during the Cold War. Moreover, in his sensational 2014 memoir, CIA counsel John Rizzo claimed that the CIA had a longstanding relationship with Hollywood and devoted considerable attention to it. In the mid-1970s, when Rizzo first joined the Agency, 'a veteran CIA liaison with Hollywood' explained the relationship to him this way:

> These are people who have made a lot of money basically creating make-believe stuff. A lot of them, at least the smarter and more self-aware ones, realize what they do makes them ridiculously rich but is also ephemeral and meaningless in the larger scheme of things. So they're receptive to helping the CIA in any way they can, probably in equal parts because they are sincerely patriotic and because it gives them a taste of real-life intrigue and excitement. And their power and international celebrity can be valuable – it gives them entrée to people and places abroad. Heads of state want to meet and get cosy with them. Their film crews are given free rein everywhere, even in places where the U.S. government doesn't normally have it. And they can be the voice of a U.S. message that will have impact with foreign audiences so long as the audience doesn't know it is coming from the U.S. government.[62]

Rizzo goes on to make the sensational claim that one of their Hollywood recruits, an unidentified 'major film star at the time', offered to work for the Agency in exchange for $50,000-worth of cocaine. Rizzo, unsurprisingly, advised against agreeing to the deal.

Rizzo's revelations are a little reminiscent of the sensational claims by game-show presenter and television producer Chuck Barris that he worked as an assassin during the sixties and seventies for the CIA.[63] His account, made into a major motion picture by George Clooney, *Confessions of a Dangerous Mind* (2002), was ridiculed by a CIA spokesman as 'ridiculous' and 'absolutely not true'.[64] Yet Barris's far-fetched secret life aside, there is likely some truth in Rizzo's claims that Hollywood has proved a useful asset for the Agency over the years. This is circumstantially supported by the admittedly few and isolated aforementioned examples, as well as the history of Hollywood's close relationship with the OSS and FBI.

Yet whatever the extent of the Hollywood–CIA relationship during the Cold War, it is unlikely that the CIA ever had a 'Hollywood formula' as Stonor Saunders claims, or that they ever controlled or directed in any kind of systematic fashion, the output of any of the major Hollywood studios and production companies. For one thing, as Hugh Wilford argues, unlike the elite cultural outfits sponsored by the CIA such as *Encounter Magazine* or the *Paris Review*, which relied upon external patronage, the 'massively profitable U.S. movie industry offered no such point of entry, even though its products had great potential for influencing – negatively as well as positively – the international image of America'.[65] For another, the CIA did not need to influence Hollywood's affairs. The American film industry, up until the mid-1960s, wilfully maintained a 'responsible' attitude towards America's Cold War foreign policy due primarily to the self-censorship of the studios both in response to HUAC, and out of the genuine patriotism of studio heads. 'CIA operations in Hollywood, such as they were,' Wilford concludes, 'originated from a shared set of assumptions and goals. Indeed, the irony was that the Agency enjoyed better relations with the movie industry than it did with several organizations it directly funded and controlled'.[66]

When Hollywood did work with the CIA, whether in attempting to bring its activities to the screen or in assisting with covert activities, it was on an ad-hoc, voluntary and cooperative basis. Never did the CIA feel the need to directly censor or compel Hollywood into compliance. To further demonstrate these claims, the remainder of this chapter will examine the attempts by director Joseph Mankiewicz, and his production company Figaro Entertainment, to portray CIA activities during the late 1950s in both film and television. In particular, his 1958 adaptation of Graham Greene's *The Quiet American*, has already, wrongly, been identified by scholars as an example of CIA interference and censorship of a potentially critical cinematic portrayal of their activities in Southeast Asia. A rereading of Mankiewicz's correspondence with CIA officer Edward Lansdale in the context of the film's wider production history, as well as his subsequent attempts to produce a TV series about the CIA, reveals not the malign hand of government interference, but, rather, an obeisant director and production company sympathetic to the CIA and America's Cold War foreign policy aims.

Joseph Mankiewicz's *The Quiet American* (1958)

Graham Greene's *The Quiet American*, first published in the UK in 1955 and released the following year in America, pulled no punches in its withering critique of US foreign policy in Southeast Asia, and its vanguard, the burgeoning covert operations of America's fledgling intelligence community. Its criticism was not taken well by many sections of the press who claimed that Greene, perhaps still bitter after being refused an entry visa to the United States only a few years previously, was simply venting his anti-American spleen. Take, for example, Robert Gorham Davis's précis of the novel for *The New York Times*:

> America is a crassly materialistic and 'innocent' nation with no understanding of other peoples. When her representatives intervene in other countries'

Figure 3.7 Michael Redgrave (left) plays British journalist Thomas Fowler alongside war hero Audie Murphy (right) as Alden Pyle, the eponymous *Quiet American*, in Joseph Mankiewicz's controversial 1958 adaptation of Graham Greene's novel. *Source:* Figaro Entertainment/Academy of Motion Picture Arts and Sciences, Beverly Hills, California.

affairs it causes only suffering. America should leave Asians to work out their own destinies, even when this means the victory of communism.[67]

Alden Pyle, the eponymous 'Quiet American', is (presumably) a CIA officer working undercover in modern-day Vietnam in the twilight of French colonial rule. In keeping with the CIA's low public profile at the time, Greene never actually identifies Pyle as CIA in the novel – rather he is described as an officer in the OSS, 'or whatever his gang were [now] called?'[68] Convinced of the need for a 'third force' in Vietnam, between communism and colonialism, Pyle supplies the Cao Đài leader, General Thế, with plastic explosives, which he then uses in a terrorist bombing of Saigon Square.

Pyle's antagonist is the world-weary opium-smoking British journalist Thomas Fowler. Fowler's Vietnamese lover, Phuong, catches the eye of the young American who wins her over with the promise of marriage, American citizenship and financial security. Fowler, who is unable to match Pyle's proposal because his pious estranged wife refuses him a divorce, grows increasingly embittered by the American's continuous proselytising for a third force and the 'whole pack' of Americans in Vietnam 'with their private stores of

Coca-Cola and their portable hospitals and their wide cars and their not quite latest guns'.[69] Fowler's growing disdain for Pyle culminates in him deciding to help a group of Vietnamese communists assassinate the young American operative. Crucially, however, in Greene's novel it is neither jealousy nor crass anti-Americanism that ultimately motivates his decision to abandon his professional commitment to neutrality and become engagé. Rather, it is only upon realising Pyle's involvement in the bombing, and witnessing 'the torso in the square, the baby on its mother's lap', that Pyle recalls the words of a French Captain in the opium-house: "one has to take sides. If one is to remain human."[70] This point, however, would be lost on Joseph Mankiewicz when he adapted Greene's novel to the screen.

Mankiewicz's alterations to Greene's novel were so significant that he effectively inverted the entire meaning of the book, creating instead a film sympathetic to American intervention in Vietnam. To begin with, Mankiewicz cast the war-hero Audie Murphy as Pyle. As America's most decorated soldier of the Second World War he was an unlikely candidate to embody the iniquities of American foreign policy that Greene found so reprehensible. Yet, from another perspective, he was perfectly cast. 'Audie Murphy accomplishes exactly what I expected him to accomplish', boasted Mankiewicz, 'a nameless symbol of the well-meaning, naïve, bewildered American do-gooder'.[71]

The effect of Murphy's casting was to emphasise the significant changes to Pyle's character that Mankiewicz had already made. Although Greene's Pyle was certainly naïve and idealistic, he was not, in the end, an innocent. Indeed, arguably the entire point of Greene's novel was that while his intentions may have been benign, by placing plastic explosives in the hands of General Thé, his actions and their consequences, and by implication American foreign policy and its consequences, was anything but.

In what was perhaps the most egregious departure from the novel, Mankiewicz exonerated Pyle from any involvement in the Saigon Square bombings. To start with he removed Pyle from any branch of government service. Instead of the CIA, or the OSS 'or whatever his gang were [now] called?', Mankiewicz's Pyle works for the 'Friends of Free Asia', 'an obvious reference to the American Friends of Vietnam' (AFV) – a non-governmental organisation dedicated to promoting American assistance to the Republic of Vietnam and whose role in the production of the film will be discussed in due course.[72] In the aftermath of the bombing, for which Greene clearly holds Pyle responsible, Mankiewicz instead shows Pyle heroically rushing to the aid of the victims with medical supplies whilst Fowler stands by, sniping his aspersions that are later shown in the film as entirely misguided. '"Why don't you shut up, for once in your life why don't you just shut up and help somebody"', Pyle chastises Fowler while rushing to the Vietnamese victims' aid – it was a line entirely of Mankiewicz's invention. As Gene Phillips has shown, the director redistributed 'the audience's sympathy more toward Pyle than Fowler' by appending choice lines to Greene's original prose that were radical departures from Greene's intent and that denied Fowler the last word.[73] The effect, particularly in this central scene, is to not only discredit Fowler's suspicions that Pyle is a government agent, but to also show Pyle, and by extension American aid, as proactive, humane and unconditionally benign – the near total opposite of Greene's intent.

If Pyle had not been involved in the bombing, then who was behind it? In Mankiewicz's final coup de grace over Greene's original meaning, he had the French police inspector Vigot instruct Fowler that he was not only wrong, but quite deliberately misled by the scheming communists who he had helped to kill Pyle. Upbraiding him for his poor French – in the novel Fowler speaks French fluently – Vigot instructs Fowler on the difference between 'plastique', or plastic explosives, and the American word 'plastics', which has nothing to do with the former. The communists had duped Fowler into thinking that the tubs of 'Dialacton', imported by the Americans, were the explosives used in the square. The implication, of course, is that the communists themselves were behind the bombing, not General Thế, and certainly not Alden Pyle. 'More crushing to you than anything else', Vigot tells Fowler with his parting shot 'must be the realization that you've simply been used, that you could be so childishly manipulated. Well if you will pardon my attempt at colloquial English Mr. Fowler, they have made a bloody fool of you.' In Mankiewicz's *Quiet American*, it is no longer Pyle, but Fowler, who is ultimately naïve.

Mankiewicz also continuously overplayed Fowler's jaundiced view of the American, and emphasised his jealousy over losing Phuong to Pyle as his principal motive for helping communist agents dispose of the American. Fowler is played by the British stage-actor Michael Redgrave. Mankiewicz initially wanted Laurence Olivier to play the role. Olivier was initially quite keen on the idea, but wrote to Mankiewicz expressing his concern that, as an Englishman, he may not win any friends in Hollywood by playing either a one-dimensional spokesperson for anti-Americanism, or if, as he suspected, 'the clever cunning of [Mankiewicz] the producer' should reverse the thrust of Greene's polemic, an anti-British caricature. Olivier told Mankiewicz, 'I am quite sure that with a little ingenuity all honours can be satisfied, all "antis" stilled, and all nationalistic heckles patted gently into place and still give them a bloody good picture.'[74] Mankiewicz tried to reassure him. Although he admitted he thought Greene's polemics 'infantile', he also told Olivier: 'I have no more intention of putting a Coca-Cola swilling, crew-cut, Mom-loving, dollar-waving Yankee on the screen, than I have of portraying an umbrella-toting, tea-and-crumpet-and-warm-beer Pukka-stout

Figure 3.8 Michael Redgrave as Thomas Fowler, inspecting a tub of 'dialacton', which he assumes to be the plastic explosive used in the bombing of Saigon Square. In Greene's original novel it is strongly inferred that Alden Pyle imported the 'dialacton' to help the Cao Đài carry out the attack. Mankiewicz, however, altered Greene's story, stressing that no such substance existed, and that the naïve Fowler had been duped by communist agents into believing this story so that he would assist them in their plot to assassinate the American. *Source:* Figaro Entertainment/Academy of Motion Picture Arts and Sciences, Beverly Hills, California.

fella Limey.'[75] But upon reading the screenplay outline, Olivier's fears were confirmed:

> I find that in exonerating Pyle to a large extent, you have obviously added blame to Fowler making him the mental case, so to speak (or is it Greene you are after?) instead of Pyle, who now becomes relatively innocent and rather characterless and Fowler a completely twisted degenerate who has no real cause to resent Pyle except through his jealousy over Phuong and his anti-American obsessions . . . In other words what I feared might take place has done so.[76]

In explaining his reasons for declining the part, Olivier concisely summarised much of the later criticism of the film. Although Greene is certainly not uncritical of Fowler's cynicism in the novel, Mankiewicz over-emphasises it, as well as his crude anti-Americanism and 'patronizing hostility to Pyle'.[77] When Fowler asks for a cigarette and Pyle tells him to keep the pack, for example, Fowler responds brusquely, 'I asked for one cigarette, not economic aid!' Phillips writes, 'Incidents of this kind tend to slant the viewer's sympathies in favor of Pyle more than Greene intends in the book, and serve to foreshadow the film's reversal of the ending.'[78]

Mankiewicz's alterations to the final exchange between Pyle and Fowler that takes place in the latter's apartment – the fateful moment when Fowler finally decides to aid the communists and become an accessory to Pyle's murder – offers the most clear-cut demonstration of how the director sought to emphasise Fowler's jealousy over Phuong as his principal motivation for assisting in Pyle's downfall. First, Mankiewicz's Pyle is nervous and wracked by indecision and premonitory guilt. Greene's Pyle is resigned, having already more-or-less accepted his complicity in the American's murder. While Fowler does pretend 'to leave the final decision of Pyle's fate to God' by telling him not to worry if he cannot make dinner that evening, it is clear from the prose, as well as Fowler's expressed atheism in the novel, that he understood it as a sophist's abnegation.[79]

Second, Greene affords Pyle little dialogue in the scene – 'I didn't hear all that he said, for my mind was elsewhere', narrates Fowler in the novel. Mankiewicz, however, allows Pyle to didactically undermine Fowler – and by implication Greene's – folly: sowing further guilt in Fowler's mind, Pyle reaffirms that he is not working for the US Government, that he doubts General Thé was even behind the bombing, and finally, in what William Bushnell described as Mankiewicz's 'most strident attack on Greene himself ... Pyle accuses the burnt-out Englishman of being "an adolescent boy who keeps on using dirty words all the time because he doesn't want anyone to think he doesn't know what it's all about. You're going to hate this"', Pyle tells Fowler in his parting shot, '"I think you're one of the most truly innocent men I'll ever know."'[80]

Fowler reaches the decision to aid the communists in the film only when Pyle tells him that he is taking Phuong with him to America. For the first time in the scene Fowler's expressions harden. Through Redgrave's accomplished performance, we briefly catch a glimmer of resolve. He takes a book to the window, the signal to the watching communists below that he has agreed to go through with the plot, and reads a passage from *Othello*:

> Though I perchance am vicious in my guess,
> As I confess it is my nature's plague
> To spy into abuses, and oft my jealousy
> Shapes faults that are not.[81]

IN SECRECY'S SHADOW

Figure 3.9 Fowler pleads with Phuong, played by Italian actress Giorgia Moll. Mankiewicz played up Fowler's jealousy of Pyle's relationship with Phuong in the film so that his principal motive for assisting the communists in Pyle's murder is not because of his political conscience, as it was in Greene's novel, but because of his personal resentment of Pyle stealing his girlfriend. *Source*: Figaro Entertainment/Academy of Motion Picture Arts and Sciences, Beverly Hills, California.

Mankiewicz here replaces a passage from Arthur Hugh Clough's 'Dipsychus' used by Greene to condemn Pyle's hubris. Then we hear a voiceover from Fowler – 'I wanted Phuong and I wanted the world to be like it was before *he* came.' As Gene Phillips writes, 'Fowler's motivation is much more ambiguous in the novel, where he says, 'I wanted him to go away quickly and die. Then I could start life again – at the point where he came in.' This ambiguity in the book was Greene's intention', continues Phillips, 'since he wanted the reader to realise that Fowler was to some extent subconsciously prejudiced against Pyle because of their mutual involvement with the same girl. Because of this very ambiguity Fowler will never be able to feel self-righteous about Pyle's death', in the same way that Pyle self-righteously proclaims in the novel that the Saigon Square victims 'died in the right cause', a moment after Fowler gives the fatal signal from his window.[82] Mankiewicz's Fowler, by contrast, as his use of the passage from *Othello* makes abundantly clear, is quite consciously motivated by jealousy.

Figure 3.10 French inspector Vigot interrogates Fowler in the final scene of *The Quiet American*. Mankiewicz significantly altered the ending of Greene's novel: in the film version, Fowler is not reunited with Phuong after Pyle's death, and he is left wracked by guilt for his participation in the American's death. Some of these changes may have been made by the director in order to appease Hollywood's censor, the Production Code Administration, which recommended that immoral acts should not go unpunished. *Source:* Figaro Entertainment/Academy of Motion Picture Arts and Sciences, Beverly Hills, California.

At the end of the novel Fowler is struck by a sense of remorse, having been reunited with Phuong, and fearing that he may have been, to an extent, subconsciously motivated by jealousy rather than purely humanitarian concerns. In the final line of the book, returning to the Catholic motifs that often defined his oeuvre, Greene ends with Fowler's contemplation: 'Everything had gone right with me since he had died, but how I wished there existed someone to whom I could say that I was sorry.'[83] In the film, however, Mankiewicz excises the opening, more sanguine clause, having Fowler say merely, 'I wished there existed someone to whom I could say I was sorry.' Unlike the novel, everything had not gone right for Fowler since Pyle had died. Phuong leaves him in the film, and, with the added humiliation of being disabused of all his pretenses by Vigot, he is left utterly despondent, and alone.

What explains this remarkable transformation of perhaps the first critique of CIA covert action by an English or American author? Recent scholarship on the film suggests a fairly unequivocal answer to this question: it was the CIA who influenced Mankiewicz to alter the novel.[84] The smoking-gun evidence for this claim is a letter to Mankiewicz from the legendary Cold Warrior and CIA operative Edward Lansdale, often presumed to be the real-life model for Pyle, although Greene always adamantly denied this. In a telling section of the letter, dated 17 March 1956, Lansdale advises Mankiewicz to 'go right ahead and let it be finally revealed that the Communists did it after all'.[85] Further credence is leant to the idea that the CIA were instrumental in altering the novel's meaning by the claims of Robert Lantz, vice-President of Mankiewicz's Figaro production company. According to his account he met with Allen Dulles at CIA headquarters in Langley who then 'cut the political red-tape to make it possible, if not "easy", to produce a picture with on-location work in Vietnam'.[86] It is difficult to gauge the extent of Dulles' involvement, as there does not appear to be any documentary record of this conversation, nor any of the subsequent assistance he may have afforded the filmmakers. Certainly Lantz's claims are not beyond the bounds of possibility, far from it. Indeed it is unlikely that the Diem government would have given Mankiewicz permission to film such a controversial novel without some kind of official sanction from his American allies. Moreover, as will shortly be discussed, many of the people that Mankiewicz met during the production either knew Dulles, or were closely associated with the CIA. What does seem apparent from the documentary record, however, is that Lansdale's and Dulles's involvement with the picture has been taken out of context from the film's wider production history. Returning their involvement to that context reveals a far more complex set of explanations for Mankiewicz's decision to change Greene's novel.

First, there is Mankiewicz himself. In the rush to emphasise the importance of the Lansdale correspondence, scholars like Jonathan Nashel, whose research uncovered the letter, appear to have lost sight of the fact that Lansdale is confirming changes to the novel that Mankiewicz had *already made*. For this reason alone, at least some of the culpability for the changes should be shifted from the CIA's to Mankiewicz's shoulders. From his correspondence with Laurence Olivier, along with other comments he made, it is clear that Mankiewicz was irked by Greene's anti-Americanism, despite his evident respect for his literary talents: 'Greene's inability to keep what must be an uncontrollably deep and bitter and consuming, but nevertheless child-like rage (and equally child-like Catholicism) from permeating his work – much like a chef who will insist upon spraying his finest dishes with insecticide before serving – is a major frustration in the literary world', Mankiewicz confided in Olivier.[87]

In a 1973 interview Mankiewicz further reflected that he thought the book bitter, and dominated by an absurd anti-Americanism. You get the impression that some idiotic bureaucrat from the State Department had refused a visa to Graham Greene who then out of anger decides to write a novel about an absolutely imbecilic American ... a virgin who drinks Coke all day while shipping plastic materials to Indochina to make bombs.[88]

In 1952 Greene was denied a visa under the McCarran Act due to his brief membership in the communist party during his youth. In his autobiography he claims he joined as a joke, and then cancelled his membership soon after when he realised he was not entitled to a free trip to Moscow and Leningrad.[89] As Gene Phillips points out, however, Greene's anti-Americanism was likely just as motivated by his vehement reaction to McCarthyism and the HUAC investigations. The same year as being denied his visa, Greene wrote an open letter in defence of his friend, Charlie Chaplin, recently exiled from the United States, which condemned HUAC's absurd inquisition in Hollywood.[90] In any case, Mankiewicz, despite his equally vocal opposition to HUAC, clearly thought that Greene had overstepped the mark with his anti-American sentiment in the novel.[91]

But Mankiewicz, despite being 'something of a dissident within the Hollywood community', was also au fait with its operating strictures. He knew, given the political climate in Hollywood, still under scrutiny by HUAC, that a faithful adaptation of Greene's novel could not get made. '"Joe would never have bent for political reasons"', insisted Mankiewicz's wife, '"nobody in Hollywood would listen at the time"' to the making of a film that skewered American actions abroad.'[92]

Along with the political climate there was also the continued presence and influence of the Production Code Administration (PCA). Indeed, as I have argued elsewhere, Mankiewicz's desire to pre-empt the PCA's inevitable objections to Greene's novel appears to explain many of the changes he made to the story.[93] Upon receiving the novel's proofs, in November 1955, Mary Pritchett and Price Chatham of Figaro productions anticipated the Code's objections, in particular Pyle's designation as a government agent, and his adulterous relationship with Phuong.[94] Pritchett and Chatham suggested resolving the problem by removing Pyle from any official government service, and having Phuong's sister live in the apartment with her and Fowler so as not to portray the two living together out of wedlock, which was strictly forbidden by the Code. Having already anticipated these objections, Mankiewicz telegrammed Geoffrey Shurlock at the PCA to inform him that he had bought the rights to Greene's novel and 'as always ... before undertaking a project I want the blessings of your office of the conditions upon which I can achieve said blessedness'.[95]

Shurlock replied with a series of potential Code violations that would have to be rewritten from the novel. 'Most serious of all is the fact that your sympathetic

Figure 3.11　Hollywood censor Geoffrey Shurlock, head of the Production Code Administration from 1954 to 1968. Shurlock replaced the puritanical Joseph Breen and oversaw the relaxing of censorship during his tenure. Nevertheless, his office played a significant role in influencing Mankiewicz to dramatically alter Greene's original novel *The Quiet American*, when transferring it to screen. *Source:* Baltimore Sun Photographic Archive.

lead throughout the story is living openly in adultery with a Vietnamese girl', he wrote, confirming the filmmakers' prognosis. 'This immoral relationship is presented most attractively, is at no point shown to be wrong, and is portrayed in much greater detail than should be approved under the requirements of the Code.'[96] He also warned, predictably, that the scenes from the novel depicting opium use and prostitution would not be acceptable under the Code. Finally, Shurlock advised that 'it would be necessary to portray the activities of the young American diplomat in such a manner that the finished picture would not be open to the criticism that it represents unfairly a prominent institution such as the Foreign Service of the United States, or any branch of it'.[97]

Mankiewicz's response to Shurlock's objections, written more than two months *before* he made contact with Lansdale, outlined almost all of the major revisions he would make to the novel:

It is my purpose, for your information, to make Pyle a thoroughly attractive young man. I shall remove him, of course, from any branch of the United States government service this will resolve any possible unfavorable portrayal of one of our governmental employees, and should remove your objection on that point.

To get back to Fowler. His marriage has ceased to exist long before he meets Phuong. There will be no doubt that it is his wife who has terminated their marriage relationship – because of his worthlessness as a human being – and her refusal to give him a divorce will be clearly indicated as a refusal to let him bring similar unhappiness to another woman. Fowler's request for the divorce will not be treated as if he wanted it truly for the purpose of marrying Phuong. He will be driven to the request in desperation – by his fear that Pyle, who has offered Phuong marriage in all honesty and love, will take her away from him. He will lie, evade, and use his own offer of marriage as a device to manipulate Phuong away from Pyle. He will represent the socially unacceptable concept of marriage as against Pyle's most worthy and acceptable one. He will not succeed. In my film treatment, Phuong will reject Fowler at the finish. Pyle, even in death, will have accomplished his purpose, he will have awakened Phuong to the necessity, in life, for the unselfishness of love and the security of marriage. Fowler will remain a bitter, hopeless man – completely and utterly alone.[98]

Mankiewicz's eagerness to please Shurlock further demonstrates his own personal antipathy towards Greene's novel. He did not require a heavy-handed PCA to encourage him to make these changes. With or without the Code, Mankiewicz would have bowdlerised Greene's novel in much the same way. Nevertheless, the nature of the Code's objections demonstrates why a faithful adaptation of Greene's novel was simply not possible in 1950s Hollywood, no matter how radical the director. *Any* film critical of the CIA, or indeed any branch of the United States Government, was unlikely to be made. Whether pre-empting the Code, or responding to its strictures, Hollywood self-censored politically subversive material and in the process kept the CIA off-screen. Without the Agency's co-operation or at least consent, which was never forthcoming, any explicit representation of the CIA was a clear-cut Code violation.

Mankiewicz had clearly already taken the decision to transform Greene's novel at the very earliest stages of pre-production. Whatever the extent of Lansdale's or indeed Allen Dulles's influence on the production, it served only to confirm and encourage Mankiewicz's freely arrived-at adaptation. Nevertheless, their involvement was not inconsequential, particularly when it came to the practical requirements of making a potentially controversial film in the politically volatile atmosphere of Ngô Đình Diệm's Vietnam. By all accounts the production was a fraught affair, beset by misfortune. Along with Vietnam's political climate, Mankiewicz had to contend with numerous illnesses in his cast and crew and other unexpected delays, such as and most significantly, the fact that Audie Murphy contracted appendicitis halfway through shooting.[99] But the lengthy delays allowed Mankiewicz the time to smooth over any potential objections to his film from the political classes, and deepen his relationship with many of the overt and indeed covert American operatives working in Vietnam at the time. He would meet many 'Quiet Americans' along the way.

Mankiewicz was introduced to a number of American and South Vietnamese officials not by Dulles, directly at least, but by Angier Biddle Duke, then President of the International Rescue Committee (IRC), an American humanitarian aid and development nongovernmental organisation.[100] With the help of Robert McAllister, head of IRC operations in Saigon, Duke furnished Mankiewicz with much of the information, contacts and access he needed to film in Vietnam. 'It is the positive and creative aspects of the struggle for Vietnamese national independence', Duke told McAllister, 'that I hope he will get the feeling of'.[101] It was indeed ironic that Mankiewicz should choose the IRC as his guide in Vietnam; they were precisely the kind of US-aid organisation that Greene had critiqued in *The Quiet American*. Moreover, as in Greene's novel, its members were intimately connected with the CIA, often serving as a front for CIA operations. In 1955, for example, the CIA funnelled money through the IRC to covertly sponsor a psychological warfare operation known as Operation Brotherhood that placed doctors, nurses and other relief workers in South Vietnam to help sure-up civilian morale at the end of French colonial rule. The operation was conceived and directed by none other than Edward Lansdale.[102]

Another IRC official that worked closely with Mankiewicz on the production was Alfred Katz – 'a freelance New York publicist and AFV [American Friends of Vietnam] member with social connections to Mankiewicz and his wife, and an IRC volunteer'.[103] Katz effectively served as Mankiewicz's envoy to the Diệm regime throughout the production. Katz, who worked with Biddle Duke out of the IRC's New York office, met Mankiewicz in February 1956 and gleefully reported that the director at once 'fell in love with Vietnam and the Vietnamese and I think we have a very important ally in someone as bright and talented as Joe Mankiewicz'.[104] Katz flew to Saigon that summer and met Lansdale the day after he arrived to discuss the project. Lansdale suggested that Katz should make a point of contacting the President in the first instance, telling him that once the project was approved by Diệm, 'everything else falls into line'. Katz approached Diệm the very next day, and dropped Mankiewicz's outline off at the American ambassador's office as well for good measure. He later heard through an embassy source that 'he [Diệm] was very pleased with

Mankiewicz's handling of the book'.[105] Lansdale helped set up a face-to-face meeting between Katz and Diệm. Katz, along with Duke and other members of the IRC, assured the President that Mankiewicz intended to transform Greene's novel 'with the aim of presenting to the world the progress made by the Vietnamese people in their struggle for freedom and independence'.[106] Convinced of the film's propaganda value, Diệm extended his full cooperation to the production. As Lansdale had predicted, once the President had given them the green light, all the other government departments fell in-line. Upon arrival in Saigon in January 1957, Mankiewicz was issued with a letter of introduction from the Special Secretary of the Presidency that requested all organisations to 'fully cooperate with and give all possible assistance' to his film company.[107]

Lansdale and the IRC may have made it easier, or indeed possible, for Mankiewicz to shoot the film in Saigon, but did they influence the actual content of the film in any way? As already stated, it is clear from the chronology of Mankiewicz's correspondence, that the fundamental decision to invert Greene's anti-Americanism had been made by the director long before he contacted Lansdale or anyone at the IRC. But Katz, Lansdale and others did offer small suggestions along the way that helped Mankiewicz build his case against Greene. For example, when Mankiewicz asked Katz whether there was anything in Greene's critique of American economic imperialism, he responded,

> America's economic stake in Vietnam is nil. There are two main exports from Vietnam – rice and rubber. America has a surplus of rice ... As far as rubber is concerned, our synthetics have answered any need for the small amount they could ship to America. Now we could never be accused of trying to be the colonial power to replace the French.[108]

Katz had missed the point of Greene's critique. Namely, that America's economic stake in Vietnam was in opening its markets to American consumer goods, not in pilfering its natural resources. This was part of the basis upon which Greene drew his distinction between old-style European colonialism, of which he was an advocate, and American 'Coca-Colonisation'. Mankiewicz, however, was undoubtedly reassured by Katz's argument for American economic disinterestedness in the region, which shored up his depiction of Pyle as entirely innocent. Yet despite this and other small suggestions made by the IRC and Lansdale, including the idea of blaming the Saigon Square bombing on the communists, Mankiewicz was always the driving force behind the changes to Greene's novel – seeking evidence and assurances to support the alterations he was already intent on making. If anything, Mankiewicz went too far, even for the IRC. 'Fowler troubled me so much', Katz wrote to Mankiewicz. 'The British have charm, too, Joe ... I'd like to see Fowler more likeable.'[109]

Along with the IRC, numerous other 'Quiet Americans' helped shape Mankiewicz's political horizons while filming in Vietnam. A telling document in his private papers, for example, is a cocktail list he drew up to celebrate the end of shooting. Members of various American 'nongovernmental' organisations such as the US Operations Missions (USOM), the Michigan State University Vietnam Advisory Group (MSU) and the Military Assistance Advisory Group (MAAG) dominate the list, along with US embassy officials and members of the Diệm regime.[110] Alden Pyle would have felt right at home in such company.

Not all of the 'Quiet Americans' that Mankiewicz met in Saigon were happy with the idea of bringing Greene's novel to the screen. Arthur G. McDowell, for example, the Executive Secretary-Treasurer of the Council against Communist Aggression, was aghast when he received news that Mankiewicz was to adapt what he described as 'Graham Greene's propaganda novel' – 'a one-sided caricature of American diplomatic and financial effort abroad on behalf of peace and liberty and against the Communist enemy ... [W]ere we interested in helping the Communist cut the throat of the freedom-loving people of Indo-China and eventually here,' he chided President of United Artists Arthur Krim, 'we would have no hesitation in recommending Mr Greene's book as the basis for a movie production by the Soviet film industry, aimed to distrust our own purposes and abandon the will to resist and help others resist the Communist aggression'.[111] Krim and Mankiewicz tried to reassure McDowell by informing him of their proposed changes to the novel that had been endorsed by the South Vietnamese Government. 'I shall await with interest the gallant attempt of United Artists and Mr Mankiewicz to draw off Mr Greene's bile and leave something constructive as well as artistic, but I remain frankly skeptical,' replied McDowell. His scepticism, however, didn't stop him forwarding to Krim a suggested alteration to Greene's novel from his friend C. Dickerman Williams that would 'show the American dying for the Diem movement, with an epilogue in which President Diem lays a wreath upon his grave. In other words, let Pyle be to the South Vietnam Government what John Reed was in its early days to the Soviet Government.'[112]

Mankiwicz did not include Dickerman Williams's suggestion, but his close contact with so many Alden Pyles during the production indeed transformed his politics vis-à-vis *The Quiet American* from anti-Greene to pro-Diệm. When the film premiered at The Playhouse Theatre in Washington, DC a year later, the proceeds from the gala performance were donated to the Republic of South Vietnam. In attendance were, among other distinguished guests: Angier Biddle Duke and numerous senior members of the IRC, including Mrs Frederick Reinhardt, who chaired the benefit performance and whose husband was the former US ambassador to Vietnam; Senator Mike Mansfield, ironically perhaps the most vocal critic of the CIA in Congress during the 1950s, but a key advocate at the time for the Diệm regime, although he who would later change his position and oppose the war in Vietnam; and Senator John McClellan.[113] Before the performance they attended a pre-theatre buffet reception hosted by the Vietnamese Ambassador whose wife took his place entertaining the esteemed guests after he was taken sick. When they arrived at the theatre, '[l]ights flooded the entrance; American flags flew from standards with the red and gold Viet Nam flags and as cymbals clashed and gongs intoned', guests were met by 'Washington's most famous hostess', Perle Mesta, alongside members of the IRC. 'Inside, Oriental music gave way to the modern tunes of Frankie Tamm and his accordion playing in the foyer. The first 200 ladies at the theater were presented with tiny red and yellow corsages distributed from upturned Viet-Namese coolie hats by flower vendors who were wives of the Viet Nam embassy staff, wearing their native costumes.'[114]

When news of the performance reached Greene, he was incensed: 'Far was it from my mind when I wrote "The Quiet America," that the book would become the source of profit to one of the most corrupt governments in Southeast Asia.'[115] Lansdale, by contrast, was jubilant: 'Just a little note to tell you that I have seen the motion picture, "The Quiet American," and that I feel it will help win more friends for you and Vietnam', he 'gleefully reported to Diệm'. He continued, 'When I first mentioned this motion picture to you last year, I had read Mr. Mankiewicz's "treatment" of the story and had thought it an excellent change from Mr. Greene's novel of despair. Mr. Mankiewicz had done much more with the picture itself, and I now feel that you will be very pleased with the reactions of those who see it.'[116]

It is tempting to conclude on the basis of Lansdale's correspondence that the CIA, or at least one of its most famous sons, was ultimately responsible for Hollywood's bowdlerisation of Greene's novel. But to do so is to misunderstand the subtler, more insidious nature and practice of American power, propaganda and ideology. As opposed to a top-down, coercive understanding of the operation of US ideology and power, and specifically the way in which the CIA sort to influence Cold War culture, the story of *The Quiet American*'s journey from novel to screen affirms Scott Lucas's notion of 'state-private networks', which goes 'beyond the simple notion of "control"' to assess, in Giles Scott-Smith's Gramscian formulation of it, the 'complex set of norms in the domain of ideas' that 'are solidified through the influence of specific elite networks operating in the interests of a ruling group'.[117] The values and ideals that made Greene's novel unacceptable to the CIA were the same values and ideals that made it unacceptable to Joseph Mankiewicz, and indeed Angier Biddle Duke, the IRC, Edward Lansdale and the Production Code Administration. At no point did the CIA, or indeed any other arm of the American Government, feel the need to intervene, censor or direct Mankiewicz into producing his version of *The Quiet American* that excised Greene's indictment of CIA covert action and American aid in South Vietnam. Yes they encouraged, facilitated, promoted and helped Mankiewicz cut through the red tape involved in getting a film made in Saigon, but the desire and imagination to counter Greene's critique existed from the start, and was shared by all.

This is not to say that the CIA, or the US Government, had no influence over the film's production, but merely to rethink the way in which that influence operates. The fundamental idea undergirding the 'state-private networks' concept is that the boundary between the US Government and private American citizens or private citizens' groups is porous. This can be understood at a practical level in terms of the 'revolving door', whereby former government employees return to non-government life, and vice versa, or more abstractly, but no less accurately, in terms of Scott-Smith's Gramscian understanding of it, or Godfrey Hodgson's related notion of 'the establishment', where 'powerful men who know each other . . . who share assumptions so deep that they do not need to be articulated; and who continue to wield power outside the constitutional or political forms . . . preserve the status quo'.[118]

Mankiewicz's *Quiet American* provides a perfect exemplification of the fluidity that existed in 1950s America between the state and the private sphere, and how this formulation helped to serve the ideological interests of the United States during the Cold War. In a letter to Allen Dulles by IRC vice-president Clairborne Pell, Mankiewicz's name appears in the margin as part of a list of the committee's board of directors – he joined the IRC after working with them on the film. It is the only time his name appears in the CIA's records. A quick glance at some of the other names alongside his, however, reveals not only that the company that Mankiewicz kept when making the film had firm links to the Agency, but also the often-blurred boundaries between the CIA, private citizens and the conduct and promotion of American aid and ideology in South Vietnam: Leo Cherne, CBS news-anchor, chairperson of the IRC and future member of the President's Foreign Intelligence Advisory Board and the Intelligence Oversight Board; Mrs Kermit Roosevelt, Secretary of the IRC and wife of CIA operative Kermit Roosevelt – key architect of the Iranian coup and supposed inspiration for Greene's choice of title for the novel after Kim Philby dubbed him the 'Quiet American'; William J. Vanden Heuvel, chairperson of the Executive Committee for the IRC, former protégé of William Donovan in the OSS and partner in his law firm; Christopher Emmet, an MI6 and CIA asset; Samuel Goldwyn, Hollywood mogul; William Merriam, future vice-president of ITT who was later enlisted by the CIA to help overthrow the Chilean President Salvador Allende; George Skouras, Hollywood mogul and former OSS officer; and Ellis Zacharias, former deputy director of US Naval Intelligence and star of the NBC espionage docudrama series *Behind Closed Doors*. These are just a handful of the names of the ostensibly private citizens who had links to American intelligence but nevertheless acted out of their own volition and shared experience in support of American ideology. CIA historian Hugh Wilford once wrote that it 'might well have been the case that the CIA tried to call the tune; but the piper did not always play it nor the audience always dance to it'.[119] In the case of Mankiewicz's adaptation of *The Quiet American*, the CIA did not call the tune, because it did not need to. The men and women who shaped the production were already playing it.

Figaro Entertainment's Unmade CIA Semi-documentary TV Series

While making *The Quiet American*, Mankiewicz's production company, Figaro Entertainment, was also working behind the scenes to produce the first officially sanctioned semi-documentary CIA television series. The proposed series was the brainchild of Mary Bancroft who had worked for Allen Dulles in OSS. They became lovers while in Switzerland during the war and remained close friends for the rest of their lives.[120] Bancroft first suggested the idea of producing a CIA television series to Figaro executive Robert Lantz in early January 1956 – about the same time that pre-production work began on *The Quiet American*. Figaro was part owned by the television network NBC. Mankiewicz regarded television as a cheaper and quicker medium that would allow his younger protégé directors to hone their skills and try out new ideas without the risks involved in a full-length feature.[121] Thus Figaro was in the market for television ideas and Bancroft, for her part, regarded the combination of 'Mankiewicz's reputation and this NBC association' as a very attractive proposition that may 'open a door for a hearing on the matter' from the CIA.[122]

Bancroft floated the idea of a CIA series that would be along the same lines as other semi-documentaries made in cooperation with various government services, such as the FBI and the Air Force, that helped 'create in the public mind an impression of their usefulness'. Bancroft noted that the most successful of these 'had a narrator in whose mouth can be put whatever ideas the services in question wishes to get across'. The Von Voorhis-inspired 'Timespeak' omniscient narrator, a key identifying feature of the semi-documentary, was, for Bancroft, little more than a mouthpiece for government.

The publicity-minded Allen Dulles, who had helped Donovan sell the American public on the idea of a central intelligence agency a decade previously, was initially keen on the idea. Since the mid-1950s the Agency had come under a degree of Congressional scrutiny, and hence the need for positive public relations became more urgent. Senator Joseph McCarthy was famously suspicious of Dulles' organisation of well-heeled Ivy League liberals, whom he suspected of leftist sympathies, and mounted one of his anti-communist crusades against the Agency – a campaign that ultimately failed and would prove the beginning of the end for McCarthy. Senator Mike Mansfield was also a vocal critic of the Agency in the mid-1950s, repeatedly urging Congress to perform better oversight of their activities.[123] Ironically, Mansfield was an admirer of Mankiewicz's *Quiet American* and attended the benefit performance in Washington. Although relatively subdued compared to the Congressional ire the CIA would encounter in subsequent decades, it was enough to give Dulles cause for concern for the Agency's public reputation and its vulnerability to attack. Bancroft and Lantz sought to exploit that vulnerability by offering Dulles a TV series that would 'serve', as Lantz put it, a 'directly useful purpose to them' in battling Mansfield in Congress.

Despite his enthusiasm for the series, Dulles did, however, give a 'flat "no" on one point – namely that current material could under no circumstances be used'.[124] Bancroft was happy to focus on past events, and drew up a proposal for a more abstract series on intelligence, with each episode focusing on a given aspect of intelligence such as 'espionage', 'counter-espionage', 'sabotage' and 'psychological warfare'. She would then furnish each themed episode with historical examples from the American Revolution to the Second World War. This historical approach was in-keeping with Dulles's public relations strategy, which, as with his *Time Magazine* cover story, stressed the long lineage of the CIA to normalise and naturalise it as part of the American system.[125] Bancroft sung from the same hymn sheet. Conceptualising the show, she noted that it would proceed from the 'fundamental concept' that 'intelligence work is an extension of life, not a thing apart'. 'A spy notices things,' she continued. 'Everyone notices things ... Therefore everyone is a spy.'[126] Rather than present the CIA as an essentially modern bureaucracy – an aberration of the Cold War – Bancroft sought, in keeping with both Dulles and Donovan's approach to public relations, to invent a tradition for American intelligence that would assuage fears that the CIA was an 'American Gestapo' and thus a threat to the American creeds of democracy and transparency. Who could argue with the concept of American intelligence if intelligence was used by George Washington himself? In this manner the historical approach not only avoided disclosing contemporary operations, but also served a vital public relations function.

OSS stories in particular would be easy to tell – 'this city is crawling with ex-OSS agents just itching to have their personal experiences dramatized so that they can brag themselves into a release of all the sufferings their wartime secrets caused them when for once in their lives they had to keep their mouths shut', she wrote disparagingly to Alfred Katz, whose work on *The Quiet American* had made him Figaro's unofficial liaison with Washington.[127] Katz later suggested 'starting the series off with a special program dealing with Operation Sunrise', the famous surrender of German troops in Northern Italy, which was personally negotiated by Dulles when he was in OSS. Like

Ellis Zacharias's role on Ziv Entertainment's *Behind Closed Doors*, Dulles would introduce and narrate the episode.[128]

Indicative of the near-fetishistic regard with which government and especially CIA endorsement was held, Bancroft and Figaro appeared more interested in gaining permission to attribute their programme to the CIA than the actual authenticity of the content. After rejecting several of Bancroft's suggestions for the wording of the attribution, Lantz proffered his own formulation: 'The producers wish to acknowledge their indebtedness to the C.I.A. for their advice and counsel.' But, Lantz quickly added, 'all that matters is to use the words CENTRAL INTELLIGENCE AGENCY, Washington D.C. in large print. It would work if we said "This series has been declared utterly incomprehensible and absurd by ALLEN DULLES, brother of JOHN FOSTER DULLES, etc . . ." What we need is the optical illusion of attribution.'[129] So unconcerned was Lantz by the accuracy of the show, so long as they could attribute it to CIA, that he even suggested that the Agency may use the series to disseminate misinformation, or as a 'testing ground for certain reaction, both here and abroad; or merely as part of a recruiting drive for special manpower'.[130] Despite the obvious and numerous public relations coups that the semi-documentary form provided various institutions of government during the 1950s, government endorsement was always conceived, at least by pioneers of the form like Louis de Rochemont, as a means to an end. Although certainly naïve in their uncritical communication of state-sourced narratives, the close contact with, for example, J. Edgar Hoover and the FBI was undertaken for the purpose of getting the inside-scoop. With Bancroft and Figaro's proposed CIA TV series, however, government endorsement appeared to be the end in itself. The epistemological barter that the semi-documentary had made, which premised its authenticity on the basis of access to state records and officials, was being undone by the slavish devotion to state endorsement that such an approach engendered.

Bancroft contacted CIA Inspector General Lyman Kirkpatrick in early June. After leaving the CIA in 1965, Kirkpatrick would become a key public spokesman for the Agency, defending it against a rising tide of public criticism from the late 1960s onwards. Although he wrote in his 1968 memoir that 'when I resigned from the Central Intelligence Agency . . . the furthest thing from my mind was to write a book about the CIA', he was evidently already publicity-savvy long before his retirement. Approving Bancroft's series, he drew up a list of conditions upon which CIA cooperation with the producers may rest. Among them, was the CIA's right to review all scripts and films before exhibition, and the guarantee that producers will ensure that 'productions will be dignified and tend to reflect credit on the intelligence profession'.[131]

The following month, Bancroft was the houseguest of Dulles and his wife in Washington, giving her the opportunity to discuss the idea with the CIA chief in depth. Dulles arranged a meeting between Bancroft and the CIA's head of public affairs, Colonel Grogan. The Colonel appeared keen on the idea, and foresaw that the series would potentially set a precedent for other producers to work with the Agency. As it happened, CBS were breathing down NBC's neck with their own proposed programme. Grogan's main cause for concern was that in helping an American television production company, the CIA may be perceived to have violated their charter, which forbade them from operating domestically. Grogan suggested that the attribution could cite the section of the 1947 National Security Act and then explicitly state that their cooperation with the production in no way violated it. Technically, the Act prevents the CIA from having 'police, subpoena, or law enforcement powers or internal security functions', which does not preclude the possibility of an open dialogue with the media for the purposes of public relations, so long as they weren't engaging in a domestic security or surveillance operation. Nevertheless, with Senator Mansfield seeking to open up the Agency to Congressional scrutiny, Grogan and Dulles preferred to err on the side of caution, in case their involvement with Figaro may be misconstrued. Nevertheless, Bancroft emerged from the meeting feeling very positive about the prospects for a cooperatively produced CIA television series and recommended a future meeting in the autumn with Mankiewicz in attendance.[132]

The meeting went ahead on 2 October. Mankiewicz, still busy with *The Quiet American*, left Robert Lantz in charge of the production. Lantz met Dulles, Grogan and Kirkpatrick in Washington along with Mary Bancroft and Alfred Katz. Dulles gave them an – uninterrupted – hour and a half of his time, and listened intently to their proposals. During the 'course of the very lively and thorough conversation', the producers stressed that 'this sensational series' would afford the CIA a public relations coup and 'would serve a long range purpose to the C.I.A.; if it could be so well done and of such public acceptance as to help the C.I.A., at least in such obvious respects as their recruiting problem'.[133] Dulles intonated that he was keen on the idea, and that 'quite a number of interested parties, including producers on other networks', were 'trying to get some kind of endorsement or authorization from the C.I.A.'. He still expressed some reservations as to the legal quandary of the CIA assisting a domestic production company, and the possibility of being attacked for it in Congress, but he nevertheless concluded the meeting by promising to give it 'some further thought' and then 'to take it up directly with the President'.[134]

What became of the proposed TV show is unclear. Perhaps Dulles got cold feet, or he was advised against it by his aids, preferring instead, in keeping with tradition, to avoid the limelight. Whatever his reasons, it was perhaps the last opportunity the CIA would have to produce an unchallenged narrative of their organisation in the domain of popular culture. Towards the end of their meeting with Figaro, Dulles, Grogan and Kirkpatrick indicated what was perhaps the most pressing reason for their receptiveness to the Figaro proposal: 'sooner or later somebody will attempt a series very close to the C.I.A., but entirely without the need for authorization, and they would rather have a responsible group on a responsible job'.[135] They were right. Just over a year later, Alfred Hitchcock's *North by Northwest* would be the first feature film to directly reference the CIA, doing so without the Agency's authorisation. Although the reference was fleeting, and Hitchcock was hardly 'irresponsible' in his representation of American intelligence, it nevertheless marked a moment of significant departure from the era of the semi-documentary that heralded the state as the arbiter of authenticity. The format it provided pointed the way to a new age of spy cinema based upon an ironic detachment, rather than a slavish devotion, to the narratives of the state.

When Roger Thornhill first uttered the near-mythical acronym 'C.I.A.' for the first time on American screens without the Agency's permission, the days of the semi-documentary were numbered. So, too, was the cherished anonymity that the CIA had hitherto managed to protect and maintain.

Notes

1. Peter Stone and Marc Behm, 'Charade First Draft Screenplay', 12 July 1962, Cary Grant Papers, The Margaret Herrick Library, The Academy of Motion Pictures Arts and Sciences (hereafter AMPAS), Beverly Hills, p. 32.
2. Bradley Smith, *The Shadow Warriors: O.S.S. and the Origins of the C.I.A.* (London: André Deutsch, 1983), p. 411.
3. See Simon Willmetts, 'The CIA and the Invention of Tradition', *Journal of Intelligence History*, 14:2 (May 2015b), pp. 112–28.
4. William Casey cited in Christopher Andrew, *For the President's Eyes Only: Secret Intelligence and the American Presidency from Washington to Bush* (New York: HarperCollins, 1996), p. 1. See also William Casey, *Where and How the War Was Fought: An Armchair Tour of the American Revolution* (New York: Morrow, 1976).
5. Bernard Porter, *Plots and Paranoia: A History of Political Espionage in Britain, 1790–1988* (Abingdon: Routledge, 1989), p. 1.
6. 'The Man with the Innocent Air', *Time Magazine*, 3 August 1953.
7. See, for example, Rhodri Jeffreys-Jones, *The CIA and American Democracy*, third edition (New Haven: Yale University Press, 2003), pp. 81–99; William Daugherty, *Executive Secrets: Covert Action and the Presidency* (Lexington: University of Kentucky Press, 2004); John Ranelagh, *The Agency: The Rise and Decline of the CIA: From Wild Bill Donovan to William Casey* (New York: Simon and Schuster, 1986); G. J. A. O'Toole, *Honorable Treachery: A History of U.S. Intelligence, Espionage, and Covert Action from the American Revolution to the CIA* (New York: Grove Press, 2014); Tim Weiner, *Legacy of Ashes: The History of the CIA* (New York: Doubleday, 2007).
8. John Foran, 'Discursive Subversions: Time Magazine, the CIA Overthrow of Mussadiq, and the Installation of the Shah', in Christian G. Appy (ed.), *Cold War Constructions: The Political Culture of U.S. Imperialism* (Amherst: University of Massachusetts Press, 2000), pp. 157–82.
9. John Prados, *The Family Jewels: The CIA, Secrecy, and Presidential Power* (Austin: University of Texas Press, 2013), p. 194.

10. David Shamus McCarthy, *The CIA and the Cult of Secrecy* (William and Mary College, Doctoral Dissertation, 2008).
11. Richard and Gladys Harkness, 'The Mysterious Doings of the CIA', *Saturday Evening Post*, 13 November 1954.
12. Don DeLillo, *Libra* (London: Penguin Modern Classics, 2006), p. 22.
13. *National Security Act of 1947*, Section 104: 'Central Intelligence Agency', 26 July 1947, Public Law 235, 61 STAT. 496.
14. General Counsel Lawrence Houston cited in David Rudgers, 'The Origins of Covert Action', *Journal of Contemporary History*, 35:2 (April 2000), p. 255.
15. Clark Clifford, cited in Ibid., p. 249.
16. DeLillo, *Libra*, p. 26.
17. Smith, *Shadow Warriors*, pp. 418–19.
18. Daniel Patrick Moynihan, *Secrecy: The American Experience* (New Haven: Yale University Press, 1999). See also the Report of the Moynihan Commission on Protecting and Reducing Government Secrecy, Senate Document 105–2, 103rd Congress (Washington, DC: United States Government Printing Office, 1997).
19. Jeffreys-Jones, *The CIA and American Democracy*, p. 117.
20. Smith, *The Shadow Warriors*, p. 413.
21. 'Memo for the DCI', 11 July 1963, CIA-RDP70-00058R000200090034-3, CIA Records Search Tool (Hereafter CREST), US National Archives, College Park, MD (hereafter NACP).
22. 'Public Affairs Advisory Group Fact Sheet', undated, CREST, CIA-RDP86 B00985R000100030010-8, NACP.
23. Eugene B. Rodney to General Walter Bedell Smith, 8 August 1951, CREST, CIA-RDP80R01731R003100150019-6, NACP.
24. 'Forthcoming Movie by Paramount Apparently Involving the Name of CIA', 3 January 1951, CREST, CIA-RDP58-00597A000100070144-7, NACP.
25. 'Daily Staff Meeting', 6 February 1952, CREST, CIA-RDP80B01676R 002300080010-0, NCAP.
26. 'Report on Principal Matters Pending', 16 June 1958, CREST, CIA-RDP75-00001 R000300340007-1, NACP.
27. Tracy Barnes to William H. Godel, 'Meeting in Pentagon on 29 September 1953', 1 October 1953, CREST, CIA-RDP80R01731R001300220008-0, NACP; the title of the MGM film that received this assistance is not mentioned in the correspondence; however, an educated guess based on the timing of this correspondence and MGM's list of releases in the following year suggests that the film was the 1954 production about a blinded US navy pilot in the Korean War, *Men of the Fighting Lady*.
28. Michael Kackman, *Citizen Spy: Television, Espionage, and Cold War Culture* (Minneapolis: University of Minnesota Press, 2005), xvii–xxxix.
29. Samuel Fuller, *A Third Face* (New York: Alfred A. Knopf, 2002), p. 308.
30. Joseph I. Breen to David O. Selznick, 25 May 1945, 'Notorious' PCA File, Motion Picture Association of America Production Code Files (hereafter MPAA-PCA), AMPAS.
31. Maurice Unger to Eddie Davis, 3 November 1955, 'Man Called X Correspondence File', Ziv Entertainment Collection, Wisconsin Center for Film and Theater Research (hereafter WCFTR), Wisconsin Historical Society, Madison. Also cited in Kackman, *Citizen Spy*, p. 17.
32. Kackman, *Citizen Spy*, pp. 14–21.
33. For more on the 'blacklist era' in Hollywood see Nora Sayre, *Running Time: Films of the Cold War* (New York: Doubleday, 1982); Tony Shaw, *Hollywood's*

Cold War (Edinburgh: Edinburgh University Press, 2007); Reynold Humphries, *Hollywood's Blacklists: A Political and Cultural History* (Edinburgh: Edinburgh University Press, 2010); Larry Ceplair and Steven Englund, *The Inquisition in Hollywood: Politics in the Film Community, 1930–60* (Champaign: University of Illinois Press, 2003); Victor S. Navasky, *Naming Names* (New York: Hill and Wang, 2003); Patrick McGilligan and Paul Buhle, *Tender Comrades: A Backstory of the Hollywood Blacklist* (Minneapolis: University of Minnesota Press, 2012).

34. Ford's politics during the Cold War are often crudely associated with those of his leading star – John Wayne. Although he never matched Wayne's jingoism and bravely opposed the HUAC inquisition, his politics undoubtedly shifted to the right in response to the Cold War, as did much of Hollywood's after the Waldorf Statement drove many of the more radical elements from its ranks. See Joseph McBride, *John Ford: A Life* (New York: Faber and Faber, 2003).
35. Andrew Sarris, *The American Cinema: Directors and Directions, 1929–1968* (New York: Da Capo Press, 1968), p. 179.
36. For more on Ziv Entertainment productions see Kackman, *Citizen Spy*, pp. 1–72.
37. For the decline of the semi-documentary format in television at the hands of parody see Kackman, *Citizen Spy*, pp. 73–112.
38. Geoffrey M Shurlock to Sol Schwartz, 23 May 1962, 'John Goldfarb, Please Come Home', PCA File, MPAA-PCA, AMPAS.
39. Jack G. Shaheen, *Reel Bad Arabs: How Hollywood Vilifies a People* (New York: Interlink Books, 2015), p. 293.
40. *The New York Times v. Sullivan*, 376 US 254 (1964).
41. For example, *Curtis Publishing Co. v. Butts*, 388 US 130 (1967).
42. P. D. Knecht to Frank Wells, 18 September 1974, Alan Pakula Papers, File 33 '*All the President's Men* Legal File', AMPAS.
43. John G. Kester to Robert F. Marshall, 20 September 1995, Richard Helms Papers, Part 1, Box 18, Folder 40, Georgetown University Manuscripts, Washington, DC.
44. The British 1956 spy film *House of Secrets* did feature an organisation called 'CIA', but significantly, the acronym referred to 'The Central Investigation Authority', not the 'Central Intelligence Agency'. *House of Secrets* (Guy Green, The Rank Organisation, 1956).
45. 'Former CIA Agent Interviewed – Radio Broadcast Transcript from Barry Gray Show on WMCA', 19 May, 1960, CREST, CIA-RDP75-00001R000200350014-3, NACP.
46. 'Forthcoming Movie by Paramount Apparently Involving the Name of CIA', 3 January, 1951, CREST, CIA-RDP58-00597A000100070144-7, NACP.
47. North by Northwest Original Manuscript, Pt. 1, 22 November 1957, Ernest Lehman Screenplays Collection, TC127, Box 1, Firestone Library Special Collections, Princeton, NJ.
48. The Professorial depiction of the head of the CIA in *North by NorthWest* was undoubtedly a reference to the longstanding and renowned CIA chief Allen Dulles, who carefully fostered his avuncular image. Leo Carroll, who played 'The Professor' would later reprise this role as Alexander Waverly in *The Man from U.N.C.L.E.*
49. *North by Northwest* (Alfred Hitchcock, MGM, 1959).
50. R. Monta to Alfred Hitchcock, 1 August 1958, Alfred Hitchcock Papers, North by Northwest Legal File, Folder 536, AMPAS.
51. Peggy Robertson to Herbert Coleman, 23 January 1959, Hitchcock Papers, Folder 542 'North by Northwest Production File', AMPAS.

52. See Hannah Arendt, *The Origins of Totalitarianism*, new edition (New York: Harcourt Brace, 1973).
53. Numerous correspondences between Dulles and Johnston can be found in the CREST files, some of which are available online. See, for example, Eric Johnston to Allen Dulles, 5 August 1960, CREST-CIA-RDP80B01676R002800220007; Allen Dulles to Harry Traynor re: Eric Johnston and Nikita Khrushchev, 10 October 1958, CREST-CIA-RDP80B01676R000700150036-2; Allen Dulles to Eric Johnston, 7 April 1959, CREST-CIA-RDP80R01731R000200130032-5, NACP.
54. Frances Stonor Saunder, *Who Paid the Piper: The CIA and the Cultural Cold War* (London: Granta, 1999), pp. 290–3.
55. Ibid.
56. David Eldridge, 'Dear Owen: The CIA, Luigi Luraschi and Hollywood, 1953', *Historical Journal of Film, Radio and Television*, 20:2 (2000), pp. 149–96.
57. Christopher Lehmann-Haupt, 'Peter Matthiessen, Lyrical Writer and Naturalist, is Dead at 86', *The New York Times*, 5 April 2014.
58. See Scott Lucas, *Freedom's War: The American Crusade against the Soviet Union* (New York: New York University Press, 1999); Helen Laville and Hugh Wilford (eds), *The US Government, Citizens Groups and the Cold War: The State-Private Network* (Abingdon: Routledge, 2006); Helen Laville, *Cold War Women: The International Activities of American Women's Organisations* (Manchester: Manchester University Press, 2009); Hugh Wilford, *The Mighty Wurlitzer: How the CIA Played America* (Cambridge, MA: Harvard University Press, 2009); Giles Scott-Smith, *The Politics of Apolitical Culture: The Congress for Cultural Freedom and the Political Economy of American Hegemony, 1945–1955* (Abingdon: Routledge, 2001).
59. George Orwell, *Animal Farm*, fiftieth anniversary edition (New York: Signet, 2004), p. 124.
60. Shaw, *Hollywood's Cold War*, p. 81.
61. For a detailed account of the CIA's role in adapting Orwell's *Animal Farm* see Daniel Leab, *Orwell Subverted: The CIA and the Filming of Animal Farm* (State College: Pennsylvania State University Press, 2008); See also Tony Shaw, *British Cinema and the Cold War: The State, Propaganda and Consensus* (London: I. B. Tauris, 2001), pp. 91–114; Shaw, *Hollywood's Cold War*, pp. 72–102.
62. John Rizzo, *Company Man: Thirty Years of Controversy and Crisis in the CIA* (New York: Scribner, 2014), p. 64.
63. Chuck Barris, *Confessions of a Dangerous Mind*, new edition (New York: Ebury Press, 2002); *Confessions of a Dangerous Mind* (George Clooney, Section Eight Productions/Miramax, 2002).
64. Paul Nowak cited in Joel Stein, 'Lying to Tell the Truth', *Time Magazine*, 13 January 2003.
65. Wilford, *The Mighty Wurlitzer*, pp. 116–17.
66. Ibid., p. 122.
67. Robert Gorham Davis, 'In Our Time No Man is Neutral', *The New York Times*, 11 March 1956.
68. Graham Greene, *The Quiet American*, Graham Greene centennial edition (London: 2004), p. 175.
69. Ibid., p. 23.
70. Ibid., p. 166.
71. Joseph Mankiewicz to Robert Lantz, 4 September 1957, Joseph Mankiewicz Papers, f. 405 – Figaro, Inc, AMPAS.
72. Jonathan Nashel, *Edward Lansdale's Cold War* (Amherst: University of Massachusetts Press, 2004), p. 167. For more on the American Friends of Vietnam

see Joseph G. Morgan, *The Vietnam Lobby: The American Friends of Vietnam, 1955–1975* (Chapel Hill: University of North Carolina Press, 1997).
73. Gene Phillips, *Graham Greene: The Films of his Fiction* (New York: Teachers College Press), pp. 141–5.
74. Laurence Olivier to Joseph Mankiewicz, 8 January 1956, Joseph Mankiewicz Papers, Laurence Olivier Correspondence, Folder 417, AMPAS.
75. Joseph Mankiewicz to Laurence Olivier, 13 January 1956, Joseph Mankiewicz Papers, Laurence Olivier Correspondence, Folder 417, AMPAS.
76. Laurence Olivier to Joseph Mankiewicz, 24 April 1956, Joseph Mankiewicz Papers, Laurence Olivier, Folder 417, AMPAS, Beverly Hills; emphasis in original.
77. Phillips, *Graham Greene*, p. 140.
78. Ibid., pp. 140–1.
79. Ibid., p. 142.
80. William S. Bushnell, 'Paying for the Damage: The Quiet American Revisited', *Film and History: An Interdisciplinary Journal of Film and Television Studies*, 36:2 (Spring 2006), pp. 42.
81. *The Quiet American* (Joseph Mankiewicz, Figaro Entertainment/United Artists, 1958).
82. Phillips, *Graham Greene*, p. 142.
83. Greene, *The Quiet American*, p. 111.
84. Nashel, *Edward Lansdale's Cold War*.
85. Edward Lansdale to Joseph Mankiewicz, 17 March 1956, Joseph Mankiewicz MSS, Research Correspondence, Folder 423, AMPAS.
86. Robert Lantz cited in William Russo, *A Thinker's Damn: Audie Murphy, Vietnam, and the Making of the Quiet American* (New York: Xlibris, 2001), p. 41.
87. Joseph Mankiewicz to Laurence Olivier, 13 January 1956, Joseph Mankiewicz Papers, Laurence Olivier Correspondence, File 417, AMPAS.
88. Joseph Mankiewicz in Brian Dauth (ed.), *Joseph L. Mankiewicz Interviews* (Jackson: University of Mississippi Press), p. 141.
89. Graham Greene, *A Sort of Life* (London: Vintage, 1999), p. 97.
90. Phillips, *Graham Greene*, p. 134.
91. For more on Greene's opposition to HUAC, see Kenneth L. Geist, *Pictures Will Talk: The Life and Films of Joseph L. Mankiewicz* (New York: Charles Scribner's Sons, 1978), pp. 173–206.
92. Rosemary Matthews cited in Nashel, *Edward Lansdale's Cold War*, p. 171.
93. Simon Willmetts, 'Quiet Americans: The CIA and Early Cold War Hollywood Cinema', *Journal of American Studies*, 47:1 (2013b), pp. 127–47.
94. Synopsis by Price Chatham of the Novel by Graham Greene, Submitted by Monica McCall, 16 November 1955, Joseph Mankiewicz MSS, Monica McCall Correspondence, Folder 413, AMPAS; Mary Pritchett to Robert Lantz, 29 November 1955, Joseph Mankiewicz MSS, Monica McCall Correspondence, AMPAS, Folder 413, Beverly Hills.
95. Joseph Mankiewicz to Geoffrey Shurlock, 23 December 1955, MPAA-PCA Records, AMPAS.
96. Geoffrey Shurlock to Joseph Mankiewicz, 5 January 1956, MPAA-PCA Records, AMPAS.
97. Ibid.
98. Joseph Mankiewicz to Geoffrey Shurlock, 9 January 1956, MPAA-PCA Records, AMPAS.
99. Russo, *A Thinker's Dream*, p. 150.
100. For more on the IRC's influence on the production of *The Quiet American*

see James T. Fisher, '"A World Made Safe for Diversity": The Vietnam Lobby and the Politics of Pluralism, 1945–1963', in Christian Appy (ed.), *Cold War Constructions: The Political Culture of U.S. Imperialism* (Amherst: University of Massachusetts Press, 2000), pp. 217–37.
101. Angier Biddle Duke to Rober McAllister, 10 January 1956, Joseph Mankiewicz MSS, f. 404 – Angier Biddle Duke, AMPAS, Beverly Hills.
102. Eric Thomas Chester, *Covert Network: Progressives, the International Rescue Committee and the CIA* (New York: M. E. Sharpe, 1995), pp. 153–6.
103. Fisher, 'A World Made Safe for Diversity', p. 230.
104. Alfred Katz to Harold Odam, 13 February 1956, Joseph Mankiewicz MSS, Alfred Katz Correspondence, Folder 408, AMPAS.
105. Alfred Katz to Joseph Mankiewicz, 9 June 1956, Joseph Mankiewicz Papers, Alfred Katz Correspondence, Folder 408, AMPAS.
106. Tranh-Chan-Thanh, Secretary of State for Information and Youth to Secretary of State for Finance, 28 December 1956, Joseph Mankiewicz Papers, Viet Nam Correspondence, Folder 429, AMPAS, Beverly Hills.
107. 'Letter of Introduction' from Vo Van Hai, Special Secretary of the Presidency, 21 January 1957, Joseph Mankiewicz Papers, Viet Nam Correspondence, Folder 429, AMPAS.
108. Alfred Katz to Joseph Mankiewicz, 9 June 1956, Joseph Mankiewicz MSS, Alfred Katz Correspondence, Folder 408, AMPAS, Beverly Hills.
109. Alfred Katez to Joseph Mankiewicz, 10 September 1956, Joseph Mankiewicz MSS, f. 408 – Alfred Katz, AMPAS.
110. Joseph Mankiewicz Coctail List, undated, Joseph Mankiewicz MSS, f. 419 – Quiet American Production File, AMPAS.
111. Arthur G. McDowell to Arthur Krim, 14 March 1956, Joseph Mankiewicz MSS, f. 403 – Quiet American Correspondence, AMPAS.
112. C. Dickerman Williams to Arthur McDowell, 9 April 1956, Joseph Mankiewicz MSS, f. 403 – Quiet American Correspondence, AMPAS.
113. For more on Mike Mansfield's opposition to the CIA see Jeffreys-Jones, *The CIA and American Democracy*, pp. 78–9.
114. Marie McNair, 'Dragon Visits "Quiet American"', *The Washington Post*, 23 January 1958.
115. Nashel, *Edward Lansdale's Cold War*, p. 168.
116. Nashel, Ibid., p. 171.
117. Giles Scott-Smith, *The Politics of Apolitical Culture: The Congress for Cultural Freedom and the Political Economy of American Hegemony, 1945–1955* (London: Routledge, 2002), p. 3.
118. Godfrey Hodgson cited in Inderjeet Parmar, 'Conceptualising the State-Private Network', in Helen Laville and Hugh Wilford (eds), *The US Government, Citizen Groups and the Cold War: The State-Private Network* (Abingdon: Routledge, 2006), pp. 14–15.
119. Hugh Wilford, *The CIA, The British Left and the Cold War: Calling the Tune?* (London: Frank Cass, 2003), p. 301.
120. Mary Bancroft, *Autobiography of a Spy* (New York: William Morrow, 1983).
121. Russo, *A Thinker's Dream*, p. 33.
122. Mary Bancroft to Robert Lantz, 11 January 1956, Mary Bancroft MSS, Box 19 – TV Series on CIA, Correspondence and Outlines – 1956–7, Schlesinger Library, Radcliffe Institute, Harvard University, Cambridge, MA.
123. Jeffreys-Jones, *The CIA and American Democracy*, pp. 78–80.
124. Mary Bancroft to Robert Lantz, 11 January 1956, Mary Bancroft MSS, Box 19 – TV Series on CIA, Correspondence and Outlines – 1956–7, Schlesinger Library.

125. Willmetts, 'The CIA and the Invention of Tradition'.
126. Mary Bancroft Notes and Ideas on Concept of TV Programme, Mary Bancroft MSS, Box 19 – TV Series on CIA, Correspondence and Outlines – 1956–7, Schlesinger Library.
127. Mary Bancroft to Alfred Katz, 10 June 1957, Mary Bancroft MSS, Box 19 – TV Series on CIA, Correspondence and Outlines – 1956–7, Schlesinger Library.
128. 'Strictly Confidential Memo' by Robert Lantz, 10 October 1957, Mary Bancroft MSS, Box 19 – TV Series on CIA, Correspondence and Outlines – 1956–7, Schlesinger Library.
129. Robert Lantz to Alfred Katz, 9 June 1957, Mary Bancroft MSS, Box 19 – TV Series on CIA, Correspondence and Outlines – 1956–7, Schlesinger Library.
130. Robert Lantz to Mary Bancroft, 8 October 1957, Mary Bancroft MSS, Box 19 – TV Series on CIA, Correspondence and Outlines – 1956–7, Schlesinger Library.
131. 'Conditions for Cooperation on TV Production' by Lyman Kirkpatrick, 14 June 1957, Mary Bancroft MSS, Box 19 – TV Series on CIA, Correspondence and Outlines – 1956–7, Schlesinger Library.
132. Mary Bancroft Memo from 1–4 July 1957, Mary Bancroft MSS, Box 19 – TV Series on CIA, Correspondence and Outlines – 1956–7, Schlesinger Library.
133. 'Strictly Confidential Memo' by Robert Lantz, 10 October 1957, Mary Bancroft MSS, Box 19 – TV Series on CIA, Correspondence and Outlines – 1956–7, Schlesinger Library.
134. Ibid.
135. Ibid.

4. THE DEATH OF THE 'BIG LIE' AND THE EMERGENCE OF POSTMODERN INCREDULITY IN THE SPY CINEMA OF THE 1960s

When covert activities go wrong, governments are supposed to respond with what James Bond author Ian Fleming called 'The Big Lie': responsibility for them had to be denied. For Fleming, this fundamental dictum of espionage had 'been so ever since the man from the opposition crept under the tent flap in the desert and listened to the plans of the enemy tribal chiefs'.[1] And so it had remained a fundamental part of the conduct of US covert activities. That is, at least, until the coming of the 1960s.

It began with Gary Powers. On 1 May 1960, a U-2 spy plane was shot down over Russia. Cunningly, Khrushchev waited for Eisenhower to issue 'The Big Lie' before revealing to the world that the pilot – Powers – and pieces of his plane were in Soviet custody. Eisenhower refused to apologise. His secretary of state, Christian Herter, unconvincingly invoked the 'circuit breaking' mechanism that provided bureaucratic distance between the President and the decision-making process that led to Powers' downed flight. 'The insulted but jubilant Russians had a show trial and put on a U-2 exhibition in Gorky Park, thus treating the episode as a propaganda victory.'[2] In the short term, the event led to the cancellation of an East–West summit, scheduled to take place two weeks after Powers' flight came down. In the long-term, however, its significance resided, as CIA historian Rhodri Jeffreys-Jones put it, in its demonstration 'to a startled American public that their president would lie to them'.[3]

For Ian Fleming, the US Government's partial and piecemeal admission represented a 'majestic mishandling' of the entire affair. James Bond's boss, M,

Fleming postulated, would have handled the affair quite differently by issuing the following denial:

> Thank you very much indeed. One of our experimental aircraft is indeed missing from our Turkish base and your description of the pilot fits in with a man who escaped yesterday from detention at that base. This man Powers is a most unreliable person who has a girl friend in Paris (to explain the foreign currency Powers carried) and he hijacked our plane with the object, presumably, of flying to her. You are quite correct to hold him in detention and he must clearly suffer all the rigours of Soviet law in the circumstances. Please return our plane and equipment in due course. Sorry you've been troubled. P.S.: Powers suffers from hallucinations and delusions of grandeur. Pay no attention to them.[4]

Fleming deemed Powers a small sacrifice in maintaining the plausibility of denial. He should be thrown 'cold bloodedly to the dogs', the British author concluded in characteristically sadistic fashion. 'He was expendable. Expend him!' But instead, what occurred? 'Endless hovering by the State Department,' lamented Fleming, 'lies, half-truths and finally admissions from on high that led at least in part to the total collapse of the Summit meeting in Paris. If the Big Lie had been spoken, and stuck to, it would have been in the true traditions of espionage.'[5]

The Powers incident was followed a year later by the CIA's disastrous attempt to invade Cuba at the Bay of Pigs. President Kennedy, who approved the operation – although he inherited the scheme from his predecessor – was a fan of the Bond novels. In March 1961 he did Fleming a 'fantastically good turn in America' by listing *From Russia with Love* in his top ten favourite books of all time in a *Life Magazine* article.[6] This led to a surge in the Bond novels' sales and helped to establish the iconic British spy as no less iconic in the United States.[7] In a much-fabled meeting between Kennedy and the British author at a dinner party hosted by the young Senator from Massachusetts at his Georgetown residence on 13 March 1960, Kennedy was apparently enthralled with Fleming's 'spoof proposal for giving Castro the James Bond treatment'. The author wryly suggested 'flooding the streets of Havana with pamphlets explaining that radioactive fallout from nuclear testing caused impotence and was known to be drawn to men who had beards. As a result, Cuban men would shave off their facial hair, thus severing a symbolic link to Castro and the revolution.'[8] Another mock scheme involved flying a giant cross over Havana to signal to a deeply Catholic populace a spiritual portentousness aggravated by the revolution.[9]

There has been an eagerness by some scholars and Fleming biographers to draw a direct line between this anecdotal and perhaps apocryphal exchange and

Operation Mongoose, the notorious CIA anti-Castro operation that famously included attempts on Castro's life – or simply his virility – via exploding clamshells, poisoned cigars and by contaminating his clothing with a depilatory that would make his beard fall out.[10] Admittedly, the excesses of Mongoose have an outlandishly fictional air, and some of the proposed schemes, particularly the plan to encourage Castro to develop facial alopecia, are uncannily similar to Fleming's humorous proposal. Moreover, Allen Dulles was said to have been greatly interested in Fleming's after-dinner performance after he learned of it via the CIA's John Bross, who attended the party. For his part Dulles recalled at least one occasion when the world of Bond had an impact on the real-world of CIA spies: after reading about it in a Bond novel, Dulles asked people within the Agency to try to develop a special kind of tracking beacon that could be installed on an enemy's car and tracked from a honing radar on the dashboard of a CIA officer's vehicle. It didn't really work out in the end as there was some difficulty in working the technology in an urban area, but, Dulles wrote, Bond's gadgets 'did get one to thinking and exploring'.[11]

Yet these amusing vignettes, as enjoyable as they must be for Bond fans, should be treated with caution. Dulles was ever astute to a public relations opportunity, especially after the Bay of Pigs when he was forced to resign from office and had to repair his own and his former Agency's beleaguered reputation; he would surely not allow a chance for the CIA to bask in the reflective glamour of Bond to pass him by. Indeed Dulles's friendship with Fleming encouraged the author to feature the CIA, via the figure of Felix Leiter, in an increasingly prominent, although still (naturally) subordinate role.[12] Perhaps more importantly, there is a danger of trivialising Mongoose, a serious and deeply morally troubling abuse of executive power, by consigning its provenance to a few glib comments in a characteristic flight-of-fancy by the Bond author who hatched his mock schemes amidst the jovial after-dinner atmosphere of Kennedy's Georgetown home. For Castro, and for the series of Congressional committees that investigated CIA assassinations programmes a decade later, not to mention an increasingly disillusioned American public, there was nothing jovial about it.

While evidence of Bond's direct intrusion onto the real world of espionage is perhaps too good to be true, stories of the Fleming–Kennedy–Dulles connection are instructive for another reason. Bond, as Nadel writes, 'was in many ways the apotheosis of the kind of leader Kennedy most admired, one who furthered the cause of containment with unlimited license, whose sexual prowess . . . was testimony to his political fitness, whose amorality was a sign of goodness'.[13] As more than one Kennedy biographer has indicated, Fleming's virile update of the knights-errand format may well have framed Kennedy's initially 'overly exalted view' of the CIA.[14] As Rhodri Jeffreys-Jones writes, '[t]he interest here lies less in the influence Fleming may have had on the CIA's depilatory plans, than in the young senator's amused curiosity about unorthodox methods'.[15] Kennedy, like Dulles and Fleming, was a romantic.[16] 'The President and his brother . . . had an interest in covert activity' recalled Thomas Lowe Hughes, former director of intelligence and research at the State Department. '[T]hey had an interest in James Bond-type activity . . . They romanticized a great deal about doing things secretly that couldn't be done openly, including some very strenuous covert activity.'[17]

'The Bay of Pigs was a severe lesson', writes Robert Kennedy's biographer Evan Thomas. 'Lacerating himself for blindly following the CIA', the president repeatedly asked, 'How could I have been so stupid?' (And, more wryly and ruefully, 'Why couldn't this have happened to James Bond?')[18] But if Kennedy should be reprimanded for falling victim to his Bond-shaped fantasies, then the CIA, on the same basis, should be apportioned at least some of that blame. 'Until the Bay of Pigs', recalled William Colby,

> indeed ever since the glory days of the OSS . . . the Agency had enjoyed a reputation with the public at large not a whit less than golden. After all, we were the derring-do boys who parachuted behind enemy lines . . . matching fire with fire in an endless round of thrilling adventures like those of the scenarios in James Bond films.[19]

It was not just a reputation, however, or a public gloss put out by the CIA's head of public affairs – although it became that as well. Rather, it was a myth, which many within the Agency bought into and sustained.

It is estimated that as much as half of the Agency's overall budget was devoted to Covert Action in the 1950s and 1960s, but 'this percentage steadily decreased in later years'.[20] Much of the early CIA and the vast majority of those who had risen to positions of seniority by the time of Kennedy's reign had served in the OSS and remained loyal to Donovan's ethos of 'shadow warfare magic'.[21] E. Howard Hunt, for example, the notoriously gung-ho covert operative who served in OSS before joining the CIA where he became intimately involved with both the Guatemalan coup and the Bay of Pigs before joining Nixon's infamous 'plumbers' unit that broke into Watergate, was a prolific spy novelist who was evidently fully invested in the myth of covert action. Dulles, himself a Donovan protégé, was inspired by the romance of espionage long before he and Ian Fleming became firm friends. Upon graduating from Princeton he bought a copy of Rudyard Kipling's *Kim*, an imperial romance that more or less invented the modern espionage novel, and read it while aboard a steamship to India. It was a formative experience. As Stephen Kinzer put it,

> *Kim* is about the glory of empire and the nasty things that must sometimes be done in secret to defend it . . . To Allie [Dulles] it was beyond

inspirational. He never parted with his copy. It was on his bedside table when he died.[22]

The mythology of covert action was not just cynically exploited by the Agency, it was wholeheartedly believed. Kennedy, it seems, was not the only one who was perhaps a little naïve. As Agency apostate Victor Marchetti later wrote in his explosive insider's history of the Agency:

> A good part of the CIA's power position is dependent upon its careful mythologizing and glorification of the exploits of the clandestine profession ... the selling of the intelligence business is designed to have us admire it as some sort of mysterious, often magical, profession capable of accomplishing terribly difficult, if not miraculous, deeds. Like most myths, the intrigues and successes of the CIA over the years have been more imaginary than real. What is real, unfortunately, is the willingness of both the public and adherents of the cult to believe the fictions that permeate the intelligence business.[23]

The Bay of Pigs marked both the culmination and the undoing of this 'cult' of covert action.[24] When Castro heard the cover story of a downed Cuban exile pilot, who claimed – on the advice of the CIA – to have escaped from a Cuban airbase and launched their insurrection from within, the Cuban President incredulously exclaimed, '[E]ven Hollywood would not try to film such a story.'[25] It was an apt response to a scheme that fell victim to the CIA's own mythmaking. For more than a decade that mythology had been allowed to develop unchecked. During the 1950s neither Hollywood nor the wider media dared risk transgressing the seemingly unassailable Cold War consensus that assumed that American foreign policy was essentially defensive in nature. The Bay of Pigs and the U-2 Spy Affair began a process that would change all of that. The fictions that sustained the cult of covert action relied upon the American public's disregard for the realities that contradicted them, and their faith in the authority of the 'official story'. But with the arrival of a new decade those realities that highlighted the duplicity of the American Government – like the pieces of Gary Powers' spy plane put on display by Khrushchev in Gorky Park, or the rounded-up Cuban exiles captured by Castro's waiting troops – became too obvious to be ignored. 'The system', wrote novelist Don DeLillo, 'would perpetuate itself in all its curious and obsessive webbings, its equivocations and patient riddles and levels of delusional thought, at least until the men were on the beach ... After the Bay of Pigs, nothing was the same.'[26]

Hollywood echoed the loss of faith in the American Government during the 1960s via an increasingly irreverent attitude towards the very things that the semi-documentaries of the previous decade had cherished: patriotism, an

Figure 4.1 Captured Cuban counter-revolutionaries after their failed invasion attempt at the Bay of Pigs. *Source:* US National Archives, College Park, Maryland.

unassailable faith in the authority of the 'official story' and an earnest commitment to realism. This growing incredulity to the semi-documentary's claims to authenticity, particularly state-sanctioned authenticity, was concomitant with the wider destabilisation of nation-centred epistemologies that became the hallmark of postmodernity. Cultural historian Alan Nadel identifies the Bay of Pigs as the 'primal scene of postmodernism' – to appropriate Peter Knight's description of the Kennedy assassination – not only because it shattered the credibility of the US government, but because it undermined the authority of the kinds of state-sourced narratives that the semi-documentaries had produced.[27] After the Bay of Pigs, and other events like it that highlighted the duplicity of American Government, 'the neat ideological package that was the 1950s spy drama', became, as Michael Kackman puts it, 'an untenable proposition'.[28] This was in part a consequence of rising production values, budgets and the use of alluring exotic locales in both the spy films and television shows of the decade that rendered the crude low-budget aesthetics of the semi-documentary obsolete. But it also marked, more significantly, an epistemological rejection of the guiding logic of the semi-documentary that equated truth with the discourses of the American Government.

In their landmark studies of post-war American culture both Nadel and Timothy Melley have argued that the emergence of postmodernism, with its attendant epistemological scepticism towards the idea of a singular, authoritative, objective and knowable past, was a direct consequence of the rise of the national security state and, in particular, government secrecy.[29] Postmodernism is of course a complex and multivalent term, and encompasses occasionally contradictory ideas, methodologies and aesthetic practices. There isn't space to do justice to these complexities here. However, one quite instructive way of situating postmodernism historically is to regard it as a product of the collapse of public trust in government, and in authority more generally, during the 1960s. As Ann Douglas put it:

> Postmodernism involves a sometimes wilful flirtation with the unknowable, even a calculated extension of it, and the CIA, in conjunction with the State and Defense Departments, matched the powers of strategic obfuscation since displayed by its ally, the transnational corporation. The doctrine of plausible deniability, promulgated by President Truman's National Security Council in 1948 and central to postmodernity, was a way of suppressing evidence and destroying knowledge ... The extreme skepticism about the possibility of disinterested knowledge and language that postmodernism sponsors ... makes most sense when taken as a straightforward description of the extremes of official dishonesty characteristic of the cold war era.[30]

In this new age of public scepticism towards government the CIA figured metonymically as a lightning rod for public anxieties about secrecy and government duplicity more generally, and its effects upon the stability and coherence of shared public truths. What was worrying about events such as the Bay of Pigs was not merely the degree of incompetence required to produce such abject operational failure, but the sense that they were just the tip of the iceberg – the most visible points of a vast and expanding labyrinth of secret corridors and private conversations that comprised an 'invisible government' – as journalists David Wise and Thomas Ross famously titled their bestselling history of CIA covert action in 1964 – that pulled the strings of American foreign policy.[31] As Timothy Melley writes, 'the early modern place of God has been assumed by the CIA, which is now seen ... as a symbol of public unknowing ... In short, the covert state has become a primary force in the postmodern "reenchantment of the world."'[32]

This postmodern state of 'public unknowing' had two immediate consequences for the representation of espionage in Hollywood cinema. First, the semi-documentary, premised as it was on a crude epistemology that authorised its didactic claims to truth by appealing to the state as the arbiter of historical authenticity, was finished. In the late 1960s, for example, Louis de Rochemont attempted to adapt Allen Dulles's account of OSS Operation Sunrise into a semi-documentary. The film was never made because, as de Rochemont was forced to concede in 1968, 'those movie executives who buy books, plays and other properties, men who actually decide what pictures are to be made – never showed serious interest in THE SECRET SURRENDER'.[33] This was because the James Bond films and the camp silliness they inspired in shows like *The Man from U.N.C.L.E.*, or spoof films like *In Like Flint*, had established what Paul Monaco described as 'a more lasting vehicle for satisfying adolescent and young adult tastes'.[34] Second, as these examples indicate, the semi-documentary was not replaced by severe criticisms of the CIA and state secrecy, with a gravity of tone that matched the didacticisms of those early Cold War espionage features. Nor did they offer anything quite so 'highbrow' as the multivalent patchworks of intertextuality that are the trademark of postmodern novelists like Thomas Pynchon and Don DeLillo. Rather, the spy films and television shows of the 1960s were, initially at least, often unashamedly 'trashy' in their playfully parodic or 'camp' rejection of the semi-documentary's state-sourced epistemology.

In her seminal essay on 'camp', Susan Sontag defined this increasingly prevalent sensibility as a 'love of the unnatural: of artifice and exaggeration'.[35] In rejecting the crude realism of the semi-documentary, spy camp celebrated artifice through improbable plotlines, impossible guns, gadgets and gizmos, villains so villainous that they'd make the sinister communists of 1950s Hollywood cinema blush, and, of course, secret lairs, femme fatales and tawdry quips. None of these tropes were new to the 1960s. In cinema many of them dated back at least as far as Fritz Lang's *Spione* (1928). But never before had they appeared with such frequency, and with such parodic intertextual reverie as to potentially upset the dominant realist aesthetic and the ideological and epistemological precepts inherent to its form. The important thing about James Bond's appeal, argued an *LA Times* columnist in 1963, is that it represents 'nothing less than a revolution in taste, a return to qualities in fiction which were all but submerged in the 20th-century vogue of realism and naturalism'.[36]

A 'revolution in taste' the camp sensibility may have been, but it was not, at least according to Sontag, a political or ideological revolution. 'It goes without saying', she wrote, 'that the Camp sensibility is disengaged, depoliticized – or at least apolitical'.[37] Indeed the crude ideology of early Cold War spy cinema was the very thing that sixties spy camp sought to escape. 'For obvious reasons', Norman Felton, the producer of *The Man from U.N.C.L.E.* instructed his writers, 'neither U.N.C.L.E. nor its antagonists are involved in international politics or diplomacy, except on those occasions where <u>wholly mythical</u> countries are involved. U.N.C.L.E. does not serve interests that are peculiarly American. The Cold War or any of its ramifications do not exist for us.'[38]

Felton understood that the success of the spy genre in the 1960s rested not

Figure 4.2 David McCallum (Illya Kuryaking), Leo Carroll (Alexander Waverley) and Robert Vaughn (Napoleon Solo) star in *The Man from U.N.C.L.E.* television series (1964–8). The show had an international flavour to appeal to growing foreign audiences. In order to maintain its global appeal producer Norman Felton instructed writers to excise any explicit mention of the Cold War from their script drafts – taking sides in an age of lucrative foreign television syndication could prove costly. Thus the spy genre shed its ideological baggage and the austere anti-communist tone of the 1950s spy melodramas was replaced by tongue in cheek international espionage organisations that operated against criminal masterminds who were deliberately not labelled as Soviet agents. *Source:* Joseph Sargent, MGM, 1966.

upon jingoistic and parochial ideology but, on the contrary, its transnational appeal. In the 1960s the fictional spy became a truly global commodity, a perfectly exploitable symbol of an increasingly interconnected age. Developments within the entertainment industry had also helped stimulate this shift outwards. In Hollywood, the break-up of the studio system had encouraged many of the majors to focus upon distribution – especially foreign distribution – and squeeze extra profits from international markets.[39] In television the birth and expansion of international syndication meant spy shows such as *U.N.C.L.E.* and *Mission Impossible* obtained vast revenues from international markets. The latter, for example, proved so popular in Iran that Iranian-born *Mission Impossible* director Reza Badiyi was flown by the Iranian Government, along with his family, babysitter and dog back to Iran first-class, where he was met at the airport at 1am by a crowd of more than 500 people, along with the National Guard, who serenaded his arrival with an out-of-tune version of the *Mission: Impossible* theme.[40]

In Europe, the spy-craze, as with the spaghetti Westerns, even spawned an entire sub-genre of internationally co-produced spy-spoofs dubbed 'Eurospy'. The global popularity of these shows also made feature-film spin-offs a lucrative proposition. Large international television audiences virtually assured the distribution of these films abroad and provided a reliable source of income.[41] Moreover, as Kackman explains, '[t]his international market was augmented by an exploding ancillary merchandising market that made outlandish gadgetry highly profitable'. Spy spoofs like *The Man from U.N.C.L.E.* offered far greater merchandising opportunities than the semi-documentaries. It is 'hard to imagine a market for a J. Edgar Hoover doll – but a *Man from U.N.C.L.E.* gun-shaped cigarette lighter, board game, or comic book generated not just free publicity, but free profits'.[42]

Where the market went, the shows' content followed. Belligerent Cold War narratives, producers knew, simply wouldn't sell so well in foreign markets. So instead of the Soviet agents working for SMERSH in the novels, Bond battled a transnational organisation, SPECTRE, which in *You Only Live Twice* (1967) even became a threat to the newfound harmony in détente between the USA and USSR. *The Man From U.N.C.L.E.*, whose title clearly evoked the United Nations, featured a Russian agent, Ilya Kuryakin, who became an increasingly prominent character in the show after becoming a 'teen pin-up idol' in America. This suggests, as one scholar has put it, 'popular renegotiations of previously rigid positions and assumptions with regard to orthodox Cold War ideology . . .'[43] As in the Bond films, *U.N.C.L.E.* also fought a transnational terrorist organisation: T.H.R.U.S.H. *Get Smart* likewise reconstructed the Manichean framework of the Cold War along depoliticised and de-territorialised lines with CONTROL battling KAOS; Amos Burke battled SEKOR; and even the *Mission Impossible* television series, whose Cold War subtext was more overt than the others, featured agents working for the IMF battling enemies from non-specific places.

Yet while the Cold War was not explicitly present in these films and television shows, its guiding narrative structure, a Manichean contest between good and evil, was. This has led some critics to claim that the politics of sixties spy fiction was almost as crudely aligned with the Cold War consensus as the anti-communist cinema of the previous era.[44] Not least because they continued to deploy what Alan Nadel has described as 'containment narratives' by pitting – except for a few notable exceptions – white, Anglo-Saxon heteronormative male heroes against orientalised and often 'homosexualised' or 'feminized' villains.[45] Hitchcock's films, for example, have come in for particular criticism for adhering to the Cold War consensus's gendered presumptions by constructing '"the homosexual" as a security risk'.[46] Occasionally, the gendered discourses of the genre were themselves subject to parody. *In Like Flint*, for example, a forerunner of the Austin

Powers series, featured the irresistible international super-spy Derek Flint, played by James Coburn, who must save the world from a global feminist conspiracy to incite the overthrow of the existing patriarchal order by brainwashing women into taking part in the revolt via subliminal messages played through salon hairdryers.

But even if one ignores the gendered ideology of these films – which, given its explicitness, may prove difficult – it is surely the most obvious reading of the binary narratives of Bond, or even *The Man from U.N.C.L.E.*, and *North by Northwest*, to see them as straightforward endorsements of the logic of the Cold War consensus.[47] To do so, however, ignores the defining feature of these spy parodies, which set them apart from their graver semi-documentary predecessors, a characteristic that Linda Hutcheon argues, in contrast to Sontag, is decidedly political: irony.

For Hutcheon, parody, which is the defining aesthetic practice of postmodern culture, challenges ideological consensus by contesting it 'from within its own assumptions'.[48] In this sense, like the tongue-in-cheek Manichean universes of *North by Northwest* or *In Like Flint*, or even Bond, it paradoxically affirms the very thing it seeks to problematise (or problematises the very thing it seeks to affirm), namely the Cold War, and can subvert 'only through irony, not through rejection'.[49] But parody is powerful precisely because, by exaggeratedly and ironically rearticulating extant forms, ideas or metanarratives, it lays bare their pretenses and assumptions as artifice, 'rendering problematic' what was once regarded as 'common-sensical' or 'natural'.[50]

With the arrival of *North by Northwest*, James Bond and all the camp spy

Figure 4.3 Camp spy satire *In Like Flint* (1967) featured James Coburn as international agent Derek Flint. The film's plot revolves around an international feminist conspiracy plotting to overthrow the American patriarchy. The feminist insurgents use salon hairdryers to brainwash recruits into compliance with their ideology. *Source:* Gordon Douglas, Twentieth Century-Fox, 1967.

romances and spoofs it inspired, the semi-documentary was no longer a credible or viable medium. If the spy cinema and television of the 1960s achieved anything that could be deemed politically radical, it was its undermining of a form that so unproblematically equated the official story with truth. As Michael Kackman writes, paraphrasing Sontag, after *North by Northwest* and James Bond, 'the seriousness of the spy's patriotism fails'.[51]

Postmodernism may not necessarily be politically revolutionary or radical, it may not lead to the overthrow of liberal capitalism, or for our more specific purposes, the curtailment of the CIA's excesses. It may not bring about something entirely new, politically or ideologically, to what had gone before, namely, the Manichean binaries of the Cold War consensus. But it may, as Hutcheon argues, mark 'the site of the struggle of the emergence of something new'.[52] That site of struggle can be located in the growing incredulity, the increasingly 'systematic incredulity', to borrow a phrase, towards the official story.[53] Fredric Jameson famously described postmodernism as 'the cultural logic of late capitalism'. This may well be so, but in a slightly less grandiose sense, it was also the cultural logic of a people who no longer trusted their government. It was this loss of faith in the official story that became the defining feature of fictional narratives about the CIA from the 1960s onwards. Spy cinema came to articulate the growing irreverence towards government that began with the U-2 Spy Affair and the Bay of Pigs and intensified throughout the decade after the assassination of Kennedy and the increasingly disastrous American involvement in Vietnam, before finding its apogee the following decade in the Watergate scandal and numerous other scandals that often involved the CIA. The scepticism of the Cold War in, for example, John Le Carré's *The Spy Who Came in from the Cold*, may have been far more scathing, and the conspiracy thrillers of the 1970s far more direct in their critique of state secrecy, but without the cleaving of 'historical truth' from 'official truth' that the spy spoofs instigated, these later forms would not have been possible. Once 'The Big Lie' was exposed, and people began consequently to distrust the validity of those 'official' truths, the stories about the CIA could never be the same again.

OUR MAN IN HAVANA AND THE ORIGINS OF COLD WAR SATIRE

If Graham Greene failed to alter the tone of Cold War espionage narratives with *The Quiet American*, he may just have achieved it with his next spy novel: *Our Man in Havana* (1958). James Wormold, the book's antihero, is a vacuum cleaner salesman operating out of the Cuban capital in the last days of Batista's rule. While there, a twittish British intelligence officer named Hawthorne thinks Wormold's profession good cover for an intelligence agent and recruits him as a spy. The ensuing plot marked out a strategy of representation that would govern the portrayal of Western intelligence in popular culture for the next decade: enthralled to his precious daughter's expensive demands, Wormold accepts the job as an espionage agent to pay for her extravagances. With no intelligence to give, he invents fictitious reports based on information from made-up agents. Increasingly brash, he decides to spice things up by sending London sketches of one of his vacuum cleaners posing as 'strange machinery' 'observed' at a secret military installation in the mountains near Santiago. Hawthorne is the only one in London who knows Wormold's profession and its striking symmetry with the drawings, but he stays quiet to avoid raising uncomfortable questions about his recruitment methods that may jeopardise his career. With the artifice of Wormold's sketches unchallenged, London draws the apocalyptic conclusion that they depict a new type of weapon 'so big that the H-bomb will become a conventional weapon', which was desirable because, according to the credulous fictional British spy chief, 'nobody worries about conventional weapons'. Eventually Wormold is found out after he confesses to his secretary, Beatrice, who has been sent by London to take over running his non-existent agents. Fearing the embarrassment of admitting Wormold's deception, headquarters decide to conceal the affair, offering Wormold a knighthood and a teaching job for his silence.[54] In exchange for helping the British secret establishment save face, Wormold is allowed to live happily ever after; he marries Beatrice, and sends his daughter to a finishing school in Switzerland.

Like *The Quiet American*, which foresaw the disastrous consequences of American entanglement in Vietnam almost a decade before it was fully entangled, *Our Man in Havana* was prophetic. For one thing it was set in Cuba – a place where events would later conspire, perhaps more than anywhere else, to encourage the kinds of parodic narratives of Cold War espionage that this book engendered. For another its parable of secrecy as the instrument for a stuffy and incompetent British intelligence establishment to save face prefigured real-life revelations that carried similar implications. In particular the ongoing Cambridge Spies scandal with the defection of Kim Philby in 1963 and the later admission in 1979 that Anthony Blunt was a known traitor, was for many a story of an insular and naïve social elite closing ranks to protect its institutions and its class. Like Wormold, Blunt was even afforded a cosy sinecure at the heart of the British establishment, despite his treachery, as the Surveyor of the Queen's Pictures. The Cambridge Spies were a significant influence upon changing conceptions of espionage in the cultural imaginary for the coming decades.[55]

But perhaps *Our Man in Havana*'s most important precedent was its irreverent tone. While *The Quiet American* was one of the first major Anglo-American critiques of the Cold War logics that guided Western intelligence, *Our Man in Havana* was one of the first satires of Cold War espionage. Greene came up with the concept for the novel as far back as the late 1930s when the climate of international relations, for Greene at least, was far less humorous: 'The shadows of the war to come in 1938 were too dark for comedy', he wrote.

> [T]he reader could feel no sympathy for a man who was cheating his country in Hitler's day for the sake of an extravagant wife. But in fantastic Havana, among the absurdities of the Cold War (for who can accept the survival of Western capitalism as a great cause?) there was a situation allowably comic, all the more if I changed the wife into a daughter.[56]

Greene's novel, published in 1958 and adapted to the cinema the following year by Carol Reed, rejected the high seriousness of the semi-documentary in favour of light parody. Wormold's timorous voice replaced the Timespeak bombast of the previous age. His motivations for spying were money and status anxiety, not duty to country or ideology. His espionage activities were bumbling, non-existent or trivial – a far cry from the entirely malicious work of communist subversives that featured in the semi-documentaries, or the vital counter-intelligence of the FBI in stopping them. Even the existential threat of nuclear annihilation – the core pillar of Hollywood's initial campaign for a permanent peacetime central intelligence agency – is trivialised in the novel as a marketing gimmick for Wormold's latest vacuum cleaner model: the Atomic Pile.

> We live in an atomic age, Mr Wormold. Push a button – piff bang – where are we? Another Scotch, please . . . Oh, of course, there's nothing atomic about it – it's only a name. Last year there was the Turbo Jet; this year it's the Atomic. It works off the light-plug just the same as any other.[57]

Like the bikini, or the emergent 'jet-set' classes, the Cold War's instruments of ultimate destruction had become mere symbols of luxury and pleasure in a late capitalist age. And like Stanley Kubrick's more sustained parody of nuclear annihilation in *Dr. Strangelove*, irreverence had replaced apocalypticism as the conventional response to the MAD logics of the Cold War. With its droll parody of the self-serving intelligence agencies and their guiding logic, secrecy, with its emphasis on artifice and performance, and its sense that the gap between the fictional and the real is hard to know – especially where the activities of the secret state are concerned – *Our Man in Havana* offered a near complete inversion and indeed rejection of the semi-documentary style that had dominated the representation of espionage onscreen in the previous decade.

In the wake of *Our Man in Havana* a new form of spy cinema that explicitly rejected its predecessor's credulous epistemology of state-sourced realism replaced the semi-documentary. 'This film has *not* been made with the consent or cooperation of the Federal Board of Regulations (F.B.R.) or the Central Enquiries Agency (C.E.A.)' proudly announced the opening title of *The President's Analyst* (1967) in a doubly ironic pastiche of the semi-documentary's government endorsements and authenticity claims. In place of state-sourced realism, the spy romances and spoofs of the 1960s exalted the exact opposite: fantasy, wish fulfilment and, above all, artifice. This is what Susan Sontag famously described as the 'essence' of a 'camp' style or sensibility, defined by 'its love of the unnatural: of artifice and exaggeration'.[58] 'Your profession has quite a natural air', Hawthorne enviously tells Wormold upon recruiting him – 'the word "natural" was a favourite adjective of his' – 'But it *is* natural', Wormold insists. At least selling vacuum cleaners would prove more natural than falsifying intelligence reports of invented Cuban military installations based on sketches of the Atomic Pile. Likewise in Hitchcock's *North by Northwest*, Roger Thornhill is thrust into this unnatural world of espionage after an entirely artificial identity as a spy – a construct of the CIA – is thrust upon him. This focus upon the artifice, fakery and duplicitousness of espionage was further emphasised by the exaggerated plotlines, the characters and, most memorably, the gadgets, guns and gizmos that by the middle of the 1960s had shifted the spy genre closer to science fiction than documentary.

Satire is always open to the charge of trivialisation. Certainly, if anything was, some of the more ludicrous spy spoofs of the era, including the increasingly tongue-in-cheek Bond films, were guilty of this. Greene himself fell afoul of the new Cuban revolutionary government, who took power a year after the publication of *Our Man in Havana*, for minimising 'the terror of Batista's rule'.[59] This, however, didn't stop the film being shot in Havana, although the authorities demanded to see early versions of the script and asked for any allusions to the new regime, including the beard of the brutal police chief Captain Segura, to be removed.[60] Curiously, as noted by Peter Hulme, perhaps the darkest sequence in the book that features the brutality of the Batista regime, when Wormold visits Santiago and is assaulted by two police officers, does not feature in the film.[61] In general, however, Carol Reed's film offered a remarkably faithful adaptation of the novel, especially when compared to Mankiewicz's *The Quiet American* (1958) that had infuriated Greene the previous year. Unlike their meddling in that production with the assistance of a friendly government in Vietnam, this time the CIA could only look on, which they did intently: CIA officer David Atlee Phillips was sent to Cuba to spy on Greene during the film's production.[62] It must have irked them to see perhaps their greatest literary bête noir cavorting with their newly arrived-upon political nemesis, Fidel Castro, who visited his friend Greene, and the cast and crew, on the set.

Yet for all the charges of trivialisation and apoliticism levelled against *Our Man in Havana*, and the camp spy parodies it inspired, they differed ideologically from their semi-documentary predecessors in at least one significant

Figure 4.4 *Our Man in Havana* (1959) co-stars Alec Guinness and Maureen O'Hara meet Fidel Castro while filming in Havana (27 May 1959). *Source*: Baltimore Sun Photographic Archive.

respect: they severed the previously unbreakable bond of loyalty and devotion between private citizens and their governments. Wormold works for British intelligence for self-serving reasons, and is perfectly prepared to deceive his handlers with faulty intelligence to get what he wants. Moreover, he is an amateur, and, initially at least, an innocent – thrown into the world of international intrigue against his will. Michael Kackman writes that the spy parodies of the 1960s 'reinvigorated espionage as a forum for the exploration of questions of citizenship and nationalism' and 'confounded the neat equation of the nation and the state' that the semi-documentaries had made.[63] Whether or not they trivialised the Cold War, they responded to, and indeed anticipated, the collapse of trust in government during the 1960s, and the fracturing of consensus that ensued.

NORTH BY NORTHWEST (1959)

Alfred Hitchcock was a great admirer of Graham Greene and was in the market for a light-hearted spy thriller when *Our Man in Havana* was published. In

1958 he tried to buy the rights to the book, but Greene refused. Perhaps still wary of Hollywood after his experience with *The Quiet American*, Greene felt that 'the book just wouldn't survive' Hitchcock's famous touch.[64] He sold the rights in the end at a cut-price to another Englishman, his friend Carol Reed, who had done a good job adapting Greene's work a decade previously with *The Fallen Idol* (1948) and *The Third Man* (1949). But despite Greene's understandable trepidation given his recent experience with Hollywood, Hitchcock and *Our Man in Havana* were ideally suited. For one thing, light-hearted spy capers were Hitchcock's specialty, or at least they had been before HUAC encouraged a caesura on all espionage features that were not wholly and unambiguously committed to the Cold War consensus and the narratives of state. He had made his name in the 1930s with films like *The 39 Steps* (1935), *Secret Agent* (1936) and *The Lady Vanishes* (1938), which, while not as scathing in their attitude towards British intelligence as *Our Man in Havana*, were nevertheless laced with an irreverent suspicion of authority – a central 'Hitchcockian' motif.

Related to that irreverence was the most persistent dilemma raised in all of Hitchcock's spy films: the conflict between the personal and the political, or between the individual and the state. It was a theme that existed in marked opposition to the ideology of the semi-documentary and the red-baiting cinema of the early Cold War that supplicated individual morality to national ideology. Hitchcock's most prolonged hiatus from the spy genre coincided with the height of McCarthyism. Explicitly political subject matter, especially that which dealt with the Cold War in anything less than un-ambiguously pro-American terms, was dangerously provocative during this period. This may well explain Hitchcock's unusual evasion of Cold War espionage thrillers until the end of the 1950s. 'The specific context invoked in *North by Northwest*', observes Pierre Lethier, 'is very clearly' that of 'a nation gradually emerging from the debilitating trauma of the witch-hunt age'.[65]

Like *Our Man in Havana, North by Northwest* (1959) was dramatically different from the narratives that preceded it in its attitude toward the Cold War and America's intelligence agencies. 'The "thaw" in the Cold War did not occur on theater screens until 1959', writes Lenny Rubenstein. '*North by Northwest* was a watershed; few films after it could treat domestic espionage with half the gravity it had formerly been accorded.'[66] The popularity of *North by Northwest*, particularly when compared with the many semi-documentary box-office flops that preceded it, surely resided in its light-hearted depiction of espionage and counter-espionage. Cary Grant's performance in particular, as the urbane fast-quipping advertising executive Roger Thornhill, drew audiences into a world of Cold War intrigue treated with wry amusement as opposed to the grave tenor of the red-baiting cinema that regarded enemy spies as a near-apocalyptic danger.[67] As Rick Worland argues, 'perhaps the most significant legacy *North by Northwest* bequeathed to the 1960s spy cycle was its overall tone'.[68]

James Mason's performance as the insouciant master spy Phillip Vandamm was a long way from the rigid and doctrinaire communist subversives of early Cold War cinema. He is assisted by Leonard and Valerian who the script implies are homosexuals – getting Hitchcock into trouble with the PCA and forcing him to remove some of the more overt references to their sexuality in the final picture.[69] The final member of the spy-ring is the matriarchal 'Mrs Townsend', or so she claims, who is redolent of Elizabeth Bentley – the infamous former Soviet agent who turned star-HUAC witness and informant for the FBI. Although Hitchcock never explicitly identifies Vandamm's spy ring as working for the Soviet Union, the Cold War subtext is fairly obvious, and Hitchcock frequently identifies them with the spy scandals from earlier in the decade. The microfilm 'MacGuffin' that all the spies are after, for example, is described by Thornhill at one point as 'the pumpkin', a clear allusion to the 'Pumpkin Papers' that implicated Alger Hiss as a communist agent – so-called because HUAC's star witness against Hiss, Whittaker Chambers, hid rolls of microfilm that implicated Hiss in a pumpkin on his farm. The baronial manor that Vandamm and his spies occupy also clearly alludes to the Soviet-owned Killenworth Estate in Glen Cove, Long Island – a site of considerable controversy in the decade leading up to the release of *North by Northwest* after the Soviets refused to pay the tax liens on the property.[70] While Hitchcock may have departed in tone from the hysteria of McCarthyist America, he still invoked some of its more provocative iconography.

The story begins with Vandamm's henchmen kidnapping Thornhill after mistakenly identifying him as a CIA (or is it FBI?) agent named George Kaplan. After a tête-à-tête between Vandamm and Thornhill at the Killenworth house, Thornhill is forced to imbibe vast quantities of liquor and is placed in a moving car heading over a cliff – an end he naturally manages to avoid right at the last minute. Unfortunately for Thornhill, Kaplan, like Wormold's plans for the 'Atomic Pile' weapons installation in Santiago, is a total fiction – an artifice of the state invented by the CIA as a decoy to deceive enemy agents. Callously, the CIA allow the Vandamm spy-ring to maintain their misperception and chase Thornhill/Kaplan to the bitter end so as not to blow the cover of their real agent, Eve Kendall, who is Vandamm's lover.

While investigating Vandamm, who was posing as a United Nations representative named Townsend, Thornhill is framed for the murder of the real Townsend in the United Nations General Assembly in New York. With events swiftly spiralling beyond his control, and with the CIA, despite their omniscience, refusing to rescue an innocent American citizen, Thornhill flees to Chicago on the 20th Century Limited from New York's Grand Central Terminal. While on-board, he is seduced, presumably on Vandamm's orders, by Kendall, who lures him to a desolate location somewhere in the Midwest. There he is attacked, in one of cinema's most iconic set pieces, by a crop-duster plane.

Eventually, the persistent Thornhill forces the CIA's hand when he casts suspicion on Kendall by catching up with her and Vandamm in Chicago. The CIA's avuncular chief, The Professor, clearly modelled on Allen Dulles and played by Leo G. Carroll who reprised much the same role as Alexander Waverly in *The Man From U.N.C.L.E.*, lets Thornhill in on the secret and enlists him in a scheme to re-ingratiate Kendall to Vandamm. But when Thornhill later learns that his government has again deceived him – by not telling him that the CIA once again intended to put an innocent's life in danger, this time Kendall's, by allowing her to leave the country with Vandamm – he confronts The Professor:

> Thornhill: I don't like the games you play.
> Professor: War is hell, Mr. Thornhill. Even when it's a cold one.
> Thornhill: If you fellows can't lick the Vandamm's of this world without asking girls like her to bed down with them and fly away with them and probably never come back, perhaps you ought to start learning how to lose a few cold wars.
> Professor: I'm afraid we're already doing that.

Perhaps Hitchcock had missile gaps, the launching of Sputnik, Hungary and the second Berlin crisis on his mind. Thornhill then becomes a direct victim of state repression when he is punched out by a police officer on The Professor's orders to prevent him from stopping Kendell. Later, however, Thornhill defies The Professor – and thereby his government – by escaping from his locked hospital room to launch a dramatic rescue mission to save Kendall from Vandamm, who soon learns of her treachery. The suspenseful sequence culminates in another of cinema's most iconic set pieces, atop the faces of Mount Rushmore where the enemy spies meet their end.

Prior to shooting, the Rushmore sequence had caused controversy in sections of the American press who reported that Hitchcock intended to deface the monument by having his characters crawl across Lincoln's nose.[71] Upon reading the reports, the monument's sculptor Lincoln Borglum, son of the original sculptor Gutzon Borglum, raised his concerns with Hitchcock that the memorial should be used 'in keeping with its concept' as a 'symbol of democracy'.[72]

Equally concerned were the former and acting superintendents of the Mount Rushmore memorial, Charles Homberger and Donald Spaulding. Producer Herbert Coleman discussed the possibility of using their influence in Washington to place pressure on Homberger and his colleagues to allow

Figure 4.5 Cary Grant as mistaken CIA agent Roger Thornhill (centre) confronting spy chief 'The Professor', played by Leo G. Carroll (left), for his callous indifference to the fate of his agent Eve Kendall (Eva Marie Saint – right) in Alfred Hitchcock's *North by Northwest* (1959). A recurring theme in Hitchcock's numerous spy dramas was the conflict between the personal and the political. *North by Northwest*, among other Hitchcock spy dramas, forces audiences to confront the utilitarian logic of the Cold War – is the life of an individual worth sacrificing for the sake of an abstract political goal? By the end of his career Hitchcock came down firmly on the side of the individual. His final unmade spy film, *The Short Night*, features a line that is quite definitive in answering this dilemma: 'Spying and espionage. Everybody suffers from it. The gains are vague and abstract. And the losses are all personal.' *Source:* Alfred Hitchcock, MGM, 1959.

filming to take place. But after seeking advice from their legal department they chose instead to try to convince Homberger and Spaulding that their use of the monument would be in keeping with the values it represents.[73] In doing so, they drafted a letter to the national park officials detailing the film's plot and emphasising the symbolic value of Mount Rushmore to the film:

> The enemies of this country fall to their deaths from the Monument of the great Presidents who gave this nation the very ideals they are seeking to subvert ... We sincerely believe it will be symbolically and dramatically

> satisfying to the people of the United States that this great National Memorial, standing there in all its granite glory, becomes the very stumbling block to those who would undermine our country. In the end, the enemies of democracy are defeated by the Shrine of Democracy itself.[74]

Homberger and Spaulding were broadly cooperative and in favour of the proposed sequence. However, they remained concerned about scenes of violence taking place on the faces of the presidents, asking that Hitchcock pan the camera so that the monument is not shown when acts of violence take place. Hitchcock adamantly attempted to convince them of the value of the scene as he had conceived it, suggesting that 'crank' letters from disgruntled citizens had influenced their opinion. Homberger and Spaulding, however, insisted that they had received their orders 'from Washington prior to receipt of any so called "crank" notes'.[75] Ultimately, Hitchcock would be frustrated in his attempts to secure shooting permission, and was forced to film the majority of the iconic sequence on a Hollywood soundstage.

The renowned Hitchcock scholar, Robin Wood, once argued that Mount Rushmore in the film 'is not a symbol of democracy standing against the wicked agents'.[76] Hitchcock and MGM's wrangling with Homberger and Spaulding, however, suggest otherwise. At the very least, this correspondence indicates that Hitchcock and his fellow producers were aware of the political resonance this scene carried, even if their patriotic invocations were born out of a pragmatic need to get filming permission. Despite the film's noteworthy departures from the red-baiting jingoism of the decade, its highly symbolic finale clearly reinforces the language and iconography of the Cold War consensus.

Nevertheless, although this finale may have gone much of the way to resolving the ideological contradictions and challenges to the prevailing logics of the Cold War within the film, as Michael Kackman has argued, the political significance of *North by Northwest* 'may have less to do with [its] mechanisms of narrative closure than with [its] chaotic disruptions'.[77] These disruptions and ambiguities opened a hitherto suppressed dialogue in Hollywood about the morality of American espionage and, in particular, the activities of the Central Intelligence Agency. Hitchcock was no radical. Indeed, he is more often than not described by scholars as either apolitical or, if anything, a champion of the Cold War consensus.[78] But Hitchcock was deviant, and operated best amidst the morally, politically and socially restrictive environment of America in the 1950s – most of his classic films were made in this period, or just after.[79] He revelled in provocation, testing the boundaries of social, moral and political decorum without ever fully transgressing them. He liked comedies of manners and films about murder where the murderer is just an average Joe, like you or me. He sought to reveal, as Richard Schickel put it, 'how thinly the membrane of civilization is stretched over an essentially irrational existence'.[80] Perhaps it was the naughty Edwardian schoolboy within him that liked to prod at the pretences and hypocrisies that papered over the moral ambiguities and contradictions of modern society. Whatever the reasons, his contrarian impulse coupled with the complex morality and playful style of his celluloid worlds would not allow him to make a Cold War spy film that was either wholeheartedly committed to the ideological precepts of its age, as some have claimed, or radically opposed to them.

Thus, in *North by Northwest*, we have a sympathetic but quite clearly villainous group of spies that recall some of the famous spy cases of the McCarthyite era, threatening to undermine national security by stealing state secrets. We have an avuncular spy-chief in the model of Allen Dulles's self-styled professorial image who is nevertheless callous, even eager, to expend the blood of an innocent American's life for sake of a higher purpose. Finally, we have that higher purpose itself, celebrated in the granite faces carved into Mount Rushmore, 'the shrine of democracy', which vanquishes the enemies of the nation, but is nevertheless called into question by the innocent individuals whose lives are threatened by it: 'perhaps you ought to start learning how to lose a few cold wars'. Few images conjure this fragility of America's democratic creed better than Roger Thornhill and Eve Kendall precariously dangling over the edge of Lincoln's nose.

So what are we to make of all these contradictions and inconsistencies in Hitchcock's political world? Is his CIA a necessary evil, or just an evil? The answer, like all of the contradictory elements within Hitchcock's films, is not a straightforward one, and Hitchcock, always an advocate of letting the audience do the job of interpretation for him, seems to have left it up to us. But for Robin Wood, one of the preeminent early auteurist Hitchcock critics, the answer was fairly clear:

> That charming father figure, the head of the C.I.A. .... seems to me to come out of things pretty badly. The film is surely solidly behind Thornhill in rejecting the use of a woman to 'get people like Vandamm': prostitution, in however admirable a cause, remains prostitution. Mixed morality – the pursuing of a good end by conventionally immoral means ... is justified by Hitchcock only as the outcome of powerful instinctive drives, of basically right feelings, not when it comes to cold calculation: justifiable, therefore, only on the personal level, not on the political.[81]

This privileging of the personal over the political, a contest that the semi-documentary's neat equation of good citizenship with the state did not allow, was increasingly stressed by Hitchcock as his career entered its twilight years. *Torn Curtain* (1966) was in part inspired by the Cambridge Spies scandal and represented the first of a series of attempts by Hitchcock during his late career to undo his own influence by producing an 'anti-Bond' spy feature that was closer to the murky moral universe of British spy realist novelists like John Le Carré. *Topaz* (1969) was even more tragic in its narrative structure, featuring the death of several innocents, who, unlike Thornhill, failed to transcend the machinations of state power and international relations with which they had become inadvertently embroiled. Hitchcock's final unmade feature, *The Short Night*, a story about a CIA agent sent to track down an escaped British defector who was modelled on the British Soviet agent George Blake, included a telling line that more or less epitomised Hitchcock's dim view of espionage by the end of his career – 'spying and espionage. Everybody suffers from it. The gains are vague and abstract. And the losses are all personal.'[82] Hitchcock's CIA was never entirely good or entirely evil – but they emerged out of an ambiguity that for the first time on American screens raised issues, tensions and contradictions between the conduct of US Cold War foreign policy and accepted standards of individual morality.

North by Northwest was arguably the single most influential spy film of the Cold War. Not only did it inspire the James Bond films and the camp spy spoofs that irreverently rejected the grave patriotism of 1950s spy cinema, but it also, for the first time, called into question the moral authority of America's national security state and the CIA in particular. It may not have been a particularly radical rejection of the Cold War consensus, and even rearticulated and re-deployed some of its key features, but in raising the prospect that the CIA could deceive and even let die its own citizens, it foregrounded some of the more far-reaching questions that began to be asked of the Agency and America's foreign policy establishment as the defining events of the long-1960s – Vietnam and Watergate – called into question the US Government's moral authority.

Hitchcock didn't express any of these political themes with anywhere near the same explicitness or seriousness of tone as the semi-documentary. Indeed it was precisely because he said it with humour and irony that it was so effective. A huge box-office success, *North by Northwest* struck a chord with an American public desperate for a more light-hearted approach to the portrayal of foreign affairs. Perhaps most significantly, however, it set the tone and the style of spy cinema and television, one of the most popular genres of the 1960s, for the next decade. Without *North by Northwest*, the James Bond films may not have been possible, and certainly would not have been the same. Nor would *The Man from U.N.C.L.E.*, *Get Smart*, *I Spy*, *In Like Flint*, the Matt Helm films, nor *Charade* (1963).

Of these, the latter was perhaps the most obviously inspired by Hitchcock's caper, although its director, Stanley Donen of *Singing in the Rain* fame, resented the idea that all light-hearted spy capers were now necessarily 'Hitchcockian'.[83] *Charade* shared with *North by Northwest*, among other things, its light-hearted plotline, its use of iconic locales – this time in Paris – its use of numerous dramatic set pieces that would have been perfectly at home in *North by Northwest*, and, most obviously, the casting of an ageing Cary Grant as an undercover CIA agent in the lead role. Grant found his distance in years from co-star Audrey Hepburn unseemly – the two reprised the roles of Thornhill and Kendall as lovers in the film.[84] Thematically, *Charade* also used Hitchcock's device of 'the innocent' – thrusting Hepburn's 'Reggie' Lampert into a world of intrigue beyond her control. It also continued Hitchcock's exploration of the moral tensions and ambiguities that arise when the 'means justifies the ends' consequentialist logic threatens innocent American lives. While Reggie dutifully tells CIA chief Bartholomew, played by Walther Mathau, 'If I'm going to die, I might as well do it for my country', she and the film also regularly call into question the amorality of the CIA. In particular, the American public's increasing concern over government duplicity in the wake of the Bay of Pigs is comically reflected in Cary Grant's four separate identities within the film, framed in a split-screen shot in the final frame. As in *North by Northwest*, *Charade* light-heartedly raises a serious political question: is the CIA and the American Government justified in lying to its people?

Although *Charade* is most obviously comparable to *North by Northwest*, almost all of the spy films and television shows of the 1960s and beyond walked in Hitchcock's shadow. *North by Northwest* gave them their mode of expression: a tongue-in-cheek world of action and movement, unbound from the discourses of the American Government, featuring innocent Americans threatened by the actions of the American Government. The age of semi-documentary innocence had drawn swiftly to a close, replaced by a form of spy cinema not necessarily radically opposed to American intelligence and the ideology that undergirded its actions, but certainly more sophisticated: appealing to increasingly younger audiences whose notions of patriotism and citizenship had not been forged by watching John Ford documentaries of the Battle of Midway, or from fighting and seeing friends die in Europe or the Pacific.

THE MAN FROM U.N.C.L.E. AND TV SPY SATIRE IN THE 1960S

Ian Fleming was a great admirer of Hitchcock. After seeing *North by Northwest* he asked the great director, via their mutual friend Eric Ambler, to direct the first James Bond film.[85] Hitchcock declined, and made *Psycho* instead, but his presence can be felt throughout the Bond series. Whether it was the more light-hearted tone of the films as compared to the novels, the emphasis on elaborate action sequences interspersed with movement through exotic or iconic locales, the sexually charged romantic sub-plots – often involving femme fatales tamed by Bond's virility and irresistible charm – or the suave unflappability of its leading hero, Bond took its cues from Hitchcock. Along with this general framework that *North by Northwest* provided Bond, the series borrowed/stole from Hitchcock quite specifically and explicitly on numerous occasions. Most famously perhaps, the helicopter chase sequence in *From Russia with Love* (1963) was so similar to the iconic crop-duster sequence in *North by Northwest* that it provoked Robin Wood into establishing Hitchcock's artistry, in his seminal book on the director, via an unfavourable comparison between the clearly superior Hitchcock sequence and the 'pandering to a debased popular taste' that Wood thought was everywhere apparent in the Bond helicopter chase scene.[86]

That Hitchcock influenced the Bond series then is undeniable. But equally undeniable is the enduring popularity of the myth that the Bond films created, and the enormity of their influence not only upon the spy genre, but cinema generally. Hitchcock may have got there first, but the Bond films adopted his formula with such panache that they would dominate the landscape of spy cinema almost completely in America for the next decade, and still prove a major influence even on the supposedly 'grittier' spy films of the present day. Yet, curiously, no American fictional spy hero ever managed to supplant Bond, although many directors tried. Perhaps this was, as Jonathan Nashel has argued, because Bond was more American than British: classless (in the films at least), consumerist, ruggedly individualistic and emblematic of a frontier spirit long evaporated from British culture but still a pervasive myth in America.[87] This may also explain why the anti-Bond films in the model of John Le Carré, reasonably popular in Britain, never really took hold in the United States.

Another explanation for the lack of any serious American rival to Bond in Hollywood may be because Americans have always felt far more uncomfortable than the British in adopting an agent of the secret state as a national icon. Admittedly the semi-documentaries did present FBI agents as 'ideal citizen types', according to Kackman, but they were no-way near as popular as the phenomenon that was Bond, and they focused on defensive counter-intelligence rather than offensive covert action. The most direct American offspring of Bond, *The Man from U.N.C.L.E.*, the *Like Flint* films and Matt Helm series, were notably more irreverent than Bond, and took the tongue-in-cheek irony to cartoonish extremes. They allowed Americans to share in the wish-fulfilment that Bond provided, while nevertheless maintaining a mocking and mildly dismissive attitude towards secrecy and intelligence agencies.

The Man from U.N.C.L.E. was actually more intimately connected with the Bond franchise than a mere semblance of style: the idea for the show came, in part, from Ian Fleming. In the autumn of 1962, at about the same time as the release of the first Bond film *Dr. No*, Ian Fleming met the British-born American television producer, Norman Felton, in New York to discuss Felton's idea for a television series based loosely on *North by Northwest* and seeking to capitalise on the popularity of Bond.[88] Vaguely interested, Fleming came up with the

Figure 4.6 Robert Vaughn as Napoleon Solo (foreground) starred alongside David McCallum as Russian-born spy Ilya Kuryakin in *The Man from U.N.C.L.E. Source:* Wikimedia Commons.

central character, Napoleon Solo, a debonair spy, like Bond, who smokes cigarillos, has 'a fine collection of bandana handkerchiefs, but otherwise dresses in dark blue, white shirt, black tie'. Crucially, however, unlike Bond, he was 'not a superman' and suffered from 'normal human frailties – hangovers, colds, corns, fibrositis, but does not take pills . . . He must be HUMAN above all else . . . Solo will sometimes win, sometimes make mistakes, be reprimanded, lose his Christmas bonus.' Fleming saw the narrative developing as 'a kind of Pilgrim's Progress, with the successes and failures, written large and dramatically, that beset the ordinary man's life'. Solo was to be popular with women, naturally, 'imbued with the power of the anonymous "HE"'. When 'not "in action", Solo is stoical, friendly, but with an inner citadel of reserve which intrigues women and dates, perhaps', like Bond, 'from [the] death of his wife and child in [an] accident'. His inner sadness, however, was not to overwhelm his '<u>zest for life and adventure</u>, which are paramount to the series and which are its basic message'. The '[s]ubsidiary message, or moral', clearing up the moral ambiguity at the heart of *North by Northwest*, 'might be the motto of the Jesuits, "When the ends are lawful, the means are also lawful."'[89]

Fleming got cold feet, perhaps because the Bond films had taken off since first meeting Felton and he was too busy capitalising on the icon he had brought into existence. He sold the rights for the character of Solo and the concept of the TV series to Felton for the princely sum of one English pound.[90] A few years later, the repeated references to his involvement with the show irritated Fleming. Suspecting that the NBC marketing department was exploiting his name without his approval, his lawyers sent the network a cease and desist letter that prompted a worried Felton to issue a stern series of warnings to all involved with the show not to mention the Fleming connection.[91] Developing Fleming's concept, Felton hired producer and screenwriter Sam Rolfe who came up with the U.N.C.L.E. acronym as well its organisational structure. Rolfe became heavily involved in the writing of the show's first season, including the show's pilot, *The Vulcan Affair*.

Felton and Rolfe fused elements of Bond and *North by Northwest* to produce a highly popular format that ran for four seasons from 1964 to 1968. From the former, it borrowed the ostensibly depoliticised and deterritorialised Manichean framework by pitting an invented international espionage organisation, U.N.C.L.E., against a nebulous globalised criminal network, T.H.R.U.S.H. From the latter, it learnt its tongue-in-cheek style and the idea of 'the innocent'. According to early notes written by Rolfe and Felton, each episode was to feature an innocent –

> frequently an attractive girl but not necessarily so. It is she – or he – who provides audience identification and empathy. The innocent might well be the viewer in Oshkosh who is suddenly thrust into a high adventure, remaining in a state of bafflement all the way.

The U.N.C.L.E. organisation, which we later learn stands for United Network Command for Law Enforcement, nevertheless evoked a kind of United Nations intelligence agency with its globalised interests and multinational staff. Aside from Ilya Kuryakin, the show's increasingly prominent Russian-born agent, the organisation was composed of 'brisk, alert young personnel of many races, creeds, colors and national origins'. Its personnel were 'peculiarly multi-national', according to Felton and Rolfe, which suited their line of work. They were required 'to cross national boundaries with such nonchalance that a daily shortwave message from the remote Himalayas fails to flutter any eyebrows'.[92] The touristic exoticism of the show was a popular device that was also borrowed from *North by Northwest* and Bond, especially because it appealed to global audiences. There was almost certainly a financial incentive for constructing *U.N.C.L.E.* to appeal to a worldwide audience, and Felton quite consciously sought to exploit foreign markets, but the multicultural composition of *U.N.C.L.E.* also responded to an NBC policy to encourage producers to cast minorities in increasingly prominent roles in order to reflect contemporary society.[93] Indeed another NBC spy show, *I Spy*, which began airing a year after *The Man from U.N.C.L.E.* in 1965, was the first

Figure 4.7   David McCallum as Russian-born U.N.C.L.E. agent Ilya Kuryakin. McCallum's Kuryakin became something of a pin-up idol during the course of the show's run, suggesting, as Rick Worland put it, 'popular renegotiations of previously rigid positions and assumptions with regard to orthodox Cold War ideology'. *Source:* Wikimedia Commons.[94]

primetime American television series to star an African American, Bill Cosby, in a prominent role.[95]

Perhaps appropriately for a 'postmodern' narrative that fulfils, supposedly, the cultural logic of late capitalism, U.N.C.L.E.'s nemesis THRUSH is also a global corporation, not a nation.[96] THRUSH threatened Soviet farmers and Latin American couples just as much as ordinary Americans. Its organisation spread supra-national tentacles around the world with each physical instance of existence termed a 'Satrap'. A Satrap 'may take the form of a manufacturing complex . . . or a school . . . or a hospital . . . or a series of underground tunnels and caverns.' Although not a nation in a traditional sense, it has, 'like many a nation', the 'national purpose . . . to dominate the earth'. Like nation states, THRUSH had 'an almost governmental structure of authority . . . At the top is the council' populated by men and women of various fields who are 'universally super-intellects and scientists'. Not that the council was strictly necessary, as all decisions were taken by the 'Ultimate Computor [sic] ... a marvellous, almost infallible thinking machine, it has been developed by the brightest minds of Thrush.' The council's job was simply to process the machine's information and carry out its recommended actions.[97] This reflected social anxieties about the dehumanising impact of science and technology, which remained a permanent feature of the Cold War.

Leo G. Carroll was obviously typecast from *North by Northwest* as the tweedy CIA-boss. He was described by Rolfe as faintly stuffy but with a 'dim' and 'dry sense of humor' that makes him immensely likeable. Waverley oversaw the two central characters – Solo, played by Robert Vaughn, an 'urbane swinger who is usually (but not always) involved with pretty girls' and Kuryakin, who Rolfe initially described as slightly jealous of Solo's womanising, but as the series ran its course, and Kuryakin became a sex symbol in his own right, would gradually become just as, if not more, promiscuous.

Vaughn's casting aligned the show with the progressive politics and student movements erupting in the period.[98] His father was a radio actor whose politics would have likely found him on the blacklist had he not died of a heart attack shortly before he was due to appear before HUAC. Like Dustin Hoffman's character in the 1976 conspiracy thriller *Marathon Man* who is writing a PhD on McCarthyism to avenge his blacklisted father, Vaughn authored an account of HUAC in Hollywood, *Only Victims*, which remains an authoritative study to this day.[99] His personal experience at the hands of McCarthyism translated into active political opposition against the 'national paranoia about communism', leading him to repeatedly denounce the war in Vietnam.[100] A friend of the Kennedy brothers, he became increasingly involved in liberal Democratic Party politics and later became the chairperson of the California Democratic Party Speakers Bureau. Once believed to have had political ambitions of his own, he apparently lost heart after Robert Kennedy's death. But he remained a vocal supporter of Senator Eugene McCarthy, who ran for the Presidency in 1968 and would become one of the CIA's most outspoken Congressional critics in the wake of the 1967 Ramparts exposé, which revealed that the CIA had infiltrated the National Student Association.

It may well have been because of his progressive politics, as well as his abhorrence towards the violence in Vietnam and the real activities of the CIA, that Vaughn grew increasingly uncomfortable with the show, and his character Solo, which he later described as 'marginally psychopathic'.[101] Certainly *U.N.C.L.E.* was not a radical departure from the glamourising exploits of Bond, perhaps the greatest recruitment tool in the history of the Western intelligence services. But *U.N.C.L.E.*'s popularity with liberal college students suggests that it offered far from a straightforward endorsement of the American intelligence community. This ambiguity over the show's politics and tone was deliberate. After the success of the first season, Felton sent the following observations to his writers:

> THE MAN FROM U.N.C.L.E. has its appeal on many levels. To youngsters and some adults, it is simply an exciting adventure story. As we move up in the 'discernment level' it becomes a comedy-adventure, a spoof, even (to the innermost of the 'in') a series offering sly commentary on our manners and morals.
>
> Our Program is, in fact, a carefully balanced blend of all these things. Its peculiar style – a mixture of physical excitement, wit, insouciant charm, parody – has evolved to the point where we are the darlings of the masses (as the ratings indicate) and of the super-sophisticates who populate Cal Tech and the space-age laboratories. And of the several groups in between.
>
> Understandably, we have no desire to tamper with this mixture.[102]

To Sam Rolfe's irritation, however, they did tamper with this mixture. In season three the show's ratings dropped as it sought to emulate the 'high camp' of the successful Batman series, which debuted in 1966. After Rolfe left the show it switched to full colour in the second season and increasingly adopted the Pop Art aesthetics and psychedelia associated with sixties camp and the counterculture. Moreover, what was once a fusion of subtle parody and drama became all out pastiche, with episodes like *Greer Window, Die Spy* and *Not So Great Escape* indulging in overt intertextual send-ups of screen culture. One episode even featured Solo dancing with a gorilla, an absurdity that tested even the most loyal fans' patience.

The show's steadily more absurdist tone was reinforced by the increasingly incredible gadgets used by U.N.C.L.E. agents and their nemeses, transforming it into something closer to science fiction than semi-documentary. Writers were encouraged to take every opportunity to insert outlandish gizmos into their scenarios, not only because of the merchandising opportunities, but also because audiences responded well to them in screen tests.[103] U.N.C.L.E. agents were issued with Walther P-38s that were augmented with scopes, barrel extensions, and a rifle that could fire sleeping darts. In addition, they occasionally used a .32 calibre pistol disguised as a cigarette lighter or a miniature camera that fired gas pellets through the lens. If their arsenal seemed a little over the top, it was only to achieve some kind of parity with THRUSH who, among other things, deployed brainwashing techniques, vaporising devices, a quartzite radiation projector, an earthquake activating machine, a volcano activating machine, laser guns, deadly hiccup gas, antimatter, a tidal-wave machine, a molecutronic gun, docility gas, a high-frequency sound machine that shattered ear drums, a brain-altering ray and radioactive bats to jam the world's radar.[104]

Despite the manifest absurdity of these devices, it didn't stop one avid U.N.C.L.E. fan writing to the FBI, the CIA and the NSA, as well as numerous electronics firms and shoe repair shops to try to track down a fountain pen transmitter and hollow-heel shoes.[105] The FBI received so many of these kinds of requests that an exasperated J. Edgar Hoover crafted a stock reply informing each enquirer that U.N.C.L.E. was a fictitious organisation with no association to the Bureau. Never missing an opportunity to promote his organisation, and perhaps envious of having to share the limelight, for once, with an entirely fictitious organisation, Hoover enclosed booklets with each letter entitled 'What It's Like to Be an FBI Agent' and 'Should You Go Into Law Enforcement?'[106] It would have proved little consolation to Hoover to know that the U.N.C.L.E. producers, for their part, were also handling enquiries for the real intelligence services. When one Michael R. Pries, for example, contacted the show with detailed designs for a new form of gas grenade, the legal department wrote back suggesting that it 'may be of possible interest for non-fictional application in the CIA which, we understand, is always on the lookout for weaponry for unusual applications'.[107] Gullible or joshing members of the public were not the only ones to fall victim to U.N.C.L.E and James Bond's fictional allure. The CIA's Office of Technical Services (OTS), the Agency's real-life Q division, found itself under increasing pressure to meet the rising expectations of real-life operatives not wishing to be outdone by Bond.[108] Along with their failed attempt to reproduce the James Bond honing beacon under Allen Dulles's command, the OTS also developed a special anti-eavesdropping 'secure room' that resembled, although not quite as ludicrously, the famous 'cone of silence' in *Get Smart*.[109]

This crossing over of factual and fictional worlds, a central feature of postmodernity, was a narrative strategy adopted by *The Man from U.N.C.L.E.*'s writers and producers that overtly mocked and subverted the semidocumentary's crude epistemology of state-source realism. The first season, for example, concluded with a credit title mocking the government endorsements of 1950s espionage shows: 'We wish to thank the United Network Command for Law and Enforcement, without whose assistance this program would not have been possible.' This fictional authorising-as-fact of a fictional text was also a technique used by the show's marketing department. Along with the toy guns, gadgets, cars, comic books, albums, novels, soundtracks, action figurines and the rest of the merchandising smorgasbord, they also produced a 'non-fictional' guide to the real world of espionage entitled *ABCs of Espionage*. It provided instruction on the real-world techniques of espionage, but did so by appealing to both real and fictional spies to verify its claims to authenticity. Illya and Solo, for example, wrote the book's introduction:

> We present herewith an ABC of espionage – based on U.N.C.L.E. files. When you read these facts – and they are all *true facts*, not fiction – you

will be studying details that are also recorded in the files of the CIA, MI5, and Deuxième Bureau.[110]

In a complete inversion of *13 Rue Madeleine*'s opening sequence, the fictional archival records of U.N.C.L.E. provide the authenticity for the supposedly 'factual' archives of the state. The effect of this inversion of the semi-documentary's appeal to the state as the arbiter of its authenticity was to call into question the credulity of such a crude authorising technique.

The Man from U.N.C.L.E. and the many espionage shows it inspired mocked the semi-documentaries in other ways. In the opening credit sequence for *U.N.C.L.E.*'s first season, for example, Solo, Ilya and Waverley directly address the camera to introduce themselves and their organisation in the same fashion as government experts like Ellis Zacharias would introduce 1950s spy shows. 'This standardized intro', writes Kackman, 'is clearly fictional, but it allows the lead characters to speak to the audience in the authoritative voices of civic leaders, reproducing the documentarist address of the semidocumentary programs from which *U.N.C.L.E.* emerged.'[111] Other spy shows of the decade such as *Get Smart* likewise parodied the authorising techniques of the semi-documentary in their opening credit sequences. Although played straight in *U.N.C.L.E.*, the 'innermost of the in', as Sam Rolfe put it, who grasped the more subtle parody in the first season, would have recognised, as Rick Worland writes, that 'the program was assuming a wry, self-conscious relationship to the cozy Hollywood/government co-operation that dates at least from World War II'.[112]

While the anti-government satire of *The Man from U.N.C.L.E.* remained subtle, even in the more 'camp' later seasons, direct criticisms of the CIA and FBI became increasingly explicit in other films and television shows as the decade wore on. In February 1967 *Ramparts Magazine* published an exposé of the CIA's covert sponsorship and infiltration of the National Student Association. Among other reasons, it was a controversial revelation because the CIA had broken its charter by targeting a domestic group. The ensuing scandal, although by no means the first to rock the CIA, galvanised public scepticism towards the CIA and the American Government more generally.[113] It also led to the unravelling of the so-called 'cultural cold war' in which the CIA covertly funnelled money to various artists, writers, musicians, filmmakers and other cultural groups and activities in order to score ideological points against the Soviet Union and try to win over the non-communist left in Europe. The Cold War, reflected Tom Braden, former head of the International Organizations Division that oversaw these operations, 'was the battle for Picasso's mind'.[114] In response to the 1967 scandal, Braden penned a widely read defence of the CIA and its covert operations that he unhelpfully titled 'I'm Glad the CIA is "Immoral"'.[115]

Not surprisingly the *Ramparts* revelations aroused particular ire in the student protest movement as well as the wider counterculture connected to it. Already a target of anti-war protestors, after *Ramparts* the CIA increasingly became a lightning rod for mushrooming student outrage at American foreign policy more generally. Leading figures in the counterculture, like Allen Ginsberg and Norman Mailer, became increasingly vocal in their opposition to the CIA after 1967.

In January 1971, for example, Ginsberg appeared as 'spokesperson for the youth' at the trial of the 'Ann Arbor Three', defending the White Panther members who bombed a CIA recruitment office in 1968.[116] The following year Ginsberg appeared on the Dick Cavett show and publicly accused the CIA of being involved with heroin trafficking in Indochina. Alongside Alfred W. McCoy, author of *The Politics of Heroin in Southeast Asia* (1972), he had spent several years researching his findings.[117] His poem 'CIA Dope Calypso' laid them out with little abstraction. In a misjudged social outing in March 1972, Richard Helms, director of the CIA, took his wife to the Corcoran Gallery in Washington where Ginsberg was giving a reading – Helms obviously hadn't researched the billing. Ginsberg confronted Helms about the Agency's drug smuggling at a reception before the reading. Helms of course denied the charges. In a surreal moment Ginsberg made a wager with the DCI: if he was right, Helms would have to meditate for one hour every day for the rest of his life. If he was wrong, he promised to give Helms his 'vajra', a brass Buddhist-Hindu ritual instrument that symbolised 'the lightning bolt doctrine of sudden illumination'. A few months later, Ginsberg sent Helms a clipping from the *Far East Economic Review* that reported a number of sightings by journalists of piles of raw opium being readied for sale in full view of CIA agents. Accompanying the clippings, a smug Ginsberg sent Helms some notes and advice on meditation techniques, including guidance on appropriate posture and proper breathing. 'It is terribly important to get him into an improved mind-consciousness', Ginsberg told reporters. 'Anything that might help save the world situation would be sheer Hari Krishna magic, the hard-headed people have brought us to such an apocalyptic mess.'[118] The more austere novelist, Norman Mailer, got back at the CIA by establishing the Fifth Estate, an organisation dedicated to exposing them. Fifth Estate magazine, *Counterspy*, later published lists of CIA agents' names – and was blamed, inaccurately, for the death of the CIA's Athens station chief, Richard Welch.[119]

The popularity of camp spy films and television shows like *U.N.C.L.E.* and *Get Smart* with student audiences allowed them to capitalise on this growing fascination by the countercultural youth in the iniquities of the CIA. Like the later seasons of *U.N.C.L.E*, shows like *Get Smart* and films such as *In Like Flint* and the Matt Helms series were infused with psychedelic imagery. But they also responded to mounting scepticism towards the Agency among the American youth. *Get Smart*, for example, directly addressed the *Ramparts* rev-

Figure 4.8 Don Adams playing Maxwell Smart in spy spoof television series *Get Smart* (1965–70). *Source:* Wikimedia Commons.

elations in an episode titled *The Groovy Guru*, which aired in the wake of the scandal. The episode, replete with countercultural stereotypes, sees Maxwell Smart and Agent 86 foil a plot by the 'Groovy Guru' radio DJ to hypnotise students via the lyrics of rock band 'The Sacred Cows' to brainwash students on campus.[120] The show also subverted the stock Allen Dulles-inspired professorial depiction of the head of the CIA by featuring Admiral Harold Harmon Hargrade, 'a doddering old man who lives on prune juice and apparently thinks that Herbert Hoover is still president' as head of CONTROL.[121] Hargrade was modelled on then CIA director Admiral William Raborn, frequently criticised as inept in the press. His tenure in office also coincided with fictional CIA chief Heinous Overreach's appearance in *John Goldfarb, Please Come Home* (1965), one of the more egregious depictions of a CIA director in the decade. The real-life Raborn and the fictional Hargarde served to undermine the generational gap that exacerbated the student movement's opposition to the CIA. Speaking at the Ann Arbor trial, Ginsberg was said to represent all youths under the age of twenty-eight in his vociferous opposition to the CIA – a lofty claim that led to numerous objections from the prosecution.[122]

Get Smart's satiric rebuke of the Agency clearly registered with student

IN SECRECY'S SHADOW

protestors at some level, when students at Michigan State University marched against the CIA's $25 million contract with the university to provide cover for operatives in Vietnam they sang a mock rendition of the *Get Smart* theme tune.[123] But perhaps the decade's most acerbic countercultural-psychedelic-infused camp satire of the CIA and the FBI that coincided with the *Ramparts* revelations was the 1967 film *The President's Analyst*.

Parody Turns Political in *The President's Analyst* (1967)

Directed by *Man from U.N.C.L.E.* scriptwriter Theodore J. Flicker, and featuring *In Like Flint* star James Coburn in the lead role, *The President's Analyst* adapted the format of the popular camp spy shows and films of the decade in the service of a withering critique of both the CIA and FBI. The plot runs along similar lines to Alfred Hitchcock's *North by Northwest*, featuring an innocent man on the run, fleeing across America from both foreign and domestic intelligence operatives. Coburn stars as psychoanalyst Dr Sidney Schaeffer, who is given the 'top job' as the President's psychoanalyst. Upon realising that both the paranoid CIA and FBI have placed him under permanent surveillance, who fear the secrets he may divulge given his access to the President's innermost thoughts, Schaeffer absconds his position and is chased across the country by the Agency, the FBI and various foreign spies who seek his unique access to classified information.

In the early screenplay drafts of *The President's Analyst*, originally titled *Don't Fool with the Phone Company*, the CIA and the FBI are directly named.[124] However, the film's director Theodore J. Flicker, and its producer,

Figure 4.9   James Coburn taking on the phone company in psychedelic 60s spy satire *The President's Analyst* (1967). *Source:* Theodore J. Flicker, Paramount, 1967.

Stanley Rubin, had not accounted for J. Edgar Hoover and the FBI's still highly influential presence in Hollywood. Neither, it turned out, had the head of Paramount studios, Robert Evans. According to his memoir, two FBI agents confronted Evans prior to the film being put into production. 'Starched collars and all,' he wrote, 'they entered my office. No smiles, just gorilla handshakes and proper identification.' J. Edgar Hoover, Evans alleged, had obtained a copy of the script for *The President's Analyst* and upon learning of its contents had furiously ordered the two agents to demand that Evans cancel the film: 'Mr Hoover doesn't appreciate having the FBI made fun of', the agents told him. After an angry dispute, during which Evans implies he was threatened, the men left the office, with Evans refusing to cancel the film. According to Evans, the following day, studio executive, Marty Davis, scolded him on the phone:

> 'Are you crazy? You don't play games with Hoover. You don't play games with the FBI.'
> 'Fuck 'em. It's a free country, isn't it?'
> 'No, it's not.'
>
> The Order was to change it. I did: to the FBE. I refused to compromise further, but I made sure anyone who read the paper knew about my story.[125]

Evans wrote that his refusal to cooperate with the FBI, 'cost me *my* privacy ... It's been over a quarter of a century now. Still my thirty-two phones at home and office share one thing – a silver anniversary of bugging.'[126] Evans' story has the air of Hollywood braggadocio, but the director of *The President's Analyst*, Theodore J. Flicker, corroborated his account. In a recent documentary biopic of his life, Flicker claimed that as a result of the film, he was effectively blacklisted from Hollywood until the death of J. Edgar Hoover in 1972.[127]

Whether or not Evans and Flicker exaggerated their account of the FBI's harassment is somewhat beside the point. Its effect upon the film's strategy of representation was to transform it into a direct parody of the semi-documentary's allegiance to state-sourced narratives. In the film's first opening sequence, a textual insert appears over a grainy image of a waving American flag, a pastiche of the patriotic iconography of the semi-documentary spy melodramas. The text reads in authoritative bold typeface:

> THIS FILM HAS NOT BEEN MADE WITH THE CONSENT OR COOPERATION OF THE FEDERAL BOARD OF REGULATIONS (F.B.R.) OR THE CENTRAL ENQUIRIES AGENCY (C.E.A.). ANY RESEMBLANCE TO PERSONS LIVING OR DEAD IS PURELY COINCIDENTAL, AND SO FORTH AND SO ON.[128]

The text offers a direct satire of the semi-documentary's tendency to laud its government endorsement through such opening textual inserts. Through this parody the semi-documentary's utilisation of state-sources and state endorsement in support of its authoritarian discourse of reality is inverted and thereby ridiculed. State endorsement is no longer an asset for filmmakers striving for historical verisimilitude; on the contrary, in this film at least, it is the rejection of the state as the arbiter of historical authenticity that is celebrated.

This opening text marks a transitional moment for the historical epistemology of the American spy thriller. While the camp spoofs of the early 1960s had revelled in the fantastical and rejected the earnestness of the semi-documentaries in their desire for authenticity, rarely had they offered such a direct, satirical critique of the state's centrality to the production of history. *The President's Analyst* thus combines the camp spy fable's celebration of artifice with a far more politicised rejection of state-sourced historical representation. It is this scepticism towards the veracity of state-sourced history that would later develop into the complete rejection of state narratives in the conspiracy thrillers of the 1970s. Yet while the conspiracy thrillers of the seventies attacked the state's monopoly on the past and the power of secrecy in distorting the historical record, they lacked the irony of the spy fables of the 1960s. *The President's Analyst* revealed the political venom of irony, its power to overturn and invert existing conventions of historical epistemology and, in so doing, lay the basis for a reaction against state power. Although the conspiracy thriller may have been more overtly political in its subject matter, it required the irony of the spy fable, and its dismantling of the state's authoritative influence of historical representation, in order to bring about a shift in the spy thriller's politics of representation.

Released in December 1967, *The President's Analyst*'s satire and rejection of state-sourced representations resonated with the prevailing counterculture and the increasing public ire towards the Vietnam War abroad, and the domestic unrest at home. The year 1967 was in many respects the turning point in terms of American public opinion towards the Vietnam War. As mass protests promulgated across the country, the anti-war effort was supported by such voices of moral authority as Martin Luther King, who denounced US involvement in Vietnam on 4 April of that year. King's speech symbolically tied the anti-war movement to the civil rights struggle, which in 1967 had turned increasingly violent with a series of race riots taking place across American cities. The violence toward African Americans at home and towards the enemies of US foreign policy abroad is a theme dealt with from the outset of *The President's Analyst*, which will be addressed later in this section.[129]

Along with its provocative political content, *The President's Analyst* is also stylistically infused with the imagery of the counterculture, which in 1967 had reached its zenith in the 'Summer of Love'. The film reflects the fashions and tastes of the swinging sixties and is set throughout to a psychedelic soundtrack. The most obvious allusion to the counterculture is the extended sequence during the film in which the central protagonist – played by James Coburn – escapes his pursuers by fleeing to the country with a group of hippies. In one of the most memorable sequences of the film Coburn frolics in the long-grass in the spirit of free love with his newly acquired hippy-lover. While the happy couple canoodle, they are oblivious to a number of spies creeping through the grass in a series of botched attempts to assassinate them. One by one, each spy is killed by the next until none are left alive. CEA agent Don Masters and his Russian counterpart eventually track Coburn and his band of countercultural stereotypes to a bar where they are playing. While listening to the music, the CEA agent realises the punch has been spiked by lysergic acid diethylamide (LSD) – a strange, although not surprising portent of the 1974–5 revelations surrounding the CIA's MK-ULTRA programme and their own experimentation with the counterculture's drug of choice.

According to the film's writer and director, Theodore J. Flicker, the idea for *The President's Analyst* came to him in the early 1960s during a dinner party with several important government officials in Washington, DC. As Flicker relayed the story, he was sat opposite 'the single most nervous human being that I ever met. The room was cool, but he was sweating and shivering. At first I thought that it was a Malaria attack, but soon it became obvious that it wasn't.' As Flicker conversed with the gentleman, he realised that he was a psychoanalyst with top-secret clearance given his responsibilities as an analyst for senior CIA officers and military officials. According to Flicker, it was this chance-encounter that became the basis for his screenplay – 'I would like to explor [sic]', he wrote 'all the comedic possibilities of this man and his peculiar problem. I don't know if it will be a chase film, or just a funny spy-story, or a comedy of character.'[130]

In the summer of 1964, Flicker put his idea into writing for submission to the studios, titling the project 'Enough is Enough is Enough'. In his brief outline of the film, he described it as a

> commercial idea combining the most saleable aspects of *Around the World in 80 Days*, *The Yellow Rolls Royce*, *007*, plus the High Camp of *Whats New Pussycat?* and *Little Orphan Annie* . . . If the most modern techniques of mobility, are used . . . the picture can have the scope of *Around the World* with production budget of a TV Show like U.N.C.L.E.

Inspired by *Little Orphan Annie*, Flicker wrote that the plot would be episodic and would see the central protagonist fleeing 'across the face of America' and constantly trying to 'melt into the backround [sic] of American life as it is lived today'. As the psychoanalyst flees across America, according to the original treatment, he is caught up in a number of topical scenarios – 'in Alabama he pigments his skin and tries to hide as a share cropper only to get involved in Civil Rights. In California he joins the Hells Angles [sic].' Agents from almost every country in the world pursue him across the US:

> Every nation in the world has their agents out to capture him alive except one. The U.S. of A. In the interests of National Security he must be killed before any foreign power can capture him and make him talk. Who are the foreign powers that want him? Russia, China, Cuba, England, Germany, France, Italy, Monaco, Israel, Egypt, Saudi Arabia, Ghana, Upper Volta, Zambeziland, India, Pakistan, North Vietnam, South Vietnam and so on, including Canada and Mexico.[131]

Already then, in the summer of 1964, Flicker had conceived of *The President's Analyst* as a politically controversial pastiche of the Cold War and the ideology of National Security. Recognising the political problems that a studio may face in producing such a film, Flicker emphasised the importance of the light-hearted camp style in conveying a serious political message. In a note titled 'the question of controversy', Flicker wrote, 'you can say anything if you do it with a smile – no one will take offence. No one minds getting satirized as long as you do his neighbor too. It is the kind of situation where no one will dare cast the first stone for fear of being called humorless.'[132] Given the reaction of J. Edgar Hoover and the FBI towards the script, Flicker, it seemed, had deeply misjudged their response. For Flicker, however, camp irony could not only satirise the semi-documentary mode of historical representation, but provided the cover of comedy for his politically controversial critique of national security and America's two most prominent intelligence agencies.

In his first full treatment of the proposed screenplay, which he submitted to Columbia Pictures, Universal and United Artists, Flicker reveals the self-referential parodic nature of the film. 'The first shot is utter chaos,' he wrote,

> and it is just one big movie cliché after another. As a matter of fact it is made entirely out of film clips. It begins with a shot of Slim Pickens riding the hydrogen bomb to earth in *Dr. Strangelove*. There is a nuclear explosion, and then there are clips of scenes from *War of the Worlds, Them, The Rains of Ranciphur*, and the like. Every manner of the world destruction, from space-monsters to a simple volcano eruption, is depicted.[133]

This cycle of self-referentiality is primarily stylistic – establishing the camp basis for the forthcoming feature, but, as discussed, it is also political, interweaving the fantastical imagery of Hollywood cinema, in the manner of Kubrick's *Dr. Strangelove*, with the purpose of parodying and ridiculing not only the ideology of national security itself, but its previous representation in

Hollywood cinema that sought out realistic footage and reconstructions from state-sources. In this proposed scene, the referents are all entirely fictional, forming a kind of Baudrillardian hyperreality, in which national security and its ultimate justification in the threat of nuclear annihilation are reduced to pure simulation – their impending reality diminished and made approachable for humour.

Following the facetious opening textual disclaimer in the final feature, the camera zooms out from the grainy image of a waiving American flag to a bustling scene of a New York city street. In the midst of this everyday urban environment, a team of 'CEA' officers are conducting an operation involving the abduction and killing of an enemy agent. In significant contrast to the semi-documentary's refusal to even acknowledge aggressive American espionage activities, this scene immediately features the violent covert intervention of the 'CEA'. Moreover, resonating with the *Ramparts* magazine revelations of the same year, it asserts that the CIA were willing to conduct illegal espionage activities on American soil. The entire operation is conducted so seamlessly that passers-by are completely unaware it is taking place, blissfully ignorant of the violent state repression occurring in front of their very eyes, providing an allegoric vision of the silent apathy of the majority of American citizens towards Vietnam and the morally questionable conduct of America's foreign policy apparatus. The scene implies that the violence of the US Government has been woven into the social fabric of America – the amorality of CIA covert action takes its place among the everyday, linking the domestic with foreign policy and the social with the political.

This theme is elaborated in the following scene in which we are first introduced to the central protagonist – psychoanalyst Dr Sidney Schaefer, played by James Coburn. The casting of Coburn in the role fulfilled a referential function as Coburn was associated with the camp spy-fable genre, having played the title-role in the Douglas Flint films along with a more peripheral role in Stanley Donen's CIA spy-caper, *Charade*. Like *The President's Analyst*, the Flint films offered a pastiche of the Bond-inspired spy format while incorporating numerous traits of the American counterculture. As producer Robert Evans said of Coburn's casting, he 'was a perfect leading man for the late sixties – rugged but irreverent. I thought it was a great coup getting him for an anti-establishment black comedy'.[134]

Schaeffer's countercultural credentials in *The President's Analyst* are established from the outset – we first see him meditatively sounding a gong in his office. Coburn is then interrupted by the entry of his patient – African American CEA officer Don Masters, played by well-known black stand-up comedian Godfrey Cambridge, whom we have already witnessed kill an enemy agent in the opening sequence. After taking his place on Schaeffer's couch, Masters begins his therapy with an extraordinary monologue, recounting his

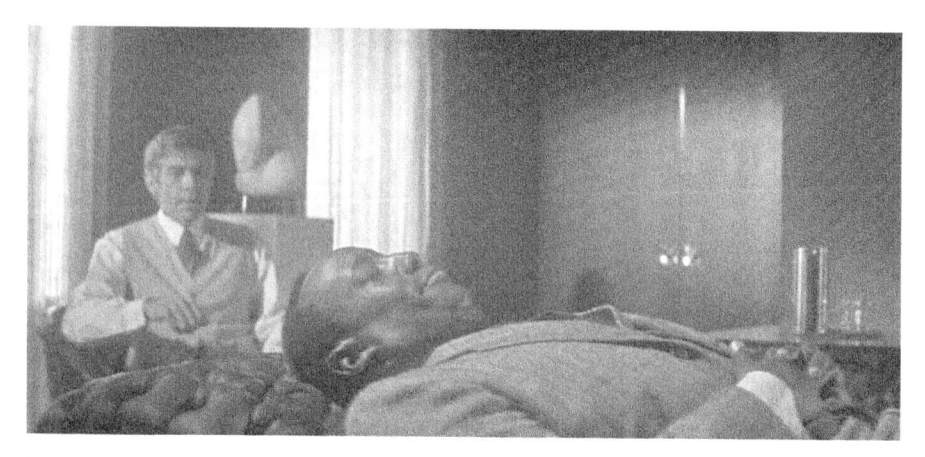

Figure 4.10 James Coburn playing psychoanalyst Dr Sidney Schaefer. In this scene he counsels CIA (called the 'CEA' in the film) agent Don Masters, played by Godfrey Cambridge. *Source:* Theodore J. Flicker, Paramount, 1967.

provocative dream of the day he first 'found out about niggers'. He was five years old and it was his second day of school. As he walked to class he was approached by some older schoolboys – 'run, run, here comes the nigger!' they taunted. Too young to understand the pejorative, the young Masters caught up with his older brother and mimicked the boys' cries – 'run, run, here comes the nigger!' His brother hit him. 'Then he did something worse,' recounted Masters, 'he told me what a nigger was, and that I was it.' Schaeffer probingly inquired, 'How do you feel about that Don?' Masters replied, 'A hate flashed in me, and I started to hate my brother.'

In stark contrast to the film's satiric tone, and Godfrey Cambridge's known credentials as a comedian, the scene is delivered straight, without a hint of irony. Cambridge's voice cracks and stutters with sorrow as he recounts the episode. As with the previous scene, Cambridge then seamlessly shifts from the violence of the social, to the violence of state: 'I hated him,' he says of his brother, 'and I hit him, and I rammed that knife into his heart.' Stunned, Schaeffer exclaims, 'What?' 'The Albanian. I killed him. I stuck that knife into him. And he was my brother and he was me, and I hated him.' 'What are you talking about?,' Schaeffer asked. 'He was an Albanian double-agent. He had secret information that threatened the security of our country, and my assignment was to kill him.' By transposing his anger at the racial abuse he suffered at school into the violence of his activities on behalf of the 'CEA', Cambridge links the racial violence of the 1960s with the violence of American foreign policy and the CIA specifically. As previously mentioned, 1967 was a year in which the external violence in Vietnam and the internal domestic unrest of black activism became increasingly associated following Martin Luther King's denunciation of the Vietnam War. Cambridge's opening monologue makes this parallel clear, offering a stark critique of US Government policy at home and abroad.

Cambridge was not the first major black spy on American screens. That accolade can be claimed by Bill Cosby's character, Alexander Scott ('Scotty') in the popular spy television series *I Spy*, which aired from 1965 to 1968. Not only was Cosby the first African American spy, but he was also the first black star of any major network television programme. In his analysis of the series, Michael Kackman argues that Cosby's character represented what Herman Gray defined as the 'Civil Rights Subject' – 'a narrowly defined African American subjectivity inscribed within a progress narrative of equal rights and gradual assimilation'.[135] Cosby's character, Kackman argued, represented an attempt by the American television industry to appropriate the critical discourses of the African American struggle by assimilating them within a framework of progressive liberal idealism and, in contrast to the increasingly internationalist critiques of leading black intellectual such as Stokeley Carmeichel, incorporate it within the dominant tropes of American history. Cosby's character was designed to alleviate white fears of an increasingly vocal African American minority by appearing as both a model agent and citizen – virtuous in his conduct and loyal to the state.

Cambridge's character in *The President's Analyst* subverts the 'civil rights citizenship' of Cosby. While he is a loyal servant of the CEA, his actions are decidedly immoral by conventional standards. The model of citizenship that Cambridge provides is one in which violence is condoned in the name of the state, but condemned in opposition to it. As a CEA officer, morality is relativised by the demands of national security. While the presumed killing of his brother is met with immediate abhorrence by Coburn, when he produces his CEA identification card to reveal his true identity, his murder of the Albanian double agent is legitimated. Coburn's reaction to this revelation vocalises the ramifications of this: 'morality is a social invention, and in this case society has not only decided that it is morally acceptable to kill people, but that it is even commendable'.[136]

Through Cambridge's inverted civil right's subjectivity, *The President's Analyst* offers a damning indictment of the immorality of the CIA and US foreign policy more broadly, while simultaneously linking it to the domestic violence towards African Americans at home. As Kackman points out, the perception of American race relations was not a peripheral concern for US foreign policy, but constituted a fundamental aspect of it. The CIA was deeply concerned with countering Soviet propaganda that portrayed America as endemically and systemically racist. The perception of racial inequality at home damaged US standing abroad, and hindered the full functioning of its liberal democratic foreign policy, which saw America intervene in the world in the name of freedom and democracy.[137] As the *London Daily Herald* put it in relation to the imposition of federal troops to impose desegregation in Little Rock – 'Racial intolerance in the South is a grave handicap to America's foreign policy, particularly as liberty is the keyword of that policy.'[138] In this vein, Cambridge's monologue in the early scene of *The President's Analyst* makes the violence of the CIA and the violence towards African Americans at home morally equivocal.

Upon arriving in Washington, DC to begin his assignment as the President's analyst, Schaefer is met by the heads of the FBR and CEA – Henry Lux and Ethen Allen Crocket. The two are clear caricatures of the popular cultural iconography of the FBI and CIA. Lux is a short and mean-spirited man, stoically dressed in a black suit and buttoned-down shirt, clearly alluding to the iconography of the G-men and their most famous advocate – J. Edgar Hoover. Resonating with the long-held notions of the FBI and CIA as the 'American Gestapo', Lux begins his briefing of Schaeffer by announcing in a sinister tone – 'the S.S.', after a dramatic pause his CEA counterpart explains 'Security and Safety'. The damning critique of American intelligence, particularly the FBI, is established from the outset. Lux, played by Walter Burke, disapproves of Schaeffer, and in a moralising tone, continually berates him for his stupidity and his lack of propriety and decency, contrasting sharply with Schaeffer's easy-going countercultural manner. Head of CEA, Ethen Allen Crocket, played by Eduard Franz, is a pastiche of the archetypal professorial Allen Dulles figure, associated most closely with the actor Leo G. Caroll who played intelligence chiefs in both *North by Northwest* and *The Man from U.N.C.L.E.* Yet while the avuncular image of the CIA-chief remains, Franz's characterisation is closer to senility than beneficent wisdom, more bumbling than omniscient, inverting this predominant representation of the DCI. As one reviewer said of the two intelligence chiefs in the film,

> The Burke and Franz dialog and acting capture perfectly the images, which, rightly or wrongly, persist in the minds of many: the hypocritical moralizing of a domestic security agency, staffed with cookie-cutter functionaries; the laissez faire, urbane foreign security agency, whose staffers are freed of justifying everything in terms of Home and Mother.[139]

Immediately, the Beltway rivalry between the FBR and CEA is established, with Lux caustically rebuking Crocket at almost every opportunity. Later in the film, when Schaefer decides to flee the grip of his overbearing security escorts who have him under constant surveillance, as well as the indefatigable demands of the President, this rivalry plays out with great satiric effect. While Lux and the FBR decide that Schaeffer must be killed to prevent foreign intelligence services from capturing him, the CEA decide to protect Schaeffer.

Figure 4.11 Dr Schaeffer (Coburn) sits in between head of the 'CEA' Ethen Allen Crcoket (Eduard Franz, left) and 'FBR' chief Henry Lux (Walter Burke, right). Crocket's character satirises the stereotypical image of the CIA, and in particular former DCI Allen Dulles, as an academic-like institution staffed by tweedy professorial types. Lux likewise satirises the public perception of the FBI as a hypocritically pious institution forged in the image of J. Edgar Hoover. *Source:* Theodore J. Flicker, Paramount, 1967.

Although this may seem admirable on the part of the CEA, their motives are driven by a desire simply to foil the plans of their FBR rivals. The intelligence services are portrayed merely as self-serving enterprises, conducting their activities not for the preservation of national security, but to sustain their own self-perpetuating rivalries and activities.

As the FBR, CEA and a number of their foreign adversaries chase Schaefer across America – a la *North by Northwest* – the film's narrative arc prefigures the paranoid conspiracy thrillers of the 1970s. Schaeffer begins, like the protagonists of the conspiracy genre, with an unambiguous devotion towards his government and a scepticism towards the paranoid logic of conspiracy. When Don Masters leaves his office after the opening scene, he reveals to Schaeffer's incredulity that his office has been bugged. This moment marks the first realisation for Schaeffer that things are not as they seem, and that he is living under a permanent state of surveillance. Nevertheless, upon learning of his assignment to be the President's analyst, the film cuts to a clichéd montage in which Schaefer joyously celebrates his appointment by roaming the iconic landmarks of New York, including a visit to the Statue of Liberty – redolent of the use of patriotic iconography by Alfred Hitchcock. By the film's conclusion, however, as with the conspiracy thriller, Schaeffer's love of country is almost completely eroded by his apprehension of the national security state that it has become.

With the growing realisation that he is under surveillance by the FBR and CEA, and later, that he is being hunted by them, Schaefer's psychological decline echoes the growing societal paranoia of the late 1960s and 1970s of an increasingly powerful intelligence bureaucracy. By the time the film reaches its peculiar conclusion, it is implied that almost every telephone in the entire country has been bugged. The bugging, however, has not been conducted by the US intelligence agencies, but by 'The Phone Company'. Schaeffer learns that he is involved in a far greater conspiracy, instigated by the sinister corporation who seek to use his position and influence in order to convince the President to pass legislation to allow for the introduction of their new 'implant' telephone technology. The film's conclusion is as convoluted and farcical as the rest of the film's camp style, but its structure anticipates the conspiracy thriller in the narrative unfolding of a multi-layered conspiracy, unveiled by the central protagonist. *The President's Analyst* thus straddles the form of the camp spy fable and the conspiracy thrillers by deploying the style of the former, and the narrative structure of the latter.

By identifying 'The Phone Company' as opposed to the American intelligence establishment as the ultimate conspirator, one may argue that it softened the film's critique of the latter. Yet *The President's Analyst* stands out in the 1960s as a camp spy-fable that dared to make the shift from apoliticism to biting satire. As one reviewer wrote, 'A significant amount of guts has been demonstrated by exec producer Howard W. Koch, producer Stanley Rubin, writer-director Theodore J. Flicker, Coburn . . . as well as bankrolling Paramount, to make such a film.'[140] Yet while *The President's Analyst* was a provocative film with limited critical success, it failed at the box-office, perhaps demonstrating the astuteness of the studio and television executives who depoliticised the spy films of the 1960s in order to avoid offending sections of both foreign and domestic audiences. *The President's Analyst* may have proved the political potency of camp satire, but it failed to prove that it could function as a lasting model of box-office success in the same manner as Bond. Nevertheless, the narrative form, the style and the political content of *The President's Analyst* marked a turning point for Hollywood, no longer beholden to the state and the demands of the semi-documentary.

By not only mocking state-endorsement, but also critiquing the state, and the US intelligence establishment in particular, *The President's Analyst* marked the moment in which the Hollywood spy thriller shifted from representational irony to direct political criticism of the CIA. From the late 1960s, through the 1970s, two new forms of the spy thriller would emerge – the realist thriller and the conspiracy thriller – that cemented this move away from irony toward criticism of the Cold War and American foreign policy. Yet as *The President's Analyst* demonstrated, it was irony that had first broken the state's grip on the representation of their intelligence agencies by both rejecting and mocking the old didacticisms of 1950s semi-documentary spy cinema. The era of irony in Hollywood spy cinema had laid the groundwork for the cynical and conspiratorial reactions against the US intelligence community, made concrete in the 1970s with the fallout from Watergate and the 1975 revelations over nefarious and illegal FBI and CIA activities. *The President's Analyst* was both a product of its times, and a sign of things to come.

Notes

1. Ian Fleming, 'Gary Powers and the Big Lie', *The Sunday Times*, 11 March 1962.
2. Rhodri Jeffreys-Jones, *The CIA and American Democracy*, third edition (New Haven: Yale University Press, 2003), p. 113.
3. Ibid.
4. Fleming, 'Gary Powers'.
5. Ibid.
6. Fleming discussed the meeting with Kennedy in a published dialogue with Allen Dulles. See 'Allen Dulles and Ian Fleming: A Redbook Dialogue', *Redbook Magazine*, June 1964.
7. Edward P. Comentale, Stephen Watt and Skip Willman (eds), *Ian Fleming and James Bond: The Cultural Politics of 007* (Bloomington: Indiana University Press, 2005), xii.
8. Christopher Moran, 'Ian Fleming and the Public Profile of the CIA', *Journal of Cold War Studies*, 15:1 (winter 2013a), pp. 119–46.
9. Ibid., p. 142.
10. Ibid.
11. Allen Dulles, 'Our Spy-Boss Who Loved Bond', *Life Magazine*, 28 August 1964.
12. 'Allen Dulles and Ian Fleming: A Redbook Dialogue', *Redbook Magazine*, June 1964.
13. Alan Nadel, *Containment Culture: American Narratives, Postmodernism and the Atomic Age* (Durham, NC: Duke University Press, 1995), p. 158.
14. See James Giglio, *The Presidency of John F. Kennedy* (Lawrence: University of Kansas Press, 1991), p. 54. Giglio is cited in Nadel, *Containment Culture*, p. 157. Evan Thomas also discusses the 'Bond effect' on the Kennedy brothers in Evan Thomas, *Robert Kennedy: His Life* (New York: Simon and Schuster, 2002), pp. 119–21.
15. Jeffreys-Jones, *The CIA and American Democracy*, p. 116.
16. For more on Kennedy's romantic framing of foreign policy see John A. McClure, *Late Imperial Romance* (London: Verso, 1994), pp. 40–9.
17. Thomas Lowe Hughes interviews in *The Man Nobody Knew: In Search of My Father, CIA Spymaster William Colby* (Carl Colby, Act 4 Entertainment, 2011).
18. Thomas, *Robert Kennedy*, p. 123.
19. William Colby and Peter Forbath, *Honorable Men: My Life in the CIA* (New York: Simon and Schuster, 1978), p. 180.
20. William J. Daugherty, *Executive Secrets: Covert Action and the Presidency* (Lexington: University of Kentucky Press, 2004), p. 34.
21. See Bradley Smith, *Shadow Warriors: O.S.S. and the Origins of the C.I.A.* (London: André Deutsch, 1983), p. 418.
22. Stephen Kinzer, *The Brothers: John Foster Dulles, Allen Dulles, and Their Secret World War* (New York: Times Books, 2013), p. 20.
23. Victor Marchetti and John D. Marks, *The CIA and the Cult of Intelligence* (New York: Coronet Books, 1974), pp. 35–6.
24. For more on the impact of the Bay of Pigs upon public and media opinion of the CIA, see Simon Willmetts, 'The Burgeoning Fissures of Dissent: Allen Dulles and

the Selling of the CIA in the Aftermath of the Bay of Pigs', *History: The Journal of the Historical Association*, 100:340 (April 2015), pp. 167–88 and Richard J. Aldrich, 'American Journalism and the Landscape of Secrecy: Tad Szulc, the CIA and Cuba', *History: The Journal of the Historical Association*, 100:340 (April 2015), pp. 189–209.
25. David Wise and Thomas Ross, *The Invisible Government* (London: Jonathon Cape, 1964), p. 19.
26. Don DeLillo, *Libra* (London: Penguin Modern Classics, 2006), p. 22. Alan Nadel identifies the Bay of Pigs as the beginning of the end of the Cold War consensus. He argues that the failed invasion precipitated a loss of faith in the authority of the official story, with its straightforward binary narratives of the Cold War, and in so doing paved the way for the postmodern scepticisim of the proceeding decade. See Nadel, *Containment Culture*, pp. 157–203. For more on the relationship between US Government secrecy, postmodernism and the breakdown of consensus see Timothy Melley, *The Covert Sphere: Secrecy, Fiction, and the National Security State* (Ithaca: Cornell University Press, 2012).
27. Nadel, *Containment Culture*, pp. 166–7; Peter Knight, *Conspiracy Culture: From Kennedy to the X-Files* (Abingdon: Routledge, 2001), pp. 112–16; Willmetts, 'The Burgeoning Fissures of Dissent'.
28. Michael Kackman, *Citizen Spy: Television, Espionage, and Cold War Culture* (Minneapolis: University of Minnesota Press, 2005), p. 76.
29. Melley, *The Covert* Sphere; Alan Nadel, *Containment Culture*.
30. Ann Douglas, 'Periodizing the American Century: Modernism, Postmodernism and Postcolonialism in the Cold War Context', *Modernism/Modernity*, 5:3 (September 1998), pp. 75–6.
31. Wise and Ross, *The Invisible Government*.
32. Melley, *The Covert Sphere*, p. 35.
33. Louis de Rochemont to John Halas and Joy Batchelor, 29 September 1968, Louis de Rochemont MSS, Box 25 Folder 7, The American Heritage Center, Laramie.
34. Paul Monaco, *The Sixties: 1960–1969*, History of the American Cinema series (Berkeley: University of California Press, 2001), pp. 192–4.
35. Susan Sontag, 'Notes on "Camp"', in Susan Sontag, *Against Interpretation and Other Essays* (London: Penguin Modern Classics, 2009), p. 275.
36. Robert Kirsch, 'James Bond Appeal?: It's Elementary, Watson', *Los Angeles Times Calendar*, 22 August 1963.
37. Sontag, 'Notes on "Camp"', p. 277.
38. 'The Man from U.N.C.L.E.', Information for Writers, Norman Felton MSS, Box 21, *The Man from U.N.C.L.E. Correspondence 1963–65*, University of Iowa Special Collections, Iowa City: IA.
39. Frederick Wasser, 'Is Hollywood America? The trans-nationalization of the American Film Industry', *Critical Studies in Mass Communication*, 12:4 (1995), pp. 423–37.
40. Reza Badiyi cited in Patrick J. White, *The Complete Mission: Impossible Dossier* (New York: Avon Books, 1996), p. 428. See also Douglas Little, 'Mission Impossible: The CIA and the Cult of Covert Action in the Middle East', *Diplomatic History*, 28:5 (2004), pp. 663–701.
41. Norman Felton himself noted that the *Man from U.N.C.L.E.* feature-films were successful primarily because of the show's popularity abroad. Norman Felton, Handwritten Note titled 'What Made The Man From UNCLE Features Phenomenal Successes in Theatrical Releases Abroad', 18 January 1968, Norman Felton Collection, Box 21, 'Man From U.N.C.L.E. General Correspondence

1966–68', University of Iowa Special Collections and University Archives (hereafter UISC), University of Iowa, Iowa City.
42. Kackman, *Citizen Spy*, p. 75.
43. Rick Worland, 'The Cold War Mannerists: The Man from U.N.C.L.E. and TV Espionage in the 1960s', *Journal of Popular Film and Television*, 21:4 (winter 1994), p. 155.
44. This is discussed in ibid, p. 152. See also Erik Barnouw, *The Image Empire: A History of Broadcasting in the United States: From 1953, Volume 3* (Oxford: Oxford University Press, 1985), p. 263.
45. Nadel, *Containment Narratives*. For more on the ideology of the spy thriller, including post-colonial interpretations, see Toby Miller, *Spyscreen: Espionage on Film and TV from the 1930s to the 1960s* (Oxford: Oxford University Press, 2003); Michael Denning, *Cover Stories: Narrative and Ideology in the British Spy Thriller* (Abingdon: Routledge, 1987); Wesley Wark, 'Introduction: Fictions of History', *Intelligence and National Security*, 5:4 (1990), pp. 7–16; Allan Hepburn, *Intrigue: Espionage and Culture* (New Haven: Yale University Press, 2005); Wesley Britton, *Beyond Bond: Spies in Fiction and Film* (New York: Praeger, 2005); Kackman, *Citizen Spy*.
46. Robert Corber, *In the Name of National Security: Hitchcock, Homophobia and the Political Construction of Gender in Postwar America* (Durham, NC: Duke University Press, 1993), p. 60.
47. See, for example, Raymond Durgnat's reading of *North by Northwest* in Raymond Durgnat, *The Strange Case of Alfred Hitchcock* (Boston: The MIT Press, 1978).
48. Linda Hutcheon, *A Poetics of Postmodernism: History, Theory, Fiction* (London: Routledge, 1988), p. 6.
49. Ibid., xii.
50. Ibid., xi.
51. Kackman, *Citizen Spy*, p. 73.
52. Hutcheon, *A Poetics of Postmodernism*, p. 4.
53. Lyotard famously defined postmodernism as 'incredulity toward metanarratives'. See Jean-François Lyotard, *The Postmodern Condition: A Report on Knowledge* (Manchester: Manchester University Press, 1984), xxiv.
54. Always the sage, Greene's scenario eerily foreshadowed British intelligence's handling of Anthony Blunt, the Soviet informer who was awarded the sinecure of Surveyor of the Queen's Pictures after his treachery was discovered by the British intelligence establishment who promptly swept the episode under the carpet until he was publicly outed by the media more than a decade later.
55. Simon Willmetts and Christopher Moran, 'Filming Treachery: British Cinema and Television's Fascination with the Cambridge Five', *The Journal of British Cinema and Television*, 10:1 (January 2013), pp. 49–70.
56. Graham Greene, *Our Man in Havana*, new edition with introduction by Graham Greene (London: Heinemann, 1970), p. ix.
57. Ibid., p. 5.
58. Sontag, 'Notes on "Camp"', p. 275.
59. Greene, *Our Man in Havana*, p. xviii.
60. Peter William Evans, *Carol Reed* (Manchester: Manchester University Press, 2005), p. 107; B. J. Bedard, 'Reunion in Havana', *Literature Film Quarterly*, 4:2 (1974), pp. 352–8.
61. Peter Hulme, 'Graham Greene and Cuba: Our Man in Havana', *New West Indian Guide*, 82:3–4 (2008), pp. 199–200.
62. Norman Sherry, *The Life of Graham Greene, Volume 3: 1955–1991* (London: Random House, 2005), pp. 142–3.

63. Kackman, *Citizen Spy*, p. 112.
64. Graham Greene cited in Neil Sinyard, *Filming Literature: The Art of Screen Adaptation* (Abingdon: Routledge, 2013), p. 108.
65. Pierre Lethier, 'The Clandestine Clapperboard: Alfred Hitchcock's Tales of the Cold War', in Robert Dover and Michael Goodman (eds), *Spinning Intelligence: Why Intelligence Needs the Media, Why the Media Needs Intelligence* (London: C. Hurst & Co., 2009), p. 188.
66. Lenny Rubenstein, 'The Politics of Spy Films', *Cineaste*, 9:3 (1979), pp. 16–21. Cited in Worland, 'The Cold War Mannerists', p. 154.
67. An exception would be the 1951 comedy, *My Favorite Spy*, starring Bob Hope, which, as mentioned in the previous chapter, the CIA found particularly egregious. *My Favorite Spy* (Norman Z. McLeod, Paramount, 1951).
68. Worland, 'The Cold War Mannerists', p. 154.
69. Geoffrey Shurlock to Joseph Vogel, 21 August 1958, North by Northwest PCA File, Motion Picture Association of America Production Code Files (hereafter MPAA-PCA), AMPAS.
70. 'Soviet Pays Taxes, Ends L.I. "Cold War"', *The New York Times*, 24 December 1955.
71. Along with 'The C.I.A. Story', 'The Man on Lincoln's Nose' was another working title for the film.
72. Lincoln Borglum to Alfred Hitchcock, 27 August 1958, Alfred Hitchcock Papers, Folder 537 'North by Northwest Miscellaneous', AMPAS.
73. R. Monta to Ernest Lehman, 4 August 1958, Alfred Hitchcock Papers, Folder 536 'North by Northwest Legal File', AMPAS.
74. R. Monta to Charles Coleman, 5 August 1958, Alfred Hitchcock Papers, Folder 536 'North by Northwest Legal File', AMPAS.
75. Howard Horton to R. Klune, R. Monta, W. Strohm and H. Coleman, 27 October 1958, Alfred Hitchcock Papers, Folder 536 'North by Northwest Legal File', AMPAS.
76. Robin Wood, *Hitchcock's Films Revisited* (New York: Columbia University Press, 2002), p. 108.
77. Kackman, *Citizen Spy*, p. 111.
78. Jane Sloan, for example, wrote that Hitchcock was in 'no way a politically active person', a sentiment echoed by his official biographer, John Taylor, who wrote that Hitchcock was 'resolutely non-political' and 'carefully avoided getting involved in anything connected with politics'. Others, such as Patricia Ferrara and Michael Walker, have argued that politics are left in the background of his films and subsumed by Hitchcock's focus on personal conflicts and a more 'universal sense of suffering and loss'. On the other hand, other scholars, most notably Robert Corber, argue that Hitchcock's films construct what Alan Nadel described as 'containment narratives', by associating threats to national security in his films with homosexuality, and thereby confirming the alterities that comprised the Cold War consensus. See Jane E. Sloan, *Alfred Hitchcock: A Filmography and Bibliography* (Berkeley: University of California Press, 1995), p. 24; John Russell Taylor, *Hitch: The Life and Times of Alfred Hitchcock* (New York: Pantheon, 1978), p. 72, 132; Patricia Ferrara, 'Discontented Bourgeois: Bourgeois Morality and the Interplay of Light and Dark Strains in Hitchcock's Films', *New Orleans Review* 14:4 (1987), p. 87; Michael Walker, 'The Old Age of Alfred Hitchcock,' *Movie*, 18:1 (1970), pp. 10–13; Robert J. Corber, *In the Name of National Security: Hitchcock, Homophobia and the Political Construction of Gender in Postwar America* (Durham, NC: Duke University Press, 1993); Some other works that focus extensively on Hitchcock's politics include Sam P. Simone, *Hitchcock*

as *Activist: Politics and the War Films* (Ann Arbor: UMI Research Press, 1985); Raymond Durgnat, *The Strange Case of Alfred Hitchcock* (Boston: The MIT Press, 1978); Jonathon Freedman and Richard Millington (eds), *Hitchcock's America* (Oxford: Oxford University Press, 1999); Ina Rae Hark, 'Keeping Your Amateur Standing: Audience Participation and Good Citizenship in Hitchcock's Political Films', *Cinema Journal*, 29:2 (winter 1990), pp. 8–22; Philip Dynia, 'Alfred Hitchcock and the Ghost of Thomas Hobbes', *Cinema Journal*, 15:2 (1976), pp. 27–41.

79. Indeed arguably Hitchcock's decline from the mid-1960s onwards was because that restrictive environment was becoming ever more permissive.
80. Richard Schickel, 'We're Living in a Hitchcock World All Right', *The New York Times*, 29 October 1972.
81. Wood, *Hitchcock's Films Revisited*, p. 109.
82. David Freeman, *The Last Days of Alfred Hitchcock: A Memoir Featuring the Entire Screenplay of 'Alfred Hitchcock's The Short Night'* (Woodstock: The Overlook Press, 1984), p. 174.
83. Stephen M. Silverman, *Dancing on the Ceiling: Stanley Donen and his Movies* (New York Alfred Knopf, 1996), pp. 284–5.
84. Ibid. p. 288.
85. See Lethier, 'The Clandestine Clapperboard', p. 190.
86. Robin Wood, *Hitchcock's Films* (New York: New York Castle Books, 1969), pp. 20–1; emphasis in original.
87. Jonathan Nashel Public Lecture, 'James Bond as an American Hero'. Available at http://www.c-span.org/video/?314705-1/james-bond-american-hero, accessed 10 March 2015.
88. Norman Felton to Ian Fleming, 7 July 1963, Norman Felton MSS, Box 22, Ian Fleming Correspondence, University of Iowa Special Collections, Iowa City; see also Kathleen Crighton's detailed and accurate production history of the show that makes extensive use of the Felton papers and is reprinted from an article in Epi-Log Journal, available on the *Man From U.N.C.L.E.* fan website http://www.manfromuncle.org/kcretro2.htm, accessed 31 July 2014.
89. 'Basic Material Pertinent to a New One Hour Television Series: "Solo"', assembled by Ian Fleming and Norman Felton, undated, Norman Felton MSS, Box 20, Character Development, University of Iowa Special Collections, Iowa City; emphasis Fleming and Felton's.
90. Ian Fleming to Norman Felton, 26 June 1963, Norman Felton MSS, Box 22, Ian Fleming Correspondence, University of Iowa Special Collections, Iowa City.
91. Graubard & Moskovitz to Norman Felton, MGM, NBC and Ashley Steiner, 19 February 1964, Norman Felton MSS, Box 22, Ian Fleming Correspondence, University of Iowa Special Collections, Iowa City.
92. 'Solo' by Norman Felton in Norman Felton MSS, Box 20, The Man from U.N.C.L.E. Character Development, University of Iowa Special Collections, Iowa City.
93. Mort Werner to Norman Felton, 17 April 1966, Norman Felton MSS, Box 5, Correspondence July–December 1966, University of Iowa Special Collections, Iowa City.
94. Rick Worland, 'The Cold War Mannerists: The Man from U.N.C.L.E. and TV Espionage in the 1960s', *Journal of Popular Film and Television*, 21:4 (winter 1994), p. 155.
95. Although Michael Kackman argues that the show's racial politics were hardly radical and constructed Cosby's character as a 'civil rights subject', incorporating the liberal tenants of civil rights into an inclusive national framework while

jettisoning the more radical elements of black emancipation that may upset the liberal order. See Kackman, *Citizen Spy*, pp. 113–43.
96. See Fredric Jameson, *Postmodernism: Or, the Cultural Logic of Late Capitalism* (London: Verso, 1992).
97. 'THRUSH', Norman Felton MSS, Box 21, General Correspondence 1963–5, University of Iowa Special Collections, Iowa City.
98. Kackman, *Citizen Spy*, pp. 86–8.
99. Robert Vaughn, *Only Victims: Study of Show Business Blacklisting*, second revised edition (New York: Limelight Editions, 1996).
100. Vaughn cited in Kackman, *Citizen Spy*, p. 86.
101. Vaughn cited in Ibid., p. 87.
102. "The Man from U.N.C.L.E.", Information for Writers, Norman Felton MSS, Box 21, *The Man from U.N.C.L.E. Correspondence 1963–65*, University of Iowa Special Collections, Iowa City: IA.
103. Norman Felton to Sam Rolfe, 10 August 1964, Norman Felton MSS, Box 21, Man from U.N.C.L.E. Correspondence File, 1964–7, University of Iowa Special Collections, Iowa City.
104. For an extensive list of UNCLE and THRUSH gadgets see http://www.tvacres.com/weapons_uncle.htm, accessed 8 July 2014.
105. Stephen Shockey to Norman Felton, 6 April 1966, Norman Felton MSS, Box 22, Man from U.N.C.L.E. Fan Mail, 1964–6, University of Iowa Special Collections, Iowa City.
106. Britten, *Beyond Bond*, p. 117.
107. Frederick C. Houghton to Michael R. Pries, 22 March 1965, Norman Felton MSS, Box 22, Man from U.N.C.L.E. Legal File, University of Iowa Special Collections, Iowa City.
108. Robert Wallace, Keith Melton and Henry Robert Schlesinger, *Spycraft: Inside the CIA's Top Secret Laboratory* (London: Bantam Press, 2009), p. 112.
109. Ibid, p. 494.
110. *The ABCs of Espionage* cited in Kackman, *Citizen Spy*, p. 85; emphasis in the original.
111. Ibid., p. 84.
112. Worland, 'The Cold War Mannerists', p. 156.
113. Tity de Vries, 'The 1967 Central Intelligence Agency Scandal: Catalyst in a Transforming Relationship between State and People', *Journal of American History*, 98:4 (2012), pp. 1,075–92.
114. Tom Braden in Hugh Wilford, 'Secret America: The CIA and American Culture', in C. W. E. Bigsby (ed.), *The Cambridge Companion to Modern American Culture* (Cambridge: Cambridge University Press, 2006), p. 278.
115. Thomas W. Braden, 'I'm Glad the CIA is Immoral', *The Saturday Evening Post*, 20 May 1967.
116. Jeffery Hadden, '"Beat" Poet Testifies in CIA Case', *The Detroit News*, 15 January 1971.
117. Alfred McCoy, *The Politics of Heroin in Southeast Asia* (New York: Harper and Row, 1972). Alexander Cockburn discusses the Ginsberg-McCoy connection in Alexander Cockburn, *Whiteout: CIA, Drugs and the Press* (New York: Verso Books, 1999), p. 249.
118. Flora Lewis, 'Ginsberg-McGovern Question CIA Smack Smuggling', *Daily Planet*, 10 June 1972.
119. John Prados, *The Family Jewels: The CIA, Secrecy, and Presidential Power* (Austin: University of Texas Press, 2013), pp. 221–2.
120. Kackman, *Citizen Spy*, p. 110.

121. Ibid., p. 107.
122. Jeffery Hadden, '"Beat" Poet Testifies in CIA Case', *The Detroit News*, 15 January 1971.
123. Kackman, *Citizen Spy*, p. 111; for details of the CIA's contract with Michigan State University see Robert Witanek, 'The CIA on Campus', *Covert Action Information Bulletin*, no. 31 (1998), pp. 25–8. For more on CIA activities on campus see Philip Zwerling (ed.), *The CIA on Campus: Essays on Academic Freedom and the National Security State* (New York: McFarland and Co., 2011).
124. 'Don't Fool with the Phone Company' Script, Theodore J. Flicker Collection, Louis B. Mayer Library Special Collections, Box 5, The American Film Institute (hereafter AFI), Hollywood.
125. Robert Evans, *The Kids Stay in the Picture* (London: Aurum Press, 1994), p. 127.
126. Ibid, pp. 126–7; emphasis in the original.
127. *Ted Flicker: A Life in Three Acts* (David Ewing, Bayside Productions, 2009).
128. *The President's Analyst* (Theodore J. Flicker, Paramount, 1967).
129. For a discussion of the relationship between domestic unrest and the war in Vietnam see Robert Buzzanco, *Vietnam and the Transformation of American Life* (Hoboken: Blackwell Publishers, 1999).
130. Theodore J. Flicker to Frank Cooper, 11 July 1964, Theodore J. Flicker Special Collections 2, Box 5 (Story Ideas), Louis B. Mayer Library, AFI.
131. 'Enough is Enough is Enough: An Original Idea for Motion Pictures by Theodore J. Flicker', undated, Theodore J. Flicker Special Collections 2, Box 5 (Story Ideas), Louis B. Mayer Library, AFI, Hollywood.
132. Ibid.
133. 'Enough is Enough is Enough Treatment by Theodore J Flicker', Summer 1964, Box 5 'Story Ideas', Theodore J. Flicker Special Collections 2, Louis B. Mayer Library, AFI, Hollywood.
134. Evans, *The Kids Stay in the Picture*, p. 126.
135. Kackman, *Citizen Spy*, p. 121.
136. *The President's Analyst* (Paramount Pictures, December 1967; Produced by Stanley Rubin; Directed by Theodore J. Flicker; Screenplay by Theodore J. Flicker).
137. Mary L. Dudziak, *Cold War Civil Rights: Race and the Image of American Democracy* (Princeton: Princeton University Press, 2002).
138. *London Daily Herald* cited in Kackman, *Citizen Spy*, p. 115.
139. 'The President's Analyst – Film Review', *Variety*, 20 December 1967.
140. Ibid.

5. SECRECY, CONSPIRACY, CINEMA AND THE CIA IN THE 1970s

In her outstanding study of the post-Watergate press scandals and Congressional investigations of the illegal, immoral or otherwise pernicious activities of the CIA and FBI, Kathryn Olmsted refutes the conventional narrative of mid-seventies American political history as that of an out-of-control executive brought to bay by courageous investigative journalists and an emboldened legislature.[1] The idea, Olmsted argues, that America's system of checks and balances saved the day, that in spite of a corrupt President and the nefarious actions of his secret intelligence services, democracy won out – indeed that the very downfall of that President and the curtailment of the CIA and FBI at the hands of a powerful fourth estate demonstrated the vitality of American democracy – was a comforting but misleading myth. This ideologically reassuring emplotment of the era was conceived in part by Hollywood. With the notable exception of *Network* (1976), journalists recurrently figured as heroes in the political cinema of the decade. Even in Alan Pakula's deeply cynical conspiracy thriller *The Parallax View* (1974), Warren Beatty plays a crusading investigative reporter; the warm hues of his newspaper office overseen by his avuncular editor contrast starkly with the 'cold and forbidding' interiors seen elsewhere in the picture.[2] Pakula, the so-called 'master of paranoia', reprised the same theme when he took Watergate on directly in *All the President's Men* (1976) a few years later. The message, as Slavoj Žižek sardonically puts it, is simple: '[W]hat a great country ours must be, when a couple of ordinary guys [Woodward and Bernstein] like you and me can bring down the president, the mightiest man on Earth!'[3]

But the reality, according to Olmsted, was very different. Tenacious investigative reporters like Woodward and Bernstein or Seymour Hersh were exceptions rather than the rule. Watergate, far from heralding a new era of aggressive advocacy journalism, encouraged trepidation from major newspaper editors who feared an anti-press reaction if they pushed their hard-won First Amendment privileges too far. Woodward and Bernstein's editor Katherine Graham at *The Washington Post*, for example, urged caution and restraint by journalists in the wake of Watergate who had become, in her words, 'too much a party to events, too much an actor in the drama'.[4] Thus, when Hersh's sensational scoop revealing the CIA's 'massive, illegal, domestic surveillance' of the anti-war movement hit the front page of *The New York Times* on 22 December 1974 – the first of a series of damning revelations of CIA misdeeds collectively known as 'The Family Jewels' that led to the Congressional investigations of CIA and FBI activities the following year – it was met with a mixture of tepid endorsement and consternation. In particular, the use of the word 'massive' proved controversial for Hersh's critics who argued that he had greatly exaggerated what the CIA claimed was a regrettable but limited transgression. When the subsequent Presidential and Congressional investigations appeared to vindicate Hersh's hyperbole, the rest of the mainstream media still refused to fully endorse Hersh's aggressive line.[5]

The Congressional committees tasked with investigating 'The Family Jewels' and other alleged abuses by the CIA and FBI, were also – contrary to popular memory – largely impotent. The Senate Church Committee, argues Olmsted, for all its media grandstanding of poisoned dart-guns and scurrilous Agency assassination plots, was predominantly political pantomime – a largely ineffectual partisan showcase for ambitious Senators, especially Senator Church himself, who cast the Agency as the 'Rogue Elephant' of American Government in order to avoid raising more troubling questions about the systemic abuse of executive power by successive administrations, including – or even especially – the Democratic presidents Kennedy and Johnson. The House Pike Committee did indeed raise some of those more troubling questions, but its chair, Otis Pike, was politically marginalised for doing so, and the findings of his committee remained classified until decades later when a Hollywood conspiracy thriller – Oliver Stone's *JFK* – helped pry open much of the official record from this period.

But perhaps the most compelling evidence that the impact of Congress and the Press upon the CIA in this period has been overblown is the largely ineffectual legislation and regulations that the various Commissions brought about. The proof, as the saying goes, is in the pudding. As CIA Director William Colby gave unusually forthright testimony to Congress about the Agency's past abuses, he was at the same time overseeing the development of major clandestine operations in Angola. Congress cut funds to the operation a year later, but

IN SECRECY'S SHADOW

Figure 5.1 Senator Frank Church holds up a CIA poisoned-dart gun during the Senate Church Committee hearings that investigated CIA and FBI wrongdoing. *Source:* United States National Archives, College Park, Maryland.

CIA activity there continued unabated. Only a few years after the investigations, the CIA began what would become its longest-running and most costly covert operation in its history in Afghanistan. Once Reagan was in power he fulfilled his electoral pledge to 'unleash' the CIA. The Agency's 'dirty wars' in Africa and Central America were at the vanguard of Reagan's more muscular foreign policy. Iran-Contra followed, repeating the now-familiar pattern of abuse – scandal – feigned penance for the cameras – repeated abuse – repeated scandal – feigned penance – ad infinitum. One need not look far in this contemporary age of rendition programmes, drone strikes and 'enhanced interrogation' that have precipitated vocal but largely ineffectual Congressional consternation to realise that the Church and Pike Committees did little to alter this pattern.

And yet, when one watches the films of the 1970s that featured the CIA and compare them to the predominantly light-hearted tone of the American spy cinema of the previous decade, it seems apparent that something did change, in American culture at least, in the way people viewed the Agency. It is tempting to regard Hollywood, with its nose for the box office, as a mirror on American society – reflecting its hopes and dreams as well as its fears and anxieties. On such a reading it seems clear that the cumulative effect of Watergate, the Family Jewels and many other revelations like them that implicated the American Government in secret scandals took their toll on the American psyche. Whether it was the CIA agent in *Breakout* (1975), who berates the head of the 'Transpacific Fruit and Steamship Corporation' for his leniency in choosing to have his own grandson jailed for 28 years instead of assassinated for compromising operational security; or the Agency chief in

Scorpio (1972) – decidedly not the avuncular Allen Dulles type that recurred in the previous era's spy films – who will stop at nothing to have one of his own agents killed, the CIA, almost without exception in the 1970s, were portrayed as sinister Machiavellians. If nothing else, it appears that Hollywood filmmakers may have been reading the newspapers when stories of CIA assassination plots and other nefarious schemes broke.

It would be a mistake, however, to regard Hollywood's increasingly tenebrous vision of the CIA in the 1970s as a straightforward translation of public opinion. Surely, the American public grew more sceptical in this period – how could it not! From June 1973 to October 1975 public approval of the Agency slumped from 67 per cent to 53 per cent – a 14-point difference. Clearly the Hersh revelations and the investigations that followed had some effect. Moreover, 61 per cent agreed in December 1975 that the CIA's and FBI's domestic surveillance of anti-war protestors constituted 'a violation of basic rights'. But, as Cynthia Nolan suggests in her analysis of public opinion of the CIA in this period, these polls cannot be viewed in isolation from the wider anxieties and scepticism towards American Government in the post-Watergate/post-Vietnam era. Moreover, other polls in the aftermath of the Church and Pike committees revealed considerable public concern that both the media and Congress's inquisition of the American intelligence community had gone too far in exposing so many government secrets.[6]

So what explains the emergence of the numerous anti-CIA films during this period in particular, and the conspiracy thriller with its attendant scepticism towards American institutions more generally? As with the declining studio system and the increasing significance of international markets in the previous decade, the new politics and aesthetic practices of Hollywood in the 1970s was substantially determined by structural changes within the motion picture industry. Cinema attendance plummeted 'to a quarter of their mid-1940s peak', allowing large conglomerates to acquire vulnerable studios. These structural upheavals provided opportunities for a younger generation of filmmakers whom producers believed could help better attract the increasingly younger audiences. Older directors and producers like John Ford, Merian Cooper, Louis B. Mayer and Cecil B. DeMille who had dominated the studio era began to retire or die. Others, like Hitchcock, were regarded as increasingly anachronistic as compared to the more innovative 'New Hollywood' usurpers. Unlike Ford and Cooper, who served in OSS, or Hitchcock, who made propaganda films during the Second World War, these younger directors did not share that formative wartime experience that instilled a sense of uncomplicated patriotism in many of their forebears. Their ideas about American foreign policy had been shaped not by the triumphant overthrow of Nazi tyranny, but by the moral quagmire of Vietnam.

Censorship, too, had loosened; the replacement of the Production Code

Administration in 1968 by the ratings system allowed for more violent and sexually explicit motion pictures. As discussed in earlier chapters the Production Code had also constrained more radical political expression, especially during the 1950s, when it effectively forbade depictions of government officials and institutions without their express permission. Although the PCA was already significantly eroded by 1968, the arrival of the ratings system sounded its final death knell. With the Production Code gone, not only did directly negative depictions of government institutions like the CIA become more permissible, but the violence perpetrated by them, whether in Vietnam or by CIA assassins, could be shown more graphically than ever. Sam Peckinpah, for example, perhaps the most well-known architect of increasing violence onscreen during this period, made two anti-CIA films towards the end of his career: *The Killer Elite* (1975) and *The Osterman Weekend* (1982). Neither of these was much good – the drugs and the alcohol had begun to catch up with his talent – but each rendered fictional visions of CIA brutality with an explicitness that would have been unthinkable in previous decades.

All this, however, fails to explain why the CIA, out of all the sullied institutions of American Government during the 1970s, was singled out by Hollywood as especially nefarious. Of all the organs of the US Government's foreign policy apparatus to have eroded America's moral authority in the sixties and seventies, the Pentagon was surely first among them. Yet with the notable exception of John Wayne's pro-military *Green Berets* (1968), no combat films were set in Vietnam during the war, and only a few that came after could be regarded as anything close to 'anti-military'. Even Francis Ford Coppola's famously bleak update of Conrad's *Heart of Darkness* in *Apocalypse Now* (1979) presented the war as a 'confusing and pointless experience'. Indeed if anything it glorified the valour of combat, made little attempt, as with Conrad's novel, to see the war through anything other than Western eyes, and, as such, failed to address the more far-reaching critiques of American imperialism that academics and members of the anti-war movement had raised.[7] Likewise the FBI, whose exposed transgressions in this period, such as the infamous COINTELPRO operation that included the bugging and blackmailing of major civil rights leaders including Martin Luther King, were surprisingly unblemished by the Hollywood cinema of the 1970s.

A key explanation for this relative difference in treatment of the various government bureaucracies by Hollywood is surely the Pentagon's and the FBI's more adept handling of public relations, particularly their longstanding relationships with Hollywood. As detailed in this chapter, the CIA began to formalise its public affairs activities in the 1970s, including officially establishing an Office of Public Affairs in 1978. They even made tentative gestures towards cooperating with filmmakers. But their first and only attempt during the 1970s to work with a major Hollywood production, *Scorpio* (1972), ended in total disaster – apparently nobody had bothered to read the script as they might have realised the filmmakers' intentions to portray the CIA as sinister and amoral. Compare these jejune efforts with the seasoned quid pro quo arrangements between the film industry and the Pentagon, or the FBI's policy, from almost the moment of its founding, of proactively sculpting its popular image, and one straightforward explanation for Hollywood's varied treatment of different government agencies swiftly emerges.[8]

In the 1970s, despite widespread anti-military sentiment in America after Vietnam, the Pentagon continued its de facto censorship of combat films by refusing technical support and the loan of its equipment to critical features while assisting those producers that supported its agenda and were compliant with its requests for script changes. As Coppola discovered, it was difficult to make any film that was even vaguely critical of the American military if expensive military equipment that could only be loaned from the US military was required for authenticity. He offered to rewrite the script of *Apocalypse Now* several times to satisfy the Pentagon, but was eventually forced to loan helicopters from the Filipino military.[9] In consequence, with little appetite for pro-military cinema and with the difficulties of getting an anti-military film made without Pentagon support, the traditional combat film effectively vanished from American screens from 1970 until the revival of American patriotism during the bicentennial celebrations of 1976.[10] Similarly, despite the exposure of COINTELPRO and other FBI scandals, the Bureau continued to work closely with the entertainment industry to produce positive depictions of its work – for example, *The F.B.I.* television series that ran until 1974, and *Dillinger* (1973) that received cooperation from J. Edgar Hoover during preproduction before he died in May 1972.

But the CIA's inexperience at public affairs alone cannot explain its unmatched status as a sinister emblem of the excesses of American foreign policy in the 1970s. 'No amount of public relations', concluded a surprisingly forthright report on the Agency's public image by its Management Advisory Group in November 1970, 'can hide or offset the damage done to our reputation by poor analysis, sloppy operations, or other forms of ineptitude'.[11] Perhaps one reason the CIA became a particular target for Hollywood cynicism during this period was that their misdeeds were especially filmic. The Agency's capacity for violence, and in particular its assassination plots, made compelling screenplay material with box-office potential. Producer Dino De Laurentiis, for example, decided to make *Three Days of the Condor* not because of any particular political persuasion, but because the opening chapter of James Grady's original novel, *Six Days of the Condor*, which saw the assassination of a whole team of CIA analysts, was such a compelling hook that he felt sure it would captivate audiences.[12] Stories of FBI surveillance and their subversion of domestic protest movements, although sinister, were perhaps less spectacular. Having said that, the 1970s did see a number of masterful films about surveillance, most notably Francis Ford Coppola's understated classic *The Conversation* (1974), which tellingly was about a private surveillance contractor, not the FBI.

To limit our analysis to a simplistic comparison between CIA revelations and Hollywood plotlines, however, overlooks the wider cultural significance that the Agency had already begun to acquire. 'The CIA is simply a tool', remarked Robert Redford during the filming of *Three Days of the Condor*. '[I]t is an instrument that lets us dig into something larger.' [13] That 'something larger', too abstract to faithfully render in a simple two-hour visual narrative, concerned the loss of American innocence in the aftermath of Watergate and Vietnam. These seminal events and others like them that 'broke the back of the American century' – many of which involved the CIA – compromised the liberal consensus notion that American politics and foreign policy was invariably honest and benign.[14] The attendant collapse of public trust in government, a process begun in the previous decade, reached its nadir after Watergate at the very moment when Hersh's Family Jewels revelations broke.

The CIA was a useful scapegoat for the more far-reaching iniquities of American foreign policy in this period, and a convenient alibi for the American public and its representatives seeking to exculpate themselves from the odious offences committed on their behalf. Indeed the concept of plausible deniability, written into the very fabric of covert action, allowed for this evasion of responsibility by America's democratically elected leaders. Church's 'Rogue Elephant' was America's deus ex machina. Many of the films of this era reinforced this proposition that it was the Agency that had gone rogue, not the American system writ large. Indeed in *Three Days of the Condor* (1975) it was not even the CIA that was at fault, but a CIA within the CIA.

But it was not just the bad timing of having so many of their past misdeeds exposed so soon after Watergate that made the CIA such a lightning rod for public scepticism towards government in this period. What all of the revelations of government corruption and immorality in this period had in common was that they revealed the corrosive effects of secrecy on American politics. It was secrecy that perpetuated the Vietnam War and allowed four consecutive administrations to mislead the American public about the US's aims and intentions there until Daniel Ellsberg blew the lid on this systematic deception by leaking the Pentagon Papers in 1971. It was secrecy that had allowed Richard Nixon to cover up the Watergate break-ins, and it was secrecy that had enabled the CIA to transgress the boundaries of morality and law. In short, unlike the momentary CIA scandals of the 1960s, the compound effect of these and other revelations like them in the decade that followed was to give an impression of secrecy's systemic corruption of American Government. It was no longer a case of a few bad apples or some errors of judgement when even the President of the United States had ordered an illegal domestic espionage operation against his political opponents by former CIA employees and then attempted to keep his abuses secret by exerting executive privilege. Secrecy and corruption had become, as the tagline for Alan Pakula's *The Parallax View* (1974) put it, 'as American as apple pie'.[15]

Since the U-2 Spy Affair in 1960 and the Bay of Pigs a year later, the CIA, paradoxically, became the public face of American secrecy. Although it was by no means the only secret institution within American Government, it was, paradoxically, the most well-known. In this sense, the position of the CIA within American culture offers a kind of synecdochal barometer of the extent of American anxieties about US Government secrecy. As previous chapters discussed, although the spy spoofs and romances broke decisively with the austere state-sourced narratives of the semi-documentary, they very rarely offered anything amounting to a radical critique of the CIA, and, by implication, American secrecy more generally. While the 1960s created conditions, to paraphrase Graham Greene, that were conducive to comedy and a light-hearted treatment of espionage, there was something much less humorous about CIA counter-insurgency operations in Southeast Asia, assassination plots, torture, attempts to overthrow the democratically elected Chilean Government, mind-control experiments and the 'massive' illegal domestic surveillance of anti-war protestors. Some elements of the humorous tone of the 1960s representations of espionage did survive into the next decade, but in films like Woody Allen's *Bananas* (1971) and *The In-Laws* (1979) it was given a more bitingly satirical edge that quite directly mocked past CIA covert operations. For the most part, however, the camp spy cinema of the 1960s was replaced with the sinister and surreal mise en scène of the conspiracy thriller – a genre that was defined by its unambiguous opposition to the disorienting effects of secrecy upon American history and democracy.

In their tone, the conspiracy thrillers of the 1970s were remarkably different from the light-hearted spy capers of the 1960s. But in their attitude towards American history, and the practice of history more generally – in their historiography if you like – the rise of the conspiracy thriller as the pre-eminent mode of representing the CIA in this period marked the culmination of a process that had begun more than a decade earlier with the rejection of the semi-documentary by the spy cinema of the 1960s. Rather than regarding the state as the arbiter of historical authenticity, as the semi-documentaries had done, the conspiracy thrillers sought to recover truth from the obfuscation of state secrecy. In doing so they provided, to borrow James Der Derian's eloquent phrasing, a 'carnival-mirror opposite' of the official story.[16]

Widespread cultural paranoia was the indivisible corollary of excessive government secrecy: an unintended though inevitable consequence of the undermining of public trust through official duplicity. From our post-Watergate perspective this causal relationship between American conspiracy culture and US Government secrecy may seem obvious. But when Richard Hofstadter delivered his seminal essay on *The Paranoid Style in American Politics* to the Oxford Union the day before President Kennedy died, a treatise that continues to define both the academic and popular conception of conspiracy culture to this day, he could not have envisaged the profound erosion of public trust in government that excessive secrecy would inspire over the next decade. For Hofstadter, the 'paranoid style' was a fringe phenomenon, not something that was apparent in the majority of the American population. It was, rather, an occasional though dangerous aberration that flared in figures like Senator McCarthy who threatened the rational 'vital centre' of American politics that was, ordinarily, forged in pragmatism and compromise, not secrecy and paranoia.[17]

Hofstadter was a member of the wartime generation, and one of the key intellectual architects of the post-war liberal consensus; his ideas about how American democracy and its political institutions functioned was thus defined in opposition to totalitarianism – of both Nazi and Soviet stripes. For Hofstadter, and other liberal consensus intellectuals like him, American democracy was exceptional and worth celebrating because, unlike the tyrannical and conspiracy-minded regimes to which it was opposed, it accommodated a melting-pot plurality of religions, ideologies and other competing creeds without the need for violent repression – needless to say, the liberal consensus historians downplayed the moments of class struggle and ethnic tension in American history that the progressive historians before them had emphasised.

This benign vision of American history became largely discredited in the decade that followed the publication of *The Paranoid Style*. Images of My Lai, or of Kim Phuc's naked screaming Christ-like icon of contorted suffering at the hands of American power as she fled her napalmed village, polluted the clean air between totalitarianism and American democracy that Hofstadter and his intellectual allies sought to conserve. More harmful still for the intellectual assumptions that underpinned Hofstadter's argument, was the recognition that the institutions of American Government were not noble, rational and transparent mechanisms that balanced the will of competing interests in American public life to produce reasonable and pragmatic policy that reflected the aggregated will of the people while steering what Buddhists refer to as the virtuous 'middle path'. But perhaps most damaging of all for Hofstadter's celebration of mainstream American politics at the expense of cultural and political paranoia was the credence that excessive US Government secrecy afforded to the latter. In an age when so many conspiracy theories about American Government were revealed as factual, and so many state-sourced narratives revealed as lies, was it more reasonable to believe the 'official story', or those who challenged it?

The paranoid vision of American history that confronted the CIA in the 1970s was doubtless a distortion of the past. It was even perhaps an unfair distortion – often casting the Agency as a convenient scapegoat for the wider failings of American foreign policy. Conspiracy theories simplify complex notions of causality, translating abstract structural causes into individual agency by assigning blame and making individuals culpable for events beyond their control. They provide easy-to-comprehend and sometimes convincing answers to troubling questions, offering what Fredric Jameson describes as a 'poor person's cognitive mapping' of an ultimately inconceivable totality.[18] They can also be dangerous: as Richard Hofstadter and Karl Popper argued, the road to Auschwitz was paved by the victory of the 'paranoid style' over reason.[19] For these reasons, the widespread cultural paranoia of the 1970s may be regarded as a deeply lamentable sullying of the enlightened 'public sphere' of reasoned discourse and debate that Jürgen Habermas has argued provides the cornerstone of a healthy democracy – certainly Hofstadter saw it this way, and for many his argument remains compelling to this day.[20]

To adopt a Hofstadterian perspective on post-Watergate America, however, is to assume that the American culture of the 1970s perverted a public sphere that was somehow still uncorrupted. But excessive government secrecy, owing to the rise of the American national security state, had long before destabilised the rational public sphere, and discredited the idea of a singular, shared and authoritative national past.[21] The conspiracy thrillers of the 1970s symbolised an America in search of a lost national past – of a past that was warped and corrupted by the sullying effects of secrecy. Its protagonists, often-investigative journalists, felt duty-bound to retrieve the truth of American history from behind the veil of secrecy. Most of these films, like *Three Days of the Condor* (1975), *The Parallax View* (1974) and *Marathon Man* (1976), were not intended as literal histories – indeed all of these examples are self-consciously fictional stories. But they did intend to say something *about* American history – about how secrecy had distorted it, and about how the American public longed for a more open and transparent past. The 'paranoid' cultural response to excessive government secrecy may not have offered an alternative history to the 'official story', but they did provide an alternative historiography that was directly opposed to the kinds of credulous patriotic narratives that the semi-documentaries had produced.[22]

In previous chapters I have traced the gradual erosion of public trust in government through its aesthetic and epistemological corollaries in Hollywood cinema. During the war and the immediate post-war period trust in government was at an all-time high, and the semi-documentary that celebrated the state as the arbiter of historical authenticity was pre-eminent. In the early 1960s the spy spoofs lampooned the credulity of such a naïve vision of America's past, particularly the history of its secret intelligence agencies. This final chapter tells the story of the culmination of this continuum – the moment when the nadir of public trust in government translated into a Hollywood aesthetic fundamentally opposed to excessive government secrecy.

SCORPIO (1973) AND CIA PUBLIC RELATIONS

The CIA's first experience of working directly with a Hollywood film crew was a bit of a disaster. *Scorpio* (1973) was the first of a new breed of films about the CIA that represented the Agency as a wholly sinister force in American life that was willing to deceive and murder American citizens, and even its own agents, in order to achieve its suitably Machiavellian ends. Emblematic of this was one of the film's promotional posters, which featured a corpse sprawled out over the CIA's official seal. It was a dramatic departure from the light-hearted spoofs of the previous era and prefigured the deeply cynical conspiracy thrillers that soon followed. Michael Winner, the film's director, later described it as prophetic – 'it showed the CIA doing things that nobody at the time believed they did'.[23] It was deeply inauspicious for CIA public relations that they allowed this film, of all the requests they had received in the past twenty-five years, to be the first to include actual location footage of Langley.

Scorpio's oftentimes-incoherent plot tells the story of a retiring assassin named Cross (Burt Lancaster), who is presumed to be a traitor and ordered dead by McLeod, his amoral former CIA boss. McLeod hires Cross's former apprentice, Jean Laurier (Alan Delon), aka 'Scorpio', to do the deed, and he embarks on a chase across Europe to hunt Cross down, visiting Paris and Vienna on the way before finally catching up with him in Washington, DC. The Hitchcockian theme of the senseless personal cost of politics and espionage is dealt with at length. Cross's wife is killed during a raid on his house by the CIA, which provokes Cross into getting even by, somewhat implausibly, killing McLeod in broad daylight after following him from Langley. Scorpio's girlfriend is also sucked into this orphic descent when she is exposed as a Czech courier who has been assisting Cross with his treachery. At the film's dénouement Scorpio catches them together and kills them both. Before he finishes Cross off, he allows him to deliver a rather strained soliloquy in which he concludes that espionage is just a game. 'There's no good, and no bad. The object is not to win, but not to lose. And the only rule is to stay in the game.'

Even though it went into production before the Watergate scandal broke, *Scorpio* may reasonably be described as the first film to address the widespread cynicism towards American Government that it inspired. As the production notes boasted, '"Scorpio" is a film right out of today's headlines.'[24] Indeed it was so timely that Burt Lancaster and Alan Delon, who were staying at the Watergate hotel during the film's production, had a chance encounter with Nixon's burglars on the night they were arrested.[25] The film even included shots

SECRECY, CONSPIRACY, CINEMA AND THE CIA IN THE 1970s

Figure 5.2 Promotional poster for *Scorpio* (1973), featuring a murdered CIA agent splayed out over the Agency's seal. *Scorpio* was the first film to be granted permission to shoot footage at the CIA's Langley headquarters. Unfortunately for the CIA it appears that nobody read the script, as it featured a nefarious CIA willing to murder its own agents to keep them silent. *Source*: MGM/Academy of Motion Picture Arts and Sciences, Beverly Hills, California.

of the Watergate hotel, although naturally Winner had no way of knowing at the time the significance that this landmark would acquire. Although this was all serendipitous, Winner had nevertheless tapped into a cultural current of cynicism that Watergate would soon bring centre stage. Arguably, however, *Scorpio* was too contemporary. It was released in the spring of 1973, when the Watergate scandal was still unfolding, and when few could have envisaged the extent of the fallout from the break-ins. Moreover, critics, whose expectations were still framed by the light-hearted capers of the previous decade, bemoaned its lack of humour and its incoherent plot. Needless to say, it fared poorly at the box-office.[26]

Given the themes of *Scorpio* and its cynical vision of espionage and the CIA in particular, why on earth did the Agency allow Winner and his crew to film at Langley? The same question was asked by Leo Cherne, then Secretariat of the President's Foreign Intelligence Advisory Board (PFIAB), and former news-anchor and chairperson of the International Rescue Committee (IRC) that had assisted Joseph Mankiewicz with his adaptation of *The Quiet American* in the 1950s. In late January 1975, less than a month after Seymour Hersh published the first of his 'family jewels' exposés of CIA misdeeds in *The New York Times*, Cherne was settling down to a Sunday night movie and TV dinner when he nearly knocked his peas all over the sofa! *Scorpio* was airing that night on NBC, and it didn't take Cherne long to realise that the external shots of Langley were authentic. Cherne was incredulous. The airing of *Scorpio* on primetime American television, a film that features amoral CIA officers assassinating their own agents at a time of increasing public pressure for a wide-ranging and far-reaching enquiry of CIA activities, including CIA assassination plots, was potentially hugely damaging for the Agency. Indeed the very next day journalist Clifton Daniel published an article in *The New York Times* that invoked *Scorpio* as an illustration of why America needed a more expansive investigation than the Rockefeller Commission's narrow focus on CIA domestic activity.[27]

Incensed by Daniel's piece, and by the idea that the Agency may have participated in the iconoclastic demise of its own reputation, Cherne asked the Agency, 'How did it come about that "Scorpio" was filmed in part at CIA headquarters at Langley – an obvious break from past CIA practice?'[28] The CIA's response betrayed the folly of their relative inexperience at liaising with Hollywood, especially when compared to the FBI's and the Pentagon's long-established engagement with the industry. The DCI at the time, Richard Helms, reluctantly agreed for the scenes to be shot at Langley after California Senator John Tunney made a request in February 1972 on behalf of the film-makers. Arthur Krim, chairperson of United Artists and personal friend of Helms, likewise approached Helms for permission. Helms' acquiescence to their requests was, as Cherne's question notes, a departure from their usual policy of refusing to work with Hollywood. Only a few years previously, for example, Helms had rejected a similar approach by John Horton on behalf of Alfred Hitchcock whose film *Topaz* was undoubtedly far more palatable for CIA public affairs than *Scorpio*.[29]

In their correspondence with the Agency, Tunney, Krim and production manager David Silver made no mention of the sinister themes of their movie, and used the production's original title 'Danger Field' that was perhaps more evocative of sixties spy capers than the darker themes that the title 'Scorpio' implies. Never did the Agency request a script, or even a treatment of the film – a standard procedure at both the FBI and the Pentagon. Nor does it appear that the filmmakers were required to enter into any formal or even tacit agreement with the Agency that would allow the CIA to raise objections and suggest script changes at a later date – again standard procedure at both the Pentagon and the FBI. Perhaps Helms and the CIA just didn't consider a fictional spy film significant enough for them to adopt the standard precautions taken by other government agencies, or perhaps they were simply too inexperienced or too trusting in this first engagement with Hollywood. Whatever the reasons behind their decision to allow the *Scorpio* crew to film Langley, they surely regretted it three years later when the film's scenes of amoral CIA assassins aired on primetime American television amidst the fallout from the 'Family Jewels' revelations.

The experience with *Scorpio* vindicated those within the Agency who feared the allure of Hollywood and its 'pot of gold'.[30] The CIA would not work again with Hollywood filmmakers for another two decades, although some television crews were allowed on to Langley but under much more strictly supervised standards. Along with the negative experience of *Scorpio* there was another reason for the CIA's suspicion of Hollywood and their initially cautious approach to public relations more generally. In contrast to the reality of their inept liaison with the *Scorpio* producers, they feared the potential public perception that they had grown too adept at public relations; they did not want to be seen to be manipulating the public record even if their efforts so far at influencing Hollywood had proved far from effective.

In 1970 Senator William Fulbright, who by the end of the 1960s had become an influential critic of the US foreign policy establishment, published a damning account of the Pentagon's public relations activities. Fulbright's *The Pentagon Propaganda Machine* decried the creeping militarism of American society and laid the blame substantially at the feet of the US military's own extensive salesmanship – 'The military has been operating for years in that Elysium of the public relations man', he lamented, 'a seller's market'.[31] The following year documentary filmmaker Peter Davis, who later directed one of the most powerful indictments of US foreign policy in Vietnam, *Hearts and Minds* (1974), made a documentary entitled *The Selling of the Pentagon* based on Fulbright's charges. The documentary struck a chord with future DCI William Colby. In the wake of the 1975 intelligence scandals Colby was approached by David Atlee Phillips, a high-ranking CIA officer who went on to found the Association of Retired Intelligence Officers (ARIO) that effectively worked as an unofficial public relations office for the CIA during the latter half of the 1970s.[32] Phillips urged Colby to initiate a more aggressive public relations campaign in response to the scandals. As David Shamus McCarthy documents,

Colby agreed in principle, but thought the approach 'too risky', and 'reminded Phillips about *The Selling of the Pentagon*'.[33] In reality, however, the CIA had a long way to go before their public relations resembled anything approaching Fulbright's account of the Pentagon's profound influence upon Hollywood and the American media. The atmosphere of scepticism and paranoia partially inspired by the Hollywood cinema of the 1970s was anything but 'an Elysium of the public relations man' for the Agency.

THE SPOOK WHO SAT BY THE DOOR (1973)

The most radical film to depict the CIA in the 1970s, and perhaps the most radical film to depict the CIA that has ever been made, was Ivan Dixon's adaptation of Sam Greenlee's novel about black insurrection in America's cities, *The Spook Who Sat by the Door* (1973). The story's protagonist, Dan Freeman, played by Lawrence Cook, becomes the first black CIA officer after the Agency are forced to adjust their 'racially discriminatory hiring policy' by an ambitious Senator who spies a cynical opportunity to court the African American vote. In response, the Agency induct a group of genial middle-class black recruits, who they are patronisingly told 'represent the best of your race', on to their rigorous and invasive training programme. Among other things, as David Shamus McCarthy notes, *The Spook* 'provides a stinging indictment of America's black bourgeoisie'. Freeman's CIA classmates chatter about fine whiskies and their alma maters – contented by their gilded cage of relative privilege within a system of white domination and heedless to the struggles of the ghetto. Freeman, however, is not like the other recruits. Although he appeases his suspicious all-white CIA recruiters with the language of liberal integrationism, a glint in his eye betrays to the audience that he has an alternate purpose for undergoing the Agency's training that, portentously, includes schooling in the techniques of guerrilla warfare.[34]

Freeman is the only one to complete the course, and is rewarded for his aptitude by being made 'reproduction section chief' – or menial Xerox dogsbody – at the Agency. His all-white superiors do, however, allow him a more expansive role as the Agency's token black man; they seat him on the front desk to impress visitors with the CIA's apparent integration and get him to guide tours of Langley for groups of liberal Senators. After five years Freeman decides to leave the Agency, telling the CIA director that he wants to return to Chicago to 'help my people help themselves' – a cause that gratifies the director's smug perception that the Agency has had a civilising effect on the young black recruit. Freeman, however, has an altogether different idea of how to help his people help themselves, although the CIA have indeed unwittingly provided him with the tools to achieve his aim of revolutionary black insurrection. Back in Chicago he passes on his CIA training in the methods

Figure 5.3 Poster for Ivan Dixon's bold adaptation of Sam Greenlee's novel, *The Spook Who Sat by the Door* (1973), which featured a black CIA recruit who uses his training to inspire an African American insurrection in cities across the US. The film was mysteriously pulled from exhibitors a few weeks after release despite its relative success at the box-office. It has been alleged by members of the production team that the FBI used its influence to convince exhibitors to remove the film due to its explosive content.
Source: United Artists/Academy of Motion Picture Arts and Sciences, Beverly Hills.

of insurgency to a group of local hustlers, transforming them from criminal Blaxploitation archetypes into a disciplined revolutionary vanguard that call themselves 'The Cobras'. They train in armed and unarmed combat, rob banks to fund their activities and raid the National Guard armoury in Chicago to stockpile weapons.

Key to The Cobras' success is their invisibility. 'Remember', Freeman tells his recruits, 'a black man with a mop, tray or broom in his hand can go damn near anywhere in this country, and a smiling black man is invisible.' To demonstrate his point he has one of them dress as a janitor and steal a pipe right from under the nose of a Chicago business executive. The white authorities never suspect that The Cobras are behind the bank robbery and the raid on the National Guard because they deem it too professional, too well organised, to be executed by African Americans. Racial prejudice produces blind spots that are easily exploited by Freeman and his followers. When The Cobras finally do fall under suspicion, they are assumed to be operating under the aegis of a Soviet agent provocateur rather than their own auspices. J. Edgar Hoover and the real FBI of the sixties and seventies held similar convictions: under their infamous COINTELPRO programme they bugged civil rights leaders, including Martin Luther King, in part because they feared the hidden hand of the Soviets.[35] The FBI and CIA thus commit to rooting out this imagined white leader of The Cobras – 'cut off the head and the snake dies' – but Freeman has carefully prepared his cadre so that 'each man is trained to handle positions three steps ahead of him in grade'.

The trope of black invisibility, and its exploitation by black power advocates to subvert the existing white power structure, evokes Ralph Ellison's *The Invisible Man*. Indeed *The Spook*'s title, along with its obvious double entendre as both a racial slur and a colloquial synonym for spying, also references Ellison's opening – 'I am an invisible man. No, I am not a spook like those who haunted Edgar Allen Poe . . . I am invisible, understand, simply because people refuse to see me.'[36] In one of the key passages of Ellison's novel, the narrator recalls his grandfather's deathbed declamation–

> [O]ur life is a war and I have been a traitor all my born days, a spy in the enemy's country . . . Live with your head in the lion's mouth. I want you to overcome 'em with yeses, undermine 'em with grins, agree 'em to death and destruction, let 'em swoller you till they vomit or bust wide open.

Freeman is the realisation of this Delphic wisdom. He grins and yesses in the Agency's training scheme in order to learn their techniques of subversion. And he lives with his 'head in the lion's mouth' long after he leaves the Agency – working as a well-attired social worker driving a smart convertible and living under the nose of his best friend and police officer Sergeant Dawson who Freeman is eventually forced to kill once Dawson discovers his deception. Freeman and The Cobras live, to evoke Mao's dictum, like fish swimming in the sea – unremarkable to the white authorities and undetectable for it.

The film's final act begins with the police shooting dead an unarmed black citizen, which leads to rioting and widespread unrest that provides the necessary conditions for Freeman's planned insurrection. When the all-white National Guard are brought in to quell the unrest, The Cobras are waiting for them, and easily outgun and outmanoeuvre them. In a particularly memorable sequence they kidnap the head of the National Guard, paint his face black and force him to take LSD before temporarily releasing him back into his unit. As he stumbles towards a pair of stunned white guardsmen, murmuring incoherently, a Cobra sniper shoots him dead. As the violence escalates, Freeman's movement gathers momentum. In the final scene, which leaves the audience guessing as to the eventual outcome of the revolt, we hear a radio announcer reporting similar uprisings across eight of America's cities as more and more 'yeses' and grins are transmuted into carefully organised screams of violent insurrection.

Greenlee wrote *The Spook Who Sat by the Door* upon leaving the United States Information Agency (USIA). During his eight years of service he had worked in a number of CIA 'hotspots', including Iraq, Pakistan, Indonesia and Greece. It is likely that he encountered the systemic racism and tokenism of American officialdom first hand during this period and Freeman's experiences in the CIA can therefore be read as partially autobiographical. He left the USIA in 1965 and returned to Chicago after studying in Greece at the Aristotle University of Thessaloniki for a few years where he wrote the first draft of *The Spook*. By the mid-1960s Chicago had become a cauldron of racial unrest and black activism. Things came to a head in 1968 following the assassination of Martin Luther King, which sparked riots on a scale that has not been seen in the United States since. The mayor of Chicago at the time, Richard Daley, became infamous for his draconian measures in response to the widespread unrest. He told a press conference, for example, that he had instructed the Chicago police to adopt a shoot-to-kill policy. Amidst this atmosphere of social turmoil Greenlee struggled to find an American publisher willing to print his incendiary novel. In 1969 he published the novel in London with 'two young British publishers', Allison and Busby.[37] The book became a bestseller in England and was awarded the Book of the Year by *The Sunday Times*.[38]

Greenlee met Ivan Dixon in Chicago after his novel's runaway success. Dixon was a well-known actor. He had starred in the 1964 film *Nothing But a Man*, a film about a young black railroad worker who struggles to maintain his identity and dignity in the racist South while at the same time falling in love with a local white schoolteacher and daughter of the town's preacher. Dixon was also a regular on the television sitcom *Hogan's Heroes* and had appeared in both *The Man from U.N.C.L.E.* and *I Spy*. He had also directed top-rated shows like *Mob Squad* and *The Bill Cosby Show* before making his feature film directorial debut with *The Spook*. Dixon said he made *The Spook* because he wanted 'to create film that projects positive Black images for the consuming public'.[39] Although many reviewers took exception to the film's advocacy of violent resistance – one even charged it with having 'no respect for human life' – the film's underlying moral is its promotion of dignity and empowerment within the black community.[40] Unlike the pimps and hustlers of Blaxploitation cinema, Freeman is educated, disciplined and abstemious. Upon taking charge of The Cobras he outlaws the use of heroin because it shows a lack of self-respect. He lectures them on the importance of education and on the need for discipline and foresight, and he forges a communal conscience sadly lacking in many African American ghettos amidst the economic and social turmoil of the 1970s. When one of his key deputies, Pretty Willie, tells Freeman that he 'hates white folks', Freeman corrects him with one of the most epigrammatic lines from the film: 'This is not about hating white folks: it's about loving freedom enough to die or kill for it if necessary.'

Dixon encountered great difficulties in getting the film made. Funding was a problem right from the start. Initially, no major studio would back the project. Finally, Dixon managed to secure a distribution deal with United Artists after he misleadingly assured them that they were planning a Blaxploitation film like *Sweet Sweetback's Baadasssss Song* (1971) and *Superfly* (1972) that had performed exceptionally well at the box-office. Dixon flew to Algiers, Ghana and Nigeria to raise additional funds for the film but his efforts were frustrated, according to his widow who was interviewed for a documentary on the making of the film, because of interference from American officials.[41] Halfway through production, with funds running out, Dixon turned to prominent members of the black community and was able to finance the final stages of the film through their donations. Getting filming permits was another major obstacle. Richard Daley was still the mayor of Chicago when the film was in production and for obvious reasons was not likely to lend municipal support to the film, especially because it includes a scene in which The Cobras burn down the Chicago Mayor's office. As a result much of the film was shot in Gary, Indiana, whose first black mayor, Richard G. Hatcher, welcomed the filmmakers with open arms, not least because it provided temporary employment for 350 to 500 Gary residents who featured as extras in the film. The riot sequences, shot in Gary, are notable for their realism – indeed their visceral nature recalls Haskell Wexler's *Medium Cool* (1969), which blended documentary with reconstruction by filming actors partaking in the real-life 1968 Chicago riots. The reverse situation was true of *The Spook* – so convincing were the staged riots that some Gary residents mistook them for spontaneous unrest and began overturning cars and lighting fires that were not part of the production – a number of real arrests were made during the shooting and can be seen in the film.[42]

Perhaps the greatest hurdle for Dixon, however, was not getting the film made in the first place, but getting it seen. In the initial weeks of its limited release the film performed very well at the box-office. A number of effusive United Artists press releases testify to this. In its first week the film grossed 'an excellent $361,636 in 13 cities' according to one statement, and grossed '$40,836 for its first three days at the De Mille and Juliet' theatres in New York.

By all accounts it was a remarkable opening performance for an independent production of this nature and logic would suggest that United Artists would continue or even expand its run. But then, only a week after performing so well at the box-office, the film was pulled from cinemas across the country under mysterious circumstances. Greenlee believes that the FBI was responsible for the film's withdrawal. He recalls a conversation with a local cinema-owner in Chicago who said that government agents had visited him and told him to stop showing the film. As yet no government documents have emerged to substantiate these claims, however, they are entirely plausible, given the FBI's history of interference with Hollywood as well as their ongoing surveillance of black power advocates and their attempts to silence civil rights leaders under their COINTELPRO programme. Whatever the reasons, *The Spook Who Sat by the Door*'s mysterious premature removal from circulation made it the most radical CIA film that most of America never saw.

Watergate, *The Parallax View* (1974) and the Emergence of the Conspiracy Thriller

Scorpio (1973) and *The Spook Who Sat by the Door* (1973) were both made early in the decade, before the Watergate saga had fully unfurled. Although they offered radically contemptuous visions of the Agency, departing from the more playful criticisms of espionage offered up in the satirical camp spy thrillers of the 1960s, they were relatively isolated examples, and were not seen by much of the American public. Yes, in literature, spy fiction had cleaved to a darker vision of espionage since the publication of John Le Carré's *The Spy Who Came in from the Cold* in 1963.[43] The 'realist' spy thriller, as it became known, rejected the unrealistic romance of Bond and the high camp of the numerous films and television shows it inspired by depicting spies as jaded and un-heroic bureaucrats who, unlike Bond, fall victim to the machinations of state power beyond their control. 'What the hell do you think spies are?' asks Richard Burton as Alec Leamas in Martin Ritt's 1965 adaptation of Le Carré's novel. 'Moral philosophers measuring everything they do against the word of God or Karl Marx? They're not. They're just a bunch of seedy squalid bastards like me: little men, drunkards, queers, hen-pecked husbands, civil servants playing cowboys and Indians to brighten their rotten little lives.'[44]

But despite the critical success of Ritt's adaptation, and other British films like *The IPCRESS File* (1965), starring Michael Caine as the jaded working-class cockney espionage agent Harry Palmer, the format never really took off in America. Perhaps their cynical visions of a moribund Western society made more sense in Britain in the context of imperial decline.[45] *Scorpio* and films like *The Kremlin Letter* (1970) are some of the very few examples of attempts to 'Americanise' the format, and neither, tellingly, performed well at the box-office. Even Alfred Hitchcock, the undisputable master of spy cinema, failed to achieve his ambition of producing a 'realistic Bond', after he began to resent the series for its increasingly cartoonish appropriation of the format he had defined with *North by Northwest*. His later spy thrillers, *Torn Curtain* (1966) and *Topaz* (1970), if remarked upon at all, are usually regarded as symptomatic of his later career decline.[46] Up until the climax of the Watergate saga in 1974, the morose vision of espionage that spy realism afforded had failed to fully take hold of the American popular imagination.

Moreover, despite the continued student agitation against the CIA in the wake of the 1967 *Ramparts* revelations, rising opposition to the war in Vietnam, and revelations in 1972 of CIA plans to overthrow Salvador Allende in Chile, the CIA still kept most of America on its side. As late as 1973, 67 per cent of respondents to a Gallup poll rated the CIA positively, with only 19 per cent regarding them negatively and 14 per cent admitting that they had not even heard of the CIA![47] Moreover, in the first third of the 1970s the scandals that did emerge in the press had negligible practical impact on the CIA or its relationship with key stakeholders. As an internal CIA report entitled 'The Agency's Image' gleefully noted in November 1970:

> We understand that at present our relationship with Congress and the White House are sound. Recent efforts by the media to involve the Agency in 'hot' press issues have had short-term impact, at most. The monthly flow of unsolicited professional applicants for employment greatly exceeds our hiring capacity. And business, alienated somewhat by the National Students Association expose [sic], is again cooperating in furnishing both non-official cover and useful information.[48]

All of this changed in the years 1974–5, following the culmination of Watergate with Nixon's resignation and then, just a few months later, the publication of the 'Family Jewels' in *The New York Times*, which precipitated years of Congressional enquiries into the nefarious activities of the CIA and FBI.

The political conspiracy thrillers that appeared with increasing frequency after 1974 were Hollywood's response to these events. Although intelligence historians are quick to dismiss conspiracy theories, following Hofstadter, as dangerously misleading and irrational, one cannot escape the fact that these films appeared at a time when such august bodies as *The Washington Post*, *The New York Times* and the United States Congress had demonstrably proven that actual conspiracies had been perpetrated at the highest levels of the American Government. In this context, the conspiracy thrillers of the 1970s provided socially symbolic negotiations of the popular anxieties about secrecy, surveillance and the uninhibited rise of the national security state since the end of the Second World War.[49]

One of the earliest, and most archetypal examples of the new breed of post-Watergate conspiracy thriller – although actually it went into production long before the culmination of the Watergate scandal – was *The Parallax View* (1974). It offered a new mode of articulation that was previously unavailable to a generation of filmmakers who came to maturity in the shadow of numerous political assassinations of progressive leaders, the civil rights movement, Vietnam, and, finally, the denouement of America's socio-political corruption: Watergate. As Pakula's biographer puts it:

> [T]he assassinations of John F. and Robert Kennedy, Martin Luther King, and Malcolm X were fresh in the minds of audience members. The Vietnam War had caused millions of citizens to distrust its government. In addition, the depravities of the Nixon administration were being systematically exposed . . . further adding to a sense among many citizens in the United States that the country had lost its moral bearings.[50]

The Parallax View drew explicitly on these events, particularly the series of assassinations of the previous decade and the inadequacy of their official explanation that was epitomised by the failings of the Warren Commission and its increasingly vocal critics. Although in early script drafts and story conferences the director, Alan Pakula, and his scriptwriter, Lorenzo Semple Jr, toyed with the idea of opening the film with scenes from Dealey Plaza, it was eventually decided that they would avoid depicting any one particular assassination but instead evoke the many assassinations 'that accrued in American history throughout the years including JFK'.[51]

The Parallax View recasts these events through the lens of post-Watergate America – and its concomitant effect upon public trust in the 'official story'. Shooting began in the spring of 1974, as Nixon's culpability for the break-ins was becoming increasingly apparent. It was released on 14 June 1974, a few months prior to Nixon's eventual resignation. Watergate demonstrated to the American public that conspiracies happen, and indeed had happened at the heart of American Government. 'This picture deals with a paranoiac delusion that turns out to be a total reality' wrote Pakula, contending that it is premised on 'the exploitation of secret plots and dangers and manipulations that may exist within society where so much has been buried and made secret in the name of preserving stability'.[52]

Pakula rendered his sullied vision of America via an idiosyncratic style that evoked the disorientating effect of government secrecy – and the conspiracies it engendered – upon the stability of the historical record and notions of truth more generally. There is a surrealistic quality to *The Parallax View*. Locations are stark and forbidding – like the dam outside the small town of Salmontail that floods and nearly kills Frady – or bizarre and eerie – like the fairground train Frady rides with his former FBI agent friend. Jump cuts are frequent and jarring, characters vanish and appear from scenes with little or no explanation or backstory, the lighting is oppressively low-key to the point of some scenes being shot almost entirely in silhouette and the soundtrack and audio effects are muted, meandering, often silent and always disconcerting. And then, of course, there is the film's most memorable scene: the Kuleshov sequence, with its jarring images of Americana seamlessly blended with scenes of violence, totalitarianism and brutality. 'To achieve in movie terms "Parallax's" uniquely contemporary paranoiac qualities', Pakula later told an interviewer, the film 'demanded a style which while seeming real and unstylized would nonetheless have a sense of the surreal about it . . . It also would give me a chance to attempt a kind of visual comment on our society . . . on the way we live and our values without ever discussing it.'[53]

By continually juxtaposing the real with the surreal, Pakula's mise en scène produces an uncanny atmosphere in which comforting images of homespun America feature as fata morganas that mask the sinister undercurrents of American life. 'THE APPEARANCE OF OPPENNESS and THE REALITY OF SECRECY are what dictate the style of your film', wrote Pakula in a handwritten note.[54] Secrecy is thus the governing logic of *The Parallax View*. The miasma of secrecy, its power to distort and to mislead generates a disorienting effect in which meanings are inverted and structures of power are unfathomable. Pakula described this as the 'Alice in Wonderland aura of secrecy'.[55]

To generate this sense of the surreal, Pakula drew inspiration from Kubrick's *A Clockwork Orange*, which was itself a form of conspiracy thriller with its central theme of the total subjugation of the individual at the hands of state power.[56] Pakula was strongly inspired by *A Clockwork Orange*'s portrayal of 'manipulation', through 'means of thought control or social discipline practiced by playing on peoples' fears and anxieties'.[57] Pakula repeatedly stated that 'the film must be played out against a background of Bread and Circuses', to demonstrate this point of social manipulation.[58] But in terms of the film's mise en scène, Pakula noted that *The Parallax View* was 'the total opposite to the bizarre quality of CLOCKWORK ORANGE', because it emphasised the 'sense of the bizarre in reality'.[59]

To achieve this effect, Pakula sought to invert Hitchcock's characteristic use of American archetypes in order to generate ulterior meanings associated with the symbols of American democracy. The effect of secrecy, as portrayed in the film, was its power to erode and undermine the historic ideals that such monuments of America came to represent. Pakula frequently likened his film to Hitchcock's *North by Northwest*, even suggesting that they replicate the Mount Rushmore finale in *The Parallax View* by ending with a chase-sequence through the Grand Canyon.[60] Unlike Hitchcock, however, Pakula sought to invest American iconography with the sinister connotations of post-Watergate

SECRECY, CONSPIRACY, CINEMA AND THE CIA IN THE 1970s

America. 'So what you're really taking', he wrote, 'are American archetypes ... figures that we all feel at home with and then twisting them'.[61] In doing so, Pakula would invert these 'symbols of American life' in order to demonstrate the bizarre and sinister undercurrent of secrecy in a 'seemingly open society' with the ultimate conclusion being that secrecy and conspiracy are, as the film's tagline put it, 'as American as apple pie'.[62]

Pakula's 'patriotic iconoclasm' was clearly demonstrated in the film's most

Figure 5.4   Poster for *The Parallax View* (1974), starring Warren Beatty as intrepid reporter Joseph Frady, featured a programme of political assassinations carried out by a shady corporation known as The Parallax Corporation. The film is considered one of the first and most archetypal films of the conspiracy thriller genre that took shape in the mid-1970s during the Watergate scandals and the revelations of CIA and FBI wrongdoing.
Source: Paramount Pictures/Academy of Motion Picture Arts and Sciences, Beverly Hills.

245

memorable sequence.[63] When central protagonist, journalist Joseph Frady, played by Warren Beatty, attempts to join the Parallax Corporation in a bid to gain knowledge of their murky operations, he is asked to undergo a series of psychological experiments to assess his suitability. In the final test, reminiscent of *A Clockwork Orange*, he is asked to watch a series of images while his responses to them are monitored. Utilising the Kuleshov effect, a series of archetypal images of America and clichéd scenes of American life are intercut with suggestive textual inserts such as 'love', 'mother' and 'God'. As the montage gathers pace and intensity a series of more violent and sexual imagery along with words such as 'enemy' begin to be juxtaposed with the earlier idyllic images of America. As the spectacle of the montage takes effect, the images of violence and the American archetypes appear to merge together – showing images of the Capitol Dome, for example, foregrounded by a Ku Klux Klan march or an American flag draped over a swastika. By the mid-section of the montage, the two sets of images – that is, of lynching and the American family, and of Lincoln and My Lai – appear inseparable. Finally, the serenity of the American archetypes return, but their connotations, as with the images of America in the film at large, have been irrevocably altered.

The net effect of this inversion of American archetypes is to produce in the individual a sense of disillusionment and a feeling of detachment from history and from the institutions that govern it. The meaning of the past is distorted by a veil of secrecy and the nefarious but nebulous intentions of unfathomable institutions. 'There should be something about PARALLAX', wrote Pakula, 'that is beyond individual people. You are being destroyed and you don't know what or who is destroying you.'[64] Although the Parallax corporation remained deliberately opaque, throughout the film it was most certainly in part modelled on the CIA and the recent revelations surrounding its activities. Indeed Pakula noted that the Parallax corporation should be 'like CIA ... which PARALLAX might use but is not directly part of it'.[65] Yet it was not the CIA itself that proved the inspiration for the Parallax Corporation, but the logic of secrecy with which the CIA had become so closely associated.

> The important point – it's a real point – is that ... semi-secret private organizations ... operating as secretly as they do, could be capable of anything. The <u>real</u> background (is) of the dangers of living in an increasingly secret society where (organisations) ... like CIA can be doing things in (the) name of American democracy.[66]

The essential unknowability of the Parallax Corporation, mimicking the unknowability of the CIA, reflects secrecy's ability to detach the ordinary

American citizen from his or her institutions, which brings about a loss of faith in the official record of their activities.

The narrative arc of the film's central protagonist, Joseph Frady, reveals this relationship between secrecy and the loss of faith in the 'official story'. The film opens with the assassination of a senator atop the Seattle Space needle – immediately investing an American monument with sinister connotations. Following the assassination, a blue-ribbon commission, evoking the Warren Commission, rules the assassination the product of a lone gunman. Frady and his newswoman colleague, Lee Carter, were present at the assassination. When Carter learns that seven of the witnesses to the assassination had mysteriously died, she confronts Frady with her suspicions that a conspiracy had taken place. Frady, however, is not convinced. In an early script draft of the scene, Frady tells Lee, 'I'm just bored with conspiracies. I have listened to conspiracy theories on every conceivable subject.' Lee replies, 'Frady, seven accidents like that. It can't be a coincidence.' He reassures her, 'Sure it can. 'You ever hear of the curse of King Tut's tomb? You think all those people died because of an ancient Egyptian curse? Or, do you figure it was the C.I.A.?'[67]

Nevertheless, Frady agrees to investigate. The 'narrative pivot', as Mark Fenster has termed it, of *The Parallax View*'s conspiratorial plot, occurs when Frady visits the small town of Salmontail to investigate the death of one of the witnesses. The Sheriff of the town attempts to kill Frady by flooding a dam in which Frady is stood. Frady is at once made aware of the conspiracy, and his perception of history is irrevocably changed. As Fenster argues, the 'narrative pivot' marks the moment of the individual's insertion into history.[68] The conclusion of the blue-ribbon commission that opens *The Parallax View* is revealed as flawed, and Frady, the individual, has become disillusioned with the validity of the 'official story', while at the same time, disoriented by the realisation that the 'truth' is masked by secrecy.

At the film's conclusion, Frady attempts to foil an assassination plot by the Parallax Corporation to kill a Senator at a campaign rally. But as Frady is hiding in the rafters, a shot rings out, killing the senator, leaving Frady, like Lee Harvey Oswald before him, as the 'patsy' of a secret conspiracy. In the final scene, the blue-ribbon commission reappears, once again confirming that the assassination was the product of a lone-gunman. Secrecy and the conspiratorial logic of history prevails in a tragic sense, over the individual's attempts to fathom and overcome the insurmountable structures of power and institutions that control the past.

Figure 5.5 Faye Dunaway and Robert Redford co-star in *Three Days of the Condor* (1975), the first conspiracy thriller explicitly about the CIA, and one of the first overtly critical films to feature the Agency. *Source:* Sydney Pollack, Paramount, 1975.

THREE DAYS OF THE CONDOR (1975)

While *The Parallax View* dealt with the malign effects of American secrecy and secret institutions at a more abstract level, *Three Days of the Condor* (1975) was the first conspiracy thriller explicitly about the CIA.[69] Although it began production prior to the publication of the Family Jewels, its release in September 1975 serendipitously coincided with the apogee of public and congressional outcry over the past activities of the Agency. In this sense the film's political significance is most easily understood as a timely and provocative critique of CIA amorality. And yet, like the Parallax Corporation, the CIA in *Three Days of the Condor*, indeed the CIA in the vast majority of Hollywood films since, has a figurative quality, tapping into wider public anxieties concerning secrecy, conspiracy and corruption. As the film's star Robert Redford remarked:

> The CIA is simply a tool, an instrument, that lets us dig into something larger. I think the movie is about trust and paranoia, it's about bureaucracy run amok ... A film that says, 'Hey, the CIA are the bad guys' wouldn't interest me. We all know that. But how frightening is it not to know how far you can trust the CIA – how big it is and what it's doing.[70]

Like *The Parallax View, Three Days of the Condor* is a film primarily concerned with the corrosive effects of secrecy upon American trust in government – a product of the widening credibility gap in the post-Vietnam/Watergate era. According to the production notes, in early 1974 producers Stanley Schneider and Dino De Laurentiis, alongside director Sydney Pollack and actor Robert Redford, 'decided to create a film that would reflect the climate of America in the aftermath of the Watergate crisis. They wanted to show how government institutions might be subverted from within to betray, not serve, the public trust.'[71] Even prior to the publication of the Family Jewels, the CIA was an obvious vessel through which to explore these symbiotic themes of excessive secrecy and the collapse of public trust in government.

Redford plays the role of Joe Turner, the heroic investigative protagonist – a core trope of the conspiracy thriller. He works as an analyst for a CIA front, the American Literary Historical Society (ALHS), which is tasked with reading both fictional and non-fictional literature from around the world in search of hidden plots and meanings that may be buried within them. Turner exudes countercultural recalcitrance and his maverick style jars with his stuffy 'Georgetown Set' superiors.[72] His nonconformist credentials are established in the film's opening shots as Redford, late for work, rides through the New York traffic on his scooter. Turner's refusal to play by the rules saves his life. At lunch he slips out his office building's 'unauthorised' back entrance, irking the security guard in the process, and in so doing avoids the watchful eyes of waiting assassins out front who are counting each employee in and out of the building. Shortly before Turner leaves, his bow-tie clad boss, peeved by Turner's wayward style, asks him if he actually enjoys working for the CIA. 'It bothers me that I can't tell people what I do', is Turner's reply, and then clarifies with: 'I actually trust people.' Before long Turner will trust very few. While out for lunch buying sandwiches, the assassins move in. Turner returns soon after to an office of murdered colleagues. The allure of this opening hook, according to Lorenzo Semple, Jr, was the overwhelming reason Dino de Laurentiis decided to adapt James Grady's *Six Days of the Condor* to the screen.[73]

Turner phones in to report the incident and the officer on the other end of the phone arranges to bring him in from the cold. The film's narrative pivot – the moment of Turner's insertion into history or his realisation that wider forces are at play – arrives when one of the officers sent to meet him shoots his colleague and tries to murder Turner. Someone working within the CIA is clearly out to get him, and was also behind the assassination of his colleagues. Turner escapes, and goes on the run.

In a scenario that the Bourne series would later emulate, Turner takes an innocent woman, Kathy Hale, played by Faye Dunaway, hostage, and hides out in her apartment. Over time Turner gains her trust and enlists her in his investigation. After kidnapping Higgins, the CIA's deputy director of the New York division, Turner becomes convinced that the conspiracy is perpetrated not by the CIA, but 'a CIA within the CIA'. Critics have argued that this aspect of the plot is indicative of the film pulling its ideological punches.

Rather than levelling its accusations at the CIA itself, or identifying more systemic abuses within the American Government, the film instead points to a few bad apples, leaving open the possibility of the essential goodness and necessity of American intelligence and US foreign policy more generally. As Tony Shaw puts it, *Condor* 'played down the extent to which covert CIA activities were a natural bi-product of America's Cold War aggression. It also fell far short of the more extreme indictments of the corporate political power system found in *The Parallax View*.'[74] Patrick McGilligan has likewise described the film as 'a wide-screen whitewash tantamount to the Rockefeller Commission' for its portrayal of 'a small, dangerous yet ultimately controllable clique'.[75]

Kathryn Olmsted has made a similar observation in her criticism of the Senate Church Committee's investigation of the CIA. She argues that Church's metaphoric assignation of the CIA as the 'rogue elephant' of American Government conveniently ignored the culpability of successive Presidents, both Democrat and Republican, for the CIA's more nefarious covert activities. Arguably then *Three Days of the Condor*, in not even blaming the CIA, but a CIA within the CIA, takes this ideological neutering of public concerns about secrecy and US foreign policy a step further. But, as David Shamus McCarthy has countered, Turner is 'unimpressed with the distinction' between the CIA and the rogue element within that he discovers is led by the Deputy Director of Operations, Leonard Attwood.[76] He tells Higgins, 'Who the hell is Atwood? He's you. He's all you guys.'[77]

McCarthy's point is further demonstrated by the CIA's response to Attwood once they discover that he is behind the conspiracy – they order him dead, and employ the same French assassin, Joubert, that Attwood had used to kill Turner's officemates, to do the deed. Before ordering Attwood's death, Higgins' superior, Wabash, reminisces for a moment about his OSS days, when lines of moral clarity seemed more determined. 'You were with Mr. Donovan's OSS, weren't you sir?' asks Higgins. 'I sailed the Adriatic with a movie star at the Helm!' Wabash replies, recalling a period in time when Hollywood had gone to work for America's intelligence service under John Ford's command before the shattering of consensus severed their wartime bond. 'You miss that kind of action, sir?' Higgins asks. 'No,' Wabash replies. '[I miss] that kind of clarity.'

Turner reaches Attwood before Joubert and interrogates him about the conspiracy – 'What's the secret worth murdering everybody for?' Finally the penny drops. 'Oil . . . This whole damn thing was about oil.' Turner realises that Attwood's plan was to take over oil fields in the Middle East, and that he had inadvertently stumbled on the plot buried within a thriller novel. When Turner had reported his suspicions about the novel, a poor-seller that had nevertheless been translated into an odd array of languages, Attwood ordered the American Literary Historical Society dead. This climax to *Three Days of the Condor* was different from the novel upon which it was based. In the book, the rogue CIA cabal smuggles drugs. James Grady, author of *Six Days of the Condor*, had read Alfred McCoy's *The Politics of Heroin*, which alleged CIA complicity in the South East Asian drugs trade, before writing the novel.[78] McCarthy argues that the changes to Grady's novel are 'obviously intended to enhance the film's political commentary'.[79] 'I didn't ever think of the CIA as an evil institution', recalled Grady, 'I thought of it as an extraordinarily necessary function of government . . . I saw the novel . . . more as like a noir – classic noir story . . . [in which] the guy goes from being an innocent to being essentially a killer.'[80] In the novel Turner, who is called Ronald Malcolm in Grady's original, kills the assassin. In the film, however, Joubert appears as Turner is interrogating Attwood and kills the latter on behalf of the Agency. He then drives Turner back to the station so that he can travel to New York to confront Higgins. On the way he delivers a world-weary speech about the virtues of being an assassin – 'It is – quite restful. Almost peaceful. No need to believe in either side, or any side. There is no cause. There is only yourself. And the belief is in your precision.'

The shift in subject from drugs to oil also capitalised on the October 1973 oil crisis, which sparked fears that America's traditional economic abundance would soon turn to scarcity.[81] It also supported a revisionist perspective on US foreign policy, by arguing, somewhat more crudely than the likes of William Appleman Williams, that the CIA and the US foreign policy establishment are motivated primarily out of economic self-interest. Both points are underlined by the film's final exchange between Turner and Higgins. The latter tells Turner that although it was a renegade operation, its principles were right – further substantiating McCarthy's argument that the film minimises the distinction between the rogue CIA and the CIA itself. 'What is it with you people?' Turner responds angrily. 'You think not getting caught in a lie is the same thing as telling the truth?' Turner's castigation triggers the following cynical homily from Higgins:

> Higgins: No, it's simple economics. Today it's oil, right? In ten or fifteen years, food, plutonium. Maybe even sooner. Now what do you think the people are going to want us to do then?
> Turner: Ask them!
> Higgins: Not now, then. Ask them when they're running out. Ask them when there's no heat in their homes and they're cold. Ask them when their engines stop. Ask them when people who've never known hunger start going hungry. You want to know something: they won't want us to ask them. They'll just want us to get it for them.

The exchange again refutes the idea that *Three Days of the Condor* limits its criticism to 'a small, dangerous yet ultimately controllable clique'.[82] It suggests instead that though Attwood may have been a malignant element within the Agency, the CIA and the US foreign policy establishment is nevertheless aligned with his ethical and political philosophy. More damningly still, it suggests that the American people or at least the system of insatiable consumption to which they acquiesce – namely capitalism – is ultimately culpable for the CIA's malevolent covert activities that were plastered all over the front pages of the newspapers on a near daily basis at the time of *Condor*'s release.

In a final coda, even *The New York Times*, the newspaper that had printed the Family Jewels that provoked the 1975 Congressional enquiries into the CIA, is implicated in the nexus of power that has enabled the CIA to run amok. Turner tells Higgins that he has given the whole story to *The New York Times*. 'How do you know they'll print it?' Higgins asks suggestively. 'They'll print it,' Turner replies, but Higgins' question casts doubt in the audience's mind and leaves the film's conclusion unsettlingly ambiguous. The idea that the CIA controlled *The New York Times*' output at a time when they were printing explosive revelations about the Agency on a near-daily basis left the new Director of Central Intelligence, George H. W. Bush, incredulous: 'Well, if we control [*The New York Times*], we're doing a hell of a job with the editorial content they're coming out with!' an exasperated Bush told a packed CIA auditorium.[83] The right-wing commentator and vocal CIA apologist William F. Buckley read the scene differently, taking umbrage at its sanctimonious exaltation of the liberal press: 'The director [Pollack] failed only to emblazon under [*The New York Times* building's logo seen in the final scene] "Daniel Ellsberg Slept Here."'[84]

Yet unlike *All the President's Men*, which Redford was busy adapting to screen as *Three Days of the Condor* went into post-production, *Condor* undermined its own sanctification of the mainstream American press by leaving open the suggestion that *The New York Times* was perhaps far more complicit in the maintenance of America's covert foreign policy than the conventional image of the crusading investigative journalism of the post-Watergate era would typically allow. As Kathryn Olmsted has shown in her analysis of the mainstream press's role in the 1975 'year of intelligence', Higgins' suggestion that *The New York Times* wouldn't print the story is arguably closer to the truth than the upbeat message of *All the President's Men*.

Three Days of the Condor was by some margin the most significant cinematic portrayal of the CIA in the post-Watergate era. In part, this was due to its star, Robert Redford, who carried the film to box-office success. It was also because of the serendipitous timing of its release, coinciding with the height of the Senate Church and House Pike Committee investigations of American intelligence. Yet Sam Peckinpah's *The Killer Elite* (1975), another thriller featuring paid CIA assassins, was released the same year and made nowhere near the same impact. Above all, it made an impact because, with the possible exception of *Scorpio*, which fared badly at the box-office, and *The Spook Who*

Sat By the Door, which was mysteriously pulled from cinemas shortly after its release, *Three Days of the Condor* was the first time a major Hollywood feature film had entirely abandoned the romantic spy formula to explicitly denounce the CIA as a dangerously Machiavellian institution. Coming at a time when reality was surpassing art, and with all the incredibly lurid accusations levelled against the Agency by *The New York Times* and the United States Congress, the accusations of *Three Days of the Condor* were almost tame by comparison, and were welcomed by a receptive American public.

Did *Condor* change people's minds about the Agency? Such a question, of any cultural artefact, is always impossible to answer without polling vast cross-sections of the audience before and after viewing the picture. But it certainly added to the climate of suspicion that was erupting everywhere around the Agency in 1975. One anecdote, however, is perhaps suggestive of the effect that cinema had upon that climate: when Emily Sheketoff, a staffer for the House Pike Committee, visited Langley for a briefing by the CIA's Director of Security Robert W. Gambino on the Agency's counter-espionage operations, she quizzed him about the existence of a 'CIA with the CIA' that she described as 'the intergroup of old CIA officers who, working together, would "take over CIA" in the event [the DCI] Mr. Colby were replaced by someone not to the liking of the group'. When an incredulous Gambino refused to even entertain the idea, Sheketoff retorted that 'everyone knew about the "CIA within the CIA" revealed in the movie "Three Days of the Condor." The meeting ended on this note.'[85]

Emile de Antonio and Philip Agee: The Radical CIA Film that Never Was

There's an image from the set of *Three Days of the Condor* of the former Director of Central Intelligence Richard Helms perched atop a director's stool in relaxed repose conversing idly with Robert Redford next to him. It's a remarkable image, and one that seems almost inexplicable given the content of the film and the aggravation it would later cause Helms' former agency. It is even more remarkable because Helms had returned from Tehran, where he was serving as United States ambassador to Iran, to defend his increasingly embattled former agency before Congress. What was he doing there? Perhaps he hadn't read the script – indeed it is almost certain that he hadn't read the script! Or perhaps he simply viewed it as a pleasant distraction, an amusing afternoon in New York, down by the East River, spent mingling with Hollywood royalty and without any sense that a fictional feature film could ever cause the CIA much flap. It is an image that could only have been taken before the release of *Condor*, in an era in which the Agency could still afford to care little about public relations.

Figure 5.6 Former CIA Director Richard Helms chats with Robert Redford on the set of *Three Days of the Condor*. *Source*: Terry O'Neill/Photographer's Gallery.

Despite the trickle of press criticism of the Agency that had gone on since the Bay of Pigs, and the momentary scandals like the 1967 *Ramparts* affair that occasionally threw the publicity-shy CIA uncomfortably into the limelight of public scrutiny, there were still relatively few critical voices of the Agency in the public domain. When James Grady was researching the CIA before writing *Six Days of the Condor*, he could only find Wise and Ross's *The Invisible Government* and Alfred McCoy's *The Politics of Heroin* in his local library.[86] '*Before* Condor', Grady wrote in a preface to a new edition of the novel, 'the average bookstore carried *zero* books about the Agency ... Fictionally, the CIA was treated like a ghost everyone tiptoed around but no one touched.'[87] In the mid-1970s this situation began to change dramatically, and in turn the CIA slowly recognised that the construction of their public image, whether through fictional or non-fictional texts, was a cause for significant concern.

In stark contrast to Helms' Saturday-afternoon demeanour on the set of *Three Days of the Condor*, the new Director of Central Intelligence George H. W. Bush was far from amused when he saw the film. 'I made the mistake over Christmas, while I was gainfully unemployed between China and here, to go see a movie called "Three Days of the Condor"', he told a packed Langley auditorium. 'I can tell some of you others have made the same mistake.' He nodded to his audience. 'I went with my daughter who is madly and passionately in love with Robert Redford, so I had to indulge her whims and went to see this thing. Well, you know,' he continued 'it's a fairly good shoot-em-up and, if I were totally untutored in this business, I might have got a yak out of it; but it was a very vicious and sinister piece because what it did was to lay at the CIA's doorstep all kinds of outrageous things that the CIA by its severest critics has never been accused of . . . This is tough propaganda', he concluded. In his speech Bush acknowledged something that evidently Helms had not, either as DCI or while sitting next to Redford on the set of *Three Days of the Condor*: 'We do have . . . a fundamental public relations problem', and his anecdotal discussion of *Condor* showed that he acknowledged Hollywood as an important part of that problem. The CIA needed to fight back, to challenge *Three Days of Condors*, or renegade CIA memoirs, or Seymour Hersh, or any criticism of the Agency in the public domain. 'This [anti-CIA "propaganda"] is tough', Bush concluded in his speech, 'and to the degree that we can be frank and open with the American people and not be afraid to appear [in public] . . . I think we can all do a whale of a job capitalizing on the fundamental support [for the CIA] that's there in the American people.'[88]

That 'fundamental support' was not always as forthcoming as perhaps the Agency would have liked in the immediate aftermath of the 'Year of Intelligence' – although, as will later be discussed, some dutiful citizens did offer to aid the Agency in rectifying its 'fundamental public relations problem', including via the production of motion pictures. But in the immediate post-Family Jewels period, it seemed, for a while, that scandal would be heaped upon scandal, and that the disclosures by journalists and Congress in this period had emboldened the Agency's critics, some of whom came from within the CIA itself.

Perhaps most bothersome for the Agency was the publication of renegade former CIA operative Philip Agee's memoir, *Inside the Company*, released the same year as the Church Committee investigations. 'In the CIA pantheon [Agee] became something close to the devil incarnate', notes John Prados. Agee's book condemned CIA policy in Latin America – he had worked in the clandestine service primarily in Uruguay, Ecuador and Mexico before

Figure 5.7 CIA apostate Philip Agee, whose memoir, *Inside the Company*, was published in 1975, which was the same year as the Church Committee's investigation of the Agency. *Source:* Wikimedia Commons.

becoming disillusioned with the Agency's policy of undermining the Latin American left to the benefit of right-wing oligarchs across the continent. Most controversially, however, Agee included a list of 250 CIA officers and agents in the book's appendix. Langley had known about Agee's plans for a critical memoir since the early 1970s, and moved aggressively against him to stymie the publication. They bugged his typewriter and assigned agents to follow him. They even had one of their agents, Sal Ferrara, win the trust of Agee by helping him escape a CIA surveillance team and provide him with funding and the bugged-typewriter with which to complete his manuscript. As Prados notes, by funding him and then provoking him once he discovered their surveillance, the CIA 'helped create its own bogeyman'.[89] Once the book was published in the summer of 1975, the CIA began a smear campaign by passing stories to the press that alleged that Agee was a Cuban agent with a dubious moral character. Their most effective tactic against Agee, and *Counterspy* magazine that likewise published CIA names and was associated with Agee, was to lay the blame of the death of CIA Athens station chief Richard Welch at their feet.

Welch's murder in December 1975 by Greek revolutionaries presented both a tragedy and an opportunity for the Agency. The CIA blamed Welch's death on *Counterspy* disclosures and used it as evidence against their critics in the press for the dangers inherent in their successive exposures of CIA activities that had taken place throughout the previous year. In reality, Welch's death had more to do with him failing to follow security protocol – he lived at the same address as his predecessor – an address well known among locals, so much so that it was included on bus tours of the city.[90] Welch's identity had also been printed in the *Athens News* prior to the *Counterspy* publication of his identity and a full month before his murder. Welch's murderers themselves also later confessed that the *Counterspy* revelations had nothing to do with their decision to target Welch.[91] But the utility of blaming Welch's murder on *Counterspy*, and the atmosphere of public disclosures more generally, was a more tempting narrative than the truth, and may well have helped silence further criticism of the Agency.

One potentially influential critique of the CIA that Welch's death did indeed help silence was a planned fictional feature film, based on Agee's memoir, by radical filmmaker Emile de Antonio. Although his intention to produce the Agee feature was earnest, de Antonio later admitted that the project was in part conceived as an elaborate red-herring to throw the FBI and the CIA off the scent of another film he was making about the radical left-wing organisation the Weather Underground.[92] The Weather Underground feature, which included interviews with insurrectionists wanted by the FBI, led to de Antonio being placed under extensive surveillance by the Bureau, and possibly the CIA as well. In the summer of 1975 de Antonio, alongside fellow documentary filmmaker Haskell Wexler and editor Mary Lampson, received a subpoena asking them to appear before a grand jury and hand over all their footage of the Weather Underground.[93] In retaliation, de Antonio launched a Freedom of Information (FOI) lawsuit against both the CIA and FBI requesting all their files on him – the FBI released more than 200 pages to him, the Agency was less forthcoming.[94] Incredibly, given the levels of surveillance that both Agee and de Antonio were under by the CIA and FBI respectively, and the fact that de Antonio had deliberately gone on record about the Agee picture to misdirect the intelligence agencies, and the fact he had launched legal proceedings against the Agency, the CIA appear to have been oblivious to de Antonio's proposed feature until it was effectively dead in the water. A CIA memo dated November 1976, more than eighteen months after de Antonio first made contact with Agee, reports that CIA veteran Jack Maury is in the process of surreptitiously obtaining a script of de Antonio's proposed feature through his contacts in the Motion Picture Association of America (MPAA). By this point, de Antonio had long since given up hope that he could get the picture made.[95]

De Antonio approached Agee in March 1975 with his proposal to make a fictionalised version of his memoir.[96] The decision to make a fictional feature

Figure 5.8 Radical filmmaker Emile de Antonio, who tried to make a fictional feature based on Agee's memoir. *Source:* Wikimedia Commons.

was an unusual move for de Antonio – all of his films to date were documentaries shot on shoestring budgets, yet now he wanted to raise more than a million dollars – small change for Hollywood but a significantly larger budget than any of de Antonio's past films – to make a fictional spy film based on a non-fictional text – why? For one thing there was little footage available to accompany Agee's account – although he wanted the final film to be 'flexible enough to include documentary material – either existing footage of Latin American political events, or interviews done expressly for the film'.[97] But perhaps more importantly, de Antonio considered Agee's book 'simply not filmic ... it is dense, too factual, none of the characters comes [sic] alive, etc'.[98]

For de Antonio the central 'dramatic thread' of Agee's biography was 'the conversion of Philip Agee from a politically naïve, twenty-one-year-old Notre Dame graduate who joins the CIA in 1956 as a "warrior against communism" to a disillusioned, self-avowed enemy of the agency and the interests it served'.[99] The numerous conspiracy narratives like *Three Days of the Condor* emerging in this period followed a similar trajectory, except Agee's story was no conspiracy theory. Still, de Antonio remained sceptical of framing Agee's conversion as a too simplistic Road-to-Damascus story – 'I was born an atheist so I'm not too much impressed with Saul-Paul tales; I believe that these things happen slowly', he told Agee.[100] De Antonio was right, even when Agee left the Agency in 1969 his letter of resignation, according to DCI William Colby at least, bore little ill-will towards the CIA.[101] As John Prados tells the story, Agee's conversion was gradual, and much of his transformation may have been a consequence of the CIA's surveillance and intimidation of him after his resignation.

De Antonio also had firm ideological and political reasons to avoid telling a neat Hollywood morality tale. He did not intend to show the heroic antics of an outraged homespun protagonist in response to a single malign event or conspiracy that could be dismissed as a sinister aberration. He did not want Agee to be cast as the heroic Robert Redford liberal crusader that holds out the possibility of redemption. Rather, he viewed Agee as a participant within a system that was itself responsible for the CIA's crimes in Latin American that de Antonio described as 'a virtual laboratory for experiments in bribery, electronic surveillance, forged documents, torture, military invasions, and assassinations'.[102] This was not about a regrettable but isolated transgression, or a few bad apples, it was, for de Antonio, the dark heart of US foreign policy.

In a published interview, de Antonio entertained the idea of casting Robert Redford in his film alongside Jane Fonda who he claimed had offered to wave her fee. This may have been a publicity stunt to try to attract potential financiers for the project, or another smokescreen for the CIA and FBI. But his musings about the possible effect of casting Redford are telling:

> Redford thinks he's against the CIA. But I'm not against the CIA, I'm against the system that produced the CIA. Redford bought the Bernstein and Woodward book and he's going to play Woodward; Watergate is a nice soft issue because it focuses on a man and not a system. Redford views Watergate as an aberration, where in my view Watergate is inherent in the system.[103]

In fairness to Robert Redford, *Three Days of the Condor*, as already discussed, had indeed considered the wider systemic causes of CIA misdeeds – in particular Higgins' final speech about the economic incentives that underline the Agency's aggressive covert activities. But Redford's liberal politics, good looks and star status were always likely to incite the derision of a radical filmmaker like de Antonio who self-consciously positioned himself as antithetical to mainstream Hollywood cinema. 'The Hollywood product', de Antonio told Agee, 'even when it is done by gifted people, is finally always controlled by the banks and the banks aren't going to like your politics one tiny bit'.[104] De Antonio sold himself to Agee on the basis of his radical credentials and appealed to his heart as opposed to his purse – 'Meredith, as a major agent, may be able to find for you what every writer wants: money, promotion, etc. He will, however, lose what is of the greatest interest in your book: its politics.'[105] De Antonio proposed to Agee instead 'a new kind of film' that rather than 'having you played by a Sean Connery type who would regret all in the end together with a sophisticated shrug to the point that, after all, everybody does it, doesn't He?

The Soviets, the etc. Why not the US[?] In other words your tale without the politics.'[106] De Antonio's film, by contrast, would be decidedly political with its focus on the systemic abuses of US foreign policy in Latin America.

Ironically, de Antonio's failure to raise the funds for the film may have been in part an indirect consequence of US foreign policy in Latin America. In June 1975 de Antonio's associates Eric Saltzman and Jeffrey Kovner flew to Peru on a fundraising mission. At this time Peru was still governed by left-wing general Juan Velasco who may well have been sympathetic towards a film critical of CIA activities in Latin America that included the ousting of left-wing leaders like himself, and their replacement with right-wing military juntas. Saltzman and Kovner met with Peruvian producer Bernardo Batievsky, whose 1972 picture *Mirage* had been met with critical acclaim. Batievsky expressed his interest in the film and raised the possibility of a 50–50 co-financing deal between himself and whichever other American partners de Antonio could source. Batievsky had little political interest in the picture, suggesting contrary to de Antonio's intentions, that they make a 'James Bond type' picture. Batievsky did, however, repeatedly stress that the film should not be anti-American and that Peru should not be specifically identified in the film.

Saltzman and Kovner then met with Luis Gerrido-Lecca, director of the Film Section in the Peruvian Ministry of Public Information. Saltzman and Kovner's account of the meeting, and of their meeting with Batievsky, is written in the style of an intelligence report, which may have been an in-joke given their accurate assumption that their correspondence was under FBI surveillance. Gerrido-Lecca offered his tacit endorsement of the project telling them that the Peruvian Government would 'smile and encourage' the picture though they could not offer financial assistance. Gerrido-Lecca also stressed that Peru should not be identified in the film and that it should not be anti-American, although 'it might reflect through CIA on American influence', he added.[107]

The planned Peruvian deal was short-lived. On 29 August General Velasco was ousted by a right-wing military coup. Although Gerrido-Lecca contacted Kovner again after the coup, extending the possibility of continuing the project, it is unlikely that the political climate was any longer conducive to a film being produced in Peru that was critical of CIA support for right-wing juntas in Latin America.[108] With or without Peruvian support, however, de Antonio would not have been able to make the picture without at least half the funding coming from American sources – Batievsky, who 'resented being used by Americans as financing of the whole', was adamant on this point. After the death of CIA Athens Station Chief Richard Welch in December 1975, however, America was likewise no longer a conducive political climate to raise funds for an anti-CIA picture. A film based on Agee in particular, whose disclosures were blamed for Welch's death, was no longer viable. His plan to raise a million dollars for such a radical project was always a long-shot, but Welch's death sealed its fate. As de Antonio later told an interviewer who asked him what became of the Agee film:

> That was shot down when CIA agent Richard Welch was killed in Athens. Nothing worse could have happened to me than having Welch killed. It's the worst that could have happened to him, too, I guess. When Welch was killed, they claimed Agee was involved in naming him, which was totally untrue. I know Greek radicals who say it was absolutely obvious to anybody who lived in Athens that that was the CIA's house. So when you read those crappy letters about what a sensitive, witty man Richard Welch was, a classical scholar and all that ... CIA guys are thugs! They are secret political police, and getting killed goes with the job, frankly. It's like being a soldier. But it destroyed the film. People are afraid to buck the CIA.[109]

Fighting Back: The Birth of CIA Public Relations

As Kathryn Olmsted's study of the post-Watergate investigations of the CIA and FBI has shown, the press and Congressional criticisms of the Agency in the wake of the Family Jewels was short-lived and changed little. After a period of public penance the CIA returned to business-as-usual. By the end of the 1970s the Agency was busy arming and financing the mujahedeen in Afghanistan in what would become the longest running covert operation in their history. In the 1980s Reagan made-good on his election promise to 'unleash the CIA' – undoing much of the limited legislation that had been brought in post-Church committee to improve oversight of CIA covert action and prevent future Agency abuses.

One thing that did change, however, was that the Agency became more conscious of the importance of public relations. In 1977 new DCI Admiral Stansfield Turner formalised the existence of the CIA's Office of Public Affairs as one of his first acts as incoming CIA chief. He employed Herbert Hetu, 'a jovial PR man with over two decades of [PR] experience in the Navy', to lead the new office in charge of selling the Agency's image.[110] Consequently, the CIA began to 'open up', or, more accurately, they opened up about things that suited a more favourable image of them, and closed down about things that did not.[111] 'Information management' had replaced their decades-old policy of blanket secrecy. As part of their new 'openness', the CIA became more receptive to overtures from film and television crews wishing to film at Langley and work with the Agency on their representations of American intelligence. Unlike the public relations disaster of allowing the *Scorpio* crew to film the Agency's headquarters, future visits to Langley were carefully choreographed. When CBS's '60 Minutes' programme came to Langley, for example, Hetu outlined a detailed filming schedule that included a tour of the statue of American spy and Revolutionary hero Nathan Hale, and the CIA's memorial wall of stars in honour of fallen officers. It also included shots of a relaxed Stansfield Turner playing tennis with CBS journalist Dan Rather – a far more amiable image of the Agency's director than of Colby or Helms hauled before the Church Committee to answer questions pertaining to CIA torture or assassinations.[112] A few years later Rather reported from the frontline in Afghanistan dressed in full Mujahedeen garb. His sympathetic portrayal of the Afghan warriors rallied support for increased CIA covert intervention in the country. One Congressman in particular, Charlie Wilson, was spurred into action by his reports, and went on to campaign tirelessly for CIA intervention in the Soviet–Afghan War. After a decade of limited press criticism of CIA activities, many within the media resumed their traditional role as spokespersons for American intervention.

Turner proved adept at handling media enquiries and was happy to appear on numerous radio and television programmes. On 19 September 1977 he appeared on ABC's *Good Morning America* programme and was asked directly about the impact of films like *The Parallax View* and *Three Days of the Condor* upon the Agency. Turner chuckled in dismissive amusement – 'Rona, Hollywood does a great job of turning intelligence into entertainment, but I don't think I could use the films you've been talking about as training films for our agents.' A couple of days later a memorandum appeared on Hetu's desk from the Chief of the Pictorial Service Branch wishing to make him 'aware of facts concerning our motion picture film holdings that vary from Admiral Turner's response to Rona'. Although the details of those holdings are redacted, it appears contextually evident that the CIA did indeed use Hollywood motion pictures as training films.[113]

In contrast to renegade memoirists like Philip Agee, numerous CIA veterans campaigned vigorously in the media on behalf of their former Agency. The desire by loyal CIA veterans to have their voices heard in defence and indeed celebration of their past intelligence activities had echoes of Donovan's postwar publicity campaign for the OSS. In particular the Association of Former Intelligence Officers (AFIO), led by CIA veteran David Atlee Phillips, effectively became surrogate spokespersons for the CIA in the aftermath of the 1975 year of intelligence.[114] Another founding member of the AFIO, Gordon McLendon, approached the Agency in 1978 with a proposal for a pro-CIA television series co-produced by former Vice-President of Warner Brothers Studios Fred Weintraub. '[I]t is worthwhile pointing out that the Agency is now being publicized, in most cases in a questionable light, by such projects as "Three Days of the Condor"', McLendon and Weintraub noted. 'We submit that there is no reason why the three individuals submitting this memorandum should not, as patriotic Americans, fight back in defense of the CIA and other

U.S. intelligence organizations.'[115] Nothing came of the proposal, but it nevertheless demonstrates the very active efforts of the AFIO alongside self-defined 'patriots' within Hollywood to try to rectify the Agency's public image.

Another self-defined patriot who tried to fight back on behalf of the Agency's tarnished reputation was a Mr Charles Felton Elkins, 'member of a wealthy California family which owns Stauffer Chemical Company', who wished to produce 'a motion picture which depicts the CIA in a favorable, perhaps romantic, light'.[116] Elkins sent a proposal to the Agency of his plan to adapt British author Roberta Lee's romantic spy thriller *Shade of the Palms*, to this purpose. In his treatment for the proposed film, Elkins outlined his motivations for wanting to produce it:

> There is no greater service or higher calling than the FBI or CIA. It is the noblest of professions and the personification of patronism [*sic*]. The destruction or harming of its operations or capability will destroy the society which it was created to serve ... I cannot understand the massive outcry from an organization which is protecting our way of life. It is my personal opinion that the actions of certain Senators to attract personal publicity to the detriment of the CIA are unconscionable and ill advised. Exposing the covers of agents borders on treason ... Their attitude of to hell with the country probably caused the death of at least one CIA agent [referring to Richard Welch] ... Unfortunately ... the support of our misguided press who attacked the CIA in every way they could [gave] the general public ... a totally distorted view of the CIA ... [T]he public was [also] deluded with secret agent movies. Robert Redford did a movie 'Three Days of the Condor' in which the CIA kills its own agent and is generally portrayed in an unfavorable light. It is unpardonable in the mind of the public for the CIA to kill other Americans who are part of their own organization. This type of film is less than helpful to the image of the CIA.[117]

For Elkins, the best way to combat this kind of 'tough propaganda', as DCI George H. W. Bush called it, was through the cinema. 'The mind of the average person is changed by emotion, dreams and hopes, not by mere facts', he asserted. '[I]f this were not true and facts spoke for themselves, the CIA would enjoy far higher public esteem than now.' Movies, Elkins concluded, were the best medium to 'reach the greatest number of people quickly for lasting effect'. *Shade of the Palms*, promised Elkins, would produce a 'hero image' for the Agency through its romantic plot. Elkins' strategy echoed that of right-wing commentator William F. Buckley, whose Blackford Oakes spy novels likewise constructed a heroic image of the CIA agent in opposition to works by Graham Greene and John Le Carré, whose representation of intelligence he despised.[118]

The Agency refused to lend their support to Elkins' project, dismissing it as a

'B-film complete with dark glasses and trench-coats'.[119] But they met him and discussed it with him. Coupled with their cooperation with television news crews – allowing them on to Langley and providing interviews and comment – it is clear that the Agency had changed its thinking on its relationship with the media. It could no longer hide in the shadows, expecting that the media's flickering torchlight would not find them. It would be another two decades, however, before the Agency began actively courting Hollywood filmmakers to help improve their public image. Then it was the existential threat of the end of the Cold War, rather than the accusations of Senators and the press, which prompted them to act.[120]

During the 1980s the Agency retreated somewhat from its first forays into public relations as their new director, Reagan aficionado William Casey, rode the wave of belligerent patriotic fervour that accompanied Reagan's re-ignition of the Cold War. As had so often been the case with CIA public relations and propaganda, private American citizens in Hollywood during the 1980s beat the drum for American nationalism and foreign policy so that the US Government didn't have to.[121] And in this way, as before, the media were complicit in the 1980s in allowing the Agency's covert activities to mushroom again to the point of scandal. History, noted Marx, repeats itself 'first as tragedy, then as farce'. He never described the nature of history in its third or fourth repetition; with the numerous scandals and enquiries that have greeted the CIA in the post-9/11 era the cycle of abuse–scandal–reprieve, abuse–scandal–reprieve has taken us somewhere beyond farce. The scandals of the 1970s, the CIA's response to them, and the failure of America's legislature to enact any lasting and effective change upon the activities of its most notorious spy agency, laid the blueprint for the 1980s, as it did for today.

As in the press and the United States Congress, criticism of the CIA in the American cinema of the 1970s was likewise limited and short-lived. Although it was a decade that did indeed witness the emergence of the first unambiguously anti-CIA movies, the more radical critiques of the Agency, like *The Spook Who Sat by the Door* or de Antonio's proposed Agee feature, were silenced. Hollywood were only prepared to go so far in their criticism of the Agency, and when filmmakers attempted to go further, their films were either mysteriously pulled from distribution or met with insurmountable obstacles – usually financial – that prevented them from being made at all. Indeed, only a single anti-CIA picture in the whole of the 1970s was widely seen by American audiences: *Three Days of the Condor* – most likely because it had Robert Redford as its star.

And yet, while the legal and political responses to the revelations of CIA misdeeds in the 1970s were muted, and the explicit criticism of the Agency in the Hollywood cinema of the era neutered, something had changed, in a wider sense, in American culture. To perceive that change it is necessary to place the paranoid cinema of the 1970s on a continuum of post-war spy cinema to reveal the broader socially symbolic currents that shifted in tandem with the evolution of its form. The starkest change can be witnessed via a simple juxtaposition, like the one with which I began this book, between the paranoid cinema of the 1970s and the semi-documentary spy films of the 1940s and 1950s. As I argued in the introduction, the paranoid aesthetic of the former completely inverted the credulous epistemology of the latter to produce a mode of popular historiography that was fundamentally at odds with government secrecy and deception. This was perhaps the most lasting cultural legacy of the 1970s: its rendering of *13 Rue Madeleine*'s unshakeable faith in the American Government as the arbiter of historical authenticity as an almost completely untenable position. Actually it was not *The Parallax View*, or *Three Days of the Condor* or any other conspiracy film of the 1970s that achieved this. Rather, it was the CIA's morally questionable activities themselves and the expansive system of government secrecy that made them possible, which were the ultimate agents of change in this destabalisation of the nation's past. Conspiracy thrillers, including those about the CIA, merely provided an appropriate vessel through which increasing social anxiety about secrecy and its effects upon the understanding of our shared history could be articulated.

As previous chapters have shown, this erosion of consensus history in the popular historical imagination captured by post-war spy films began in the 1960s, with 'camp' cinema's parodic rejection of the semi-documentary's earnest commitment to government-endorsed nationalist historiography. The conspiracy thrillers of the 1970s completed this trend towards epistemological scepticism that is the hallmark of postmodernity. Unlike their 1960s forebears, however, the critical vision of consensus history they provided, with a few notable exceptions, was not delivered as irony. They offered instead an unequivocal vision of the slide into social fragmentation, political paranoia and the collapsing authority of the 'official story' that the post-war expansion of US Government secrecy and the national security state had enabled.

Although the repeated scandals of the sixties and seventies involving the US intelligence community may not have forced them to alter their behaviour, except in providing an impetus for more effective CIA public relations, they altered American culture, and Americans' understanding of their history, profoundly. The ramifications of this, from a near-complete breakdown of public trust in our leaders to the erosion of all forms of authoritative knowledge with the onset of postmodernity, are still with us to this day. No wonder then, that in the wake of the 9/11 attacks, an event that once again drove American policymakers, in the words of Dick Cheney, 'to spend time in the shadows in the intelligence world', the conspiracy thriller witnessed a powerful revival.[122] That the semi-documentary is all but extinct as a form of historical representation while the conspiracy thriller continues to thrive is revealing. We live in the shadow of the

1970s, not the 1950s. Our collective cultural response to excessive government secrecy remains the same as the post-Watergate era: paranoia, scepticism and perhaps most profoundly, a loss of faith in the authority and the relevance of history.

Notes

1. Kathryn Olmsted, *Challenging the Secret Government: The Post-Watergate Investigations of the CIA and FBI* (Chapel Hill: University of North Carolina Press, 1996).
2. Jared Brown, *Alan J. Pakula: His Films and His Life* (New York: Backstage Books, 2005), p. 128.
3. Slavoj Žižek, 'Good Manners in the Age of Wikileaks', *London Review of Books*, 33:2, 20 January 2011, pp. 9–10.
4. Olmsted, *Challenging the Secret Government*, p. 26.
5. Ibid., pp. 35–6.
6. Cynthia M. Nolan, 'Seymour Hersh's Impact on the CIA', *International Journal of Intelligence and Counterintelligence*, 12:1 (1999), pp. 21–3.
7. Tony Shaw, *Hollywood's Cold War*, p. 226. The most famous critique of Conrad's implicit racism and imperialism in *The Heart of Darkness*, despite its ostensible anti-imperialist narrative, is Chinua Achebe, 'An Image of Africa: Racism in Conrad's "Heart of Darkness"', *Massachusetts Review*, 18:4 (1977), pp. 782–94.
8. See Lawrence Suid, *Guts and Glory: The Making of the American Military Image in Film*, second revised edition (Lexington: University of Kentucky Press, 2002); Richard Gid Powers, *G-Men: Hoover's FBI in American Popular Culture* (Carbondale: Southern Illinois University Press, 1983); John Sbardellati, *J. Edgar Hoover Goes to the Movies: The FBI and the Origins of Hollywood's Cold War* (Ithaca: Cornell University Press, 2012).
9. Suid, *Guts and Glory*, p. 337.
10. Ibid., pp. 295–304.
11. 'The Agency's Image', 18 November 1970, CIA-RDP80-00473A000600080041-7, CIA Records Search Tool (hereafter CREST), US National Archives, College Park, MD (hereafter NACP).
12. Lorenzo Semple Jr interview with author.
13. 'Robert Redford Struggles to Stay in Touch With the Real Man: When the Press has the Power, it's Easy to Become the Heavy', *Three Days of the Condor*, Pressbook, Clippings File, University of Southern California Cinematic Arts Library (hereafter USCAL), Los Angeles.
14. Don DeLillo, *Libra* (London: Penguin Modern Classics, 2006), p. 181.
15. 'Scene Outline: Parallax View', 1 January 1973, Alan Pakula Papers, Folder 374 'Story Notes', AMPAS, Beverly Hills.
16. James Der Derian, *Virtuous War: Mapping the Military-Industrial-Media-Entertainment Network* (New York: Routledge, 2009), p. 228.
17. Richard Hofstadter, *The Paranoid Style in American Politics and Other Essays* (New York: Random House, [1964] 2008). Hofstadter's fellow liberal consensus intellectual Arthur Schlesinger Jr offered perhaps the most well-known defence of centrist pragmatism, an ideal that underlines Hofstadter's essay, in Arthur M. Schlesinger Jr, *The Vital Center: The Politics of Freedom*, new edition (New York: Da Capo Press, 1988).
18. Fredric Jameson, 'Totality as Conspiracy', in Fredric Jameson, *The Geopolitical Aesthetic: Cinema and Space in the World System* (Bloomington: Indiana University Press, 1992), pp. 9–84.

19. Hofstadter, *The Paranoid Style in American Politics*; Karl Popper, *The Open Society and Its Enemies*, new edition (Abingdon: Routledge Classics, 2011), pp. 307–8.
20. Jürgen Habermas, *The Structural Transformation of the Public Sphere: An Inquiry into a Category of Bourgeois Society*, trans. Thomas Burger (Cambridge, MA: MIT Press, 1989).
21. Timothy Melley discusses the impact of secrecy upon the public sphere in Timothy Melley, *The Covert Sphere: Secrecy, Fiction, and the National Security State* (Ithaca: Cornell University Press, 2012), pp. 1–34.
22. See Simon Willmetts 'Reconceiving Realism: Intelligence Historians and the Fact/Fiction Dichotomy', in Christopher Moran and Christopher J. Murphy (eds), *Intelligence Studies in Britain and the US: Historiography since 1945* (Edinburgh: Edinburgh University Press, 2013), pp. 146–71.
23. Gary Fishgall, *Against Type: The Biography of Burt Lancaster* (New York: Scribner, 1995), p. 285.
24. United Artists Production Notes in 'Scorpion Clippings Files', *The British Film Institute*, London, UK.
25. Fred Emery, *Watergate: The Corruption of American Politics and the Fall of Richard Nixon* (New York: Touchstone, 1994), p. 130.
26. Fishgall, *Against Type*, p. 291.
27. Clifton Daniel, 'Rockefeller Panel and its C.I.A. Mission', *The New York Times*, 20 January 1975.
28. Memorandum for Angus Thuermer, 27 January 1975, CIA-RDP88-01365R000300210001-3, CREST, NACP.
29. John E. Horton to Donald E. Baruch, 21 August 1968, Hitchcock Papers, Folder 761 'Washington Research File', AMPAS, Beverly Hills.
30. 'Memorandum for the DCI', 11 July 1963, CREST, CIA-RDP70-00058R000200090034-3, NACP.
31. Senator William Fulbright, *The Pentagon Propaganda Machine* (New York: Liverlight Publishing, 1970), p. 12.
32. See Christopher R. Moran, 'The Last Assignment: David Atlee Phillips and the Birth of CIA Public Relations', *International History Review*, 35:2 (2013b), pp. 337–55.
33. David Shamus McCarthy, *The CIA and the Cult of Secrecy* (William and Mary College, Doctoral Dissertation, 2008), p. 110.
34. On 'liberal integrationism' see Manning Marable, 'Race, Identity, and Political Culture', in Michele Wallace (ed.), *Black Popular Culture* (Seattle: Bay Press, 1992), p. 292.
35. Nelson Blackstock, *Cointelpro: The FBI's Secret War on Political Freedom* (New York: Pathfinder Press, 1988); David Garrow, *The FBI and Martin Luther King, Jr.* revised edition (New Haven: Yale University Press, 2006).
36. Ralph Ellison, *The Invisible Man* (New York: Penguin Modern Classics, 2001), p. 7.
37. United Artists Production Notes in 'Scorpion Clippings Files', The British Film Institute, London, UK.
38. Ibid.
39. Ibid.
40. Meyer Kantor, 'This "Spook" Has No Respect for Human Life', *The New York Times*, 11 November 1973; Fran Well, '"The Spook Who Sat By the Door" Director Shocked by "Extreme Reaction" to Film', *The Boston Herald Traveller and Record American*, 5 October 1973.
41. *Infiltrating Hollywood: The Rise and Fall of the Spook Who Sat by the Door* (Christine Acham and Clifford Ward, ChiTrini Productions, 2011).

42. Ibid.
43. John Le Carré, *The Spy Who Came in from the Cold* (London: Victor Gollancz and Pan, 1963).
44. *The Spy Who Came in from the Cold* (Martin Ritt, Salem Films, 1965).
45. Tony Shaw, *British Cinema and the Cold War: The State, Propaganda and Consensus* (London: I. B. Tauris, 2001), pp. 60–2; Michael Denning, *Cover Stories: Narrative and Ideology in the British Spy Thriller* (Abingdon: Routledge, 1987).
46. Hitchcock's last unmade film before he died, *Short Night*, also featured the CIA. For more see David Freeman, *The Last Days of Alfred Hitchcock: A Memoir Featuring the Entire Screenplay of Alfred Hitchcock's 'The Short Night'* (Woodstock: Overlook Press, 1984).
47. Cynthia M. Nolan, 'Seymour Hersh's Impact on the CIA'.
48. 'The Agency's Image', 18 November 1970, CREST – CIA-RDP80-00473A 000600080041-7, NACP.
49. On conspiracy cinema as socially symbolic see Ray Pratt, *Projecting Paranoia: Conspiratorial Visions in American Film* (Lawrence: University of Kansas Press, 2002).
50. Brown, *Alan J. Pakula*, p. 125.
51. Alan Pakula to Mr Lorts, 26 July 1974, Alan Pakula Papers Mss, Folder 345 'correspondence', AMPAS, Beverly Hills.
52. 'It Could Only Be A Movie', Says Alan Pakula about his Suspense Film, 'The Parallax View', Alan Pakula Papers, Folder 363 'Publicity', AMPAS, Beverly Hills.
53. 'It Could Only Be A Movie', Says Alan Pakula about his Suspense Film, 'The Parallax View', Alan Pakula Papers, Folder 363 'Publicity', AMPAS, Beverly Hills.
54. 'Handwritten Notes', 21 February 1973, Alan Pakula Papers, Folder 373 'Story Notes', AMPAS, Beverly Hills.
55. 'Notes on the Parallax View', 8 August 1972, Alan Pakula Papers, Folder 374 'Story Notes', AMPAS, Beverly Hills.
56. In his biography of Anthony Burgess, Roger Lewis claimed that Burgess was inspired to write *A Clockwork Orange* following his involvement with CIA mind-control experiments while working as a colonial officer in Malaya. See Roger Lewis, *Anthony Burgess* (New York: Faber and Faber, 2002).
57. 'Handwritten Script Notes', Alan Pakula Papers, Folder 369 'Script Notes', AMPAS, Beverly Hills.
58. 'Notes on the Parallax View', 19 October 1972, Alan Pakula Papers, Folder 374 'Story Notes', AMPAS, Beverly Hills.
59. 'General Observations on Script and Book', 24 July 1972, Alan Pakula Papers, Folder 373 'Story Notes', AMPAS, Beverly Hills; 'Scene Outline: Parallax View', 1 January 1973, Alan Pakula Papers, Folder 374 'Story Notes', AMPAS, Beverly Hills.
60. 'General Observations on Script and Book', 24 July 1972, Alan Pakula Papers, Folder 373 'Story Notes', AMPAS, Beverly Hills.
61. 'Scene Outline: Parallax View', 1 January 1973, Alan Pakula Papers, Folder 374 'Story Notes', AMPAS, Beverly Hills.
62. Ibid.
63. Albert Boime, *The Unveilling of the National Icons: A Plea for Patriotic Iconoclasm in a Nationalist Era* (Cambridge: Cambridge University Press, 1997).
64. 'General Observations on Script and Book', 24 July 1972, Alan Pakula Papers, Folder 373 'Story Notes', AMPAS, Beverly Hills.
65. 'Notes on Parallax View', 11 October 1972, Alan Pakula Papers, Folder 374 'Story Notes', AMPAS, Beverly Hills.

66. 'Script Notes', undated, Alan Pakula Papers, Folder 369 'Script Notes', AMPAS, Beverly Hills.
67. 'Parallax View Screenplay Draft', Alan Pakula Papers, Folder 327 'Parallax View Script', AMPAS, Beverly Hills.
68. Mark Fenster, *Conspiracy Theories: Secrecy and Power in American Culture* (Minneapolis: University of Minnesota Press, 2001), pp. 111–12.
69. Other films of the era that featured the CIA or a shady American intelligence outfit with clear allusions to the CIA included: *Day of the Dolphin* (Mike Nichols, AVCO Embassy Pictures, 1973); *Scorpio* (Michael Winner, MGM, 1973); *Marathon Man* (John Schlesinger, Paramount, 1976); *All the President's Men* (Alan J. Pakula, Warner Brothers, 1976); *The Godfather Part II* (Francis Ford Coppola, Paramount, 1974); *Winter Kills* (William Richert, AVCO Embassy Pictures, 1979); *The Killer Elite* (Sam Peckinpah, United Artists, 1975); *Telefon* (Don Siegel, MGM, 1977).
70. 'Robert Redford Struggles to Stay in Touch With the Real Man: When the Press has the Power, it's Easy to Become the Heavy', *Three Days of the Condor* Pressbook, Clippings File, University of Southern California Cinematic Arts Library, Los Angeles.
71. *Three Days of the Condor* Production Notes, Clippings Files, Museum of Modern Art, New York.
72. For more on the 'Georgetown set' and their influence during the Cold War see Gregg Herken, *The Georgetown Set: Friends and Rivals in Cold War Washington* (New York: Knopf Publishing, 2014).
73. Lorenzo Semple Jr, interview with author, 12 June 2009.
74. Tony Shaw, *Hollywood's Cold War* (Edinburgh: Edinburgh University Press, 2007), p. 260.
75. Patrick McGilligan, '*Three Days of the Condor*: Hollywood Uncovers the CIA, Sidney Pollack Interviewed', *Jump Cut*, 10–11 (1976), p. 11.
76. McCarthy, *The CIA and the Cult of Secrecy*, p. 91.
77. *Three Days of the Condor* (Sydney Pollack, Paramount, 1975).
78. James Grady interview with author, 10 October 2009.
79. McCarthy, *The CIA and the Cult of Secrecy*, p. 89.
80. James Grady interview with the author, 10 October 2009.
81. David Potter, *People of Plenty: Economic Abundance and the American Character* (Chicago: University of Chicago Press, 1958).
82. McGilligan, '*Three Days of the Condor*', p. 11.
83. 'DCI Speech to CIA: Today and Tommorrow', Headquarters Auditorium, 4 March 1976, CREST: CIA-RDP79-00498A000700040003-7, NACP.
84. William F. Buckley Jr, 'The Case of Robert Redford vs. the C.I.A.', *The New York Times*, 28 September 1975, p. 13.
85. Robert W. Gambino, 'Memorandum for the Record: Conversation with Emily Sheketoff, Staff Member of House Select Committee', CREST, CIA-RDP89B00552R000100100016-1, NACP.
86. James Grady interview with author.
87. James Grady, 'Rhyme', preface to Grady, *Six Days of The Condor* (Aylesbury: No Exit Press, 2007), pp. xiii–xiv; my emphasis.
88. 'DCI Speech to CIA: Today and Tomorrow', Headquarters Auditorium, 4 March 1976, CREST: CIA-RDP79-00498A000700040003-7, NACP.
89. Prados, *The Family Jewels*, p. 244.
90. Prados, *The Family Jewels*, p. 222.
91. Ibid.
92. Michael Fellner, 'Emile de Antonio's CIA Diary (1975)', in Douglas Kellner and

Dan Streible (eds), *Emile de Antonio: A Reader* (Minneapolis: University of Minnesota Press, 2000), p. 361.
93. 'Statement by Haskell Wexler at Press Conference in Los Angeles, 6 June 1975, On Grand Jury Subpoenas', Emile de Antonio MSS, Box 80, Folder 10 – Weather Underground Correspondence 1976, Wisconsin Center for Film and Theater Research (hereafter WCFTR), Madison; Peter Biskind, 'Does the U.S. Have the Right to Subpoena a Film in Progress', *The New York Times*, 22 June 1975.
94. 'Emile de Antonio Biographical Material', Emile de Antonio MSS, Box 80, Folder 9 – Weather Underground Correspondence 1974–5, WCFTR, Madison.
95. 'Motion Picture Film Based on Agee Book – Inside the Company: CIA Diary', 8 November 1976, CREST, CIA-RDP88-01365R000300110002-3.
96. Emile de Antonio to Philip Agee, 5 March 1975, Emile de Antonio MSS, Box 46, Folder 18 – 'Inside the Company' Correspondence, WCFTR, Madison.
97. 'Film Treatment for "Inside the Company", Emile de Antonio MSS', Box 46, Folder 19 – '"Inside the Company" Treatment and Prospectives', WCFTR, Madison.
98. Emile de Antonio to Robert Boehm, 10 November 1975, Emile de Antonio MSS, Box 46, Folder 18 – 'Inside the Company' Correspondence, WCFTR, Madison.
99. 'Film Treatment for 'Inside the Company', Emile de Antonio MSS, Box 46, Folder 19 – '"Inside the Company" Treatment and Prospectives', WCFTR, Madison, WI.
100. Emile de Antonio to Philip Agee, 21 December 1975, Emile de Antonio MSS, Box 46, Folder 18 – 'Inside the Company' Correspondence, WCFTR, Madison.
101. Prados, *The Family Jewels*, 242.
102. 'Film Treatment for "Inside the Company", Emile de Antonio MSS', Box 46, Folder 19 – '"Inside the Company" Treatment and Prospectives', WCFTR, Madison.
103. Michael Fellner, 'Emile de Antonio's CIA Diary (1975)', in Douglas Kellner and Dan Streible (eds), *Emile de Antonio: A Reader* (Minneapolis: University of Minnesota Press, 2000), p. 362.
104. Emile de Antonio to Philip Agee, 5 March 1975, Emile de Antonio MSS, Box 46, Folder 18 – 'Inside the Company' Correspondence, WCFTR, Madison.
105. Ibid.
106. Ibid.
107. 'Meetings on Agee Film in Lima, Peru June 13–17, 1975', 11 July 1975, Emile de Antonio MSS, Box 46, Folder 18 – 'Inside the Company' Correspondence, WCFTR, Madison.
108. Luis Gerrido-Lecca to Jeffrey Kovner, 29 September 1975, Emile de Antonio MSS, Box 46, Folder 18 – 'Inside the Company' Correspondence, WCFTR, Madison, WI.
109. Susan Linfield, 'Irrepressible Emile de Antonio Speaks (1982)', in Douglas Kellner and Dan Streible (eds), *Emile de Antonio: A Reader* (Minneapolis: University of Minnesota Press, 2000), p. 121.
110. McCarthy, *The CIA and the Cult of Secrecy*, p. 135.
111. In an interview for 'Good Morning America' in 1977, for example, Director of Central Intelligence Admiral Stansfield Turner explained to his interviewers that he was instigating a new 'American model of intelligence, which, on the one hand, shares all that we can with the public ... But on the other', involved the issuance of 'some very Draconian rules ... about tightening security'. 'Good Morning America Transcript', 19 September 1977, CREST, CIA-RDP99-00498R0003000300040012-5, NACP.
112. 'CBS-TV "60-Minutes" Filming Schedule', 6 June 1977, CREST, CIA-RDP80M00165A002400130019-5, NACP.

113. 'Memo for Assistant to the DCI (Public Affairs) re: Rona Barrett's Comments about Hollywood Films on "Good Morning America"', 19 September 1977, CREST, CIA-RDP88-01365R000300010001-5, NACP.
114. Moran, Christopher R., 'The Last Assignment: David Atlee Phillips and the Birth of CIA Public Relations', *International History Review*, 35:2 (2013b), pp. 337–55.
115. Memo for Admiral Stansfield Turner re: 'Proposed TV Series as Outlined Herein', 3 March 1978, CREST, CIA-RDP81M00980R001700080050-1, NACP.
116. Elmer Linberg to 'Bob', 30 March 1977, CREST, CIA-RDP88-01314R000300010028-2, NACP.
117. 'Presentations for Shade of the Palms', undated, CREST, CIA-RDP88-01314R000300010029-1, NACP.
118. Peggy Whitman Prenshaw (ed.), *Conversations with William Buckley* (Minneapolis: University of Minnesota Press, 2009), p. 123.
119. Memo for Deputy Director of Central Intelligence re: 'Shade of the Palms', 18 April 1977, CREST, CIA-RDP88-01314R000300010027-3.
120. Tricia Jenkins, *The CIA in Hollywood: How the Agency Shapes Film and Television* (Austin: University of Texas Press, 2012).
121. Tony Shaw, *Hollywood's Cold War*, pp. 267–300.
122. Dick Cheney on NBC's Meet the Press with Tim Russert, 16 September 2001. Available online at http://georgewbush-whitehouse.archives.gov/vicepresident/news-speeches/speeches/vp20010916.html, accessed 31 March 2015. On the return of the conspiracy thriller post-9/11 see Ross Douthat, 'The Return of the Paranoid Style: How the Iraq War and George W. Bush Sent the Movie Industry Back to its Favorite Era – The 1970s', *The Atlantic*, April 2008.

CONCLUSION

In his introduction to Senator Daniel Patrick Moynihan's cogent critique of excessive US Government secrecy, FBI historian Richard Gid Powers wrote: 'If official secrecy had a devastating impact on American history, its impact on Americans' understanding of that history was a collateral disaster.'[1] From the very beginnings of history as a professional discipline in the nineteenth century, indeed, since the time of the ancients and the first known works of source-based historical narrative by Herodotus and Thucydides, history has always existed, as Lynn Hunt put it, 'in a symbiotic relationship with nationalism'.[2] In this sense, the function of history was to provide unifying and guiding stories of our collective past that may bind us up in a national community. In so doing, these stories not only buttressed the authority of the nation state, and of our national leaders, by entrenching their lineage, but also gave us, the citizens of that national community, a sense of our common destiny. In the United States, a young nation of colonising immigrants and dispersed communities with different customs, creeds, languages and ethnicities, such unifying stories of a shared national past and manifest future were all the more needed. 'The story of the nation's rise provided the common threads to bind together disparate peoples, whether of different ethnic groups, different classes, or different regions.'[3]

Along with nationalism there was another tradition of the nineteenth century within which the historical profession took root: positivism. This was especially the case in the United States where the German idealism of Leopold Von Ranke was misappropriated as the basis of a new 'scientific' approach to history.[4] The adoption of the scientific method, with its attendant advocacy of empiricism, led to the exaltation of the archive, which provided the firm empirical ground upon which the newly professionalised historians could apply Ranke's rigorous philological and documentary methods. Thus, since governments were the most meticulous record-keepers, and since the nation-state was, until the 1960s, the prevailing subject of interest for the historian, the bureaucratic records of the national government found in the national archives so exalted by *13 Rue Madeleine*'s opening scene, became the mainspring of history. Even in the nineteenth century American historians were never so naïve as to take everything they found in the national archive, or every politicians' speech and official utterance, at face value. Indeed one of Ranke's great legacies was his shift away from the simple idolisation of Prussian nationalism – although the nationalist project remained at the heart of his idealism – towards a more interrogative historical method that questioned and rigorously challenged evidence in order to affirm the validity of individual documents. But there was nevertheless a general faith, which persists to this day among diplomatic historians, that the aggregated contents of the official record, once appropriate checks have been performed to weed out deceptive material, would faithfully illuminate the past. The massive expansion of American government secrecy in the second half of the twentieth century, in the popular historiography of Hollywood cinema at least, fundamentally undermined this trust in the authority of the official record.

This is not to argue that American secrecy was a post-war invention. Governments, including the US government, have always kept things secret from their people. The nineteenth-century philosopher Max Weber wrote eloquently on the subject, arguing that secrecy was essential to the effective functioning of the modern bureaucratic state: how could civil servants engage in candid deliberation if they knew that every idea and suggestion they made was a matter for the public record?[5] But something was different about the nature and levels of government secrecy in post-war America. First and most obviously, the scale of US government classification in the post-war era dwarfed anything that had gone before it.

> From the beginning of classification in 1907 to the end of World War II, the [US] government generated only 325,000 cubic feet of classified documents. But between 1946 and 1958 an estimated one million cubic feet of classified documents were created.[6]

Those cubic feet have grown exponentially ever since.[7] Second, thanks to the rise of new mass media, including Hollywood, as well as their more adversarial relationship with government from the 1960s onwards, the American public became more aware of official deception, especially because the CIA produced a litany of spectacular failures from the Gary Powers affair and Bay of Pigs on, which increasingly brought the US Government's secret and often nefarious activities to public attention.

Finally, and this I think has had the most profound effect as far as American trust in the official record is concerned, deception and official duplicity took on such significant proportions during the Cold War that at times it was almost as if there existed two entirely separate US foreign policies – one overt, the other covert. Occasionally, during the Vietnam War, for example, as revealed by Daniel Ellsberg's leak of the Pentagon Papers, the avowed policy of the United States and its covert reality were fundamentally at odds with each other. There is a major difference between secrecy of a tactical nature, whereby sources, methods and individual covert operations are concealed in order to maintain the element of surprise but without fundamentally contradicting the overt policies of the United States Government, and deception of a more strategic nature, where, for example, the US Congress can declare official neutrality in the Iran–Iraq war while the President's National Security Council sells weapons to Iran while funnelling money into the hands of the Nicaraguan Contras – an activity that was likewise officially outlawed. There is, in short, a fundamental difference, between necessary secrecy and outright deception that goes against the grain of official policy. The former may inspire limited scepticism toward the official record, generating a concern for the comprehensiveness of its coverage in certain areas, but the latter generates an almost unbounded paranoia and suspicion that the official record is, *in toto*, corrupted and therefore wholly unreliable.

There are more than enough examples of this kind of systematic strategic deception in post-war American history to make the paranoid conspiracy theorist, so maligned by Richard Hofstadter and many historians since, appear almost reasonable.[8] For there is a thin line between, for example, the healthy scepticism of Woodward and Bernstein that revealed the existence of a real conspiracy at the highest levels of American Government, and the delusions of the paranoid. Hofstadter, of course, had a ready-made answer to this challenge:

> One may object that there *are* conspiratorial acts in history, and there is nothing paranoid about taking note of them . . . The distinguishing thing about the paranoid style is not that its exponents see conspiracies or plots here and there in history, but they regard a 'vast' or 'gigantic' conspiracy as the *motive force* in historical events. History *is* a conspiracy, set in motion by demonic forces of almost transcendent power, and what is felt to be needed to defeat it is not the usual methods of political give-and-take, but an all-out crusade.[9]

It's an important distinction, and for the most part, a convincing one, which provides comfort to the merely astute historian who maintains a healthy scepticism towards the official record without slipping into outright paranoia. But Hofstadter was a signed-up member of the liberal consensus, a philosophy that had guided Hollywood's representation of secrecy and espionage from the Second World War up to the arrival of the irreverent camp spy thrillers of the 1960s. For Hofstadter, who first delivered his famous essay on the paranoid style a day before President Kennedy was killed, American democracy, and her democratic institutions, represented a bulwark of pragmatism and reason against the irrational, indeed paranoid, totalitarian threats of Nazi fascism and Soviet communism.[10] How different Hofstadter's argument may have been had he made it fifteen years later, from the vantage of post-Watergate America, when official secrecy had fundamentally eroded that consensus vision of American democracy as transparent, rational and benign.

The society that produced both Richard Hofstadter and *13 Rue Madeleine* feels distant, even antiquated. Theirs was a special time, forged in the embers of a global war whose moral lines, even discounting the advantage of victors writing their own history, were clear. John Ford may have 'soft-soaped' his OSS film about the Battle of Midway to try to appeal – unsuccessfully in the case of Josephine MacNab – to the mothers of America, and his deputy Ray Kellogg may have carefully edited the films of Nazi atrocities at the Nuremberg trials, but who could doubt their validity? The images the OSS Field Photographic Unit produced and edited together during the war were so vivid, so real, unlike anything the American public had ever seen before. Their power was such that they even helped elevate the epistemic authority of cinema as a medium. By the end of the Second World War, cinema, previously regarded by many in and outside the industry as a form of entertainment and nothing more, provided vital evidence at the most significant trial of the twentieth century. These were government-produced films, their official provenance proudly proclaimed, just like the post-war semi-documentaries. Their content remains compelling. But they are also relics of a bygone age, products of an epoch that existed before excessive government secrecy had fundamentally sullied the official story.

The erosion of Hollywood cinema's faith in the official record was a gradual process. During the 1950s, haunted by the spectres of HUAC and McCarthyism, Hollywood stayed loyal to the official story. So much so that by the end of the decade there existed a conspicuous vacuum in their output: why were there so many domestic FBI agents in the Hollywood films of the 1950s but *no* foreign CIA agents? At a time when US covert action was entering its so-called 'golden age', this disparity was hardly representative. J. Edgar Hoover and the FBI's overbearing cooperation with filmmakers in this period compared with the CIA's 'cherishment of anonymity' provide one explanation. The other is that the US Government refused to officially acknowledge the existence of its covert operations, and Hollywood, along with the rest of the American media, up until the Bay of Pigs, helped facilitate this state of denial.

When the first challenge to consensus history and the official story finally did come it was not in the form of explicitly political content that was radically opposed to the existing Cold War ideology. The tongue-in-cheek 'camp' romance narratives of the 1960s were wilfully apolitical, even to the point of denying the existence of the Cold War. What they were, however, was deliberately incredulous – consciously rejecting the austere commitment of the semi-documentary to state-sourced realism. By breaking with the dominant form of realist representation – bound as it was to the official story – they opened up a space for later critical voices by cleaving away from and even consciously rejecting nationalist discourses.

The conspiracy thrillers of the 1970s marked the culmination of Hollywood's shift away from state-sourced realism. These narratives were infused with a suspicion of the official story inspired by repeated revelations of government deception in the period that culminated with Watergate and the 1975 investigations of the US intelligence community. The sanctity of the government archives and advisors that were the wellspring of the semi-documentaries was entirely debased in these stories. Their emergence signified a new dominant cultural logic that replaced the credulous epistemology of the early Cold War consensus that had relied upon public trust in government. In this respect the CIA, which became synonymous with excessive government secrecy in this period, had a profound effect upon American culture. Although the Agency scrambled to repair their public image in the wake of the 1975 Congressional investigations, and were even successful, indirectly, in silencing some of the most critical voices in the American filmmaking community, it was too late to reverse the much broader cultural current towards widespread public scepticism of the official record that their activities had inspired. It is no coincidence that while the semi-documentary is today an anachronism, the paranoid tropes of 1970s conspiracy cinema have been continually recycled, especially in the aftermath of 9/11.[11]

Despite this widespread cultural scepticism towards the official record that reached its zenith in the 1970s but has never really dissipated since, professional intelligence historians continue to exalt the official record as if nothing has changed since the age of Leopold von Ranke. One recent history of British Government secrecy in the Cold War, for example, begins with an encomium to the official records and the UK national archive not a whit less idolatry than the opening scene of *13 Rue Madeleine*.[12] In Britain, government-anointed historians have been provided with privileged access to write official histories of the intelligence agencies while offering precious little reflection upon the difficult political and epistemological questions that must accompany such a task.[13] In America the relationship between scholarship and government is arguably even closer; the emphasis there is often on policy prescription as opposed to more humanistic studies.[14] The CIA has worked hard to build links with the academy since the turmoil of post-*Ramparts* 1960s through, among other initiatives, its 'Scholars in Residence' programme that places avowed CIA officers in academic departments who often teach intelligence studies.[15] The revolving door has benefited academics, too, who occasionally receive lucrative contracts to advise US intelligence agencies. It is almost as if the atmosphere of cultural scepticism that exists everywhere around them has simply hardened the resolve of professional scholars to work more closely with governments. As discussed in the introduction this is not to say that national archives, and even maintaining close links with intelligence agencies, has no use. But to adopt such an approach without reflection and to continue to exalt the epistemological supremacy of professional scholarship over vernacular concerns about intelligence history seems almost wilfully naïve.

Hollywood has thus presented what Wesley Wark termed a 'counter-history' of intelligence.[16] Or more precisely, following Linda Hutcheon's study of postmodern fiction as a mode of critical historiography, it has provided much-needed reflection upon the inescapable challenge that government secrecy has posed to the official story. Scholarship, by contrast, has remained relatively silent on this issue.[17] As Dominick LaCapra put it in his discussion of the relationship between history and the novel:

> In fact the most telling question posed by the novel to historiography may be whether contemporary historical writing can learn something of a self-critical nature from a mode of discourse it has often tried to use or to explain in overly reductive fashion. A different way of reading novels may alert us not only to the contestatory voices and counter-discourses of the past but to the ways in which historiography itself may become a more critical voice in the 'human sciences.'[18]

Perhaps historians still yearn for a simpler time, where, as in *13 Rue Madeleine*, they could enter the National Archives and find out clearly and unequivocally 'what the CIA and the FBI knew'. Perhaps, like Wabash in *Three Days of the Condor*, they 'miss that kind of clarity'. But the rise and rise of US Government secrecy in the second half of the twentieth century has made such yearning appear hopelessly nostalgic. We cannot return to the age of consensus history that began the Cold War: the scale of government secrecy and duplicity won't allow us. Nor would we want to. If intelligence historians really want to come to terms with the challenge that spy fiction has posed to their craft, then they must first address the implications of government secrecy for traditional historiography. Neither naivety nor nihilism is a satisfactory response. For the epistemological challenge that secrecy has posed, to the historian, to the public and to our shared national culture, may just be the most disruptive legacy of the twentieth century for American democracy. Fiction has not provided the answers either, but it has raised the question and highlighted the problem much more than the academy has done. It is time for us to listen to fiction, and not just dismiss it as bunk, for its concerns about the past are, in the end, our own.

Notes

1. Richard Gid Powers introduction to Daniel Patrick Moynihan, *Secrecy: The American Experience* (New Haven: Yale University Press, 1999), p. 17.
2. Lynn Hunt, *Writing History in the Global Era* (New York: W. W. Norton and Company, 2014), p. 3.
3. Ibid.
4. Peter Novick, *That Noble Dream: The 'Objectivity Question' and the American Historical Profession* (Cambridge: Cambridge University Press, 1988), pp. 21–60.
5. H. H. Gerth (ed.), *From Max Weber: Essays in Sociology*, new edition (Abingdon: Routledge, 1991), pp. 233–5.
6. John E. Moss, 'The Crisis of Sececy', *Bulletin of the Atomic Scientists*, 17:1 (January 1961), p. 9.
7. See, for example, Information Security Oversight Office's (ISOO) Report to the President for Fiscal Year 2009. Available online at http://www.archives.gov/isoo/reports/2009-annual-report.pdf, accessed 6 April 2015.
8. The occurrence of real conspiracies in post-war America coupled with the proliferation of US Government secrecy has been a noted counterpoint to Hofstadter's argument by a number of recent works on conspiracy theory including Kathryn Olmsted, *Real Enemies: Conspiracy Theories and American Democracy, World War I to 9/11* (Oxford: Oxford University Press, 2010); Mark Fenster, *Conspiracy Theories: Secrecy and Power in American Culture* (Minneapolis: University of Minnesota Press, 2001), and Peter Knight, *Conspiracy Culture: From Kennedy to the X-Files* (Abingdon: Routledge, 2001).
9. Richard Hofstadter, *The Paranoid Style in American Politics and Other Essays* (New York: Random House, [1964] 2008), p. 29; my emphasis.
10. Karl Popper also famously raised the spectre of totalitarianism in his discussion of conspiracy theories. See Karl Popper, *The Open Society and Its Enemies*, new edition (Abingdon: Routledge Classics, 2011), pp. 307–8.
11. Ross Douthat, 'The Return of the Paranoid Style: How the Iraq War and George W. Bush Sent the Movie Industry Back to its Favorite Era – The 1970s', *The Atlantic*, April 2008.
12. Peter Hennessy, for example, one of the leading historians of British secrecy, is so enamoured with archival research that he devotes an entire chapter to it in *The Secret State*. Significantly, he describes the experience in the quasi-religious terms of 'pure elation and illumination' and praises the 'god of the archives' who was with him that day. See Peter Hennessy, *The Secret State: Whitehall and the Cold War*, (London, UK: Penguin Press, 2002), xv–xxi.
13. Christopher Andrew, *The Defence of the Realm: The Authorized History of MI5* (London: Penguin, 2010); Keith Jeffrey, *MI6: The History of the Secret Intelligence Service, 1909–1949* (London: Bloomsbury, 2011).
14. On differences between US and British approaches to intelligence studies see Richard Immerman, 'Intelligence Studies: The British Invasion', *History: The Journal of the Historical Association*, 100:340 (April 2015), pp. 163–6; Simon Willmetts, 'Reconceiving Realism: Intelligence Historians and the Fact/Fiction

Dichotomy', in Christopher Moran and Christopher J. Murphy (eds), *Intelligence Studies in Britain and the US: Historiography since 1945* (Edinburgh: Edinburgh University Press, 2013), pp. 146–7.
15. See John Hollister Hedley, 'Twenty Years of the Officers in Residence: CIA in the Classroom', *Studies in Intelligence*, 94:4 (November 2005), pp. 31–40.
16. Wesley Wark, 'Introduction: Fictions of History', *Intelligence and National Security*, 5:4 (1990), p. 12.
17. Linda Hutcheon, *A Poetics of Postmodernism: History, Theory, Fiction* (London: Routledge, 1988).
18. Dominick LaCapra, *History and Criticism*, (Ithaca: Cornell University Press, 1985), p. 132.

SELECT FILMOGRAPHY

IN CHRONOLOGICAL ORDER

The Battle of Midway (John Ford, OSS Field Photographic Unit Film, 1942).
December 7th (John Ford and Gregg Toland, OSS Field Photographic Unit Film, 1943).
At the Front in North Africa with the US Army (Darryl F. Zanuck, United States Government, 1943).
The Nazi Concentration Camps (Ray Kellogg and George Stevens, OSS Field Photographic Unit Film, 1945).
They Were Expendable (John Ford, MGM, 1945).
Cloak and Dagger (Fritz Lang, United States Pictures/Warner Brothers, 1946).
O.S.S. (Irving Pichel, Paramount Pictures, 1946).
13 Rue Madeleine (Henry Hathaway, Twentieth Century-Fox, 1947).
Captain Carey, U.S.A. (Mitchell Leisen, Paramount, 1950).
My Favorite Spy (Norman Z. McLeod, Paramount, 1951).
House of Secrets (Guy Green, The Rank Organisation, 1956).
The Quiet American (Joseph Mankiewicz, Figaro Entertainment/United Artists, 1958).
North by Northwest (Alfred Hitchcock, MGM, 1959).
Man on a String (André de Toth, RD-DR Production Company, 1961).
Dr. No (Terrence Young, United Artists, 1962).
Charade (Stanley Donen, Stanley Donen Productions/Universal, 1963).
From Russia with Love (Terence Young, MGM, 1963).
To Trap a Spy (Don Medford, MGM, 1964).
The IPCRESS File (Sidney Furie, Rank, 1965).
Operation C.I.A. (Christian Nyby, Allied Artists, 1965).
The Spy Who Came in from the Cold (Martin Ritt, Salem Films, 1965).
Arabesque (Stanley Donen, Universal, 1966).
The Defector (Raoul Levy, Gaumont, 1966).
Our Man Flint (Daniel Mann, Twentieth Century-Fox, 1966).

SELECT FILMOGRAPHY

Murderers Row (Henry Levin, Columbia, 1966).
One Spy Too Many (Joseph Sargent, MGM, 1966).
Torn Curtain (Alfred Hitchcock, Universal, 1966).
The Ambushers (Henry Levin, Columbia, 1967).
In Like Flint (Gordon Douglas, MGM, 1967).
The President's Analyst (Theodore J. Flicker, Paramount, 1967).
The Spy in the Green Hat (Joseph Sargent, MGM, 1967).
The Helicopter Spies (Barry Shear, MGM, 1968).
The Wrecking Crew (Phil Karlson, Columbia, 1969).
How to Steal the World (Sutton Roley, MGM, 1969).
Topaz (Alfred Hitchcock, Universal, 1969).
The Kremlin Letter (John Huston, Twentieth Century-Fox, 1970).
The Losers (Jack Starret, Fanfare Films, 1970).
Bananas (Woody Allen, United Artists, 1971).
Day of the Dolphin, (Mike Nichols, AVCO Embassy Pictures, 1973).
Executive Action (David Miller, National General Pictures, 1973).
Scorpio (Michael Winner, MGM, 1973).
The Spook Who Sat by the Door (Ivan Dixon, United Artists, 1973).
The Conversation (Francis Ford Coppola, Paramount, 1974).
The Godfather Part II (Francis Ford Coppola, Paramount, 1974).
Three Days of the Condor (Sydney Pollack, Paramount, 1975).
The Killer Elite (Sam Peckinpah, United Artists, 1975).
Marathon Man (John Schlesinger, Paramount, 1976).
All the President's Men (Alan J. Pakula, Warner Brothers, 1976).
Telefon (Don Siegel, MGM, 1977).
Winter Kills (William Richert, AVCO Embassy Pictures, 1979).
JFK (Oliver Stone, Warner Brothers, 1991).
Confessions of a Dangerous Mind (George Clooney, Section Eight Productions/ Miramax, 2002).
Ted Flicker: A Life in Three Acts (David Ewing, Bayside Productions, 2009).
Thomas Lowe Hughes interviews in *The Man Nobody Knew: In Search of My Father, CIA Spymaster William Colby* (Carl Colby, Act 4 Entertainment, 2011).
Infiltrating Hollywood: The Rise and Fall of the Spook Who Sat by the Door (Christine Acham and Clifford Ward, ChiTrini Productions, 2011).

BIBLIOGRAPHY

Manuscript Collections

American Heritage Center, University of Wyoming, Laramie, Wyoming, USA (AHCW):
  Louis de Rochemont Collection.
  Richard de Rochemont Collection.
British Film Institute, London, UK:
  Assorted Clippings Files.
Cinematic Arts Library, University of Southern California, Los Angeles, California, USA:
  Pressbook Clippings.
  Twentieth Century-Fox Collection.
  Warner Brothers Archive.
Firestone Library Special Collections, Princeton, New Jersey, USA:
  Ernest Lehman Screenplays Collection.
Georgetown University Manuscripts, Washington, DC, USA:
  Richard Helms Papers.
Harold B. Lee Library, Brigham Young University, Provo, Utah, USA:
  Argosy Pictures Collection.
  Merian C. Cooper Collection.
The Hoover Institute, Stanford University, Stanford, California, USA:
  Russell J. Forgan Collection.
Lilly Library, University of Indiana, Bloomington, Indiana, USA:
  John Ford Papers.
Louis B. Mayer Library, The American Film Institute, Hollywood, California, USA:
  Theodore J. Flicker Papers.
Margaret Herrick Library, Academy of Motion Pictures Arts and Sciences, Los Angeles, California, USA (AMPAS):
  Alan Pakula Papers.

Alfred Hitchcock Collection.
Cary Grant Papers.
Joseph Mankiewicz Papers.
Motion Picture Association of America Production Code Files (MPAA-PCA).
Paramount Pictures Press Sheets.
Schlesinger Library, Radcliffe Institute, Harvard University, Cambridge, Massachusetts, USA:
Mary Bancroft Papers.
University of Iowa Special Collections and University Archives, University of Iowa, Iowa City, Iowa, USA (UISC):
Norman Felton Papers.
Richard Maibaum Papers.
US National Archives, College Park, Maryland, USA (NACP):
CIA Records Search Tool (CREST).
Wisconsin Center for Film and Theater Research (Hereafter WCFTR), Wisconsin State Historical Society, Madison, WI:
Emile de Antonio Papers.
Ziv Entertainment Collection.

Government Reports, Legislation and Court Cases

In Chronological Order

National Security Act of 1947, Section 104: 'Central Intelligence Agency', 26 July 1947, Public Law 235, 61 STAT. 496.

'Report on the Activities of the Central Intelligence Agency' by Special Panel of Consultants Chaired by Lieutenant General James Doolittle, September 1954. Available online at <http://www.foia.cia.gov/sites/default/files/document_conversions/45/doolittle_report.pdf>, accessed 31 March 2015.

The New York Times Co. v. Sullivan, 376 US 254 (1964).

Curtis Publishing Co. v. Butts, 388 US 130 (1967).

Report of the Moynihan Commission on Protecting and Reducing Government Secrecy, Senate Document 105–2, 103rd Congress (Washington, DC: United States Government Printing Office, 1997).

Information Security Oversight Office's (ISOO) Report to the President for fiscal year 2009. Available online at <http://www.archives.gov/isoo/reports/2009-annual-report.pdf>, accessed 6 April 2015.

Interviews Conducted by Author

Lorenzo Semple Jr, 12 June 2009.
James Grady, 10 October 2009.

Newspaper and Periodical Articles

In Chronological Order

Zanuck, Darryl F. 'Do Writers Know Hollywood?: The Message Cannot Overwhelm the Technique', *The Saturday Review*, 30 October 1943, p. 12.

Pryor, Thomas M., 'By Way of Report; Checking Up on U.S. Movies Abroad – A Note on the Atom Secret – Other Items', *The New York Times*, 12 August 1945.
'U.S. Pictures Sets "Cloak and Dagger"', *Hollywood Reporter*, 3 October 1945.
Ford, Corey, and MacBain, Alistair, 'Cloak and Dagger', *Collier's*, 6 October 1945.
Carroll, Harrison, 'House on 92nd St. Is Greatest Spy Picture', *Herald Express*, 19 October 1945.
Schallert, Edwin, 'Gen. Donovan Will Play "Cloak and Dagger" Role', *Los Angeles Times*, 30 November 1945.
'Five 20th-Fox Employees to Aid "O.S.S." Advisors', *Hollywood Reporter*, 30 April 1946.
Crowther, Bosley, 'The Screen: "O.S.S." War Spy Thriller, with Alan Ladd, Miss Fitzgerald in Leading Roles, Makes its Appearance at the Gotham', *The New York Times*, 27 May 1946.
'Cloak and Dagger', *Independent Film Journal*, 14 September 1946.
'"Cloak and Dagger" Story of OSS Agent Has Excitement', *Film Bulletin*, 14 September 1946.
Crowther, Bosley, 'The Screen: "Cloak and Dagger," with Gary Cooper and Lilli Palmer, New Actress from England, in the Lead Roles, Arrives at Strand', *The New York Times*, 5 October 1946.
'Lang Strives for Reality: Director is Unique for Mastery of Violence, Tense Action in Films', *Morning Telegraph*, 29 October 1946.
Barnes, Howard, 'On the Screen', *New York Herald Tribune*, 16 January 1947.
Crowther, Bosley, 'The Screen', *The New York Times*, 16 January 1947.
Hale, Wand, '"13 Rue Madeleine" is Thrilling OSS Drama', *Daily News*, 16 January 1947.
'The Man with the Innocent Air', *Time Magazine*, 3 August 1953.
Harkness, Richard and Harkness, Gladys, 'The Mysterious Doings of the CIA', *Saturday Evening Post*, 13 November 1954.
'Soviet Pays Taxes, Ends L.I. "Cold War"', *The New York Times*, 24 December 1955.
Davis, Robert Gorham, 'In Our Time No Man is Neutral', *The New York Times*, 11 March 1956.
McNair, Marie, 'Dragon Visits "Quiet American"', *The Washington Post*, 23 January 1958.
Fleming, Ian, 'Gary Powers and the Big Lie', *The Sunday Times*, 11 March 1962.
Kirsch, Robert, 'James Bond Appeal?: It's Elementary, Watson', *Los Angeles Times Calendar*, 22 August 1963.
'Allen Dulles and Ian Fleming: A Redbook Dialogue', *Redbook Magazine*, June 1964.
Dulles, Allen, 'Our Spy-Boss Who Loved Bond', *Life Magazine*, 28 August 1964.
Braden, Thomas W., 'I'm Glad the CIA is Immoral', *The Saturday Evening Post*, 20 May 1967.
'The President's Analyst – Film Review', *Variety*, 20 December 1967.
Hadden, Jeffery, '"Beat" Poet Testifies in CIA Case', *The Detroit News*, 15 January 1971.
Lewis, Flora, 'Ginsberg-McGovern Question CIA Smack Smuggling', *Daily Planet*, 10 June 1972.
Schickel, Richard, 'We're Living in a Hitchcock World All Right', *The New York Times*, 29 October 1972.
Well, Fran, '"The Spook Who Sat By the Door" Director Shocked by "Extreme Reaction" to Film', *The Boston Herald Traveller and Record American*, 5 October 1973.
Meyer, Kantor, 'This "Spook" Has No Respect for Human Life', *The New York Times*, 11 November 1973.

Daniel, Clifton, 'Rockefeller Panel and its C.I.A. Mission', *The New York Times*, 20 January 1975.
Biskind, Peter, 'Does the U.S. Have the Right to Subpoena a Film in Progress', *The New York Times*, 22 June 1975.
Buckley Jr, William F., 'The Case of Robert Redford vs. the C.I.A.', *The New York Times*, 28 September 1975.
Folkart, Burt A., 'Alvah Bessie, Blacklisted By Studies, Dies', *Los Angeles Times*, 24 July 1985.
'Obituary of Michael Burke, 70; Spy, Ex-N.Y. Yankees President', *Los Angeles Times*, 7 February 1987.
Vosburgh, Dick, 'Obituary: Ben Maddow', *The Independent*, 14 October 1992.
Stein, Joel, 'Lying to Tell the Truth', *Time Magazine*, 13 January 2003.
Douthat, Ross, 'The Return of the Paranoid Style: How the Iraq War and George W. Bush Sent the Movie Industry Back to its Favorite Era – The 1970s', *The Atlantic*, April 2008.
Žižek, Slavoj, 'Good Manners in the Age of Wikileaks', *London Review of Books*, 33:2, 20 January 2011, pp. 9–10.
Xan Brooks, 'John McCain Criticises *Zero Dark Thirty*'s Depiction of Torture', *The Guardian*, 20 December 2012. Available online at <http://www.theguardian.com/film/2012/dec/20/john-mccain-zero-dark-thirty>, accessed 28 July 2015.
Mark Hosenball, 'Senate Panel to Examine CIA Contacts with "Zero Dark Thirty" Filmmakers', *Reuters*, 2 January 2013. Available online at <http://www.reuters.com/article/2013/01/03/us-usa-ciafilm-idUSBRE90200420130103>, accessed 28 July 2015.
Lehmann-Haupt, Christopher, 'Peter Matthiessen, Lyrical Writer and Naturalist, is Dead at 86', *The New York Times*, 5 April 2014.

Unpublished Master's and PhD Theses

McCarthy, David Shamus, *The CIA and the Cult of Secrecy* (William and Mary College, Doctoral Dissertation, 2008).
Petrocalli, Heather Oriana, *Portland's 'Refugee from Occupied Hollywood': Andries Deinum, his Center for the Moving Image, and Film Education in the United States* (Department of History, Portland State University, Master's Thesis). Available online at http://pdxscholar.library.pdx.edu/open_access_etds/608, accessed 27 February 2014.

Books

Alsop, Stewart and Braden, Thomas, *Sub Rosa: The O.S.S. and American Espionage* (New York: Reynal and Hitchcock, 1946).
Andrew, Christopher, *For the President's Eyes Only: Secret Intelligence and the American Presidency from Washington to Bush* (New York: HarperCollins, 1996).
Andrew, Christopher, *The Defence of the Realm: The Authorized History of MI5* (London: Penguin, 2010).
Ankersmit, Frank, *History and Tropology: The Rise and Fall of Metaphor* (Berkeley: University of California Press, 1994).
Arendt, Hannah, *The Origins of Totalitarianism*, new edition (New York: Harcourt Brace, 1973).
Badiou, Alan, *The Century*, trans. Alberto Toscano (New York: Polity Press, 2007).

Ballard, J. G. *Miracles of Life: An Autobiography* (New York: Liveright, 2013).
Bancroft, Mary, *Autobiography of a Spy* (New York: William Morrow, 1983).
Barnouw, Erik, *The Image Empire: A History of Broadcasting in the United States: From 1953, Volume 3* (Oxford: Oxford University Press, 1985).
Barris, Chuck, *Confessions of a Dangerous Mind*, new edition (New York: Ebury Press, 2002).
Bazin, André, *What is Cinema*, volume one, revised edition (Berkeley: University of California Press, 2004).
Bigger, Phillip J., *Negotiator: The Life and Career of James B. Donovan* (Crenbury: Associated University Presses, 2006).
Bird, Kai, *American Prometheus: The Triumph and Tragedy of J. Robert Oppenheimer* (New York: Atlantic Books, 2009).
Birdwell, Michael E., *Celluloid Soldiers: Warner Brothers' Campaign against Nazism* (New York: New York University Press, 2001).
Blackstock, Nelson, *Cointelpro: The FBI's Secret War on Political Freedom* (New York: Pathfinder Press, 1988).
Bogdanovich, Peter, *Fritz Lang in America* (London: Studio Vista Limited, 1967).
Boime, Albert, *The Unveilling of the National Icons: A Plea for Patriotic Iconoclasm in a Nationalist Era* (Cambridge: Cambridge University Press, 1997).
Boyer, Paul, *By the Bomb's Early Light: American Thought and Culture at the Dawn of the Atomic Age* (Chapel Hill: The University of North Carolina Press, 1994).
Britton, Wesley, *Beyond Bond: Spies in Fiction and Film* (New York: Praeger, 2005).
Brooker, Keith, *Film and the American Left: A Research Guide* (Westport: Greenwood Publishing Group, 1999).
Brown, Anthony Cave, *The Last Hero: Wild Bill Donovan* (London: Times Books, 1982).
Brown, David S., *Richard Hofstadter: An Intellectual Biography* (Chicago: University of Chicago Press, 2006).
Brown, Jared, *Alan J. Pakula: His Films and His Life* (New York: Backstage Books, 2005).
Burgoyne, Robert, *Film Nation: Hollywood Looks at U.S. History*, second revised edition (Minneapolis: University of Minnesota Press, 2010).
Burke, Michael, *Outrageous Good Fortune* (New York: Little, Brown and Company, 1984).
Buzzanco, Robert, *Vietnam and the Transformation of American Life* (Hoboken: Blackwell Publishers, 1999).
Carré, John Le, *The Spy Who Came in from the Cold* (London: Victor Gollancz and Pan, 1963).
Casey, William, *Where and How the War Was Fought: An Armchair Tour of the American Revolution* (New York: Morrow, 1976).
Ceplair, Larry and Englund, Steven, *The Inquisition in Hollywood: Politics in the Film Community, 1930–60* (Champaign: University of Illinois Press, 2003).
Chester, Eric Thomas, *Covert Network: Progressives, the International Rescue Committee and the CIA* (New York: M. E. Sharpe, 1995).
Cockburn, Alexander, *Whiteout: CIA, Drugs and the Press* (New York: Verso Books, 1999).
Coffin, Lesley L., *Hitchcock's Stars: Alfred Hitchcock and the Hollywood Studio System* (Lanham: Rowman and Littlefield, 2014).
Colby, William and Forbath, Peter, *Honorable Men: My Life in the CIA* (New York: Simon and Schuster, 1978).
Comentale, Edward P., Stephen Watt and Skip Willman (eds), *Ian Fleming and James Bond: The Cultural Politics of 007* (Bloomington: Indiana University Press, 2005).

Corber, Robert J., *In the Name of National Security: Hitchcock, Homophobia and the Political Construction of Gender in Postwar America* (Durham, NC: Duke University Press, 1993).
Custen, George, *Bio/Pics: How Hollywood Constructed Public History*, (New Brunswick, NJ: Rutgers University Press, 1992).
Custen, George F., *Twentieth Century's Fox: Darryl F. Zanuck and the Culture of Hollywood* (New York: Basic Books, 1998).
Daugherty, William J., *Executive Secrets: Covert Action and the Presidency* (Lexington: University of Kentucky Press, 2004).
Dauth, Brian (ed.), *Joseph L. Mankiewicz Interviews* (Jackson: University of Mississippi Press, 2008).
Dawidoff, Nicholas, *The Catcher Was a Spy: The Mysterious Life of Moe Berg* (New York: Vintage, 2011).
Dean, Robert D., *Imperial Brotherhood: Gender and the Making of Cold War Foreign Policy* (Amherst: University of Massachusetts Press, 2003).
Delage, Christian, *Caught on Camera: Film in the Courtroom from the Nuremberg Trials to the Khmer Rouge*, trans Ralph Schoolcraft and Mary Byrd Kelly (Philadelphia: University of Pennsylvania Press, 2013).
DeLillo, Don, *The Names* (New York: Knopf, 1982).
DeLillo, Don, *Running Dog*, vintage reissue edition (New York: Vintage, 1989).
DeLillo, Don, *Libra* (London: Penguin Modern Classics, 2006).
Denning, Michael, *Cover Stories: Narrative and Ideology in the British Spy Thriller* (Abingdon: Routledge, 1987).
Derian, James Der, *Virtuous War: Mapping the Military-Industrial-Media-Entertainment Network* (New York: Routledge, 2009).
Diggins, John Patrick, *The Proud Decades: America in War and Peace, 1941–1960: America in War and Peace, 1941–1960* (New York: W. W. Norton and Company, 1989).
Douglas, Lawrence, *The Memory of Judgment: Making Law and History in the Trials of the Holocaust* (New Haven: Yale University Press, 2001).
Dudziak, Mary L., *Cold War Civil Rights: Race and the Image of American Democracy* (Princeton: Princeton University Press, 2002).
Dunlop, Richard, *Donovan: America's Master Spy* (New York: Skyhorse Publishing, 2014).
Durgnat, Raymond, *The Strange Case of Alfred Hitchcock*, (Boston: The MIT Press, 1978).
Eldridge, David, *Hollywood's History Films* (London: I. B. Tauris, 2006).
Ellison, Ralph, *The Invisible Man* (New York: Penguin Modern Classics, 2001).
Emery, Fred, *Watergate: The Corruption of American Politics and the Fall of Richard Nixon* (New York: Touchstone, 1994).
Engelhardt, Tom, *The End of Victory Culture: Cold War America and the Disillusioning of a Generation* (New York: Basic Books, 1996).
Evans, Peter William, *Carol Reed* (Manchester: Manchester University Press, 2005).
Evans, Robert, *The Kids Stay in the Picture*, (London: Aurum Press, 1994).
Fenster, Mark, *Conspiracy Theories: Secrecy and Power in American Culture* (Minneapolis: University of Minnesota Press, 2001).
Ferro, Marc, *Cinema and History*, trans. Naomi Greene (Detroit: Wayne State University Press, 1988).
Fielding, Raymond, *The American Newsreel, 1911–1967* (Norman: Oklahoma University Press, 1972).
Fielding, Raymond, *The March of Time, 1935–1951* (New York: Oxford University Press, 1978).

Fishgall, Gary, *Against Type: The Biography of Burt Lancaster* (New York: Scribner, 1995).
Ford, Corey and MacBain, Alistair, *Cloak and Dagger: The Secret Story of OSS* (New York: Random House, 1946).
Fousek, John, *To Lead the Free World: American Nationalism and the Cultural Roots of the Cold War* (Chapel Hill: University of North Carolina Press, 2000).
Freedman, Jonathon and Millington, Richard (eds), *Hitchcock's America* (Oxford, Oxford University Press, 1999).
Freeman, David, *The Last Days of Alfred Hitchcock: A Memoir Featuring the Entire Screenplay of Alfred Hitchcock's 'The Short Night'* (Woodstock: The Overlook Press, 1984).
Fulbright, Senator William, *The Pentagon Propaganda Machine* (New York: Liverlight Publishing, 1970).
Fuller, Samuel, *A Third Face* (New York: Alfred A. Knopf, 2002).
Garrow, David, *The FBI and Martin Luther King, Jr.* revised edition (New Haven: Yale University Press, 2006).
Geist, Kenneth L., *Pictures Will Talk: The Life and Films of Joseph L. Mankiewicz* (New York: Charles Scribner's Sons, 1978).
Gerth, H. H., (ed.), *From Max Weber: Essays in Sociology*, new edition (Abingdon: Routledge, 1991).
Giglio, James, *The Presidency of John F. Kennedy* (Lawrence: University of Kansas Press, 1991).
Greene, Graham, *Our Man in Havana*, new edition with introduction by Graham Greene (London: Heinemann, 1970).
Greene, Graham, *A Sort of Life* (London: Vintage, 1999).
Greene, Graham, *The Quiet American*, Graham Greene centennial edition (London: 2004).
Habermas, Jürgen, *The Structural Transformation of the Public Sphere: An Inquiry into a Category of Bourgeois Society*, trans. Thomas Burger (Cambridge, MA: MIT Press, 1989).
Hall, Roger, *You're Stepping on My Cloak and Dagger* (London: William Kimber and Co., 1958).
Harris, Mark, *Five Came Back: A Story of Hollywood and the Second World War* (New York: Penguin, 2014).
Hennessy, Peter, *The Secret State: Whitehall and the Cold War* (London: Penguin Press, 2002).
Hepburn, Allan, *Intrigue: Espionage and Culture* (New Haven: Yale University Press, 2005).
Herken, Gregg, *The Georgetown Set: Friends and Rivals in Cold War Washington* (New York: Knopf Publishing, 2014).
Hitz, Frederick P., *The Great Game: The Myths and Reality of Espionage* (New York: Vintage Press, 2005).
Hodgson, Geoffrey, *America in Our Time: From World War II to Nixon: What Happened and Why* (Princeton: Princeton University Press, 2005).
Hofstadter, Richard, *The Paranoid Style in American Politics and Other Essays* (New York: Random House, [1964] 2008).
Humphries, Reynold, *Hollywood's Blacklists: A Political and Cultural History* (Edinburgh: Edinburgh University Press, 2010).
Hunt, Lynn, *Writing History in the Global Era* (New York: W. W. Norton and Company, 2014).
Hutcheon, Linda, *A Poetics of Postmodernism: History, Theory, Fiction* (London: Routledge, 1988).

Jameson, Fredric, *The Political Unconscious: Narrative as a Socially Symbolic Act* (Ithaca: Cornell University Press, 1981).

Jameson, Fredric, *Postmodernism: Or, the Cultural Logic of Late Capitalism* (London: Verso, 1992).

Jeffrey, Keith, *MI6: The History of the Secret Intelligence Service, 1909–1949* (London: Bloomsbury, 2011).

Jeffreys-Jones, Rhodri, *Cloak and Doller: A History of American Secret Intelligence* (New Haven: Yale University Press, 2002).

Jeffreys-Jones, Rhodri, *The CIA and American Democracy*, third edition (New Haven: Yale University Press, 2003).

Jenkins, Tricia, *The CIA in Hollywood: How the Agency Shapes Film and Television* (Austin: University of Texas Press, 2012).

Johnson, Chalmers, *Blowback: The Costs and Consequences of American Empire* (London: Time Warner Paperbacks, 2002).

Kackman, Michael, *Citizen Spy: Television, Espionage, and Cold War Culture* (Minneapolis: University of Minnesota Press, 2005).

Kalat, David, *The Strange Case of Dr. Mabuse: A Study of the Twelve Films and Five Novels* (New York: McFarland and Company, 2005).

Katz, Barry, *Foreign Intelligence: Research and Analysis in the Office of Strategic Services, 1942–1945* (Cambridge, MA: Harvard University Press, 2013).

Kellner, Douglas and Streible, Dan (eds), *Emile de Antonio: A Reader* (Minneapolis: University of Minnesota Press, 2000).

Kinzer, Stephen, *The Brothers: John Foster Dulles, Allen Dulles, and Their Secret World War* (New York: Times Books, 2013).

Knight, Peter, *Conspiracy Culture: From Kennedy to the X-Files* (Abingdon: Routledge, 2001).

Koppes, Clayton and Black, Gregory, *Hollywood Goes to War: How Politics, Profits, and Propaganda Shaped World War II Movies* (Berkeley: The Free Press, 1987).

LaCapra, Dominick, *History and Criticism*, (Ithaca: Cornell University Press, 1985).

Landsberg, Alison, *Prosthetic Memory: The Transformation of American Remembrance in the Age of Mass Culture* (New York: Columbia University Press, 2004).

Laville, Helen, *Cold War Women: The International Activities of American Women's Organisations* (Manchester: Manchester University Press, 2009).

Laville, Helen and Wilford, Hugh (eds), *The US Government, Citizens Groups and the Cold War: The State-Private Network* (Abingdon: Routledge, 2006).

Leab, Daniel, *Orwell Subverted: The CIA and the Filming of Animal Farm* (State College: Pennsylvania State University Press, 2008).

Levi, Primo, *The Drowned and the Saved*, trans. R. Rosenthal (New York: Vintage, 1989).

Lewis, Roger, *Anthony Burgess* (New York: Faber and Faber, 2002).

Lucas, Scott, *Freedom's War: The American Crusade against the Soviet Union* (New York: New York University Press, 1999).

Lyotard, Jean-François, *The Postmodern Condition: A Report on Knowledge* (Manchester: Manchester University Press, 1984).

MacDonald, Elizabeth, *Undercover Girl* (New York: Macmillan, 1947).

McBride, Joseph, *John Ford: A Life* (New York: Faber and Faber, 2003).

McClure, John A., *Late Imperial Romance* (London: Verso, 1994).

McCoy, Alfred, *The Politics of Heroin in Southeast Asia* (New York: Harper and Row, 1972).

McGilligan, Patrick, *Fritz Lang: The Nature of the Beast* (Minneapolis: University of Minnesota Press, 2013).

McGilligan, Patrick and Buhle, Paul, *Tender Comrades: A Backstory of the Hollywood Blacklist* (Minneapolis: University of Minnesota Press, 2012).
McIntosh, Elizabeth P., *Sisterhood of Spies: The Women of the OSS* (Annapolis: Naval Institute Press, 2009).
Marchetti, Victor and Marks, John D., *The CIA and the Cult of Intelligence* (New York: Coronet Books, 1974).
Marwick, Arthur, *The Sixties: Social and Cultural Transformation in Britain, France, Italy and the United States, 1958–74* (Oxford: Oxford University Press, 1999).
Melley, Timothy, *The Covert Sphere: Secrecy, Fiction, and the National Security State* (Ithaca: Cornell University Press, 2012).
Miller, Toby, *Spyscreen: Espionage on Film and TV from the 1930s to the 1960s* (Oxford: Oxford University Press, 2003).
Monaco, Paul, *The Sixties: 1960–1969*, History of the American Cinema series (Berkeley: University of California Press, 2001).
Morgan, Iwan W., *Beyond the Liberal Consensus: A Political History of the United States since 1965* (London: Palgrave Macmillan, 1994).
Morgan, Joseph G., *The Vietnam Lobby: The American Friends of Vietnam, 1955–1975* (Chapel Hill: University of North Carolina Press, 1997).
Moynihan, Daniel Patrick, *Secrecy: The American Experience* (New Haven: Yale University Press, 1999).
Nadel, Alan, *Containment Culture: American Narratives, Postmodernism and the Atomic Age* (Durham, NC: Duke University Press, 1995).
Nashel, Jonathan, *Edward Lansdale's Cold War* (Amherst: University of Massachusetts Press, 2004).
Navasky, Victor S., *Naming Names* (New York: Hill and Wang, 2003).
Novick, Peter, *That Noble Dream: The 'Objectivity Question' and the American Historical Profession* (Cambridge: Cambridge University Press, 1988).
O'Donnell, Patrick K., *Operatives, Spies and Saboteurs: The Unknown Story of the Men and Women of World War II's OSS* (New York: Free Press, 2004).
Olmsted, Kathryn, *Challenging the Secret Government: The Post-Watergate Investigations of the CIA and FBI* (Chapel Hill: University of North Carolina Press, 1996).
Olmsted, Kathryn, *Real Enemies: Conspiracy Theories and American Democracy, World War I to 9/11* (Oxford: Oxford University Press, 2010).
Orwell, George, *Animal Farm*, fiftieth anniversary edition (New York: Signet, 2004).
O'Toole, G. J. A., *Honorable Treachery: A History of U.S. Intelligence, Espionage, and Covert Action from the American Revolution to the CIA* (New York: Grove Press, 2014).
Parish, James Robert and Pitts, Michael R., *The Great Spy Pictures* (Metuchen: Scarecrow Press, 1974).
Parrish, Robert, *Growing Up in Hollywood* (St Albans: Triad Paperbacks, 1976).
Parrish, Robert, *Hollywood Doesn't Live Here Anymore* (Boston: Little, Brown and Company, 1988).
Perlstein, Rick, *Nixonland: The Rise of a President and the Fracturing of America* (New York: Scribner, 2008).
Phillips, Gene, *Graham Greene: The Films of his Fiction* (New York: Teachers College Press).
Popper, Karl, *The Open Society and Its Enemies*, new edition (Abingdon: Routledge Classics, 2011).
Porter, Bernard, *Plots and Paranoia: A History of Political Espionage in Britain, 1790–1988* (Abingdon: Routledge, 1989).
Potter, David, *People of Plenty: Economic Abundance and the American Character* (Chicago: University of Chicago Press, 1958).

Powers, Richard Gid, *G-Men: Hoover's FBI in American Popular Culture* (Carbondale: Southern Illinois University Press, 1983).
Prados, John, *The Family Jewels: The CIA, Secrecy, and Presidential Power* (Austin: University of Texas Press, 2013).
Pratt, Ray, *Projecting Paranoia: Conspiratorial Visions in American Film* (Lawrence: University of Kansas Press, 2002).
Prenshaw, Peggy Whitman (ed.), *Conversations with William Buckley* (Minneapolis: University of Minnesota Press, 2009).
Radosh, Ronald and Radosh, Allis, *Red Star over Hollywood: The Film Conlony's Long Romance with the Left* (New York: Encounter Books, 2006).
Ranelagh, John, *The Agency: The Rise and Decline of the CIA: From Wild Bill Donovan to William Casey* (New York: Simon and Schuster, 1986).
Rentschler, Eric, *The Ministry of Illusion: Nazi Cinema and Its Afterlife* (New Haven: Yale University Press, 1996).
Resch, Robert Paul, *Althusser and the Renewal of Marxist Social Theory* (Berkeley: University of California Press, 1992).
Ricoeur, Paul, *Time and Narrative*, three volumes (Chicago: University of Chicago Press, 1984, 1985, 1988).
Rizzo, John, *Company Man: Thirty Years of Controversy and Crisis in the CIA* (New York: Scribner, 2014).
Rogers, Daniel T., *Age of Fracture* (Cambridge, MA: Harvard University Press, 2012).
Rollins, Peter C., (ed.), *The Columbia Companion to American History on Film* (New York: Columbia University Press, 2005).
Rosenstone, Robert, *Visions of the Past: The Challenge of Film to Our Idea of History* (Boston: Harvard University Press, 1995).
Rosenstone, Robert, *History on Film/Film on History* (London: Longman Pearson, 2006).
Russo, William, *A Thinker's Damn: Audie Murphy, Vietnam, and the Making of the Quiet American* (New York: Xlibris, 2001).
Salter, Michael, *Nazi War Crimes: US Intelligence and Selective Prosecution at Nuremberg: Controversies Regarding the Role of the Office of Strategic Services* (Abingdon: Routledge, 2007).
Sarris, Andrew, *The American Cinema: Directors and Directions, 1929–1968* (New York: Da Capo Press, 1968).
Saunders, Frances Stonor, *Who Paid the Piper: The CIA and the Cultural Cold War* (London: Granta, 1999).
Sayre, Nora, *Running Time: Films of the Cold War* (New York: Doubleday, 1982).
Sbardellati, John, *J. Edgar Hoover Goes to the Movies: The FBI and the Origins of Hollywood's Cold War* (Ithaca: Cornell University Press, 2012).
Schlesinger Jr, Arthur M., *The Vital Center: The Politics of Freedom*, new edition (New York: Da Capo Press, 1988).
Schwartz, Rosalie, *Flying Down to Rio: Hollywood, Tourists, and Yankee Clippers* (College Station: A&M University Press, 2004).
Scott-Smith, Giles, *The Politics of Apolitical Culture: The Congress for Cultural Freedom and the Political Economy of American Hegemony, 1945–1955* (Abingdon: Routledge, 2001).
Shaheen, Jack G., *Reel Bad Arabs: How Hollywood Vilifies a People* (New York: Interlink Books, 2015).
Shapiro, Jerome F., *Atomic Bomb Cinema* (London: Routledge, 2002).
Shaw, Tony, *British Cinema and the Cold War: The State, Propaganda and Consensus* (London: I. B. Tauris, 2001).
Shaw, Tony, *Hollywood's Cold War* (Edinburgh: Edinburgh University Press, 2007).

Sherry, Norman, *The Life of Graham Greene, Volume 3: 1955–1991* (London: Random House, 2005).
Silverman, Stephen M., *Dancing on the Ceiling: Stanley Donen and his Movies* (New York: Alfred Knopf, 1996).
Simone, Sam P., *Hitchcock as Activist: Politics and the War Films* (Ann Arbor: UMI Research Press, 1985).
Sinyard, Neil, *Filming Literature: The Art of Screen Adaptation* (Abingdon: Routledge, 2013).
Sloan, Jane E., *Alfred Hitchcock: A Filmography and Bibliography* (Berkeley: University of California Press, 1995).
Smith, Bradley F., *The Shadow Warriors: O.S.S. and the Origins of the C.I.A.* (London: André Deutsch, 1983).
Smith, Richard Harris, *OSS: The Secret History of America's First Central Intelligence Agency* (Berkeley: University of California Press, 1972).
Smyth, Jennifer E., *Reconstructing American Historical Cinema from Cimarron to Citizen Kane* (Lexington: University Press of Kentucky, 2006).
Smyth, Jennifer E. (ed.), *Hollywood and the American Historical Film* (London: Palgrave Macmillan, 2011).
Stafford, David, *The Silent Game: The Real World of Imaginary Spies*, (London: Viking Press, 1989).
Stephanson, Anders, *Manifest Destiny: American Expansion and the Empire of Rights* (New York: Hill and Wang Critical Issues, 1996).
Suid, Lawrence, *Guts and Glory: The Making of the American Military Image in Film*, second revised edition (Lexington: University of Kentucky Press, 2002).
Taylor, John Russell, *Hitch: The Life and Times of Alfred Hitchcock* (New York: Pantheon, 1978).
Tegel, Susan, *Nazis and the Cinema* (London: Bloomsbury Continuum, 2007).
Thomas, Evan, *Robert Kennedy: His Life* (New York: Simon and Schuster, 2002).
Toplin, Robert Brent, *Reel History: In Defense of Hollywood* (Lawrence: University Press of Kansas, 2002).
Troy, Thomas F., *Donovan and the CIA: A History of the Establishment of the Central Intelligence Agency* (Frederick: University Publication of America, 1996).
Vaughn, Robert, *Only Victims: Study of Show Business Blacklisting*, second revised edition (New York: Limelight Editions, 1996).
Virilio, Paul, *War and Cinema: The Logistics of Perception* (London: Verso, 2009).
Wallace, Robert, Melton, Keith and Schlesinger, Henry Robert, *Spycraft: Inside the CIA's Top Secret Laboratory* (London: Bantam Press, 2009).
Waller, Douglas, *Wild Bill Donovan: The Spymaster Who Created the OSS and Modern American Espionage* (New York: Simon and Schuster, 2012).
Weiner, Tim, *Legacy of Ashes: The History of the CIA* (New York: Doubleday, 2007).
Welky, David, *The Moguls and the Dictators: Hollywood and the Coming of World War II* (Baltimore: Johns Hopkins University Press, 2008).
White, Hayden, *Metahistory: The Historical Imagination in the Nineteenth Century* (Baltimore: Johns Hopkins University Press, 1973).
White, Hayden, *Tropics of Discourse: Essays in Cultural Criticism* (Baltimore: Johns Hopkins University Press, 1978).
White, Hayden, *The Content of the Form: Narrative Discourse and Historical Representation*, paperback edition (London: Johns Hopkins University Press, 1990).
White, Patrick J., *The Complete Mission: Impossible Dossier* (New York: Avon Books, 1996).
Wilford, Hugh, *The CIA, The British Left and the Cold War: Calling the Tune?* (London: Frank Cass, 2003).

Wilford, Hugh, *The Mighty Wurlitzer: How the CIA Played America* (Cambridge, MA: Harvard University Press, 2009).
Winks, Robin, *Cloak and Gown: Scholars in America's Secret War* (London: The Harvill Press, 1987).
Wise, David and Ross, Thomas, *The Invisible Government* (London: Jonathon Cape, 1964).
Wood, Robin, *Hitchcock's Films* (New York: New York Castle Books, 1969).
Wood, Robin, *Hitchcock's Films Revisited* (New York: Columbia University Press, 2002).
Zanuck, Darryl F., *Tunis Expedition* (New York: Random House, 1943).
Zwerling, Philip (ed.), *The CIA on Campus: Essays on Academic Freedom and the National Security State* (New York: McFarland and Co., 2011).

Scholarly Articles and Book Chapters

Achebe, Chinua, 'An Image of Africa: Racism in Conrad's "Heart of Darkness"', *Massachusetts Review*, 18:4 (1977), pp. 782–94.
Aldrich, Richard J., 'Policing the Past: Official History, Secrecy and British Intelligence since 1945', *English Historical Review*, 119:483 (2004), pp. 922–53.
Aldrich, Richard J., 'American Journalism and the Landscape of Secrecy: Tad Szulc, the CIA and Cuba', *History: The Journal of the Historical Association*, 100:340 (April 2015), pp. 189–209.
Bazin, André, 'On Why We Fight: History, Documentation, and the Newsreel (1946)', trans. and ed. Bert Cardullo, reprinted in *Film and History: An Interdisciplinary Journal of Film and Television Studies*, 31:1 (2001), pp. 60–2.
Bedard, B. J., 'Reunion in Havana', *Literature Film Quarterly*, 4:2 (1974), pp. 352–8.
Braun, Robert, 'The Holocaust and the Problems of Historical Representation', *History and Theory*, 33:2 (May 1994), pp. 172–97.
Bushnell, William S., 'Paying for the Damage: The Quiet American Revisited', *Film and History: An Interdisciplinary Journal of Film and Television Studies*, 36:2 (spring 2006), pp. 38–44.
Cady, Susan A., 'Microfilm Technology and Information Systems', in Mary Bowden, Trudi Hahn and Robert Williams (eds), *Proceedings of the 1998 Conferences on the History and Heritage of Science Information Systems* (Melford: Information Today ASIS Monograph Series, 1999), pp. 182–4.
Deutsch, James, '"I Was a Hollywood Agent": Cinematic Representations of the Office of Strategic Services in 1946', *Intelligence and National Security*, 13:2 (1998), pp. 85–99.
Douglas, Ann, 'Periodizing the American Century: Modernism, Postmodernism and Postcolonialism in the Cold War Context', *Modernism/Modernity*, 5:3 (September 1998), pp. 71–98.
Douglas, Lawrence, 'Film as Witness: Screening *Nazi Concentration Camps* before the Nuremberg Tribunal', *Yale Law Journal*, 105 (1994), pp. 449–81.
Dujmovic, Nicholas, '"Hollywood, Don't You Go Disrepectin My Culture": *The Good Shepherd* versus Real CIA History', *Intelligence and National Security: Special Issue on Spying in Film and Fiction*, 23:1 (February 2008), pp. 25–41.
Dunne, Phillip, 'The Documentary and Hollywood', *Hollywood Quarterly*, 1:2 (January 1946), pp. 166–72.
Dynia, Philip, 'Alfred Hitchcock and the Ghost of Thomas Hobbes', *Cinema Journal*, 15:2 (1976), pp. 27–41.
Eldridge, David, 'Dear Owen: The CIA, Luigi Luraschi and Hollywood, 1953', *Historical Journal of Film, Radio and Television*, 20:2 (2000), pp. 149–96.

Fellner, Michael, 'Emile de Antonio's CIA Diary (1975)', in Douglas Kellner and Dan Streible (eds), *Emile de Antonio: A Reader* (Minneapolis: University of Minnesota Press, 2000), pp. 361–4.

Ferrara, Patricia, 'Discontented Bourgeois: Bourgeois Morality and the Interplay of Light and Dark Strains in Hitchcock's Films', *New Orleans Review* 14:4 (1987), pp. 79–87.

Fisher, James T., '"A World Made Safe for Diversity": The Vietnam Lobby and the Politics of Pluralism, 1945–1963', in Christian Appy (ed.), *Cold War Constructions: The Political Culture of U.S. Imperialism* (Amherst: University of Massachusetts Press, 2000), pp. 217–37.

Foran, John, 'Discursive Subversions: Time Magazine, the CIA Overthrow of Mussadiq, and the Installation of the Shah', in Christian G. Appy (ed.), *Cold War Constructions: The Political Culture of U.S. Imperialism* (Amherst: University of Massachusetts Press, 2000), pp. 157–82.

Grady, James, 'Rhyme', preface to Grady, *Six Days of The Condor* (Aylesbury: No Exit Press, 2007), pp. i–xvi.

Hark, Ina Rae, 'Keeping Your Amateur Standing: Audience Participation and Good Citizenship in Hitchcock's Political Films', *Cinema Journal*, 29:2 (winter 1990), pp. 8–22.

Hedley, John Hollister, 'Twenty Years of the Officers in Residence: CIA in the Classroom', *Studies in Intelligence*, 94:4 (November 2005), pp. 31–40.

Hulme, Peter, 'Graham Greene and Cuba: Our Man in Havana', *New West Indian Guide*, 82:3–4 (2008), pp. 185–209.

Immerman, Richard, 'Intelligence Studies: The British Invasion', *History: The Journal of the Historical Association*, 100:340 (April 2015), pp. 163–6.

Jameson, Fredric, 'Periodizing the 60s', *Social Text*, 9:10 (1984), pp. 178–209.

Jameson, Fredric, 'Totality as Conspiracy', in Fredric Jameson, *The Geopolitical Aesthetic: Cinema and Space in the World System* (Bloomington: Indiana University Press, 1992), pp. 9–84.

Katz, Barry, 'The Arts of War: "Visual Presentation" and National Intelligence', *Design Issues*, 12:2 (summer 1996), pp. 3–21.

Lethier, Pierre, 'The Clandestine Clapperboard: Alfred Hitchcock's Tales of the Cold War', in Robert Dover and Michael Goodman (eds), *Spinning Intelligence: Why Intelligence Needs the Media, Why the Media Needs Intelligence* (London: C. Hurst & Co., 2009), pp. 185–200.

Linfield, Susan, 'Irrepressible Emile de Antonio Speaks (1982)', in Douglas Kellner and Dan Streible (eds), *Emile de Antonio: A Reader* (Minneapolis: University of Minnesota Press, 2000), pp. 113–23.

Little, Douglas, 'Mission Impossible: The CIA and the Cult of Covert Action in the Middle East', *Diplomatic History*, 28:5 (2004), pp. 663–701.

McGilligan, Patrick, '*Three Days of the Condor*: Hollywood Uncovers the CIA, Sidney Pollack Interviewed', *Jump Cut*, 10–11 (1976), pp. 11–12.

Marable, Manning, 'Race, Identity, and Political Culture', in Michele Wallace (ed.), *Black Popular Culture* (Seattle: Bay Press, 1992), p. 292.

Moran, Christopher, 'The Pursuit of Intelligence History: Methods, Sources, and Trajectories in the United Kingdom', *Studies in Intelligence*, 55:2 (June 2011), pp. 33–5.

Moran, Christopher R., 'Ian Fleming and the Public Profile of the CIA', *Journal of Cold War Studies*, 15:1 (winter 2013a), pp. 119–46.

Moran, Christopher R., 'The Last Assignment: David Atlee Phillips and the Birth of CIA Public Relations', *International History Review*, 35:2 (2013b), pp. 337–55.

Moss, John E., 'The Crisis of Sececy', *Bulletin of the Atomic Scientists*, 17:1 (January 1961), pp. 8–11.

Nolan, Cynthia M., 'Seymour Hersh's Impact on the CIA', *International Journal of Intelligence and Counterintelligence*, 12:1 (1999), pp. 18–34.

Parmar, Inderjeet, 'Conceptualising the State-Private Network', in Helen Laville and Hugh Wilford (eds), *The US Government, Citizen Groups and the Cold War: The State-Private Network* (Abingdon: Routledge, 2006), pp. 14–15.

Rosenstone, Robert, 'History in Images/History in Words: Reflections on the Possibility of Really Putting History onto Film', *American Historical Review*, 93:5 (1988), pp. 1,173–85.

Rubenstein, Lenny, 'The Politics of Spy Films', *Cineaste*, 9:3 (1979), pp. 16–21.

Rudgers, David, 'The Origins of Covert Action', *Journal of Contemporary History*, 35:2 (April 2000), pp. 249–62.

Salt, Barry, 'Film Style and Technology in the Forties', *Film Quarterly*, 31:1 (1977), pp. 46–57.

Sklar, Bob, 'Does Film History Need a Crisis?', *Cinema Journal*, 44:1 (autumn 2004), pp. 134–8.

Sobchack, Vivian C., '*The Grapes of Wrath* (1940): Thematic Emphasis through Visual Style', *American Quarterly*, 31:5 (winter 1976), pp. 596–615.

Sontag, Susan, 'Notes on "Camp"', in Susan Sontag, *Against Interpretation and Other Essays* (London: Penguin Modern Classics, 2009), pp. 275–92.

Susman, Warren, 'Film and History: Artifact and Experience', *Film and History*, 15:2 (May 1985), pp. 26–36.

Taylor, Stan A., 'Introduction: Spying in Film and Fiction', *Intelligence and National Security: Special Issue on Spying in Film and Fiction*, 23:1 (2008), p. 1–4.

Urban, Hugh, 'The Torment of Secrecy: Ethical and Epistemological Problems in the Study of Esoteric Traditions', *History of Religions*, 37:3 (February 1998), pp. 209–48.

Valero, Larry, '"We Need Our New OSS, Our New General Donovan, Now . . .": The Public Discourse over American Intelligence, 1944–53', *Intelligence and National Security*, 18:1 (2003), pp. 91–118.

Vries, Tity de, 'The 1967 Central Intelligence Agency Scandal: Catalyst in a Transforming Relationship between State and People', *Journal of American History*, 98:4 (2012), pp. 1,075–92.

Walker, Michael, 'The Old Age of Alfred Hitchcock,' *Movie*, 18:1 (1970), pp. 10–13.

Wark, Wesley, 'Introduction: Fictions of History', *Intelligence and National Security*, 5:4 (1990), pp. 7–16.

Wasser, Frederick, 'Is Hollywood America? The Trans-nationalization of the American Film Industry', *Critical Studies in Mass Communication*, 12:4 (1995), pp. 423–37.

Wesley Wark, 'Introduction: Fictions of History', *Intelligence and National Security*, 5:4 (1990), pp. 7–16.

White, Hayden, 'Historiography and Historiophoty', *American Historical Review*, 93:5, (1988), pp. 1,193–9.

Wilford, Hugh, 'Secret America: The CIA and American Culture', in C. W. E. Bigsby (ed.), *The Cambridge Companion to Modern American Culture* (Cambridge: Cambridge University Press, 2006), p. 278.

Willmetts, Simon, 'Reconceiving Realism: Intelligence Historians and the Fact/Fiction Dichotomy', in Christopher Moran and Christopher J. Murphy (eds), *Intelligence Studies in Britain and the US: Historiography since 1945* (Edinburgh: Edinburgh University Press, 2013a), pp. 146–71.

Willmetts, Simon, 'Quiet Americans: The CIA and Early Cold War Hollywood Cinema', *Journal of American Studies*, 47:1 (2013b), pp. 127–47.

Willmetts, Simon, 'The Burgeoning Fissures of Dissent: Allen Dulles and the Selling of the CIA in the Aftermath of the Bay of Pigs', *History: The Journal of the Historical Association*, 100:340 (April 2015a), pp. 167–88.

Willmetts, Simon, 'The CIA and the Invention of Tradition', *Journal of Intelligence History*, 14:2 (May 2015b), pp. 112–28.
Willmetts, Simon and Moran, Christopher, 'Filming Treachery: British Cinema and Television's Fascination with the Cambridge Five', *The Journal of British Cinema and Television*, 10:1 (January 2013), pp. 49–70.
Witanek, Robert, 'The CIA on Campus', *Covert Action Information Bulletin*, no. 31 (1998), pp. 25–8.
Woodward, Comer Vann, 'The Age of Reinterpretation', *American Historical Review*, 66:1 (October 1960), pp. 1–19.
Worland, Rick, 'The Cold War Mannerists: The Man from U.N.C.L.E. and TV Espionage in the 1960s', *Journal of Popular Film and Television*, 21:4 (winter 1994), pp. 150–61.
Zegart, Amy, 'Cloaks, Daggers, and Ivory Towers: Why Academics Don't Study U.S. Intelligence', in Loch Johnson (ed.), *Strategic Intelligence: Understanding the Hidden Side of Government*, volume one (Westport: Praeger Publishers, 2006), pp. 21–32.
Zone, Ray, 'Vintage Instruments', *American Cinematographer* 84:1 (2003), p. 104.

Websites

Jonathan Nashel Public Lecture, 'James Bond as an American Hero'. Available online at <http://www.c-span.org/video/?314705-1/james-bond-american-hero>, accessed 10 March 2015.
'Nuremberg: Its Lessons for Today'. Available online at <http://www.nurembergfilm.org/films_within_film.shtml> accessed 31 March 2015.
Proceedings of the Nuremberg Trials at 'The Avalon Project: Documents in Law, History and Diplomacy', Yale Law School. Available online at <http://avalon.law.yale.edu/subject_menus/imtproc_v1menu.asp>, accessed 31 March 2015.
'Public Trust in Government: 1958–2014', Pew Research Center US Politics and Policy. Available online at <http://www.people-press.org/2014/11/13/public-trust-in-government>, accessed 30 March 2015.
'The Fans from U.N.C.L.E.' Available online at <http://www.manfromuncle.org>, accessed 20 November 2014.

FILM AND TELEVISION INDEX

13 Rue Madeleine, 1–5, 7–10, 13, 18, 78, 85–6, 93–4, 102–14, 131, 201, 265, 273, 275–7
39 Steps, The, 186

All the President's Men, 134, 222, 252
Animal Farm, 139–40
Apocalypse Now, 226–7
Argo, 140–1
At the Front in North Africa, 55–7

Bananas, 229
Batman (TV series), 199
Battle of Midway, 23–9, 46, 47, 49–50, 55, 84, 193, 275
Behind Closed Doors, 131, 160
Breakout, 224

Charade, 121, 134, 192–3, 209
Citizen Kane, 33, 103, 131, 192, 193, 209
Cloak and Dagger, 78, 84–5, 89–102, 105, 107, 110, 113
Clockwork Orange, A, 244, 246
Confessions of a Dangerous Mind, 141
Confessions of a Nazi Spy, 53, 60, 103, 141

Conversation, The, 228
Counterfeit Traitor, The, 128

December 7th, 46–51
Desert Victory, 55
Dillinger, 227
Dirty Dozen, The, 94
Dr. Mabuse, 89
Dr. No, 194
Dr. Strangelove, 37, 183, 208

Fallen Idol, The, 186
F.B.I., The (TV series), 227
FBI Story, The, 128
Fighting 69th, 44
From Russia With Love, 194

Get Smart (TV series), 179, 192, 200–4
Grapes of Wrath, The, 25–7, 33, 130
Green Berets, 226

Hearts and Minds, 235
Heroes of Telemark, 98
Hotel Berlin, 92
House on 92nd Street, The, 103–5, 108, 131

297

I Led Three Lives, 128
I Spy (TV series), 192, 196, 211, 239
In-Laws, The, 229
In Like Flint, 177, 179–80, 192, 202, 204
IPCRESS File, The, 11, 241

JFK, 4–5
John Goldfarb, Please Come Home, 132–3, 203

Killer Elite, The, 226, 252
King Kong, 30
Kremlin Letter, The, 241

Lady Vanishes, The, 186
Lost Patrol, The, 30

M, 89
Man Called X, The, 129–30
Man from U.N.C.L.E., The (TV series), 122–3, 177–80, 188, 192–202, 204, 207, 212, 239
Man on a String, 134
Marathon Man, 198, 231
Medium Cool, 240
Metropolis, 89
Mission Impossible (TV series), 178–9
Monuments Men, The, 94
My Favorite Spy, 127
My Son John, 95

Native Land, 93
Nazi Concentration Camps, 62–70, 88
Nazi Supreme Court Trial of the Anti-Hitler Plot, 59–60
Network, 222
Nixon, 134
North by Northwest, 11–12, 114, 121–2, 135–6, 163, 180–1, 184–98, 204, 212–13, 242, 244
Northern Pursuit, 92
Nothing But a Man, 239
Notorious, 98, 128

Objective Burma, 92
Operation C.I.A., 134
O.S.S., 78, 84–9, 107, 110
Osterman Weekend, 226
Our Man in Havana, 14, 181–5

Parallax View, The, 12, 222, 229, 231, 241–8
Pick Up On South Street, 128
President's Analyst, The, 11, 134, 184, 204–15

Quiet American, The, 14, 142–63, 181–2, 184, 186, 234

Rio Grande, 84

Scorpio, 225–6, 232–6, 241, 252, 261
Secret Agent, 186
Selling of the Pentagon, The, 235–6
Short Night, The, 12, 192
Spione, 89, 177
Spook Who Sat by the Door, The, 236–41, 252, 264
Spy Who Came in from the Cold, The, 11, 181, 241
Superfly, 240
Sweet Sweetback's Baadasssss Song, 240

That Justice Be Done, 60
They Were Expendable, 58
Third Man, The, 186
Three Days of the Condor, 227–8, 231, 248–55, 258–9, 262–5, 277
Triumph of the Will, 59
Topaz, 12, 192, 234, 242
Torn Curtain, 12, 191, 242

Walk East on Beacon, 105, 128, 131
Why We Fight, 26

Zero Dark Thirty, 8, 15, 46

GENERAL INDEX

Academy of Motion Pictures Arts and Sciences (includes Academy Awards), 47, 52, 141
Afghanistan, CIA covert action in, 224, 261
African Americans, representation of, 206, 210–12, 236–41
Agee, Philip, 255–64
Allen, Woody, 229
Allende, Salvadore, 158, 242
Alsop, Carleton, 138
Alsop, Stewart, 79
Althusser, Louis, 16–17
Ambler, Eric, 193
American Friends of Vietnam (AFV), 144, 154
'Ann Arbor Three', 202–3
Araner (yacht), 30
Arbenz, Jacobo, 124–5
Argosy Pictures, 44, 80, 84
Armistead, Mark, 24, 32
assassination, 6, 13, 130, 172, 223, 225, 227, 229, 234, 239, 243, 245, 247, 249, 259, 262; *see also* Kennedy, President John F.

Association of Former Intelligence Officers (AFIO), 235, 262–3
atomic weapons (representation of), 93, 95–102, 104, 122, 183–4, 187, 208–9
August, Joseph, 33

Badiyi, Reza, 178
Ballard, J. G., 22
Bancroft, Mary, 159–62
Barnes, Tracy, 128
Bartlett, Sy, 105–6
Batievsky, Bernardo, 260
Baudrillard, Jean, 209
Bay of Pigs, 14–16, 124–6, 132, 171–6, 181, 193, 229, 254, 273, 276
Bazin, André, 28, 35, 69
Beatty, Warren, 222, 245–6
Bentley, Elizabeth, 187
Berg, Moe, 45
Bessie, Alvah, 90, 92–4
Beugnon, Raphael, 83
Blake, George, 192
Blaxploitation, 237–40
Blunt, Anthony, 182
Bogdanovich, Peter, 98, 101

Bolton, Alfred J., 33–4
Bond, James, 11–12, 15, 88, 134, 170–3, 179–81, 184, 192–6, 198, 200, 209, 214, 241–2, 260
Bourne, Jason, 7, 249
Boyer, Paul, 99–101
Braden, Thomas, 79, 201
Breen, Joseph, 108, 124–5
Britain, 35, 66
  relations with US, 22, 40, 43–4, 53, 55, 82, 88, 96, 107, 124, 155
  spy fiction of, 11–12, 14, 16, 30, 139, 143, 145, 171, 181, 182, 185–6, 192–4, 241
Brown, Anthony Cave, 43, 44, 48, 81
Bruce, David, 80
Buckley, William F., 252, 263
Burke, Amos, 179
Burke, Michael, 84, 93, 96–8
Burke, Walter, 212–13
Burton, Richard, 241
Bush, George H. W., 252, 255, 263

Cagney, James, 44, 56, 86, 102, 106
Caine, Michael, 241
Cambridge, Godfrey, 209–12
Cambridge Spies, 12, 14, 182, 191
camp style (politics and aesthetics of), 11, 177, 180, 184, 192, 199, 201–2, 204–9, 214, 229, 241, 264, 275–6
Carroll, Leo G., 122, 178, 188–9, 198
Carroll, Mike, 80, 84, 106–7, 110
Casey, William, 41, 122, 264
Castro, Fidel
  CIA assassination attempts on, 124, 171–2
  and Hollywood, 174, 184–5
Central Intelligence Agency (CIA)
  and American core values, 6, 160
  Congressional oversight of, 5, 125–6, 159–60, 172, 215, 222–5, 234; *see also* Church Committee *and* Pike Committee
  covert action (and myth of), 10, 15, 124–7, 129–30, 170–5, 223–4, 228–9, 250, 252, 259, 261, 264, 274–6
  establishment of and campaign for, 9, 16, 78–84, 111
  Office of Public Affairs, 226, 261–5
  Office of Technical Services (OTS), 200
  public perception of, 6, 10, 15, 173, 224–5, 227–8, 231–2, 242
  relationship with academia, 276–7
  relationship with Hollywood, 15, 127–63, 231–6
  relationship with press, 121–7, 252, 261–83
Central Intelligence Group (CIG), 111
Chambers, Whitaker, 187
Cheney, Richard (Dick), 265
Cherne, Leo, 158, 234
Church Committee, 223–5, 228, 250, 252, 255, 256, 261–2
Clifford, Clark, 125
Coburn, James, 180, 204, 207–14
COINTELPRO, 226–7, 238, 241
Colby, William, 14, 173, 223, 235–6, 253, 258, 262
Coleman, Herbert, 188
Conrad, Joseph, 226
conspiracy theories
  conspiracy cinema, 12–13, 229, 241–53
  explanation for widespread belief in, 12, 229–32, 265, 274–8; *see also* secrecy
Cook, Lawrence, 236
Cooper, Gary, 90, 93, 96–7
Cooper, Merian C., 30–1, 34–7, 42–4, 80, 225
Coppola, Francis Ford, 226–8
Cosby, Bill, 197, 211, 239
Counterspy Magazine, 202, 256–7
counter-subversion (fear of enemies within)
  Communist, 85, 92, 94–5, 128, 151, 155–6, 159, 177–9, 183, 187; *see also* House Un-American Activities
  Japanese-Americans, 47–9
  Nazi, 53, 60, 98, 103, 106
Crowther, Bosley, 89, 101–2, 113–14

GENERAL INDEX

Cuba, 15, 124–6, 171–5, 181–4, 256
Cunningham Combat Camera, 23–4

Daley, Richard, 239–40
Darwell, Jane, 25
Davenport, Henry, 48
Davis, Peter, 235
D-Day, 57–8, 87–8, 105–7
de Antonio, Emile, 257–61, 264
De Laurentiis, Dino, 227, 249
de Rochemont, Louis, 8–10, 37, 56, 77, 80–3, 102–14, 128, 131, 134, 139, 161, 176–7
de Rochemont, Richard, 37–42, 102
Dean, Gordon, 61
Deinum, Andries, 84, 90, 96
DeLillo, Don, 5, 18, 125–6, 174, 177
Delon, Alan, 232
Democratic Convention (1968), 239–40
Department of Defense, relationship with Hollywood, 226–7, 234–6
Diem, Ngo Dinh, 150, 153–7
Dixon, Ivan, 236–40
documentary, 8, 10, 25–6, 28–9, 35–41, 46–7, 51, 55–8, 63, 68–9, 80, 82, 88–9, 93, 96, 102–3, 105, 108, 112, 113, 131, 205, 235, 240, 257–258; *see also* semi-documentary
Dodds, Thomas, 57
Doering, Otto C., 42, 84, 109–10
Donen, Stanley, 192, 209
Donovan, James, 58, 60, 66
Donovan, William J.
  and campaign for permanent peacetime intelligence agency, 8, 10, 16, 44, 56, 77–84, 137, 262
  influence upon *13 Rue Madeleine* (1947), 104–14
  influence upon *Cloak and Dagger* (1946), 93–7, 101
  influence upon *O.S.S.* (1946), 85–9
  legacy of public relations activities for CIA, 122, 125–7, 159, 160, 173, 250, 262
  and Field Photographic Unit, 24, 30, 36–8, 42–8, 101, 104–14
Doolittle Report, 86

Douglas, Ann, 16, 176
Douglas, Lawrence, 58, 69
Duke, Angier Biddle, 154–7
Dulles, Allen
  and OSS/CIA public relations, 79–80, 121–7, 137–8, 150, 153–4, 158–62, 176
  relationship with Ian Fleming, 172–3
  representations of, 188, 191, 200, 203, 212–13, 225
Dunaway, Faye, 248–9
Dunne, Philip, 10, 51

Early, Stephen, 27
Eisenhower, Dwight D., 64, 107, 170
Elkins, Charles Felton, 263
Ellison, Ralph, 238
Ellsberg, Daniel, 228, 252, 274
Encounter Magazine, 142
'Eurospy', 179
Evans, Robert, 205, 209

'Family Jewels' Revelations, 223–4, 228, 234–5, 242, 248–9, 252, 255, 261
Fax Dean, 32
Federal Bureau of Investigation (FBI), 37
  Congressional oversight of, 5, 222–5, 261
  and Hollywood, 78, 83, 91–4, 103–4, 109, 112, 114, 128–31, 139, 141, 184, 159, 161, 183, 187, 200, 203–15, 226–8, 234–5, 237–8, 241–5, 257–60
Felton, Norman, 177, 194–6, 199
Fenster, Mark, 247
Ferrara, Sal, 256
Field Photographic Unit, OSS (FPU)
  legacy of, 78, 80, 81, 82, 88, 111, 275
  origins of, 30–6, 42–6
  wartime activities of, 9, 23–9, 46–70
Figaro Entertainment, 142–63
'Fighting 69th' (military regiment), 30, 43; *see also Fighting 69th* in film index
First World War, 16, 30–1, 43–5, 123
Fitzgerald, Geraldine, 84, 86–7, 89
Flicker, Theodore J., 204–10, 213–14

301

Fonda, Henry, 27
Fonda, Jane, 259
Ford, Corey, 84, 95–6
Ford, John, 9, 23–36, 42–61, 65, 78, 80–2, 88–9, 95, 111, 114, 130–1, 192, 225, 275
Forgan, Russell J., 80, 107–11
Frankfurt School, 45
Franz, Eduard, 212–13
Freisler, Roland, 59–60
Fulbright, William, 235–6
Fulton, John, 33

gadgets, 80, 89, 172, 177, 184, 199–201
gender (representations of), 86–9, 179–80
Gerrido-Lecca, Luis, 260
Gestapo, 64, 66
  media comparison of US intelligence with, 78, 86, 89, 122, 160, 212
  representation of, 87, 92, 106
Ghormley, Robert L., 34
Gilbert, Gustave, 67–8
Gilks, Alfred, 33
Ginsberg, Allen, 202–203
Goldstein, Lloyd, 53
Göring, Hermann, 62–3, 67
Grady, James *see* Six Days of the Condor
Graham, Katherine, 262, 223
Grant, Cary, 186, 189, 193
Greene, Graham, 14, 142–58, 181–6, 229, 263
Greenlee, Sam, 236–41
Griffis, Stanton, 88
Grogan, Stanley, 162
Grotsky, Ben, 33
Gruson, Sydney, 124
Guatemalan Coup (1954), 123–6, 173

Habermas, Jürgen, 231
Halas and Batchelor, 139–40
Hall, Roger, 79
Halprin, Sol, 81
Hansen, Edmund H., 33–4
Hari, Mata, 90, 123
Harkness, Gladys, 125
Harkness, Richard, 125

Hatcher, Richard G., 240
Hathaway, Henry, 112
Helm, Matt, 192, 194, 202
Helms, Richard, 134, 202, 234–5, 253–5, 262
Hepburn, Audrey, 193
Herodotus, 272
Hersh, Seymour, 130, 223, 225, 228, 234, 255
Hetu, Herbert, 261–2
Hickox, Sid, 33
Hillenkoetter, Roscoe H., 125
Hiss, Alger, 187
Hitchcock, Alfred, 11–12, 98–9, 104, 114, 121, 128, 135–6, 163, 179, 184–94, 204, 213, 225, 232, 234, 242, 244
Hoffman, Heinrich, 59–60
Hofstadter, Richard, 17, 94, 230–1, 242, 274–5
'Hollywood Ten', 85, 90–1, 95
Holocaust
  and the paranoid style, 231
  representation of, 57–70
homosexuality as national security threat
  in Cold War Hollywood cinema, 12, 179
Hood, Richard, 92
Hoover, J. Edgar, 8, 44, 83, 92, 94, 103–5, 128–9, 139, 161, 179, 200, 205, 208, 212–13, 227, 238, 275
Horton, John, 234
House Un-American Activities Committee (HUAC), 8, 85–6, 91–4, 100, 124, 130–1, 142, 151, 186–7, 198, 275
Hubbard, Bernard R., 39
Hunt, E. Howard, 173
Hunt, Lynn, 272
Huston, Walter, 48
Hutcheon, Linda, 180–1

Iliad, The (epic poem), 16
Inside the Company (book) *see* Philip Agee
International Rescue Committee (IRC), 154–8

interventionism, 29, 44–5, 56, 85, 94, 125, 144,
Invisible Government, The (book), 176
Invisible Man, The, 238
Iran-Contra, 224, 274
Iranian coup (1953), 124–6, 158

Jackson, C. D., 138
Jackson, Robert H., 58, 61–2
Jameson, Fredric, 16–17, 74n 181, 231
Jeffreys-Jones, Rhodri, 127, 170, 172
Jenkins, Tricia, 15
Johannes, Robert, 52–3
Johnson, President Lyndon Baines, 45, 222
Johnston, Eric, 138
Joy, Jason, 108, 111
Jutland, Battle of, 35–6

Kackman, Michael, 128–9, 175, 179, 181, 185, 190, 194, 201, 211
Katz, Alfred, 154–5, 160, 162
King, Martin Luther, 206, 210, 226, 238–9, 243
Kellogg, Ray, 34, 53–4, 59–63, 81–2, 88, 275
Kennedy, John F.
  assassination of, 4–5, 130, 181, 230, 243, 275
  fondness for James Bond novels and relationship with Ian Fleming, 15, 172–4
  foreign policy of, 45, 170, 223
Kennedy, Robert, 173, 198, 243
Khrushchev, Nikita, 138, 170, 174
Kiley, Dan, 60–1
Killenworth Estate, 187
Kim (novel), 173–4
Kimmel, Husband E., 47
Kirkpatrick, Lyman, 161–2
Knox, Frank, 46
Kovner, Jeffrey, 260
Krim, Arthur, 156, 234
Kubrick, Stanley, 37, 183, 208, 244
Kuleshov Effect, 244, 246

LaCapra, Dominick, 277
Ladd, Alan, 84–6, 88
Lampson, Mary, 257
Lancaster, Burt, 232
Lanf, Fritz, 84, 89–91, 96–102, 105, 177
Langan, John F., 40
Langley, USS, 35
Lansdale, Edward, 142, 150, 152–7
Lantz, Robert, 150, 159–62
Lardner, Ring, 85, 91
Le Carré, John, 194
Leahy, William, 27–8
Leary, Robert, 34
Lee, Roberta *see Shade of the Palms*
Leeds, Bert, 81
Leiter, Felix, 134, 172
Levi, Primo, 58
libel *see* tort law and Hollywood representation of government officials
liberal consensus, 5–8, 10–11, 16, 29, 45, 82, 130, 174, 179–81, 185–6, 190, 192, 228, 230, 265, 275–7
Life, meaning of, 42
Litvak, Anatole, 53
Lovering, Otho, 34
Lorentz, Pare, 25, 61
Lucas, Scott, 9, 69, 139, 157

McAllister, Robert, 154
MacBain, Alistair, 84, 95–6
McBride, Joseph, 25–6, 42, 47, 50, 55
McCallum, David, 178, 195, 197
McCarthy, David Shamus, 125, 235–6, 250
McCarthy, Joseph, and McCarthyism, 8, 94, 124, 130–1, 151, 159, 186–7, 191, 198, 230, 275
McCoy, Alfred W. *see The Politics of Heroin in Southeast Asia*
MacDonald, Elizabeth, 86–7
McDowell, Arthur G., 156
McGilligan, Patrick, 96–8, 250
McGuinness, Kevin, 26, 49–50
Mackenzie, Jack, 23–4
McLendon, Gordon, 262

MacNab, Josephine, 22–9, 49, 51, 55, 69, 275
Maddow, Ben, 90, 92–4
Maibaum, Richard, 88
Mailer, Norman, 202
Maltz, Albert, 85, 91
Mankiewicz, Joseph, 14, 142–62, 184, 234
Mansfield, Mike, 124, 156, 160, 162
March of Time (newsreel), 8, 37, 46, 55–6, 66, 80, 82, 102–3, 105, 109
Marcuse, Herbert, 45
Martin, John Stuart, 105
Marxism, 16, 45, 85, 92–4, 241, 264
Mason, James, 187
Mathau, Walter, 193
Maury, Jack, 257
Melley, Timothy, 6, 8, 175–6
Metro-Goldwyn-Mayer (MGM), 26, 39, 128, 135–6, 190
Midway, Battle of, 23–7
MK-ULTRA, 207
Monat, Pawel, 127
Monks, John, 105–6
Mosaddegh, Mohammad, 124–5
Motion Pictures Association of America (MPAA), 137–8, 257
Mount Rushmore (representation in *North by Northwest*), 188–90, 244
Moynihan, Daniel Patrick, 1, 126, 272
Murphy, Audie, 143–4, 154
My Lai Massacre, 230, 246

Nadel, Alan, 172, 175, 179
Nashel, Jonathan, 150, 194
National Broadcasting Company (NBC), 158–9, 162 196, 234
National Security Act (1947), 10, 78, 111, 121, 125, 162
National Student Association (NSA), 198, 201, 242
nationalism (US), 8
Nazi Germany
  Cold War framing of, 137, 225, 230, 275
  propaganda *see* propaganda

representations of, 44, 49, 53, 57–70, 78, 87–91, 94–101, 103–6, 112–13
Neuman, Franz, 45
newsreel, 1, 8, 22–3, 39–40, 46–50, 53, 55, 61, 66, 68, 70, 80, 82, 103, 109; *see also* March of Time
New York Times v. *Sullivan* (1964), 9, 133–4
Nixon, President Richard, 94, 173, 228, 232, 242–3
North African Campaign (WW2) *see* Operation Torch
Nuremberg Trials (OSS role in), 57–70, 77–9, 81, 84, 88, 112, 275

Oakes, Blackford, 263
Office of Naval Intelligence (ONI), 34, 37, 93, 131, 158
Office of Strategic Services (OSS)
  dissolution of, 9, 68, 77
  establishment of, 36, 42
  Field Photographic Unit (FPU) see Field Photographic Unit
  Office of the Coordinator of Information (COI), 36–40
  'Oh So Social' Moniker, 45, 79, 83, 88–9, 93
  post-war campaign for permanent peacetime intelligence agency *see* Donovan, William J.
  recruitment strategy of, 45
  Reports Declassification Division, 79–81
  relationship with Hollywood, 9, 10, 42–70, 77–120, 139, 158–9, 160, 176; *see also* Donovan, William J. (campaign for permanent peacetime intelligence)
  representation of, 1–3, 9, 45, 77–120, 143–4, 160, 173, 176
  Visual Presentation Branch (VPB), 37–42, 57, 60–1, 102
Office of War Information (OWI), 10, 29, 49, 51
Olivier, Laurence, 145–6, 150
Olmsted, Kathryn, 222–3, 250, 252, 261
Operation Brotherhood, 154

Operation McGregor, 96
Operation Mongoose *see* Castro, Fidel (CIA assassination attempts of)
Operation Overlord *see* D-Day
Operation Sunrise, 79, 160, 176
Operation Torch, 36, 39, 51–7, 111
Oppenheimer, Robert J., 100
Ortiz, Peter, 84
Orwell, George, 139–40
Oswald, Lee Harvey, 247

Pakula, Alan, 13, 222, 229, 243–6
Palmer, Lilli, 97
Paramount, 39, 56, 78, 80, 83–9, 93, 96, 102, 109, 113, 127–8, 138, 205, 214
Paranoid Style in American Politics, The (essay) *see* Richard Hofstadter
Paris Review, 139, 142
Parrish, Robert, 24, 25–8, 34, 47, 49, 58, 60–1, 65, 68
Pearl Harbor Attack, 44, 46–51, 78, 86, 97, 111
Pearson, Drew, 45
Peckinpah, Sam, 226, 252
Pennick, Jack, 33, 53
Pentagon Papers, 12, 228, 274
Pentagon Propaganda Machine, The (book), 235
Pershing, General 'Black Jack', 31, 43
Phenix, Richard, 82
Philby, Kim, 158, 182
Phillips, David Atlee, 126, 184, 235, 262
Pichel, Irving, 27, 85
Pike Committee, 223–5, 252–3
Polish–Soviet War, 31, 42
The Politics of Heroin in Southeast Asia (book), 202, 251, 254
Pollack, Sydney, 130, 248–52
postmodernism, 8, 11, 175–6, 181, 208–9, 265
Powers, Gary *see* U-2 Incident (1960)
Powers, Richard Gid, 1, 272
Prados, John, 255–6, 258
Production Code Administration (PCA), 9–10, 108, 124, 128, 132, 136, 138, 149, 151–3, 156, 187, 225–6

propaganda
  Nazi propaganda, 34, 59
  Soviet propaganda, 92, 138, 170
  US propaganda during Cold War, 125, 138, 154, 157, 235; *see also* Central Intelligence Agency (Cultural Cold War), 44, 138–1
  US propaganda during Second World War, 10, 26, 36–7, 40, 45–6, 51, 58, 67–9, 80, 111, 225, 264
psychedelia, 199, 202, 204, 207
Pynchon, Thomas, 177

Radar, William, 81
Radio-Keith-Orpheum Pictures (RKO), 30, 39
Ramparts Magazine, 198, 201–4, 209, 242, 254, 277
Ranke, Leopold von, 272–3
Rather, Dan, 262
Reagan, President Ronald, 41, 224, 261, 264
realism
  as authorised by the US government *see* semi-documentary
  demand for during and after Second World War, 9, 10, 22–9, 49–51, 55–7, 82, 105
  as narrative or cinematic technique, 8, 13, 25–6, 29, 49–51, 55, 68–9, 103–10, 161, 175
  reaction against, 174–215; *see also* semi-documentary (declining credibility of)
  realist spy cinema, 7, 11–12, 232–6
  relationship between fiction and reality, 13–18, 22–3, 51, 57, 199–201
  theories of, 13–14, 16–18, 35–6, 180–1
Redford, Robert, 228, 248–55, 259, 263–4
Redgrave, Michael, 143, 145–7
Reed, Carol, 183–4, 186
Rees, John E., 83
Ribbentropp, Joachim von, 62–3, 67
Richards, Atherton, 37–41

Riefenstahl, Leni, 59
Ritt, Martin, 11, 241
Rizzo, John, 141
Robinson, Edward G., 60
Rockefeller Commision, 234, 250
Rogers, Andy, 79
Rolfe, Sam, 196–201
Roosevelt, Eleanor, 27–8
Roosevelt, President Franklin D., 27–8, 36–7, 44, 93
Roosevelt, Kermit, 158
Rosenstone, Robert, 14
Rosson, Harold, 33
Rostow, Walt, 45
Rubin, Stanley, 205, 214

Saint, Eva Marie, 189
Salter, Michael, 51, 61, 67
Saltzman, Eric, 260
Sarris, Andrew, 131
Saturday Evening Post
  relationship with OSS and CIA, 79, 125
Saunders, Frances Stonor, 44, 138–41
Schlesinger Jr, Arthur, 45
Schneider, Stanley, 248
Schulberg, Bud, 58–61
secrecy
  implications for history and national memory, 4–8, 18, 176, 181, 229–31, 244, 265, 273–8
  and public trust in government, 4–8, 12–13, 17, 176, 181, 185, 228–31, 243, 248–9, 265
  theories of, 126–7, 273
Secret Surrender, The (book), 176–7
semi-documentary, 1–3, 8–11, 53, 56, 80, 82, 93–5, 102–14, 131–2, 136, 159–63, 186, 191–2, 194, 264
  declining credibility of, 174–85, 193, 200–1, 205–6, 209, 214, 229, 231, 265, 273–6
Semple Jr., Lorenzo, 243, 249
Shade of the Palms (novel), 263
Shaheen, John, 79, 80–1, 83, 88–9, 96, 109
Shaw, Tony, 77, 139, 250

Sheketoff, Emily, 253
Shurlock, Geoffrey, 151–3
Signal Corps (US Army), 32, 52, 54, 58, 61, 63
Six Days of the Condor (novel), 227, 249, 251, 254
Skouras, George, 83, 104, 110, 158
slander *see* tort law and Hollywood representation of government officials
Smith, Bradley, 88, 126
Smith, Walter Bedell, 127, 132
Sontag, Susan, 177, 180–1, 184
Spanish Civil War, 92–3
Special Operations Executive (SOE), 88, 107
Sperling, Milton, 90, 95–101, 113
state–private networks, 139, 157–8
Stevens, George, 58, 63
Stimson, Henry, 47
Stone, Oliver, 4–5, 130, 134, 223
Strategic Services Unit (SSU), 77, 89

Taylor, Jack, 66
Thomason, John W., 34
Thucydides, 272
'Timespeak' *see* Voorhis, Westbrook von
Toland, Gregg, 33, 46–50
tort law and Hollywood representation of government officials, 10, 133–6; *see also New York Times* v. *Sullivan* (1964)
Truman Committee (Senate Special Committee to Investigate the National Defense Program), 52
Truman, President Harry S., 9, 52, 78–9, 99–100, 125, 129, 176
Tunney, John, 234
Turner, Stansfield, 261–2
Twentieth Century-Fox, 8–9, 32–3, 39, 51–2, 78–82, 88, 102, 105, 111, 180
Tzu, Sun, 122

U-2 Incident (1960), 132–3, 170–1, 174, 273
United Artists, 39, 156, 208, 240–1

United States Information Agency (USIA), 239
United States Pictures, 78, 95
Universal Studios, 39, 208

Valenti, Jack, 138
Vaughn, Robert, 178, 195, 198
Velasco, Juan Alvarado, 260
Vietnam War, 5, 45, 130, 143–59, 181–2, 184, 192, 198, 204, 206, 208–10, 225–8, 242–3, 274
Villa, Pancho, 31, 43
Virilio, Paul, 35–6, 42, 70
Voorhis, Westbrook von, 65, 103, 131, 159

war and cinema, relationship between, 9, 23–9, 34–42, 69–70; *see also* realism
Wark, Wesley, 277
Warner Brothers, 39, 44, 78, 80, 84, 89, 92, 95, 127, 262
Warren Commission, 13, 243, 247; *see also* Kennedy, John F. (assassination of)
Watergate scandal, 5, 7, 12, 16–17, 130, 134, 173, 181, 192, 215, 222–5, 228–33, 241–52, 261, 265, 275–6
Wayne, John, 165n, 226

Wead, Frank 'Spig', 34
Weather Underground, The, 257
Webb, Bob, 58
Weber, Max, 273
Weintraub, Fred, 262
Welch, Richard, 202, 256–7, 260–1, 263
Welles, Orson, 33
Wexler, Haskell, 240, 257
White, Hayden, 14
White Panther Party *see* 'Ann Arbor Three'
Wilford, Hugh, 139, 141–2, 159
Wilkie, Wendell, 56
Williams, Dickerman, 156
Williams, William Appleman, 251
Wilson, President Woodrow, 56, 85
Winner, Michael, 232–4
Wisner, Frank, 128
Wood, Robin, 190–1, 194
Woodward, Robert and Bernstein, Carl, 130, 134, 222–3, 259, 274

Zacharias, Ellis, 34, 131, 158, 160, 201
Zanuck, Darryl F., 8–10, 32, 51–6, 58, 80–1, 88, 102, 105–13, 128, 139
Zigman, Joe, 58
Ziv Entertainment, 128–1, 160
Žižek, Slavoj, 222